T0360945

RECENT DEVELOPMENTS IN
NON-NEOCLASSICAL ECONOMICS

In Memory of Marilyn

Recent Developments in Non-Neoclassical Economics

STANLEY BOBER

Routledge
Taylor & Francis Group

LONDON AND NEW YORK

First published 1997 by Ashgate Publishing

Reissued 2018 by Routledge
2 Park Square, Milton Park, Abingdon, Oxon, OX14 4RN
711 Third Avenue, New York, NY 10017, USA

Routledge is an imprint of the Taylor & Francis Group, an informa business

Copyright © Stanley Bober 1997

All rights reserved. No part of this book may be reprinted or reproduced or utilised in any form or by any electronic, mechanical, or other means, now known or hereafter invented, including photocopying and recording, or in any information storage or retrieval system, without permission in writing from the publishers.

Notice:
Product or corporate names may be trademarks or registered trademarks, and are used only for identification and explanation without intent to infringe.

Publisher's Note
The publisher has gone to great lengths to ensure the quality of this reprint but points out that some imperfections in the original copies may be apparent.

Disclaimer
The publisher has made every effort to trace copyright holders and welcomes correspondence from those they have been unable to contact.

A Library of Congress record exists under LC control number: 96079840

ISBN 13: 978-0-367-00013-4 (hbk)
ISBN 13: 978-0-429-44500-2 (ebk)

Contents

v

Preface

This book was undertaken with the intention of providing a means to introduce various strands of new thinking in economics which, in an overall sense, can be said to constitute a counter-revolution with regard to the core framework of economic analysis. What is to be placed at the center of economic reality is the understanding of the forces that maintain the economy in a state of economic growth, and to account for such a condition within a realistic institutional basis.

What has been happening in recent years is a movement to refocus the essence of economic reasoning away from the conventional (neoclassical) approach where the core of the science, the unifying principle if you will, is the concern with the allocation of scarce resources, to an analysis of reproducibility and growth where the discussion is not tied to the characteristics of scarcity. It is not a matter, as economic texts normally tell it, of doing the best with what we have; but it is a matter of viewing an economic system in its fundamental activity of increasing what we have over time. The revolution is then to return the central theme of the science of economics to its classical-Marxian roots where the essential understanding dealt with the growth in the wealth of nations. So this book begins with its first chapter entitled "What is economics about?"

The standard marginalist view is to reckon the whole of economic reality as wrapped around the rational problem of maximization under constraints; with students generally beginning their study of economics with the notion of "unlimited wants" versus mankind's limited productive capability as essentially imposed by "nature's" restraint on economic resources. The conception which has thereby arisen is that of a world where the material goods, which are the object of man's desire, and technical knowledge, have been shaped by some kind of external agent — let us simply call it 'nature' — and given to man in scarce quantities, with a haphazard distribution and an immutable form. All that remains then is for the society to work out the mechanics for a series of exchanges for the existing goods; the problem of economics is the problem of allocation. Certainly classical economics would not have denied that there exists a problem of rational allocation, but they would have relegated it to the status of a minor problem and not the essence of what economics is about.

It is this kind of schematization that the non-neoclassical (or perhaps better put as 'post-classical') approach would discard in order to bring the study of economics in line with the social and political forces in practically all parts of the world that have as their goal the economic growth of societies. There is the realization that the modern world is increasingly becoming one of a man-made world, where the elements of knowledge and technology are developed from 'within' the system and have greatly replaced the normally understood notion of resources as given by nature. Whatever economic limitations a society faces, it is to a great extent man-made, resulting from perverse institutional arrangements that deny a material betterment to a wide range of society. As well, society may put in place 'misguided' policies as a result of a wrong reading of how the economy works and in that way inhibit economic growth. And this latter consideration emerges from a type of economic modelling that is not grounded in the operations of economic institutions as they exist.

Several heterodox theoretical perspectives have emerged in the last decade to challenge various aspects of mainstream neoclassical economics; be it an understanding of the determination and role of prices or that of the distribution of income, or the role of money, or the idea and construction of a production function, or, indeed, the very basic idea of independent supply and demand functions. From these as well as other challenges to the theoretical foundation of conventional economics, there have emerged two broad strands of non-neoclassical analysis under the labelling of post-Keynesian and neo-Ricardian economics.

The latter looks at the historical experience of western capitalist societies and sees long-term economic growth in conjunction with repetitive shorter-term cyclical variations in output. The center of their analysis is based on models of steady-state growth; certainly as a device to capture the long-run experience, and to serve as a framework to consider the required economic relationships that would maintain a system on such a path. The neo-Ricardian attitude would be to consider the cyclical fluctuations or deviations around the trend line as interruptions of the growth pattern traceable to a mis-alignment of economic elements. However the reasoning for the short-term experience, neo-Ricardians would argue for beginning from a basis of an equilibrium growth model.

Post-Keynesians by contrast tend to put at the center the reality of the non-equilibrium cyclical experience which, of course, can be summed up in terms of the upward secular trend. But the essential approach is a realistic explanation of the cycle itself including the Keynesian mechanics of restating full employment. As will be pointed out throughout this book, these frameworks should be considered as complementary to one another; for particular economic elements such as distribution and investment are instrumental to an understanding of both movements.

The challenges that we spoke of above have given rise to a non-neoclassical set of 'tools' with which to understand the realistic workings of the economy. And it bears stating that they have not come from conventional neoclassical (marginal) economic analysis. On the contrary, they have mainly come out in bitter polemic with and as a challenge to it. Moreover, they all deal with problems of production. None of them touch on problems of optimum allocation of scarce goods. We mention some, and await their full elaboration as we begin to travel this different (non-mainstream) road of economic reasoning. We will encounter the Kaldor-Pasinetti income distribution models as they relate to aggregate savings and the accumulation of capital. Also we will, as the basic framework for models of growth, look at the Harrod-Domar macro-dynamic growth paths. We will need to rethink our understanding about the determination of prices and the mechanics of production, and here we analyze the Kaleckian pricing approach and the Sraffian production and value models. We might also add, with particular reference to the short term, that in the penultimate chapter of this book the reader will find some questioning of the usual Keynesian framework especially with regard to the role of money and the functioning of the labor market. This book strives to weave together these and other recent developments so that at the end, the reader will come away with an appreciation of an alternative way.

Acknowledgements

I give special and heartfelt praise to Ms. Linda Cuda for transforming an illegible hand into finished typescript. She has been very patient and forgiving with what, at times, must have seemed as overdemanding behavior. The making of the manuscript into a ready-for-publication form owes everything to her professionalism and care.

Also a thank you to Mr. Carlo Valeri whose computer genius has produced professional draftsman-like diagrams from those rather amateur hand-drawn figures by the author.

1　What is economics about?

What is now thoroughly ingrained and accorded universal acceptance (until quite recently) is the idea that the central concern of the study of economics is that of designing a mechanism to produce an optimum allocation of scarce resources. As economics textbooks are all too eager to point out, the decisions of economic units, whether we speak in terms of individual consumers, individual resource owners, business firms or indeed units of government, are all undertaken within the 'unpleasant' environment of scarcity; therefore, all economic decisions within the context of limited choices are viewed through a similar prism based on the concept of opportunity cost. Thus the study of economics is how best to make use of limited means in the pursuit of almost unlimited ends; or, to put the matter more formally, it is the study of the logic of how rational decisions can be made from among the competing alternatives. The overriding principle governing this logic is, to reiterate, that of opportunity cost which in well functioning markets is closely akin to money costs. Overall, the framework is one of choice under constraint, with the economic system being viewed essentially as an allocative mechanism.

It is within the framework of restriction that one chooses the option that maximally advances one's own gain — a choice which we may label 'economizing behavior' to reflect the flip-side of the choice which involves the embodiment of least cost. But the taking of a decision involves a change in the allocation of the resource from the status-quo; therefore, decisions are marginal in nature since they involve the addition to or subtraction from an existing condition. Decision making that is carried out by means of marginal analysis means a process of making a choice between alternatives by considering small changes in the end outcome resulting from small changes in the combination of alternatives. When carried to its logical limit this kind of analysis deals with infinitesimal changes associated with a continuous function; thus, for a continuous total utility function, we can define the marginal utility as the rate of change in total utility with respect to the change in the independent variable. Should the total utility function not be continuous but defined for a discrete set of values of the independent variable, then the incremental change in the total utility corresponding to a unit change in the independent variable would be the discrete analog of the marginal utility.

This constant rearrangement as a result of this decision process is carried on within an exchange economy or what we may consider as a marginalist scheme of general equilibrium. It is a scheme by which the economic system find those prices (equilibrium prices) which bring about, via this exchange, the optimum allocation of the existing resources. This optimum is defined as that condition that results in individual economic units maximizing their utility with respect to the distribution of resources among them. Maximization under the constraint of scarcity would appear to be the very foundation of the discipline of economics.

This notion that the whole of economic analysis can be reduced to, as explained by, this principle of marginalism, i.e. the understanding of human behavior as a relationship between ends and scarce means which have alternative uses, is, it must be emphasized, a particular approach to economic reality. It is not the only approach, though one would think that it is, considering the way it has so thoroughly permeated economic reasoning. In recent years there has emerged a strong challenge to this orthodoxy that offers a replacement paradigm as the core of what economics is about. This different approach takes as its central focus that of a class relationship-production-distribution structure that has as its message the maintenance and over time the advancement of production levels; the primary concern here is with understanding the mechanism of economic growth and not, to reiterate, with the solution to the problem of optimum allocation of scarce goods. What is being asked of the discipline of economics is to return to its classical-Marxian roots; to put at the core the hallmark of what economics was all about at the very beginning. This means that coming to grips with such matters as the distribution of output, the determination of savings and investment, the mechanism of price determination must have as its starting point the socio-economic relations between individuals within a process of production. That is, that an analysis of an economy that is operating within a capitalist mode of production must explicitly treat the environment as one of a class society; where the output is produced by one class and is planned and directed by another class. Social relationships between 'constituencies' of the economy and the resulting distributional effects as well as pricing behavior, flow from the productive process and its inherent 'class conflict'.

This starting point is to be juxtaposed with that which underlies the current orthodoxy of marginalism that sees the behavior of economic units within a framework of the causal relation between goods and the satisfaction of human needs. And thereby the starting point for marginalism becomes the psychological relation between individuals and finished goods. This conventional attitude leads to particular characterizations of economic analysis. For example, a theory of value is grounded in conditions of demand as represented by utility to consumers. Individuals and their wants are treated as the ultimate data of the analysis; they are the atoms of the essential process of exchange with the explanation of value to be found in the 'behavior equations' of these economic particles. This places price in the role of an allocating agent, hence telling us that commodities whose prices are positive are then by definition considered 'scarce goods'; and these are the goods that are economically relevant. Individuals behaving in a rational self-serving (natural law) way will exchange the given final goods among themselves up to the point where the ratios of marginal utilities are equal to the corresponding ratio of prices.

Furthermore, this attitude of considering prices as an 'index of scarcity' applies as well, in a more general system, to scarce resources used as means of production, e.g. capital and labor. While productive resources are exchanged in their own special markets guided by similar rational laws of maximizing behavior, the price outcome of these goods of a 'higher order' and, by imputation of resources generally, are determined from the goods of the 'first order', i.e. products sold to final consumers. Marginalists see the producing unit as a consumer of a different kind engaged in the process of exchange that fulfills a production goal rather than a utility goal; but the rational guidelines and maximization principles are equally applicable to both. Thus another characterization stemming from the orthodox construction is that one derives a theory of distribution, i.e. an explanation of the various category of income (wages, rents and profits) as incidental to the pricing process as determined by the conditions of exchange. It comes down to having one accept a theory of income distribution that is based upon a theory of value which results from natural law in the relation of man's rational behavior to maximization considerations.

As this behavior is assumed general in all arenas of exchange, there is no need to particularize the explanation of the income to any unit of input, since all incomes flow from the same explanatory principle. Hence whatever the social or power relationship between people in the production

3

activity, it has essentially nothing to do with the respective rewards that are afforded by the market process. It is important to stress that the neoclassical attitude considers the decisions to buy and sell as impelling and determining production; production is animated by and takes the form of an exchange process. If all action is based in exchange, and exchange involves transforming one property into another, then labor or work itself is part of an exchange or market process. The term 'work' is what one labels the hourly or daily consumption of what has been purchased by the producing unit — all income is then simply the result of an exchange of property.

It is then but a short step to seeing the relationship between the inputs as a harmonious one; each makes his distinct contribution to production and receives his appropriate reward. Whatever conflict emerges results from differences over which contributing factors should get more of the value they jointly create. There is then cooperation in the act of production and the struggle over distribution is merely the manifestation of an underlying community of interest to bring about a higher level of output. This 'cooperative vision' is at the heart of neoclassical distribution analysis; constituencies are to be considered on the same plane and rewards to not flow from what may be considered as a hierarchy class position traceable to the ownership or lack thereof of the means of production. It is telling that current theory talks in terms of non-descriptive factors of production without reference to the specificity of labor or, indeed, the 'means of production'; and while one may use the term labor, it is simply a way to designate a factor. This is, of course, quite different from that 'other' challenging approach that draws its essential structure from the classical-Marxian scheme where we do not even find the term 'factors of production' in the economics vocabulary, and where there was not any consideration of placing the various categories of income on the same analytical level and dissolving any distinction between income from work and income from property. In the 'modern' agenda, such a distinction is returned to the forefront of analysis as it becomes fundamental to questions concerning capital accumulation and distribution of income. This non-neoclassical approach has taken on the umbrella title of post-Keynesian:neo-Ricardian economics under which one finds diverse routes leading away from the commonly accepted orthodoxy. We will, in this book, travel along some of them.

In this section we want to highlight additional differences so as to set the stage for the analysis of some of the principles of this non-marginalist economics; let us say of this 'production approach' to economic reality.

4

Consider the term 'scarce goods' in its original usage by the classicists and how it has come to be employed in current economic reasoning. There are goods (resources) whose availability is insufficient to meet the need for them. They may be commodities that are in demand as requirements for production, but they are inherently limited and must be taken as given either due to natural circumstances or perhaps due to peculiar skills that cannot be multiplied and enhanced. We can consider such goods as those of the 'natural endowment type'. While these goods are not irrelevant, they are of little economic importance compared to the mass of goods that are exchanged which are commodities that are produced by other commodities and the application of labor. Let us refer to these latter goods as those of the 'production type'.

With regard to goods of the endowment type, Ricardo had this to say:[1]

> There are some commodities, the value of which is determined by their scarcity alone. No labor can increase the quantity of such goods, and therefore their value cannot be lowered by an increased supply. Some rare statues and pictures, scarce books and coins, wines of a peculiar quality, which can be made only from grapes grown on a particular soil, of which there is a very limited quantity, are all of this description. Their value is wholly independent of the quantity of labor originally necessary to produce them, and varies with the varying wealth and inclinations of those who are desirous to possess them.

Going on to compare with goods of the production type, Ricardo observes:[2]

> By far the greatest part of those goods which are the objects of desire are procured by labor and they may be multiplied, not in one country alone, but in many almost without any assignable limit, if we are disposed to bestow the labor necessary to obtain them.

Let us append in the modern vein; if we are disposed to bestow the labor and technology necessary to obtain them, continuing with Ricardo's thinking:[3]

> In speaking, then, of commodities, of their exchangeable value, and of the laws which regulate their relative prices, we mean always such commodities only as can be increased in quantity by the exertion of

5

human industry, and on the production of which competition operates without restraint.

It is clear that for the classicists the notion of scarcity followed 'accepted' usage and was relegated to goods of the endowment type which are not augmentable given the desire for them. Their price is wholly reflective of demand as evidenced by the market process. One can formulate a pure exchange model from which equilibrium or utility maximization prices can be extracted. Certainly, then, the marginalist notion holds in the 'narrow' in that goods that have positive prices are scarce goods; but it does not hold in the 'general' attitude which proclaims that scarce goods are those goods that have positive prices.

The classical approach never considered designating goods of the production type as 'scarce'. Hence, their value while subject to the influence of exchange cannot be wholly dependent on it. Indeed, these goods are seen to be producible 'almost without limit' and their value must fundamentally reflect what we might consider as the inherent 'difficulty' in bringing them into being and is thus determined on the basis of their costs of production. It bears re-emphasizing that the classicists do not use the term scarcity as reflecting the availability of goods generally, but use the term simply as a prerequisite for defining economic goods by virtue of the costs involved in their production. Thus, in fact, one should not construct a pure exchange model that purports to develop a theory of relative prices independent of the 'mechanism' of production. The principles which explain prices must be in terms of man's activities and relations within the act of production and not within the act of exchange; the analysis should be based on the characteristics of reproducibility rather than that of scarcity.

Consider the following telling observation by Professor Luigi Pasinetti,[4] concerning the apparent 'overlooking' of the Ricardian distinction between scarce commodities and produced commodities:

> The process through which this has happened is itself very interesting. Economic goods have positive prices. Now, within a pure exchange model, the only goods that have positive prices are the 'scarce' goods. The marginalists have therefore turned things upside down and defined the scarce goods as those goods that have positive prices. But this procedure, though justified in a pure exchange model, is illegitimate in general. All the produced commodities do have positive prices, and yet they are not 'scarce' in

6

the classical sense of the word. But the marginalists did not go back to check their definitions. The consequence has been that they went on to (illegitimately) apply to produced goods the conclusions of their theories about scarce goods. For the marginalists, all economic goods have become scarce — not because they really are scarce but simply because they have been called so.

Has it not been promulgated that maximization is the very foundation of the subject of economics, and that economics is the science which studies human behavior as a relationship between ends and scarce means which have alternative uses? Well, one does not deny that economics is about this, but the current and expanding critical inquiry denies that optimization within the exchange environment is all that it is about. Indeed, optimization may be considered a minor issue easily solvable, and far from the whole of economic reality.

Marginalists may well respond by claiming that scarce (economic) goods are really what they are and not what they are called, because the basis for them is found in the limited resources given by nature. Man's productive capability is limited by the material resources that are essentially given to him so that the notion of 'unlimited production' even if applicable to any one good cannot be applied generally. Thus society in an overall way is always facing a limited set of possibilities.

However, this seemingly plausible attitude which is currently at the core does, I believe, prevent an adequate understanding of real world economics. What the analysis has to be built around is the constant and increasingly accelerated pace of technology that has been freeing society from its bounds of nature. For example, that traditional agricultural sector used by text authors as an example of a 'competitive sector' and to demonstrate how returns to production are constrained by nature, is now a very minor part of society, and it is so because technology has freed-up production to the point where is most of the world populations are unburdened from the threat of hunger and starvation. And where these difficulties persist it is the result of internal strife and a lack of political will to form a cohesive society such that modern know-how can be applied.

One comes across the idea that the law of diminishing returns (the basis for the traditional cost curve configuration) reflects a constraint imposed by nature. For if the laws were not valid, it would possible to produce all the required foodstuff on currently cultivated land or for that matter in a 'flowerpot'. And the argument for this constrained limit is that if it were not so, then why does society resort to less fertile land over time as it

7

seems to increase production; it would make no sense to do so if all can be gotten from what society is currently doing.

But this illustration of how man is constrained is itself a victim of a very limited view. The application of increased knowledge regarding planting techniques, seed development and the reclamation of non-fertile land does away with appreciable differences in growing capability so that one brings into production additional land of somewhat equal fertility as needed. A decision may be made to apply know-how to less fertile land in order to enhance its capability and bring it up to par rather than to apply further technology on currently used land to bolster its productivity even further. Certainly, though, one should not realistically think in terms of fixation of fertility or productive capability formed by natural limits — if the flowerpot is too small to absorb the new developments we can fabricate a larger one if we turn the 'lab' towards that end. Textbooks consider the law of diminishing returns to be as famous as the law of gravity in physics, which is to say the least a somewhat exaggerated claim, for the latter is immutable (in this world) while the former depends on heroic assumptions such as that of a 'fixed factor'. The point is made that not to adhere to the law would be a fairy tale; well, perhaps its very adherence is the fairy tale.

Turning to Professor Pasinetti's remarks along these lines we find:[5]

> Even the raw materials and the traditional sources of energy, which at the beginning of the industrial revolution absolutely conditioned the rise of industries, are becoming less and less important, as man learns how to make, in whatever place they like, a great part of the raw materials (or their synthetic substitute), and are moreover developing entirely new sources of energy.

Thus technical progress comes to the forefront; it is not a complication but at the heart of economic activity, and its presence impacts on society through the mechanics of production. If economic analysis is to be relevant in a world which is more and more a man-made world where knowledge is greatly replacing nature, then the focus has got to be on the theoretical framework that deals with the essential concern of production and growth. And it is around this core that one explains the behavior of such matters as pricing, the distribution of the output, the recurrent instability of the economy and the determinants of investment and its relationship to savings. One does suspect that the forces which drive capital accumulation affect employment through the change in the capital stock, and through the technical change that is imparted to the system via

8

the act of accumulation itself. These realities can only be understood within a framework of production models that allows the construction of 'different' principles of economics which are developed independent of the problem of optimum allocation of scarce resources.

The primary issue then is how can society maintain itself materially? And the mechanics for the analysis is through what has been labeled 'structured models' that set out rules revealing the behavior of economic constituencies, e.g. the savings pattern, pricing behavior or the method of production. These rules reflect the realities of existing institutions and what must be done to perpetuate them and thereby the existence and growth of the material output. This approach differs from the 'behavior models' of the neoclassical attitude that 'calculates' outcomes based on a predictable 'rational' behavior pattern reflecting the balancing of optimality activities. This latter mechanism demonstrates a real world if only the real world would resemble the model, while the structural (neo-Keynesian) alternative demonstrates a model to capture the real world that resembles the model.

There is a further difference that should be mentioned concerning the use of time in economic analysis. Marginalist economics commonly employ the tool of 'mechanical' or 'abstract' time that has the hallmark of reversibility of outcomes or behavior. This is observed in analysis that begins by specifying a sufficient number of equations to determine its unknowns so as to find the compatible or equilibrium outcome for the equations; we observe a result at a point in time predicated on the structure of the behavioral equations. Subsequent to a parametric change, a different outcome is prescribed at a different point in time, and should the change be reversed, the outcome reverts to the original position at a later point in time; though with regard to the outcome it is as though time were reversed — one goes forward to the past. Such analysis is not confined to comparative static models but applies as well to dynamic systems where equations trace a path through time such as the cobweb analysis, or a particular pattern of output fluctuations, or the working-out of the multiplier mechanism.

What is particular about this is the lack of uncertainty or, let us say, the presence of complete foresight that allowed reversibility; telling us that decisions and accompanying undesirable outcomes can be reversed. This, it seems, is indicative of systematic or predictable behavior based on 'universal laws'; thus we have knowledge not only of what happened but of what will happen — we go from a revocable past to a known future. While this makes for presumably very neat cause and effect relationships which is at the base of equilibrium mechanics, realism does dictate that uncertainty pervades much of decision making, and economic activity stemming from past decisions are to a considerable degree not reversible. Thus time should be treated in terms of historical time, where irreversibility and uncertainty provide the framework for decision making. 'Time' flows in one direction — forward; there is no changing of what is only an awareness of its impact on decisions regarding a future outcome which is uncertain, but is certain not to be a replica of the past. In historical time modeling one goes from an irrevocable past to an uncertain future.

Certainly decisions with regard to whether or not to increase production and thereby utilize a greater degree of existing capacity will greatly depend on 'short-term' profit expectations; and this in turn depends upon the given price arrangements and some conjecture about wage rates, assuming that productivity is prescribed by the technology in place. But over the longer term one encounters a decision as to whether to expand capacity which involves a greater degree of uncertainty since one is projecting profit expectations over a much longer time horizon so that past experiences, while totally not irrelevant, is less a consideration than the current state of the economic and political situation. And assuming that one does undertake the investments, this will over the 'long' period of time produce future capacity which may or may not be justified by events at the forward period in time. But the outcome of the past decision is at hand and cannot be reversed; one can certainly reduce investment levels to what they were prior to the previous decision, but profit expectations would not be the same as if investment were at that lower position all along. Even if one were to imagine the physical destruction of the existing capacity so as to obliterate the mistake, the effect of having made it would affect decisions about the future. As another case in point, consider a change in the technique of production in response to an altered price circumstance. This change results in a new environment — one will have learned to do things differently. Then if one were again to confront the original circumstance there would be no question of going back to a replica of the original production mechanics.

So for the state of the economy at a point in time, let us say for its technical base and capital structure, the savings and investment flows are the result of past decisions impacted upon by conditions at the time decisions are made and past experiences. The development of the economy is an historical process resulting from decisions made at every point in the face of uncertainty about the future given the irrevocable

10

results of past decisions. At every point one has to reconsider what has been done at a previous point and gather in current information to decide upon the next step; there is no 'automatic' response mechanism with its inherent predictability as in neoclassical, closed behavior models. Joan Robinson sets out this 'time matter' clearly when she tells us:[6]

In a world depicting equilibrium positions there is no causation. It consists of a closed circle of simultaneous equations. The value of each element is entailed by the values of the rest. At any moment in logical time, the past is determined just as much as the future. In a historical model causal relations have to be specific. Today is a break in time between an unknown future and an irrevocable past. What happens next will result from the inter-actions of the behavior of human beings within the economy. Movement can only be forward.

Our understanding of economic events within the reality of historical time would then have us come to grips with the one overriding development that is clearly discernable from historical data, and that is the long term uneven expansion of the economy. This alternative paradigm to neoclassical economics that we have been talking about places the study of economic growth, the study of this overriding development, at the core of what economics is about. And the many principles for analysis such as the formulation of prices, the impact of technical change on demand for labor and on effective demand and production arrangements, all must be seen to play their role in the historical expansionary evolvement of the economy.

So within the reality of the 'forward movement', how should the analysis be modeled so as to capture this historical process? For post-Keynesians the construct is a dynamic system that incorporates time in a manner that propels the system into a state of perpetual change. But what type of change? If the effort is to explain history via the observed secular trend, then the analysis is frequently based on models of steady-state growth in which the variables are growing at the same constant rate so that all the variables under consideration remain in the same proportion to each other (steady-state growth is defined in an equivalent way to what has been called balanced growth). In this construction, the functional relations including expectational considerations are explicitly specific to yield a definite configuration for the dependent variables associated with given data variables. The steady-state outcome is then the core movement corresponding to an average position around which one perceives the actual oscillatory movements of the economy. The aim being that we have to first come to grips with the balances that maintain the growth condition in order to appreciate what can throw the system off the track and produce the observed cyclical movements — the cycle emerges as a 'miscalculation' that produces a departure from the underlying core movement.

Yet another way to get hold of the change through time is in the effort to explain the short period analysis; that is, to model the system as it fluctuates around the trend line. And there has been some controversy as to which approach should take center stage. Those concerned with the dynamics emphasizing the short period see the trend as a consequence of successive short-span movements, while others (the neo-Ricardian branch of the overall non-neoclassical upheaval) see the long period as basic arguing that there are forces in the system that make for sustained movement and can be studied independent of the shorter period fluctuation and which can be best viewed within a steady-state model.

Though this difference in emphasis may be overblown, as a case can be made that both analyses are essential and are indeed complementary to one another. Both the trend which the long period analysis is supposed to shed light on, and the cyclical fluctuations meant to be explained by shorter period models, both depend on similar determinants such as expectation considerations and the rate of investment. Yet steady-state models which can be considered as a fair approximation (real economics are not in steady-state) are logical time constructions as the causal relations can apply to a reverse movement through time. This device would seem to run counter to the post-Keynesian framework of an actual or historical movement of the economy. But this ought not to dissuade the use of this approach. Actual movements will not reflect this 'steady condition'; but what the latter modeling does is provide a way to organize and relate the economic balances that are fundamental to the forward historical progress, even though such progress may not be manifested by a steady-state image. Consider that while the steady-state allows reversibility, the system is not going to be reversed but will use the track for forward movement reasoning only. Indeed the reality of an oscillatory economy can perhaps be best understood in terms of temporary occurrences such as expectational errors which cause the deviation from the long period position, which though exercising a gravitational pull does not necessarily lock the system on to it.

We mention two considerations relating to the study of growth economics. One is what can be referred to as the problem of existence. That is, given the structure of the model and its parameters, are there

12

meaningful values for the variables that allow the system to grow at a steady pace (though this is not the only type of equilibrium path that can be generated). Secondly, given existence and should the economy find itself off the path, is the reaction to this 'disequilibrium' such as to bring the system back to the growth trajectory or to propel the system further away from it. And should the reaction be one of divergence, it may be possible to limit such movements away from the center of gravity. One can of course construct a theory of the business cycle on the basis of an unstable growth path.

All these matters will come to the fore as we set forth a study of economics that has at the core the long-term material growth of society. But first we must become aware of a different understanding of what heretofore has been some of the accepted principles of economics. This will then allow us to weave together realistic underpinnings upon which to come to grips with the historical growth process.

NOTES

1. David Ricardo, *The Principles of Political Economy*, E.P. Dutton, New York, Everyman's Library, #590, 1957, p. 6.

2. Ibid.

3. Ibid.

4. Luigi L. Pasinetti, *Structural Change and Economic Growth*, Cambridge University Press, 1985, footnote #11, p. 11.

5. Ibid., p. 21.

6. Joan Robinson, *The Accumulation of Capital*, Richard D. Irwin, Homewood, Illinois, 1956, p. 26.

2 Theory of household demand

The theory of consumer behavior deals with the consumer's decision making process, that is, the way one chooses among available alternatives. This process which is reflected in demand functions is designed to explain observed individual behavior; and we might add is important to firms who need to know how the market will react to a change in price as they contemplate their market strategies. How 'real' is demand theory as it is now commonly understood and promulgated as a part of the general neoclassical model? Does it carry much relevance in a world where firms have much market power with price being only one, and perhaps not even the essential ingredient in influencing consumer behavior, and where consumers increasingly do not see themselves as 'individuals' but as part of a larger social class with particular consumption patterns and a hierarchical arrangement within the social group itself? There have been questions of late whether the demand functions in the different forums in which they have been shaped in conventional analysis have an adequate theoretical justification.

Demand curves have been derived from 'utility maps' which serve as basis for the cardinal utility and ordinal utility (indifference curve) approaches. These have been the two basic paths to the study of consumer demand and they are imbued with a rather elusive concept, e.g., that of the measurement of utility in the cardinal or the ordinal sense. By utility maps we refer to the plotting of individual utility functions which when aggregated for all households are presumed to represent the relative preference for two or more goods by society as a whole.

Yet a 'utility surface' represents an introspective notion; and introspection cannot be accepted as scientific proof of the existence of utility functions. This phenomenon is assumed to exist as a law of nature governing the psychology of consumption and whose existence need not be proved. The argument that utility functions are imaginary constructions is seen by the fact that they cannot be identified independently of the behavior of the consumer. But if utility observations are derived, or to be inferred, from consumer demand, then it would be circular reasoning to state that the demand curve can be derived on the basis of utility — we are deducing utility maps from the same data that it is intended to explain. Professor Roncaglia in his work on Sraffian economics observes that:

> It would then seem impossible to demonstrate that a 'utility map' is anything more than a purely mental construction devised by marginal theorists to provide a basis for the subjective theory of value. But to say that utility is the cause of demand on this basis represents nothing more than a simple definition, and to say that demand depends on utility, after giving this definition, constitutes nothing more than a simple 'tautology'.

Thus utility theory cannot be the explanatory agent for consumer demand functions and hence cannot provide a basis for the explanation of the formation of prices.

But certainly the utilitarian theory must have been telling us something over all this time. What does it mean to say, for example, in terms of indifference analysis, that the consumer when ranking combination of goods that lie on the curve compared to being off the curve sees some combinations that are more or less preferable to other combinations? That they would purchase those combinations that are more 'useful' or 'pleasurable' before they would consume those they consider less useful, i.e. carrying less utility. All this is saying, however this decision is reached, is that consumers act rationally driven by some internal individual calculation which can be inferred from behavior patterns, but which may not explain it. We get an ordering of preferences for various combinations of goods but no criterion of explanation of the order. If we call the explanation of behavior by indifference analysis as 'rationality' or 'natural behavior', then the analysis demonstrates what is meant by these descriptive terms; this much it does tell us. But a description of something is not an explanation save if one insists on the imaginatory utility calculation fall back. And this brings up a further consideration. convention tells us that no two indifference curves can be represented by the same combination of goods, the indifference curves cannot cross without violating the rationality assumption. But what if an individual's consumption pattern reflects that of a larger social group with whom he associates, then the same combination of goods may place the person on a lower indifference curve if he perceives himself to be 'out of step'. At different points in time the same combination of goods may yield different satisfaction levels.

We turn to a somewhat detailed look at one response to the criticism of the utilitarian theory of demand, which has been to reformulate the theory in terms of revealed preverences. The idea here is that without any reference to an imaginary utility surface, each individual's demand function could be constructed by simply observing behavior in the market; to put the matter somewhat differently, that it is possible to construct a consumer's indifference map without the characteristic of an ordinal measurement of utility.

Consider that an individual purchases a basket of goods (A) rather than a basket of goods (B); one could, it would seem, conclude that there is a revealed preference for basket (A). However, it may be that it is not that (A) is preferred, but that it is (B) that one cannot afford to purchase. We obviously need some price information before making definitive statements about preference from observed behavior. So if (A) is more expensive than (B) and the consumer purchases (A), then we can say that (A) has been revealed preferred to (B).

Consider figure 2.1 where we have a budget line PP BB and points which represent different baskets of goods.

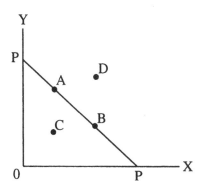

Figure 2.1

Given price and income information, the consumer faces a budget constraint line PP revealing the different baskets of goods X and Y that can be purchased were the consumer to spend all of his income. If point (A) is chosen, it is revealed preferred to (B) and all other points on PP. A point such as (C) is revealed inferior to basket A since the former represents a less expensive basket; that it is not purchased is a revelation

17

of the assumption that the consumer considers it preferable to expend all resources and obtain the basket with the maximum combination of goods. A point such as (D) above the constraint line represents a more expensive basket of goods and cannot be revealed to be inferior to (A) but can certainly be revealed to be superior to (A) as it contains at least more of one of the two goods but not less of either X or Y.

With these considerations in mind we can state the three criteria underpinning the revealed preference theory of demand. The first is that the individual always behaves consistently in the sense that he should never prefer (A) to (B) and then find (B) revealed preferred to (A). This consistence criterion would seem to rule out quality judgments on the basis of price. For example, (A) is revealed preferred to (B), but a sudden increase in the price of (B) by which (B) becomes more expensive than (A) would reveal (B) superior and preferred to (A). Secondly there is the idea of transitivity of preferences. By this we mean that should (A) be revealed preferred to (B) and (B) shown to be preferred to (C), then the consumption of (A) would also reveal it is preferred to the (C) basket. And thirdly, given any particular combination of goods, there does exist a budget constraint line that brings about the consumption of those goods.

Consider figure 2.2 with a price line PP' upon which the consumer chooses a point B which is then revealed preferred to all other points on PP'. Now a point such as X which lies above and to the right of B would by consumer behavior be seen to be preferred to B as there is a corresponding budget line that allows its purchase; and all points on this budget line will lie above that of PP' making all points on such a line preferred to PP'. Thus since all points above B are preferred to it, and B is the preferred basket to all others on PP', then a preference curve through point B would have to be drawn so as to lie below CBD and above PP' as any basket that is preferred to B is also preferred to all other baskets on PP'.

To construct such a preference curve let us pass a budget line VV' through point B and have the consumer choose a basket represented by point Q on VV'. Consumer behavior tells us that at the prices reflected an VV' basket Q is revealed preferred to B, although Q is no more expensive than B. And by similar reasoning all points within the area $C'QD'$ are preferred to Q and thereby as well preferred to point B; thus a preference curve showing a revealed preference for Q upon a change in the budget line would have to pass through Q from point B.

We can repeat this process by passing another budget line such as FF' through B and observe consumer behavior. Say that the consumer chooses

18

point G on FF' rather than B, we find that G must be revealed preferred to B, since, at these prices B is no more expensive than G. Again, given FF' we would rule out all points above and to the right of point G since they would be preferred to basket G given the appropriate budget line; thus a curve showing a preference for G would have to pass through point G from point Q.

We do want to demonstrate that points on PP' are revealed inferior to B, though there are budget lines which will lead to their being purchased. Consider a point H on budget line PP' which is revealed inferior to B but will be purchased under constraint line UU'. All points on UU' are revealed inferior to H, and H basket itself is revealed inferior to B. Hence the altered budget line to PP' would reveal a preference for B basket. Thus all points above H on UU' would thus be eliminated as a base from which preference changes would be revealed (note that as well all areas below UU' are revealed inferior). Now consider a point such as A on PP' which is revealed inferior to point B, though the A basket would be purchased given price line RR' and is thus revealed preferred to all other baskets on RR'. But we have observed that A is preferred inferior to B, hence a change in the budget line to PP' would reveal a preference for point B. All points below RR' are as well inferior to A so that altered prices would 'move' the consumer to the B point.

Thus alternate budget lines reveal different preferences so that one can, it would seem, construct a demand relationship from observed behavior. We observe market behavior that reflects a rational consumer without having to account for it in utilitarian terms, and if preferences remain unchanged for the time under observation (tastes and incomes are given) then the revealed choices will correspond to one's preferences. What the SS' line shows are the observed preferences for different basket of goods under different price regimes. The central point being that the consumer does reveal a set of preferences through observed behavior.

But is the revealed-preference approach to consumer demand really different from the more conventional utilitarian attitudes? Do we gain anything by focusing on the choices themselves as against examining the implication of utility maximization for choices, if all that we are doing is substituting the term 'preferences' for 'utility maps'?

Let us see the relation between the consistency criterion of revealed preference which is a postulate concerning consumer choice, and the view of the consumer as a utility maximizer. We reiterate the consistency condition: that if B and A are two different baskets, and if B is revealed preferred to A then A is never revealed preferred to B. This consistency condition is known as the 'weak axiom of revealed preference'. Figure (2.3) demonstrates this.

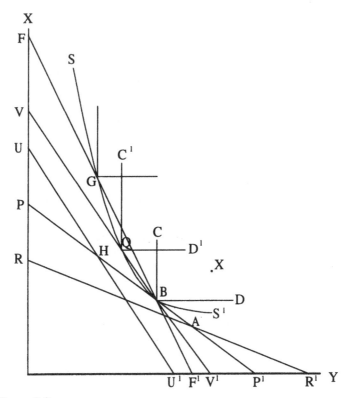

Figure 2.2

II' is the budget line when B is chosen and is thus revealed preferred to all other bundle of goods, on this budget line; but when B is chosen, the A basket is available to be purchased. The A basket lies within the area bounded by II'. On the other hand when A is chosen on $IIII'$, the basket of B goods is not available as it lies outside the bounds of the budget line. Thus when A is available one reveals a preference for the B basket, and when B is available one chooses it over A (one only chooses A, to reiterate, when B is not available). It is the nature of 'weak ordering' that there is no rejected basket that is preferred to B.

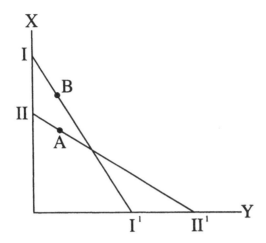

Figure 2.3

Now consider point B in Figure (2.4) which gives a point of tangency between the budget constraint line and an indifference curve showing the highest level of utility (indifference curve) that the consumer can reach.

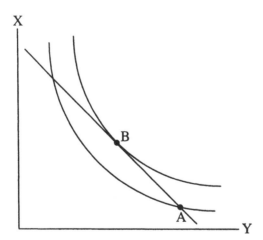

Figure 2.4

But A is another bundle of goods that is on the constraint line and thereby available but is revealed not preferred to B. This signifies that A must have a lower total utility than B so that the indifference curve through

A is below that through B. Thus if A is chosen in a particular market situation, then B cannot be available, otherwise A would not be the maximizing utility choice. The revealed preference approach reflecting the consistency criterion is compatible with the individual's maximization of utility.

We relate this preference approach to the downward sloping demand curve.[2] Consider figure (2.5) where we have a consumer's budget distribution between a good (Y) on the horizontal axis and money income on the vertical axis.

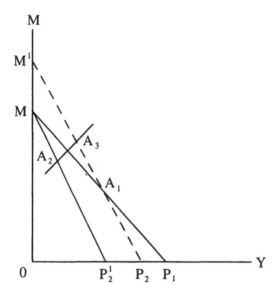

Figure 2.5

Assume an initial environment represented by constraint line MP_1. The consumer has OM of money with which he can attain any combination of money and good (Y) on the constraint line ranging from purchasing no (Y) and being at point (M) to having no money (spending all income) and purchasing OP_1 of good (Y). Suppose that the revealed preference places the consumer at point A_1; then on the consistency assumption we can suppose that combination A_1 will be chosen at any future time if the possibility of that choice comes up again.

Now say that the consumer confronts an increase in the price of good (Y) which clearly alters the constraint line from MP_1 to MP_2. How does the consumer respond, that is, where will he go to on the new budget line?

22

In order to understand the move, let us presume a hypothetical increase in our consumer's income which completely compensates for the higher price and enables the attainment of the original combination at the new price of P_2. This leads to 'supposed' constraint line $M'P_2$ with a slope determined by the P_2 price and intersecting the original constraint line at A_1. Note that all points on our hypothetical option line are possible; but some of the new possibilities were not attainable in the original budget circumstance, those lying on the segment $M'A_1$. But there are other options that were attainable in the original circumstance, those lying on segment A_1P_2 which is to the left and within the MP area. Yet the consumer in having revealed a preference for combination A_1 in the original circumstance, implies a rejection of positions that lie within or on the triangle OMP_1. In other words, the consumer will have rejected the options along A_1P_2 when these were at the same time available to him.

Thus in response to our hypothetical altered constraint line, the consumer will be found to continue the combination at A_1 (he is consistent) or indeed, a preference could be revealed for options along segment A_1M'. This latter move would not make for inconsistency as these options were not attainable in the original environment.

Let us suppose, perhaps somewhat more realistically, that the move is to point A_3 revealing a smaller amount of (Y) purchased. Now the essential question is what would be the move if there is a real reduction in income which alters the constraint line from our hypothetical $M'P_2$ to MP_2, i.e. we have a fall in income while prices remain constant at P_2? Clearly the consumer would have to move to some combination such as A_2 to the left of A_3 (prices are not falling to compensate for the reduced income level). Note that as good (Y) at A_2 is less than at A_3 which is less than at A_1, then the purchase of (Y) at A_2 is less than at A_1. Thus an increase in the price level from P_1 to P_2 reduces the quantity of (Y) purchased.

Of course, this argument would hold even if we were to presume that the consumer remains at his original revealed preference point A_1 when we hypothetically increase his income in the face of the higher price. A reduction in income would necessarily move him to a point to the left of A_1 since points on $M'P_2$ are unattainable. If we assume the move to A_2 it would necessarily contain less (Y) than at A_1; and we find a positive income elasticity for good Y which must translate into an inverse relation between price and quality demanded.

Assuming that most goods have a positive income elasticity, we then have a revealed preference and consistency behavior supporting basis for the laws of demand.

This approach does give us definite pieces of information about the consumer's preferences from the observation of behavior; and by comparing preferences revealed under different conditions, i.e. in different price-income situations, a preference scale can be drawn up leading to the construction of the demand curve. But does this mechanism address the problem or does it show even more clearly the tautological character of the subjective theory of demand. What we have is a description of observations but no theory explaining these conditions other than to say that if preferences remain unchanged, and the individual acts rationally, then his choices will correspond to his preferences. We are still lacking the cause of the preferences or, for that matter, for the existence of a utility map.

If utility or revealed preference are factors that are deduced from consumer demand behavior, then how can they serve to explain that very behavior? There is a circularity of reasoning here as the cause is deduced from the same phenomenon (demand) that it is supposed to explain. Furthermore, we should note the static nature of revealed preferences. Consistency reads that the consumer cannot prefer B to A at the same time as he prefers A to B; and then does away with the reality that the state of the world changes over time by referring to a single moment in time. But consumer actions are separated by the passage of time within which 'tastes' may change; thus a switching of preferences does not allow a rejection of rational behavior with any degree of certainty. If it is misleading to read inconsistency between B and A as irrationality, then we have no certain criterion that might be used to test the assumption of rationality except under a most restrictive time condition. Thus a derivation of the rational laws of demand from consistency tests is not on firm ground.

Another critique leveled at the presumed empirical verification of the consistency hypothesis was put forward by Hicks who makes the point that the aim of a theory of demand should be to explain the behavior of groups of individuals. "It is always material of this character which we have to test; and indeed it is material of this kind which we want to test, for the preference hypothesis only acquires a prima facie plausibility when it is applied to a statistical average".[3] Thus the theory wants to address the 'average' or 'representative' consumer which emerges from an analysis applied to a group large enough to be of economic interest. But if the consistency test is applied to a group of consumers, it is necessary for the

24

group to possess a most remarkable homogeneity if it is to give us a rigorous test of the preference hypothesis. If all the members of the group are economically identical, the test is valid; but if they are not identical, the test breaks down. After going through an illustration of this, Hicks concludes:

> It accordingly appears that if apparent inconsistency is to be ruled out, the group to which the test is applied must be homogenous not only in wants, but also in income. We shall, I should suppose, rarely desire to assume such homogeneity. But if we do not assume it, the consistency test is not an infallible check. I feel obliged to conclude from this that there is in practice no direct test of the preference hypothesis.[4]

Thus the theory of revealed preference has no operative significance in that it can be tested against reality and thereby form a means or basis for the generalized law of demand; for the evidence of consistency we would need, it seems, ideal observational conditions.

Perhaps then we ought not to be concerned with the supposed universally recognized truth of rational consumer behavior in whatever form as the underpinning of demand theory, and simply accept the observation of the law of demand itself. For the law does apply, with full force, to the behavior of groups as much as to individuals, and it is this characteristic which gives the law its special importance. Though Hicks does make the point that the derivation of the law from consistency tests is the best way of establishing the law, yet the law which reflects or registers such behavior cannot be said to be explained or caused by what it is describing.

What is needed is some sort of objective standard by which one can establish an ordering of goods which would correspond to the one established by consumer behavior, and which, of course, is derived apart from the observations themselves. To reiterate, one does not have a theory of demand if such a theory is deduced from the observations of behavior which is the very phenomenon to be explained by the theory.

We then can accept the demand curve as a descriptive curve from which we can draw no explanatory power (except on an introspective basis), and consider its relative importance within the framework of the long-term analysis. Post-Keynesians would argue that in an economy that is expanding over time the importance of consumer behavior from the vantage point of the law of demand, that is, in terms of the substitution effect, is less than that from a basis of the income effect. "Indeed, any substitution, based on a change in relative prices, is likely to be of only minor importance and, if ignored altogether, will be less disastrous to the argument than if, as the typical neoclassical model, the income effects are ignored instead".[5] This approach rests on two considerations: one that prices are, in the main, not of the marginalist's demand responsive phenomena, and secondly that consumers do not generally order goods on the basis of price driven substitutability. Let us here look into the lack of substitution characteristic leaving a theory of pricing for a later discussion.

Household expenditures normally consist of the purchase of a set of goods that satisfy different needs. In choosing such a set or 'basket' consumers would include, for example, food, personal care materials, clothing, transportation and other items which clearly fall into different categories of need satisfaction and would result in little if any substitutability between an item of one category of need and that of another. Whatever substitutability does exist occurs within extremely narrow subcategories. The procedure of structuring a demand curve in terms of a particular good supposes that the consumer is generally determining expenditures within the framework of a subcategory and is thus not very helpful in explaining actual demand behavior. And it is questionable even within a subcategory whether the essential element is the relative price change, or acquired taste as a result of social convention and 'class' affiliation.

The consumer orders up a set of purchases where the bundles or categories comprising the set are hierarchically grouped (along with sets of sub-groupings) to reflect consumer preferences of need fulfillment — certain needs are put before others. The level of income and social 'necessity' are the primary determining features of the number of bundles that yield total need fulfillment; and it is also of crucial influence in determining the extend to which combinations of different subgroups will serve to satisfy a particular need category.

As an example, consider the stacking of bundles beginning with food receiving the highest preference or ranking and bundles consisting of clothing, personal care, transportation, etc. receiving lower rankings. Imagine these bundles being stacked from highest to lowest ranking as sandbags on a levee with the water level representing that of income. As income rises the first bundle is being submerged with the second remaining dry until the first is entirely 'consumed'. The third bundle likewise remains dry until the second is submerged and so forth. The threshold level of income for bundle three is that which satisfies the need fulfillment of bundle-type two; and consumers in their consumption patterns do not substitute lower ranked categories for higher ones.

We find that price changes essentially effect the substitutability of goods through the position of the budget line; i.e. through the income rather than the substitution (price) impact, or via its effect on threshold income for different bundles. The goal of the consumer in the face of price changes is to try and maintain their established consumption pattern reflective of their social position. If the price of bundle-rank one rises, the consumer will purchase less of the lower regarded goods so as to be able to maintain the higher regarded category. However, should the price of bundle-rank two fall, the consumer does not purchase less of the higher ranked goods; indeed, the purchase of bundle two will increase as a result of the increase in real income and not as a matter of substitution of goods.

In general, as the prices of lower regarded needs fall (and beyond some minimum need the normally presumed highest priority food category may rapidly fall to a low ranking), the consumer advances into higher regarded categories of need. The point is that lower prices of goods of certain rankings will, via the income impact, propel the consumer towards higher ranked goods that is so regarded because of the effect these goods have on the consumer's social standing. Once we get beyond the 'minimum' food and shelter needs (and this is very much a variable greatly determined by income and convention) the hierarchy of categories of wants can go any which way and is subject to rapid change resulting from the constant creation of needs and introduction of different goods.

Consumer demands are then the result of learned social behavior, they are not given or 'ordered' by natural law — certainly in a modern society. Preferences are mainly driven by external psychological factors rather than by some internal rational mechanism. This will cause rapid demand shifts that become even more so in response to income changes.

This attitude is not new; but it has been largely viewed as a means to explain the behavior of consumption expenditures over the business cycle, in particular the buoyant behavior of such expenditures during downtowns in economic activity and, as well, to shed some light on the long term constancy of consumption spending as a proportion of income. The modern explanation of household expenditures as it is observed aggregately somehow did not filter down to a different emphasis regarding the theory of demand.

Let us consider such an explanation in terms of the 'relative income hypothesis'.[6] Suppose two households #1 and #2 have identical incomes of $50,000 per year at a point in time, and that family #1 maintains this level for the next five years. However, family #2 realizes an income increase of $10,000 in the following year which is maintained for three subsequent years and then in the fifth year only its earnings fall back to $50,000, that is, equal to what household #1 has been earning all along.

Furthermore say that #1 has maintained a balanced budget with zero savings throughout, while household #2 in the face of its higher income increases its spending by 80 percent. Then for household #1 we have:

$$\frac{C}{Y} = 1$$

and for #2:

$$\frac{\Delta C}{\Delta Y} = \frac{8000}{10000} = .8$$

$$\frac{C}{Y} = \frac{58000}{60000} = .966$$

$$\frac{S}{Y} = \frac{2000}{60000} = .033$$

The question confronting household #2 when its income falls is whether it would reduce its expenditures by 8000 so as to behave like household #1, that is, to behave in the manner prior to its increase in income. It would be surprising if a family in these circumstances succeeded in reducing its consumption sufficiently to balance its budget. We would suppose that its consumption pattern (its ordering of goods) reflecting its social standing which it strives to maintain would be greatly molded during its high income years.

What we find is quite low income elasticity of demand in the aggregate reflecting the desire of households to maintain establish patterns which, as well, implies hesitancy even within narrow subgroups to engage in price driven substitution. Our second household can be expected to sacrifice savings to protect its living standard as this standard mirrors the consumption of particular goods. When the water recedes, the sandbags of wants do not fall with it — at least not for a good while.

What this means in terms of an aggregate consumption relationship is to write:

$$C_t = f(Y_t, \frac{Y_t}{Y_o})$$

28

where Y_0 is the highest income obtained in previous years, i.e. the last cyclical peak, which establishes one's relative position with associated households. When income begins to recover from a level below Y_0 consumption expenditures do not fully adjust as households rebuild their savings position; but as incomes grow to exceed the previous high each yearly income level is that of Y_0 and households find themselves with different consumption patterns that reflect their relative income position in the overall distribution. Income elasticity takes on a fully adjusted value which tells us something about the evidence concerning the long-term ratio of consumption to output.

It is our concern to understand 'principles' of economics with the context of the long-term movement of the economy. And a factor characteristic of the growth path of the economy is the system's absorption of the continuous changes in technology. This factor of technical change has generally been discussed in its relation to the production process as it impacts upon distribution and employment. We will, at a later point, consider the matter in this light, but here we want to emphasize the effect of technical change on demand. This will provide a further supportive argument for our approach to consumer demand, where we bring to the forefront the evolution of demand in response to the long-term characteristic of increases in income.

We can say that technical change yields persistent increases in real output per capita; this change permeates the system through the adoption of innovations that increase productivity. This growth in output means higher wages for the household sector as well as higher profits; and it is this higher real income via its impact on aggregate demand that fuels the long-term growth in aggregate secular output. Thus the economy's secular rate of growth depends on the growth of productivity, and we want to capture the particular aspect of consumer demand as it relates to this long-term development.

As income increases, consumers will be making new decisions as to how to use their greater spending capability; and in general these decisions will be strongly influenced by external societal factors. Now to relate technical progress as the driving force underlying a growth vector implies that this increase in productivity is taking place over a broad range of relevant sectors, in that such sectors have high income elasticities. "The relevance itself of technical progress depends on potential demand: an increase in productivity however large it may be, loses much or even all of its meaning, if it takes place in the productive process of a commodity for which demand can only be small or negligible".[7] Hence an investigation

29

of the impact of technical progress on the growth path of the economy must imply some assumption concerning the unfolding of household demand on income increases. Consider the following example where we have three sectors (a, b, c). We can set up an R vector representing the respective income elasticities which, when taken with the growth rate reflective of the technical process (G_S) will yield a G vector representing the growth rate of each of the sectors.[8] Thus:

	$\eta_a = 1.5$				.045	
R Vector	$\eta_b = 1$	·	$G_S = .03$	=	.03	= G Vector
	$\eta_c = .8$				.024	

What the R Vector tells us is the rate of growth in output experienced by each sector in order to accommodate the increase in demand resulting from the growth in productivity. What emerges as a result of different empirical investigations is that as per capita income increases due to technical progress, the demand for the output of the different sectors do not expand proportionally. These investigations support the observation made over one hundred years ago by Ernst Engle now known as Engle's law, which states that the proportion of means spent on food declines as income increases; but the law can be generalized to state that the proportion of income spent on any type of commodity changes as income increases.

Since technical change forms an essential underpinning, via its impact on per capita income, of the secular growth characteristic of the system, and since this growth rate of output reflects in part the expanding consumer goods sector, then consumer demand theory as commonly set out is of little help in understanding what is happening. Household demand theory is promulgated on a static basis where preferences are defined at a given level of income with the emphasis being placed on the consequences of price changes. Even if we were to put aside our doubts concerning an explanation for the 'laws of demand', this way of emphasizing consumer behavior is wrongly placed. Increases in productivity implies increases in per capita income, but it is the composition of the latter with attendant different sector demands that feeds back to the system in terms of non-uniform promotion for further technical progress. One might paraphrase Adam Smith and say that technical progress depends on the relevance of the market. And since our approach is that the study of economics is essentially about the long-term evolvement, then the role played by household expenditures in this process cannot be understood within the static framework of demand theory. So we turn to a different way of reckoning consumer behavior.

In the conventional analysis the absolute level of utility reflects the level of consumption already taken place — it is as if the good in the example is the only one being consumed. But what we are emphasizing is that the level of satisfaction observed from the consumption of a particular amount of a good depends on the order or where on the priority list it is. The higher the order the higher the total satisfaction conveyed at any given level of purchases. In a dynamic environment, needs (or satisfaction levels) saturate very rapidly; and this has nothing to do with the conventional notion of the rapidity of the decline of 'marginal utility', but has everything to do with the rapid shift or the ordering of goods as income changes.

Note that a given level of real income assumes a particular composition of the goods basket reflective of a particular ordering; but as incomes change the priorities will be altered, the tendency is not to increase proportionately the consumption of goods already being purchased. Yet how do particular goods respond to income changes? We can classify goods of a type (a) which are those basic items required to satisfy physiological needs. Secondly there are goods of a type (b) which households consider as telling of their status and relative position in society, and greatly reflects needs that are acquired via learned behavior. This (b) category represents the vast number of goods, and we can also identify a (c) type classification designated as 'inferior' goods. Each of these types can be represented by Engle curves as seen in Fig. (2.6).[9]

From the household's point of view there are goods for whichever Engle curve they relate to, that are at the bottom of the curve; the consumer faces them with a zero demand stance. There are other goods corresponding to their particular curve that lie somewhere in the middle of the curve, that is, goods for which income and price changes play a relevant role in their consumption. And there is a third category of goods that are at the top of their corresponding curve in that their consumption does not respond any more to income and price changes — consumption here has come to depend on the nature of consumer's preferences. Indeed goods of this characteristic may take on an inferior position.

31

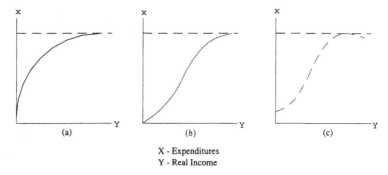

X - Expenditures
Y - Real Income

Figure 2.6

Now which goods fall into which category of position on the corresponding curve very much depends on the level of real income. Certain goods which may have a zero demand quite irrespective of income and price changes up to a threshold income level could very well enter into the second category once the threshold has been crossed. But then other previously purchased goods may suddenly enter the saturation condition (come to the top of the curve) rendering their purchase level unaffected by price and income changes or they may fall into the inferior category. Income changes will cause structural charges in the composition of the three categories of goods; the basket of goods does not change proportionately over time.

Price changes will more quickly move certain goods to the saturation point which was going to occur anyhow as incomes increase. The important factor is that price changes cannot affect the basic shape of those Engle curves though they may steepen the relations on the curve. Conceivably, if the price were to fall for a particular good, one could always find a high enough level of real income that could cancel out the supposed effect of the price change by relegating the good in question to the saturation or inferior category. For goods in the second category the dependency of demand on price (the substitution effect) will vary along the corresponding Engle curve. As income increases a good can shift in category making negligible any relationship between price and demand. In general, elasticities of demand with respect to price are critically dependent on the level or real income. Increases in real income brings new 'needs' into existence rendering the price change effect less meaningful as the goods satisfying the old need fall away in desirability. One now can appreciate the rather limited analysis of conventional static demand theory which treats the income and price impacts separately, if the income aspect is paid much attention to at all.

To say that new needs arise and priorities rearranged is to note that consumer preferences are less and less dominated by the physiological or intuitive drive, and increasingly dominated by social pressure and knowledge about what is new. "And if real per capita incomes are continually rising, and consumers are enjoying extra amounts of incomes over time, they are indeed continually facing new situations. Even if they are reasonably aware of their preferences at the old levels of income, they cannot be so aware of them at higher levels because they have never experienced such levels before — they must learn their new preferences".[10] Households will continually be educating themselves as to different needs and choices of goods. Thus it is the changing levels of real income with the attendant expansion of knowledge and experience that forms the realistic focal point for an understanding of household demand behavior.

NOTES

1. A. Roncaglia, *Sraffa and the Theory of Prices*, John Wiley, New York, 1978, p. 106.

2. For a detailed discussion of this way of deriving the demand curve see J. R. Hicks' *A Revision of Demand Theory*, Oxford Press, London, 1956, Chapter VII. Also see discussion in R. K. Armey, *Price Theory*, Prentice Hall, Englewood Cliffs, New Jersey, 1977.

3. Hicks, op.cit., p. 36.

4. Ibid., p. 58.

5. Alfred S. Eichner, *Toward a New Economics*, M. E. Sharpe, Inc., Armonk, New York, p. 160.

6. See James S. Duesenberry, *Income, Savings and the Theory of Consumer Behavior*, Harvard University Press, Cambridge, Mass. 1952, for the 'Macro' application.

7. Luigi L. Pasinette, *Structural Change and Economic Growth*, Cambridge University Press, Cambridge, England, 1981, p. 68.

8. Drawn from Stanley Bober, *Pricing and Growth*, M. E. Sharpe, Armonk, New York, 1992, Chapter 4.

9. Based on Pasinetti, op.cit., pp. 72-73.

10. Ibid., p. 76.

3 The distribution of income

The conventional (neoclassical) story

David Ricardo observed that the principal purpose of political economy was to determine the laws which regulate the distribution of income. This highlights the point that while the neo-Keynesian paradigm parts company with the orthodox neoclassical approach in many ways, it may be fair to say that it is in the area of income distribution where the schism is most profound since what is involved is a difference in the explanation of the driving force of capitalism.

We begin by setting out the essentials of the neoclassical theory of income determination so as to have on hand the 'conventional' principles that will be put into question. The neoclassical approach determines the distribution of income between 'factors of production' within the realm of microeconomics. This is to say that distribution theory is to be treated as a facet of price determination. To state this somewhat differently: one derives a theory of distribution as incidental to the pricing mechanics in that income distribution is determined by the conditions of exchange. The concern is with the individual as personal distribution of income as determined by economic agents trading in specific markets. One then should be able to relate the pricing of input factors in factor markets to the pricing of goods in specific goods markets. While this sounds perfectly plausible, it will require, as we shall see, a degree of exercising the imagination.

The system produces an output (a good) as a result of an infusion of factors of production into a production process or an aggregate production function. To these factors we assign the names capital and labor that earn incomes called profits and wages respectively. The firm, in its quest to achieve least cost production, is seen to be continuously varying the combination of inputs in response to differences in relative factor prices that are, to reiterate, determined in specific factor markets.

Stepping back from the production side of matters to the factor pricing issue, we find less of a problem, if you will, in contemplating the competitive market for the labor factor. This input can be presented in a technical measurable unit such as hours worked which can be aggregated into an homogenized whole and provided independent of its price. The demand for this factor's services is seen as being ultimately derived from labor's contribution to output at the margin of output, i.e. from its 'marginal productivity'. And profit maximization requires that the 'firm' pay the labor factor no more than what the use of that input in the production process will contribute to the receipts of the firm. This is, the price of the labor factor and thus its income will be equal to the value of its marginal product. For a given wage the firm will continue employment to the point where:

$$W = P \cdot \frac{\Delta Y}{\Delta N} \quad \text{or} \quad \frac{W}{P} = \frac{\Delta Y}{\Delta N} \tag{1}$$

P = price level
N = labor employed
Y = level of output
W = money wage

We can then draw a demand function in money wage-employment space as:

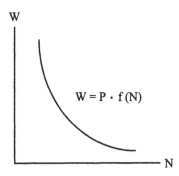

Figure 3.1

Accepting that $\frac{\Delta Y}{\Delta N} = f(N)$.

36

On the supply side the traditional story is told in terms of the labor factor being an 'independent supplier' operating in a competitive market for his services and making judgments concerning the mix of real income and leisure that is anticipated to be most satisfactory. Our labor factor works up a utility function (U) as:

$$U = U(y^e, S)$$

where

$$\frac{dU}{Iy^e}, \frac{dU}{dS} > 0 \qquad (2)$$

which is to be maximized subject to the constraint that:

$$y^e = \frac{W}{P^e} \cdot (T-S) \equiv w^e \cdot (T-S) \qquad (3)$$

where (T) is the total hours available to be employed and (S) is the number of hours devoted to leisure, so that T-S gives the number of working hours (n). A point to bear in mind is that the worker is in all likelihood uncertain about future prices that converts nominal income (the money wage) into real income; thus the use of the expected price (P^e) level entering the expected real income (y^e) and expected real wage (w^e).

Note the similarity of thinking: the factor when encountered as consumer in the previous chapter is conventionally seen to be governed by the 'utility calculus' to maximize satisfaction from a given mix of goods; and now we see him or her as seller governed by similar principles to maximize satisfaction of what is being sold (labor service) for a given mix of real income and leisure. Let us follow the orthodox mechanics in Fig. (3.2) to see how this approach forms the supply function.

Each U (indifference curve) indicates all the combinations of expected real income and leisure that results in the same level of satisfaction (utility); with higher curves representing higher levels of such utility. Our labor unit would like to reach the highest satisfaction curve possible, but is limited by the constraint line which is determined by the available hours of work and the expected real wage. At an expected real wage of w_o^e, the factor can work up to the full number of available hours and earn real income of $w_o^e \cdot T$. Thus one can trade income for leisure along the constraint line $w_o^e \cdot T - T$. The tangency position such as Y_o^e, S_o shows the highest level of satisfaction from a particular choice of real wage and leisure.

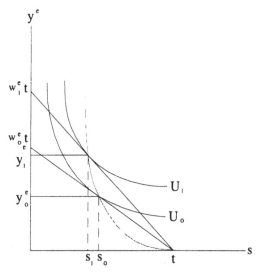

Figure 3.2

Now an increase in the expected real wage alters the shape of the constraint line allowing a higher level of satisfaction to be attained at the expense of the consumption of leisure and therefore paid for in terms of the number of hours worked, i.e. $T-S$ increases. There is, one can say, a disutility associated with the foregoing of a greater amount of leisure; so that more hours worked will be forthcoming up to the point where the increment in expected real income is equal to the incremental disutility. The price of the labor service must offset the marginal disutility of supplying the service.

By connecting all such points we have the relationship between expected real income and the amount of labor offered by the individual as n; and assuming a homogeneous labor force with a single wage rate (to get at the basic notion here) we can sum up to an aggregate labor supply curve in Fig. (3.3).

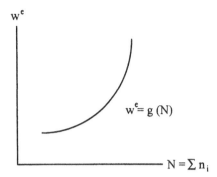

Figure 3.3

Thus for a given expected price level P^e, the amount of labor supplied is shown to be a function of the expected real income. Then

$$N = N(w^e) \qquad (4)$$

but

$$w^e = \frac{W}{P^e} = g(N)$$

and

$$\frac{dw^e}{dN} > 0 \qquad (5)$$

Or, in a similar fashion to Fig. (3.1) where it is the nominal wage and the vertical axis we can see this relation in Fig. (3.4) in terms of $W = P^e \cdot g(N)$.

The graphing of our two functions in W,N space shows their intersection point which determines the price and the quantity of the labor factor sold; and it is on this that one determines the income received by labor. Thus we have the conventional labor market outcome in terms of:

$$P \cdot f(N) = P^e \cdot g(N) \qquad (6)$$

implying

$$\frac{P^e}{P_o} = 1$$

39

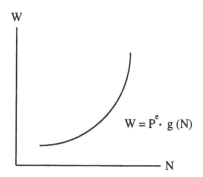

Figure 3.4

We see this in Figure (3.5).[1]

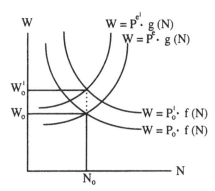

Figure 3.5

Let us reiterate an essential point that the demand for labor is viewed as varying inversely with the real wage, hence a lower ratio of money wages to the rice level has the effect of shaping the demand curve to the right. But this, in the immediate term, reduces purchasing power which flattens the contraint line, resulting in more leisure taken and which is reflected in a shift of the supply curve to the left at the given nominal wage. This has the outcome of a labor shortage that causes a higher money wage which wipes away the demand incentive of the lower real wage resulting in no change in employment as the original ratio of money wages to prices is restored. What we are saying is that labor is able to calculate the full effect of the price level change by increasing price expectations to the same degree, and being able to bring about money wage increases to maintain real wages in the face of such expectations, though one can certainly argue conditions where the increase in the demand for labor at the nominal wage will reflect a reduction in the real wage and an increase in employment. This orthodox theory relying on equilibrium prices set in competitive markets to determine the pricing of inputs has been subject to some trenchant criticism and certainly with regard to the labor factor. Yet what we do have in regard to the pricing of this factor is that it can be represented by, as we have pointed out, a measurable unit of itself that can be put into a market structure for which a value can be determined — though doubt has been raised about the very logic of a demand curve based on marginal productivity considerations for factor services generally. The question for us at this point is whether we can apply this same market reasoning to the earnings of capital. We began by considering this approach, and to do this we need to recall some basic ideas.

Capital goods are durable assets that produce a stream of earnings over time. For example, if one owned an apartment building that generates rental payments over the life of the building, and if one contemplated selling the building, one would need to determine the value today (to set a price) of that future income stream. The value of that future income is what is called the present value of the capital asset. In general, the present value of an asset is that amount of money that would need to be invested today at the current rate of interest to generate the assets future income stream. The formula for determining the present value (V) is:

$$V = \frac{R}{1+r} \qquad (7)$$

where (r) is the rate of interest and (R) is the expexcted future net receipts. The interest rate (r) is used to evaluate, in the present, the worth of the future return. For example, if A were to offer B$104, payable one year into the future in exchange for cash now, B would have to determine the present value of that future $104 — how much would B have to invest now to generate 104 a year from now. Should the rate of interest be 5%, then B would have to invest $99 to realize $104 and B would give A no more than $99.00 currently to obtain that future sum of money.

But let us see a somewhat more realistic application. Suppose we have a piece of capital that has a projected "life" of four years with projections of earning a stream of income of $100.00 in each of its earning years; and let us consider the "worth" of this investment under interest rates of 3%, 5%, and 6%, as shown in table (3.1).

Table (3.1)
Present Value Table

Year	Earnings	Discounted at r of: 3%	5%	6%
1	100	97.09	95.23	94.33
2	100	94.25	90.90	89.04
3	100	91.74	86.43	83.96
4	100	88.89	82.30	79.23
Σ of Present Values		371.97	354.86	346.56
Cost of Capital		354.46	354.86	354.86

Using our formula we can generate the present value of the expected income from our piece of capital as follows assuming a 3% interest rate,

$$V = \frac{100}{1.03} + \frac{100}{(1.03)^2} + \frac{100}{(1.03)^3} + \frac{100}{(1.03)^4} = 371.97 \tag{8}$$

and likewise for the 5% and 6% regimes.

Under the 6% condition we find that the sum of the present values is less than the cost of capital. What this calculation is saying is that the quantity of dollars today that would be sufficient to generate the asset's stream of income at the going interest rate is less than the cost of acquiring the capital good as the vehicle to generate this future income. Investment in this piece of capital is decidedly not worthwhile in the light of alternative means of generating income. However, should the interest rate be 3% then one is positively motivated to undertake this investment as the value of the income stream today exceeds the cost of capital — it is less costly to generate the income via the investment in this capital good than alternatively.

Now at the 5% rate one is, so to speak, indifferent as to this investment; but this borderline rate has an important economic role. It is that percent which equates the sum of the present values to the cost of the investment, and it may or may not be equal to the existing interest rate. Yet it is a rate that is 'internal' to the piece of equipment itself; given the expected net yield and the cost one can then find the internal rate of return for a particular piece of equipment. This rate has been referred to as the marginal efficiency or capital rate; and it bears reiterating that although both the mec (m) and rate of interest (r) are percentages we must not think of them the say way — the estimate of the former in no way depends upon the latter. We can consider this internal rate as one which maximizes the present net worth of an investment, and which provides a guide to the worthwhileness or incentive of a particular investment undertaking. This internal rate (m) equates the present value of receipts to the present value of costs, so that this is the rate which sets net present worth (NPV) equal to zero. We have:

$$NPV = V - C$$

then:

$$V - C = 0, r = m \qquad (9)$$
$$V - C > 0, r < m$$
$$V - C < 0, r > m$$

Thus the lower the rate of interest the higher the NPV and the greater the incentive to undertake the project given the project's (m).

For a given rate of interest one can imagine arraying potential investments ranked according to their (m) rate (or positive NPV), and investing first in that capital good whose worthwhileness is most positive, i.e., whose (m) exceeds (r) by the most, and then bringing less worthy investments into being until one exhausts all positive incentive at the ruling interest rate. The stimulant for further investment beyond the point of zero net present value would require a lowering of the rate of interest so as to have it fall below the existing (m) rate; or some combination of higher expected net receipts and/or a lower capital cost which would drive the (m) rate above the existing market rate of interest. Putting the latter possibility to aside, then the lower the rate of interest the greater the number of capital goods whose internal m-rates will lie above the (r) and the greater will be the amount of investment undertaken.

The greater the level of capital accumulation (the more roundabout production) the lower the internal rate of return for additional investment, and the lower the rate of interest needs to be to stimulate the additional accumulation. And in the usual way of thinking, the lower net receipt flow and rate of return is attributable to the operation of the law of diminishing returns that is ultimately derived from the marginal product of capital, unless offset by technological change (which could come through an

43

increase in net income flows). We can now structure this discussion within a demand for capital schedule.

In Fig. (3.6) we have a curve relating the demand for capital, i.e. investment, to the rate of interest. Let us assume an equilibrium position in that the rate of accumulation has resulted in a stock of capital such that the mec-rate is equal to the rate of interest; in other words, that the desired capital stock at that interest rate is the amount of capital already in place.

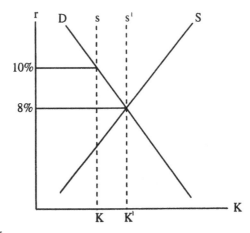

Figure 3.6

This level of capital is represented by the vertical ss line which intersects a point on the demand curve that represents a rate of return, so the point of intersection is one where the rate of profit (the rate of return) is equal to the rate of interest.

Yet this 10% interest may result in a supply of loanable funds that exceeds demand as determined by desired investments, leading to a fall in (r) to say .08 which would then call forth a greater level of investment as more pieces of capital yield rates of return in excess of the now lower interest rate. Additional investment is undertaken (the s line shifts to s') driving down the rate of profit until it equates the interest rate at .08 and thus removing the incentive for further capital accumulation. We can consider this latter intersection point as the long-term position in that the amount of 'capital' (i.e. net savings) that is forthcoming at this interest rate is equal to the demand for capital, that is, the amount of investment that the system wants to undertake. Our 8% rate will permit the capital stock to remain intact thereby resulting in zero net capital formation.

44

In laying-out this conventional story we do not want to lose sight of a basic point that will be important in later discussions. As capital is increasing from k to k' the rate of profit on the increased capital is being driven down as derived from the declining marginal product of capital; and since investment levels reflect the equality of the rate of profit and the rate of interest where the latter is determined in the loanable funds market, then the rate of profit, that is, the earnings to 'capital', can be said to be a market determined outcome. So we have a sequence whereby the rate of interest falls stimulating an increase in capital accumulation which results in declining marginal productivities that brings about declines in the rate of profit until incentive for additional accumulation ceases. The story here is quite similar to our labor market story as we now talk in terms of the economy accumulating capital up to the point where the rate of interest is and to the marginal productivity of capital, as it demands labor up to the point of equality of the real wage and the marginal productivity of labor.

Before engaging in critical analyses of these outcomes let us see how it all plays out within the neoclassical apparatus of production and distribution.

Approaching the discussion from an aggregative perspective we have the economy viewed as a single producing unit seeking to determine the least cost method of producing a level of output. This involves arriving at the correct combination of the productive factors labor and capital, both of which are assumed to be capable of variation in their application to produce the output, and we suppose that all of the labor and that of capital are each of a homogenous kind capable of being related to each other in different quantities. Furthermore, it would be best at this opening of the analyses to conceive of the capital good as a sort of natural agent that while it receives a reward as it is brought into the production process is itself not a produced means of production. This is like our market discussion involving capital where the incentive for investment results in more capital goods on the scene in a sort of 'out-of-the-blue' manner. Certainly these are simplifying assumptions, but rather appropriate at this point so as not to obscure the essential neoclassical message.

The variation of inputs is represented by an isoquant diagram which illustrates all possible combinations of capital and labor by which it is possible to produce a given level of output. As we can see from the smooth contour of the curve in Fig. (3.7) there is the implication of an infinite number of such combinations; but to engage a degree of realism we would in place of the smooth curve portray production in terms of multiple faceted lines where each line represents a production process with a technologically fixed combination of inputs to produce a level of output. Hence in the quest to determine the desired (least-cost) input ratio, the latter approach would necessitate the finding of the proper mixtures of processes, rather than, for the former, the proper capital-labor ratio.

Generally the neoclassical analysis has been framed around the smooth production curve, and we will follow this routine approach to a production function, leaving the fixed-proportion process approach for a later time.

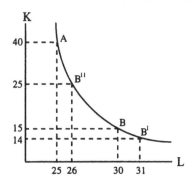

Figure 3.7

That our curve is negatively sloped tells us that one factor can be substituted for another in such a way as to maintain a constant level of output. But the convexity of the isoquant tells us that the amount of capital saved (machine hours) due to the substitution of labor for capital becomes increasingly less the greater the labor input (or smaller amount of capital) when the substitution occurs. The curve reflects the notion that the productivity of an additional input of a factor (and we reckon this productivity here in terms of the amount of savings in another input use that it gives rise to) becomes increasingly smaller the greater the amount of the particular factor in use. The isoquant's slope is a measure of such a move between inputs and it is referred to as the marginal rate of technical substitution (MRTS); as it is the ratio of the change in capital divided by the change in labor. At point B' the MRTS of capital for labor is 1:1 but at B'' the rate of substitution is 15:1 which is a reflection of the greater productivity of labor. This technical rate of substitution is simply another way of using the concept of marginal product, and it may be expressed as a ratio of the marginal productivities of labor and capital. Thus a move say from (A) to (B') tells us that the change in capital multiplied by the marginal product of capital must equal the change in labor multiplied by the marginal productivity of labor. So as between any two points we find:

$$\Delta Q = MP_K \cdot \Delta K + MP_L \cdot \Delta L \tag{10}$$

as $\Delta Q = 0$, the isoquant equation is:

$$MP_K \cdot \Delta K + MP_L \cdot \Delta L = 0$$

then:

$$-\frac{\Delta K}{\Delta L} = \frac{MP_L}{MP_K} = MRTS \tag{11}$$

The objective of this conventional exposition is not only to determine the optimum or least-cost position for a given level of output, i.e. on a given isoquant, but to understand the impact of factor-price changes on the factor input ratios and on production expenditures as the output levels change. Now consider Fig. (3.8) where it is point (A) which represents a least cost factor combination for an output level of 100; then the production of 200 output will see exactly twice labor and machinery as the corresponding point on the 100 output isoquant. A field of isoquants reflects the notion that the further removed from the origin the higher the level of total product represented by the curve; and a characteristic of such a set of curves is that they show complete proportionality. Thus a ray from the origin such as OAB defines a constant input ratio but, of course, an increase in the magnitudes of the inputs along the ray. As contrasted with a movement on the isoquant where it is the level of output that remains constant, but the ratio of inputs producing this output changes.

The extent of increase in factor magnitude as production levels change is a matter of what is referred to as returns to scale. If all inputs were to be increased in the same proportion, and this led to an equal proportional increase in production, then the relationship between input and output is characterized by constant returns to scale. This relationship can be put within an explicit form of a production function set out as:

$$Q = F(K, L) \tag{12}$$

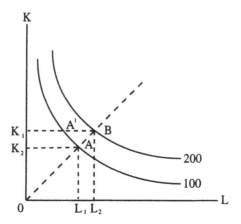

Figure 3.8

This very aggregative expression does create, as we will see, some insurmountable problems; but for now we suspend critical judgement. Where the production function has the property of proportionality, we say that it is homogeneous of the first degree. To reiterate, this property of homogeneity means that equal percentage increases in each input will cause an increase of the same percentage in the output. Thus:

$$Q = F(K, L) \tag{13}$$

and

$$F(ZK, ZL) = Z^{n}Q$$

where Z is an arbitrary number. The function is homogeneous of degree (n), with the constant returns function having $n = 1$. If $n > 1$ we find increasing returns to scale, and if smaller than one we have decreasing returns to scale.

We can engage this production function on a basis where the two variable inputs are not used in fixed proportions as production levels change. A particular case being where we have one fixed and one variable factor; and the usual approach here is to restate the function in terms of per capita output as a function of per capita capital. As (Z) is an arbitrary positive number we can let $Z = 1/L$ which implies that the function works with one unit of labor, then by substituting into the function we have:

48

$$ZQ = F(ZK, ZL) \qquad (14)$$

$$\frac{Z}{L} = F(\frac{K}{L}, 1)$$

and in per capita terms

$$q = f(k) \qquad (15)$$

The shape of this output per unit of labor function is seen in Fig. (3.9) and it follows the usual neoclassical production blueprint when the economy is able to vary a single input. The configuration tells us that capital per unit of labor increases, i.e. that of capital intensity, output will begin to exhibit decreasing marginal returns. We will be able, from a particular form of this function, to read the curve for determination of the marginal product curve of the inputs and for the relative shares of wages and profits in output. That is, a point on the function will give us the distribution of the output commensurate with the least cost or optimum utilization of the inputs. But let us get to the distributional aspect of our traditional story in a somewhat fuller way by first setting out the mechanics of the attainment of an optimal combination of resources.

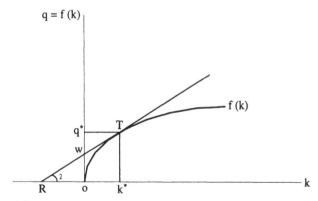

Figure 3.9

Turning to the financial side let us suppose a wage rate (w) of 10.00 per unit of labor and a cost of capital (r) of 5.00 per unit. The total cost (C) is:

49

$$C=wL+rK \qquad (16)$$

giving the combination of resources that can be employed for a given outlay. For example, for an outlay of 100.00 we find:

$$100=5K+10L$$

$$K=2o-2L \qquad (17)$$

it is possible to employ 20 machines and no labor or 10 labor and no machines or some combination of inputs. A curve that reveals possible purchase options is labeled an isocost curve and depicted in Fig. (3.10). Note that the cost line is drawn with a particular slope reflecting the relative input prices, and thereby the extent to which one factor can be substituted for in purchasing — keeping in mind that the slope of an isoquant tells us the degree to which one factor can be substituted for another in production, i.e. from the technical side. We restate the isocost equation as follows:

$$rK=C-wL \qquad (18)$$

$$K=\frac{C}{r}-\frac{w}{r}(L)$$

$$=\frac{100}{5}-\frac{10}{5}(L) \qquad (19)$$

thus if L = 0, K = 20, and for every unit increase in labor the system foregoes two units of capital (or equal to w/r). The slope of our curve is -2 which is the negative of the ratio of input prices.

A change in relative factor prices for a given level of outlays alters the slope of the isocost line affording the economy a changed set of input combinations. Say that the price of labor falls to 8 and that of capital to 3, then:

$$K=\frac{100}{3}-\frac{8}{3}(L)=33.3-2.6(L) \qquad (20)$$

The slope of this cost line is -2.6; for every unit of labor hired the system now foregoes 2.6 units of capital or, to look at this another way, along the first cost line the value of a unit of capital was equivalent to 1/2 unit of labor while along the second line a unit of capital is equivalent to 2.6 units of labor. One would assume that the 'firm' would try and seek out a more labor using production technique with possible distribution effects.

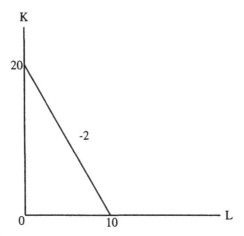

Figure 3.10

To find the lowest cost for any given output, we superimpose a set of isocost lines on the production function, i.e. on an isoquant curve. In Fig. (3.11) we find such a construction for a set of isocost lines of slope (-2) reflecting expenditures of $50, $100, and $200 represented by C_1, C_2 and C_3 lines respectively.

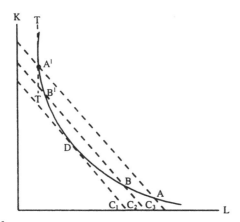

Figure 3.11

At (A) and (A') the resource combinations to produce the output I_1 are available for the given outlay; but we also see that starting from either point the cost can be reduced without incurring reductions in output by selecting a different mix of inputs. Indeed costs can be reduced in such a manner until point (D) reflecting a particular input combination at the C_1 expenditure level. Clearly every other point on the isoquant will involve a higher cost. But let us look behind the obvious.

Starting from a point such as A' we find the marginal rate of technical substitution of capital for labor is relatively high as given by the slope of the tangent TT at point A. Based on this information the move from A' to B' will find the system making a smaller expenditure. The slope of the cost line tells us that one unit of labor costs the same as two units of capital, and in the above move one unit of labor replaces three units of capital. In other words, the amount of money saved by employing less capital more than offsets the increase in labor costs. Thus as long as the MRTS is greater than the input price ratio, the substitution of labor for capital carries the 'firm' to lower isocosts such as a move to point D.

At a point such as D lowest cost is realized when the slope of the isoquant at that point is equal to the slope of the isocost. This is a limiting point, in that in moving to it one is closing the difference between the rate at which capital can be substituted for labor in production and the rate at which they can be substituted in expenditures. That is we have the quality of:

$$\frac{MP_L}{MP_K} = \frac{w}{r} \tag{21}$$

Of course, the same approach holds from the other side starting from a point such as (A) where lower expenditures result from the substitution of capital for labor.

Putting some numbers to equation (22) suppose:

$$\frac{50}{25} = \frac{10}{5} \left(\frac{MP_L}{MP_K} = \frac{w}{r} \right) \tag{22}$$

which can be put as:

$$\frac{50}{10} = \frac{25}{5} \left(\frac{MP_L}{w} = \frac{MP_K}{r} \right) \tag{23}$$

telling us that the ratio of labor's contribution to production to its price is identical to that of capital. In simpler terms that the return for the expenditure on each unit of input is the same. One cannot therefore improve one's optimum position by altering the proportion of resources employed. Unless confronted with changes in labor prices or productivity, expansion in production will be undertaken with the same factor ratio in use.

This finally brings us to statements revealing the distribution of income as a reflection of having achieved an optimum combination. Recalling our individual factor market outcomes, we have that the price of each factor of production is equal to its marginal product (keeping in mind that conventional analysis assumes the economy composed of price taking producing units) so that:

$$w = \frac{\Delta Y}{\Delta L}, wL = \frac{\Delta Y}{\Delta L} \cdot L \tag{24}$$

$$r = \frac{\Delta Y}{\Delta K}, rK = \frac{\Delta Y}{\Delta K} \cdot K \tag{25}$$

$$\frac{wL}{Y} = \frac{\frac{\Delta Y}{\Delta L} \cdot L}{Y} \tag{26}$$

and

$$\frac{rK}{Y} = \frac{\frac{\Delta Y}{\Delta K} \cdot K}{Y} \tag{27}$$

It is on the basis of factor endowment (and through this on productivity), and on its price that the income to each factor is fixed determining distribution of income.

Now suppose an increase in the productivity of 'capital' so that equation (24) is no longer an equality, but now reads:

$$\frac{50}{10} < \frac{30}{5} \tag{28}$$

The addition to production per dollar spent on capital exceeds that of labor; the release of one unit of labor permitting the purchase of two additional units of capital will increase output by 10. Thus for the same expenditure the firm realizes greater output. And this drive to alter the mix of resources may, of course, flow from a change in factor pricing due to a supply change. In general, the lower the price of a factor relative to its productivity, the greater the number of units employed; and given the factor substitution capability of this discussion, will then affect the employment of other factors with which it works. But the degree of this capability is a technical matter relating to production.

We should be able then to set up a guide as to what happens to the distribution between profits and wages upon a change in the factor price ratio. Such a guide is provided by the elasticity of substitution which is a central concept related to the production and generally measures the degree of substitutability between factors. More specifically, it measures the proportional change in the capital to labor ratio (which is a reflection of the marginal rate of technical substitution) brought on by a proportional change in the input price ratio. Thus:

$$\sigma = \frac{\Delta\%(\frac{K}{L})}{\Delta\%(\frac{w}{r})} \tag{29}$$

with the ratio of relative shares being:

$$\frac{WL}{rK} \tag{30}$$

As an example, suppose an increase in the wage rate to rate of interest ratio of 10% which will prompt an increase in the capital to labor ratio. Should the technical possibility along the isoquant at this point allow for an increase in the capital labor ratio of 10%, then the substitution for the relatively expensive factor totally compensates for its higher price resulting in no change in the value of the factors employed, i.e. no change in relative shares. As we can see from (31) if w/r increases by 10%, and $L|K$ falls by 10%, it follows that ratio (31) remains constant.

But the degree of substitution represents the MRTS between the factors at a point on the isoquant. Recalling equation 12 one can then find the ratio of the marginal productivities for each value of the capital to labor ratio; and this could allow for the degree of substitutability at that point that yields the value $\sigma=1$. However, it is quite possible that an increase in the relative price of labor will find the MRTS such as to represent 'inelastic substitutability' meaning that capital cannot be substituted for labor in the same proportion as the relative increase in the wage rate, thus resulting in a higher wage share relative to that of capital ($\sigma<1$). Overall, when the ratio of capital to labor increases, the relative share of labor falls, rises or remains constant as the elasticity of substitution is more than, less than, or equal to one. Again we reiterate the point that in this discussion the elasticity of substitution will be different for every combination of inputs. So income distribution is linked to the mechanics of production in that it depends on the elasticity of substitution allowed for by the technology in use.

A particular case though would be one where the elasticity of substitution remains the same for every factor ratio, that is, (σ) can take on any real value. And a special value of this case is where the elasticity is equal to unity and is represented by a production function of a specific form known as the Cobb-Douglas function. We can portray the neoclassical framework with the use of this form of the linear homogeneous production function; it is a useful tool to express the ideas that we have been discussing and will serve as lead-in to some critical analyses of this orthodox approach. The Cobb-Douglas is a widely used production function; and not only is the elasticity of substitution of this form of the function equal to one, but it is the only form which a constant returns to scale function with a value $\sigma=1$ can take.

Translating the production function from its general expression (that of equation 13) into the specific form of Cobb-Douglas, we write:

$$Q = AK^{\alpha}L^{\beta} \tag{31}$$

where A is any positive number usually handled as an indicator of technological change attributable to 'autonomous' growth factors, and (α) and (β) are numbers between zero and one that add to one.

The first matter is to show that these exponents (α) and (β) are the output elasticities of capital and labor respectively which, when factors are paid their marginal product (as convention tells us) will yield the relative shares of profits and wages in output. With regard to 'capital' we arrive at its marginal product from (32) as:

$$\frac{dQ}{dK} = \alpha K^{\alpha-1}L^{\beta} \tag{32}$$

neglecting the (A) term and with the rate of interest equal to the marginal product the profits share in output is:

$$\frac{rK}{Q} = \frac{\alpha K^{\alpha-1} L^{\beta} \cdot K}{K^{\alpha} L^{\beta}}. \tag{33}$$

$$= \frac{\alpha K^{\alpha-1} \cdot K}{K^{\alpha}} \tag{34}$$

which by the law of exponents yields

$$\frac{\alpha K^{\alpha}}{K^{\alpha}} = \alpha \tag{35}$$

for labor's share, following the same mechanics we get:

$$\frac{dQ}{dL} = \beta K^{\alpha} L^{\beta-1} = w \tag{36}$$

and

$$\frac{wL}{Q} = \frac{\beta L^{\beta-1} \cdot L}{L^{\beta}} = \beta \tag{37}$$

The sum of these output elasticities must equal, to the totality of the output. We are saying that as each factor is paid to its marginal product as reflected in the respective output elasticities, then the respective marginal product times the amount of the factors employed exhausts the total output.

This Euler's theorem can be demonstrated directly from the general expression of the per capita function (16) where we have:

$$Q = Lf(k) \tag{38}$$

Determining the marginal productivity of capital which is equal to the return to capital or the rate of profit we find:

$$\frac{dQ}{dK} = Lf'(\frac{K}{L}) \cdot \frac{1}{L} = f'(k) \tag{39}$$

and

$$r = f'(k) \tag{40}$$

The marginal product of labor is seen as:

$$\frac{dQ}{dL} = Lf'(\frac{K}{L}) \cdot (\frac{K}{L^2}) + f(k) \tag{41}$$

$$= f(k) - kf'(k) = w \tag{42}$$

telling us that wages per capita is equal to output per capita minus profits per capita. Relating (39), (40) and (43) we see:

$$Kf'(k) + Lf(k) - Kf'(k) = Lf(k) = Q \tag{43}$$

And this result requires, to reiterate, that the output elasticities add up to one so that constant returns to scale prevails; and these characteristics mirror an elasticity of substitution equal to unity. There remains the task of demonstrating the value $\sigma = 1$ from a Cobb-Douglas function. Let us restate the elasticity of substitution equation as:

$$\frac{d(k) \cdot \frac{w}{r}}{d(\frac{w}{r}) \cdot k} \tag{44}$$

And as the factor price ratio is equal to the ratio of the respective marginal productivities we can write:

$$\frac{w}{r} = \frac{\beta K^{\alpha} L^{\beta-1}}{\alpha K^{\alpha-1} L^{\beta}} = \frac{\beta}{\alpha}(K \cdot L^{-1}) \tag{45}$$

$$= \frac{\beta}{\alpha}(K \cdot \frac{1}{L})$$

$$= \frac{\beta}{\alpha}(k)$$

Then using (44):

$$\frac{d(k) \cdot \frac{\beta}{\alpha}(k)}{d(\frac{\beta}{\alpha} \cdot k) \cdot k} = 1 \qquad (46)$$

So we now have before us the neoclassical apparatus which creates a link from a position on the production function to the distribution of income; and supposedly one is satisfied to accept such a 'productivity' (or rational?) explanation. However, this is far from the case; though before beginning to question one of these underpinnings let us picture this marginalist approach to distribution via the production function diagram in Fig. (3.9).

Increasing the scale of the operation by increasing capital and labor proportionately will not affect output per capita. There is no gain in $Q|L$ as long as capital to labor ratio is the same because the function is one of constant returns as we have been saying. We see that the marginal product of capital is positive in that output per capita increases with higher ratios of capital per capita, but, with diminishing intensity. That is:

$$f'(k) > 0, f''(k) < 0 \qquad (47)$$

Or directly from the expression of the function in (31):

$$\frac{Q}{L} = \frac{K^\alpha L^\beta}{L} = \frac{K^\alpha}{L^\alpha} = (k)^\alpha \qquad (48)$$

$$\text{as } \beta = 1 - \alpha$$

and

$$MP_K = \frac{dQ}{dk} = \alpha k^{\alpha - 1} \qquad (49)$$

with

$$\frac{dMP_K}{dk} = \alpha(\alpha - 1)k^{\alpha - 2} \qquad (50)$$

which is negative as $\alpha - 1$ is negative.

The rate of profit being equal to the marginal product of capital is simply equal to the slope of our per capita production function by equations (33) or (41). One then reads the rate of profit via the slope of the tangent (RT) to a point on the function as given by k, q* — in Fig. (3.9) this is represented by the slope θ. The rate of profit is:

$$\frac{wo}{oR} = \frac{wq*}{Tq*} = r \tag{51}$$

with profits per capita being:

$$\frac{rk}{L} = \frac{wq*}{Tq*}(ok*) = wq* \tag{52}$$

then

$$oq* - wq* = ow = w \tag{53}$$

Per capita wages, i.e. the wage rate, is the difference between oq* and the q-axis intercept of the tangent to the production function. And one reads relative shares of capital and labor directly from Fig. (3.9) as $wq*/oq*$ and $ow/oq*$ respectively.

Starting from an 'equilibrium' position which is one of an input ratio reflective of optimum efficiency where factors are paid their marginal product, there exists a particular level of employment and relative income ratio. The determinants of income distribution in this conventional story are, to reiterate, factors endowments, the marginal physical product of each factor achievable with the existing technology, and the competitively determined output prices. Distribution comes out of the production process via the factor input ratio reflective of the technology in use.

As this result is read from Fig. (3.9), we can employ the same type diagram to see differences in distribution associated with a different input ratio and technology.

With a ratio k_1 the wage rate is w_1 with the rate of profit given by the slope $θ_1$, and the ratio of profits to wages is shown by the distance OR_1. For a higher capital to labor ratio we see the rate of profit given by the tangent R_2T_2 of a smaller slope $θ_2$ with profits per capita being $w\,q_2$ associated with a higher wage rate w_2. The more capital intensive condition carries with it a lower rate of profit (as it does a higher wage rate). Or, to put this another way, we see a relation between a lower rate

59

of profit and a higher ratio of capital per capita to output per capita. What emerges is a 'wage curve' that shows a negative relationship between (w) and (r) as factor proportions change. Thus the slope of such a curve at a point gives the ratio of the wage rate to the rate of profit that reflects the respective marginal productivities and thereby the factor ratio in use, giving a particular point in the production function. For the given income distribution at hand, the technique that is in use is most profitable.

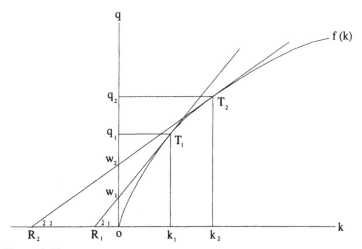

Figure 3.12

We will look at such a curve in detail later on, but for now if we set it out along the following notation we will have another way of reckoning the neoclassical approach to distribution.

Thus:

$$q = f(k), r = f'(k)$$

$$w = f(k) - kf'(k)$$

and

$$\frac{dw}{dk} = -kf''(k) > 0 \tag{54}$$

$$\frac{dr}{dk} = f''(k) < 0$$

$$\frac{dw}{dr} = -k = \text{slope of wage curve}$$

with

$$\frac{\dfrac{dw}{w}}{\dfrac{dr}{r}} = \frac{dw}{dr} \cdot \frac{r}{w}$$

so that the elasticity at a point on the wage curve represents relative factor shares. As:

$$-\frac{r}{w}\left(-\frac{kf''(k)}{f''(k)}\right) = -k \tag{55}$$

or

$$\frac{r}{w} \cdot \frac{K}{L} = \frac{rK}{wL} \tag{56}$$

Thus from a point on the wage curve one reads a relation between the factor price ratio, the factor input ratio (the particular technique reflecting a point on the production function) and relative shares.

Some critical analysis

The foregoing discussion presents us with a 'mechanistic' explanation for income distribution. The production apparatus employs nondescript 'factors' who come on an alike basis in that each will make its distinct contribution and receive the appropriate reward. Neoclassicals viewed the relationship between capital and labor as an essentially harmonious one. In so far as there is any antagonism between them, it arises merely from the competition as to which factor should get more of the value which they have jointly created. There is here a double harmony between factors: they cooperate in the act of production and in distribution their struggle is the manifestation of an underlying sameness of interest to bring about a higher level of output. This cooperative design is at the center of the conventional explanation which sees the economy as a constant circular flow of goods and productive services. There is always a stream of items, let us say factors, moving in one direction balanced by a corresponding flow of income moving in the other, with the market mechanics determining the flows of both quantities and payments. But if income is only to be explained via the market interplay, then factors of production are to be molded as items of production analagous to finished goods as items of consumption.

It is this fundamental approach that is rejected by neo-Keynesian analysis; the central point in the distribution of the output is not cooperation but 'conflict'. Capital has a presence in the productive process not as 'items' but as an income-bearing property; and income derived from it is to be understood as a payment to those who have property rights and will be paid in accordance with the extent of their holdings. The payment to capital (which is the disposition of a surplus) is the result of a property relation; it is not the result of an exchange environment in which productivity is gauged and reward based on it. Labor does receive a reward in 'exchange' for work, but the reward is the outcome of the conflict between labor and the holders of property rights within the context of existing institutional arrangements and the technique of production.

Thus the neo-Keynesian approach brings the realism of the ongoing conflict between 'capital' and labor to the foreground of analysis. It does not smother this conflict by talking in terms of households (rather than social classes) that sell their productive services in markets. The conventional approach maintains an analogy between the factor and product markets with the same principles operating in both; neo-Keynesians reject this approach and the notion that one should even refer to a 'factor market' — income earned in the productive process is not simply a facet of general price determination. There does not exist any 'natural' solution that implies optimality in establishing values for the distributive variables. So that in rejecting the approach of determining distribution within the framework of market pricing analysis, neo-Keynesians can then allow for the inherent conflict between factors and expose this 'power struggle' in the determination of relative shares.

It should be emphasized that the payment to a factor, e.g. the wage, is not an 'exchange' even though the amount will be determined through a bargaining process. The reward stems from the power that the factor possesses to extract a portion of the income that might exist after there is replacement of what has been used for production. The payment is then related to the surplus and the factor's position in its creation, that is, it is dependent to a degree in the way production is organized. One would certainly think that there are institutional and historical arrangements between the productive constituencies that bear on the distributive outcome.

We begin the inquiry of the orthodox approach by considering the return to capital. As we have seen, the neoclassical cooperative view finds its expression in an aggregative production function associated with marginal productivity theory. This function places something called 'capital' (in conjunction with labor) into an aggregative production arrangement to explain the flow of output; and then considers the marginal product of this capital in response to changes in its quantity per capita to determining the rate of profit and the level of profits. This required that capital be capable of being treated as an instrument that creates output the value of which can then be judged to determine its 'reward', i.e. the price. In order for 'capital' to be both a productive item as well as an instrument in determining distribution it needs to be able to stand apart in some sense from its own value, so that one can change its quantity without first having to price it in order to determine the quantity. But this is clearly not possible: capital is not a 'natural' unit such as land that can be measured in terms of a given fertility, nor is it like labor that can be measured in terms of productivity or efficiency units or in terms of hourly units. Capital as a produced means of production, which is to say tht it is created out of labor and other capital goods so that it has no existence 'outside' of the cost of bringing it into being. Thus capital has to be measured in terms of value units which immediately solves one problem as it simultaneously creates another.

This value measure is uniform for all the diversity of capital goods and hence allows for a composite measure of capital that enters into our aggregate production function; but it is not possible to arrive at such a composite without first knowing what the distribution of income is. It is impossible to conceive of a quantity of homogeneous capital that has a measure which is independent of the rate of profit and wages, and thereby relative prices; how then can we talk in terms of the slope of the production function now for a given value of capital per capita, determining the rate of profit, when the value is itself not determinable in the absence of knowing what the rate of profit it — three is nothing in and of itself that we can take the marginal product of. The production function leads us in circular reasoning in that we have to know the rate of profit in order to determine what it is.

Joan Robinson in her trenchant article on the production function and capital theory posed a seemingly harmless question concerning the unit in which one measures a quantity of capital; but in doing so she paved the way for a complete rethinking as to how to structure the production function and caused the traditional type function to be put aside. It is instructive to read her words as she tells us that:[2]

> Moreover, the production function has been a powerful instrument of mis-education. The student of economic theory is taught to write O = f(L,C) where L is a quantity of labor, C a quantity of capital, and O a rate of output of commodities. He is instructed to assume all workers are alike and to measure L on man-hours of labor; he is told something about the index-number problem involved in choosing a unit of output; and then he is hurried on to the next question, in the hope that he will forget to ask in what units C is measured. Before ever he does ask, he has become a professor, and so sloppy habits of thought are handed on from one generation to the next. (I use the original notation in the quote.)

Yet it should be possible to meet the question head on and to devise a number for capital in the aggregate that is independent of income distribution so as to be put into a production function with labor suitably measured. The function can then emerge as a useful tool in that it will allow us to see how capital — and in the production process this is in the form of produced means of production — is an aid to and makes labor more productive; and at the same time to explain how the ownership of property in value capital lays claim to a portion of the current output by receiving profits as a return on invested capital which at a previous time was in the form of 'finance capital'.

Joan Robinson's response was to measure capital in terms of labor time; but before we delve into this approach and observe the formation of a different type of production function let us point up a further aspect of mis-education by the conventional function. A change in the capital to labor ratio results from the spending of finance capital that has a value and is specified in its natural unit. But when profits are earned and capital is no longer money, it is a produced item, say, a plant. 'Capital' as money cannot co-exist with profits as money, and quite possibly the value of capital in the form of the plant will differ from the value of capital in the form of invested finance. As Mrs. Robinson puts it, "When an event has occurred, say, a fall in prices which was not foreseen when investment was made, how do we regard the capital represented by the plant?"[3] Which value of capital represents the change in capital intensity of which we are to take the marginal product of? Of course, capital as invested money can be expressed in an appropriate independent measure, but when receiving money profits such is not the case. The problem has been that we have become accustomed to talk of the rate of profit as though profits and capital were both sums of money at the same time. Yet even when capital is aggregated in value terms the value capital may differ from invested capital.

The traditional production function abstracts from the entire problem either by considering capital as a produced means of production but treating it as a sort of natural agent that at different points in time can be molded to reflect different capital to labor ratios in response to changes in the factor price ratio; or does away with uncertainty about the value outcome by implicitly assuming that no event occurs so that anticipations at the time of invested money are out of step with activity at the time profits are taken. Well, it would seem that the neoclassical apparatus cannot stand the test of close scrutiny nor deliver the explanation for income distribution that it was supposedly intended to do. So we turn to Joan Robinson's redesign of the production function and observe what message a production process can convey.

The basic question is whether capital should be valued according to its future earning power or its past costs. The former approach, which we demonstrated early in this chapter, arrives at capital's value via a calculation of the project's present value which, we can say, represents maximally what would be paid for the project. This requires the calculation of an expected stream of net revenue and a given rate of interest; and the value of the capital is given by the sum of the discounted stream of future profits. But to do so one has to begin with a rate of interest which is what the production function, into which this value of capital is to be put, was supposed to determine.

On this basis a given array of equipment represents an amount of capital; but at a different point in time the same array will represent a different amount of 'capital' reflective of a different rate of interest as well as of a change in the wage rate. The difference in the rate of interest (profit) cannot be ascribed to the difference in the 'amount' of capital in the production function which, as we now see again, cannot be determined until the rate of interest is known beforehand. It is to past costs that we must turn.

There is a stock of physical capital in existence with a particular productive capability, and this stock is to be valued in terms of the labor time required to produce it — one treats capital as a quantity of labor time expended in the past. We can think of investment as the employment of labor in a way that yields the 'fruit' of this employment in the future. The productivity of capital consists of the notion that a unit of labor expended in the past is more valuable today than a unit expended today because its fruit is already ripe; i.e., capital is that good which allows past labor to increase the output of current labor.

Yet a value of capital to be reckoned in terms of labor time never comes to us solely composed of labor time. Past labor embodied in today's capital must itself be thought of as having worked with existing capital or, if we go back to the 'beginning' and some 'natural type' capital. As Mrs. Robinson points out, "When Adam delved and Eve span there were evidently a spade and a spindle already in existence".[4] In a production process today's labor is being added to the product of past labor which, in its own time, was added to the product of still earlier labor, and so on. The rate of profit earned will then form part of the cost price of the capital good used to produce other capital goods (it is the 'price' of capital that is to be added to that of labor). Then the value of a piece of apparatus at a point in time is the result of previous outlays compounded at a particular rate of profit. At every step the cost of capital exceeds the 'direct' outlay required to bring it into being by the ruling rate of profit. And it is this cost that is to be reckoned in labor time, which means that this valuation will be expressed as a function of the rate of profit (interest). To reiterate, the value of capital as expressed in past labor time includes an allowance for profit on the costs incurred to create today's capital stock. Thus an array of 'machines' at a point in time is the physical capital, and its value in terms of wage units is considered as real capital; with the factor ratio being that of real capital to manhours of current employment. The same physical stock will therefore represent a larger amount of real capital when produced under a higher rate of profit and a lower amount when produced under a lower rate. To see this matter from a 'looking-back' perspective, the real capital today is the result of work done over a previous number of periods cumulatively brought forward at a given rate of profit.

Let us conjure up an economy in an equilibrium position of a 'stationary state'. In such a state the economy is evidencing increasing output but without any changes in the conditions of production or in the distribution of the output. Were one to take a snapshot of the system, one would find a ruling rate of profit and wage rate that has existed for a time into the past and is expected to remain so. Furthermore, one could find a level of capital accumulation and growing labor force that permits the increasing output through time. Thus if one were to take another snapshot at a later

66

time period, one would find a larger level of employment, capital stock and output, but otherwise no other changes. We can consider the output of this system in terms of some composite good of which net investment would be a part. Another view of this equilibrium state is a condition in which net investment is zero so that gross investment is equal to depreciation and workers enter the labor force at the correct replacement rate. Techniques of production are not changing and every unit of labor is contributing to the flow of output and maintaining the capital stock. In this condition, the two snapshots of the economy would look exactly the same. There is also the assumption of no economies or diseconomies of scale so that the factor ratio remains unchanged at any scale of operation.

Thus equilibrium conditions are prevailing in the internal structure of the system. To relay Mrs. Robinson's description:[5]

> Each type of product sells at its normal long-run supply price. For any one type of commodity, profit of the rate ruling in the system as a whole, on the cost of capital equipment engaged in producing it, is part of the long-run supply price of the commodity, for no commodity will continue to be produced unless capital invested for the purpose producing it yields at least the same rate of profit. Thus the costs of production which determine the supply price consists of wages and profits. . . . .
> Since the system is in equilibrium in all its parts, the ruling rate of profit is being obtained on capital which is being used to produce capital goods and enters their costs of production. Profit on that part of the cost of capital represented by this profit is then a component of the cost of production of final output.

Consider different islands having different economic conditions with regard to the factor ratio and production techniques in use and with regard to the distribution of the output. However, all islands are in a condition of stationary equilibrium. What we want to reveal is the interplay between the rate of profit, the wage rate, and the technique of production that give rise to the different factor input and distribution characteristics of the various equilibrium states.

We use the following notation.

K	-	capital stock in terms of output
w	-	wage rate
r	-	rate of profit

L_K -   input of labor (t) periods ago to produce a unit of capital

L   -   current labor employed per unit of output

The capital stock is given as:

$$K = wL_K(1+r)^t \qquad (57)$$

where, to reiterate, the value of capital reckoned in past labor time includes an allowance for profit incurred in the past (t periods ago) to create the current stock. In terms of labor time we have:

$$K_L = \frac{K}{w} = L_K(1+r)^t \qquad (58)$$

showing the value of capital to be an increasing function of the rate of profit.

From (57) we can write:

$$K = \frac{rK}{r} = \frac{Y - wL}{r}$$

Y being the output of the composite good with a particular technique in use, then:

$$Y - wL - rwL_K(1+r)^t$$

$$Y = wL + rwL_K(1+r)^t \qquad (59)$$

which gives the equilibrium product exhausted condition corresponding to the capital employed. But more telling will be to rearrange (60) to state:

$$w = \frac{Y}{rL_K(1+r)^t + L} \qquad (60)$$

which tells us that for a given value of the wage rate the system will have in use that productive process which yields the greatest surplus over costs and hence the highest rate of profit.

In table (3.2) we lay out the 'engineering data' for an island where the ruling wage rate is (1) and there are (4) units of alike labor working a normal number of hours.

Table (3.2)

Technique	α	β	γ	δ
Wage Rate	1	1	1	1
Capital	20	29	44.4	72.8
Product	10	12	14	16
Wage Bill	4	4	4	4
Profit	6	8	10	12
Rate of Profit	0.3	0.27	0.22	0.16
$\dfrac{Y}{L}$	2.5	3	3.5	4
$\dfrac{K_L}{L}$	5	7.3	11.1	18.2
K_L	20	29	44.4	72.8

For each of the four techniques the labor input t-periods ago are 10, 20, 22.924, 29.840 and 40.216 respectively with the respective gestation periods (the t's) being 0, 1, 2, and 4. These techniques from (α) to (δ) show an ascending order of the ratio of real capital to current employment as well as any increasing levels of output per unit of labor.

We see that the set of equipment carrying the largest capital cost per man reveals the highest rate of output, but the surplus earned with this (δ) technique results in the lowest rate of profit. Were we to parachute into an economy with the data in table (1) we would find the (α) production process in use with the system earning a rate of profit of 30%. Reflecting this stationary equilibrium in equation (61) we have:

$$1 = \frac{10}{.30(20)+4} \tag{61}$$

69

Another island with similar data in terms of sets of equipment, employment and output but with a ruling wage rate of 1.25 will exhibit results as seen in table (3.3).

Table (3.3)

Technique	α	β	γ	δ
Wage Rate	1.25	1.25	1.25	1.25
Capital	25	34.38	51	82
Product	10	12	14	16
Wage Bill	5	5	5	5
Profit	5	7	9	11
Rate of Profit	.20	.20	.17	.13
$\dfrac{Y}{L}$	2.5	3	3.5	4
$\dfrac{K_L}{L}$	5	6.9	10.2	16.4
K_L	20	27.5	40.8	65.6

Here we find equi-profitable techniques (α) and (β) at rates of profit of 20% so that dropping in on the system will find the operation of either technique or a possible combination of the two.

We might even visit a third island where the ruling wage rate is 1.50 and find via table (3.4) that it is the (β) technique that holds sway with a rate of profit of 15%.

On a fourth and fifth island with wage rates of 2.0 and 3.00 respectively we would find the corresponding techniques to be (α) and (δ). Should a ruling wage rate be 1.83 then a system would confront equi-profitable techniques of (β) and (α) at 10%.

Table (3.4)

Technique	α	β	γ	δ
Wage Rate	1.50	1.50	1.50	1.25
Capital	30	39.6	57.15	88.35
Product	10	12	14	16
Wage Bill	6	6	6	6
Profit	4	6	8	10
Rate of Profit	.13	.15	.14	.11
$\dfrac{Y}{L}$	2.5	3	3.5	4
$\dfrac{K_L}{L}$	5	6.6	9.5	14.7
K_L	20	27.5	38.1	58.9

From these observations of different existing conditions we can draw a Robinsonian production function relating output per unit of labor (Y/L) to capital (suitably measured) per unit of labor (K_L/L). Each point on this curve is one of an equilibrium condition: the rate of interest which enters into the cost of the technique is equal to the rate of profit actually ruling and expected to remain so; it is a rate that reflects the system having chosen the production process which is best given the ruling wage rate. The production function comes into view in Fig. (13) as the solid zig-zag line connecting different islands with different wage rates.

Visiting the island where w = 1 finds technique (α) in place with the relationship of output per capita to that of capital per capita being 2.5 to 5. Passing to the island where the wage rate is 1.25 we observe equi-profitable techniques (α) and (β) process in use with the output per capita and capital intensity ratios being 3 and 6.6 as shown by the connecting 'zag-line' to the third point. As Professor Harcourt points out, "It is we who are moving, through — not the islands — they are in positions of long-run stationary equilibrium".[6]

71

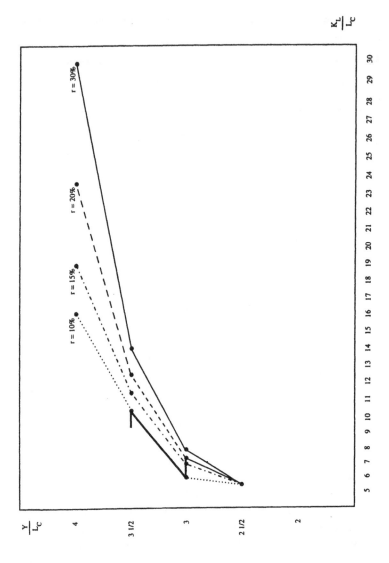

Figure 3.13

We have also drawn in outward 'moving' dashed lines of different slopes that give the relationship between an output per head and real capital per head when the rate of profit is constant. On each of the islands we have costed different equipments (productive processes) at the ruling rate of profit, and for this calculation one does get something akin to the smooth sweep of the orthodox production function. But we must not read any causality doing such a curve; different real capital to labor ratios will not be engaged on the basis of an existing rate of profit unless the two processes were equally as 'good'. What we see is that different sets of equipment costed at the same rate of profit represents different values of capital along this curve due to different 'roundaboutness' of their production. But then the same physical capital on two islands will represent different real capital because each is associated with different ruling rates of wages and profits. What we get hold of is a point on the curve (considered as the productivity curve) which tells us of the stationary condition of the economy at the time we visit it. The production system is determined for an exisitng distribution of income; we then need to come up with an explanation for the rate of profit.

At this point we should consider briefly a reinforcing criticism of the orthodox 'mechanistic' way of explaining income shares. A way, to reiterate, that related a command of the share of output to the productivity of the input; where this productivity is reckoned within a 'fantasy framework' of homogeneity of factors and single output, and, in general, continuous variability of factor use. We consider the attack that has been launched under the banners of 'capital reversing' and 'technique reswitching'. By the latter we mean that a given technique is preferable both at high and low rates of profit, while other available techniques being preferable at the intermediate rates. By preferable we mean an ordering of techniques such that the economy will be able to pay a higher wage rate corresponding to a given rate of profit, or an ordering that relates to the earning of a higher rate of profit corresponding to a given wage. Thus a technique which is preferred (considered more efficient) at the higher rate of profit returns to be preferred — is reswitched to — at the lower rate of profit. We look at the mechanics of this and what it means for the orthodox theory.

Consider a consumption good (A) that is producible by alternative techniques (α) and (β), and where the production with either technique is of a two-step sequence. There is first the direct production of the consumption good say with the (α) technique, thus (A^α); using a fixed quantity of labor (l_A^α) and capital (k_A^α) — considered in the equipment sense as a number of machines. Secondly there is the production of the capital goods input appropriate to the (α) technique, thus (K^{α}); itself produced by means of fixed labor input (l_K^{α}) and a fixed amount of the capital itself (k_K^{α}). Thus a reference to a production system refers to the production of a final good and a capital good that serves as input for the production of itself and that of the final good. We can suppose that capital depreciates at some constant rate (d) and production is carried on under constant returns.

As we are considering two sectors producing different goods we will need to express the 'value' of the output of one sector in terms of the output of the other (the latter being considered the 'numeraire') so as to be able to obtain a total value of production and to compare the output of one sector to the other. Expressing value in terms of the consumption good would have the value of a unit of consumption output equal to itself, i.e. equal to 1 (it is the numeraire) and express the value of the capital output in terms of the consumption good. We have the following equations for both sectors where this value is 'exhausted' by the cost of production; which is equal to the labor cost plus the cost of capital composed of the physical input of capital per unit of output of the sector multiplied by its price (in terms of the consumption good) all multiplied by the rate of profit earned on this capital investment. Of course, the return on investment must provide for the replacement of depreciated stock as well as the normal rate of profit which will go to augment the capital stock, thus the return on investment is equal to ($r+d$). Our two price equations are:

$$1 = l_A w + k_A p_K (r+d) \tag{62}$$

$$p_K = l_K w + k_K p_K (r+d) \tag{63}$$

We presume at this point that we are dealing with a single system utilizing a particular technique that may or may not be the same in both sectors. For a level of production in the A-sector there must correspond a level of production in the capital sector sufficient to replace the capital used up in the production of the 'consumption sector' plus that which is necessary to replace the capital used to produce the capital input to the A-sector. Total output consists of consumption output plus replacement capital so that in this discussion there is zero net accumulation of capital. However, there is a net output for the whole production system consisting of the output of the consumption sector which is to be distributed between the 'capitalists' and workers. The unknowns of the system consists of the w, r

74

and p_K while the knowns, reflecting the technique in use, are l_A, k_A, l_K, k_K, and d.

We can from the system defined by statements 62 and 63 determine the relations between (r) and (w) as:[7]

$$w = \frac{1 - k_K(r+d)}{l_A + (l_K k_A - l_A k_K)(r+d)} \qquad (64)$$

Equation (64) presents a wage-profit curve resulting from the given technique that shows the trade-off in the division of the net output of the system, i.e. that of a physical quantity of the consumption good.

When the rate of profit is zero there is some positive wage rate (w*) which reflects the maximum net output attainable per unit of labor with the given technique; and as the rate of profit rises from zero the wage falls as a continuous function of the change in (r) reaching zero for a finite maximum rate of profit (r*) where all of the net product goes to 'capital'. The maximum wage is:

$$w* = \frac{1 - k_K d}{l_A(1 - k_K d) - l_K k_A d} \qquad (65)$$

That w* is positive is seen by the numerator being positive in that the capital sector produces in excess of its own replacement needs, thus allowing production in the consumption sector; and that it is finite results from the technology that capital enters the production of both goods (k_A and k_K are both greater than zero). Similarly with a wage of zero we have a corresponding maximum rate of profit (r*) as:

$$r* = \frac{1 - k_K d}{k_K} \qquad (66)$$

And what statement (66) is saying to us is that capitalists are acting to maximally reproduce the capital stock.

The way is now clear to diagramatically set out the $w-r$ curve, but how shall we depict it? Does equation (63) define a straight line relationship or that of a non-linear (rectangular hyperbole) function? The answer will depend on what happens to relative prices, indeed, on how p_K changes, with changes in the division of the surplus between wages and profits. And this in turn depends on the technology of the system, i.e. on the proportion between physical capital and labor in the two sectors. Let us first consider the 'simple' case where the input ratios are equal in both sectors, so that:

$$\frac{k_K}{l_K} = \frac{k_A}{l_A}$$

and

$$l_K k_A = l_A k_K \tag{67}$$

which causes the relationship (65) to read:

$$w = \frac{1 - k_K d}{l_A} - \frac{k_K}{l_A}(r) \tag{68}$$

and we have a decreasing straight line from a maximum w^* when $r = 0$. The slope of the line being determined by the ratio of capital used in one sector to labor used in another sector.

What happens to p_K in this case? If we rearrange (63) and substitute from (64) we arrive at p_K as a function of (r) in the form of:[8]

$$p_K = \frac{l_K}{l_A + (l_K k_A - l_A k_K)(r + d)} \tag{69}$$

With equal input ratios the relative value p_K is constant for variations in the value of (r). As the rate of profit changes the resulting changes in the distribution of the surplus (the change in profit costs relative to wage costs) affects both sectors equally.

Perhaps more realistically (less simply) we would take up the case when the physical capital to labor ratio is greater in the capital goods sector than in the consumption sector. Thus:

$$\frac{k_K}{l_K} > \frac{k_A}{l_A} \tag{70}$$

and

$$l_K k_A > l_A k_K$$

Equation (64) would now read a bit more complex revealing an outward bending or concave relationship along the w - r curve.[9] In this case p_K as positive for different positive values for the rate of profit; and this tells us that an increase in the rate of profit affects the capital goods sector more than the consumption goods sector.

We examine this particular case in Fig. (3.14).

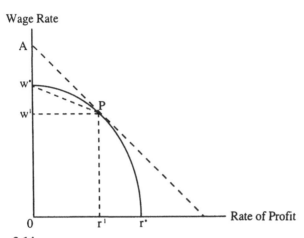

Figure 3.14

The segment ow^* measures the wage rate when the rate of profit is (approaches) zero and is therefore also a measure of the maximum net physical output per unit of labor obtainable from the system. Then a segment such as w^*w^1 measures the amount of the surplus per worker that is taken in the form of profits and corresponds to a rate of profit (or^1), it is as if in understanding the ow^* segment all of the net product was produced by labor only, and therefore it was 'entitled' to all of it. But 'capital' is, of course, part of the production process, and the owners of this capital input share in the surplus as a mirror of the rate of profit earned on their 'contribution'.

The tangency to the w^*-r^* curve at P can be read as a measure of the 'value' of capital per worker when the rate of profit is (or^1). Note that the tangency is:

$$\frac{w^1w^*}{w^1P} = \frac{w^1w^*}{or^1} \tag{71}$$

77

and as $w'w^*$ is profit per worker and or' is the rate of profit we have:

$$\frac{rK}{rL} = \frac{K}{L} \qquad (72)$$

with the tangency being the slope of the 'wage curve' (w^*P). Clearly then, from the assumption of 70, as we move down the w^*-r^* curve with the rate of profit increasing, costs in the capital goods sector will increase by more than in the consumption sector. So that a move along the curve gives evidence of how relative prices between the sectors change in response to changes in the division of the net product between profits and wages.

Such is the analysis when the consumption good is produced in the confines of a single system — the A^α. But suppose that there are two ways to produce the consumption good, designating the second system by (A^β).[10] And consider that the β-system yields a $w-r$ curve that is convex or inward bending so that the ratio of capital to labor is higher in the consumption sector than in the capital sector. Again let us bear in mind that the wage/rate is measured in terms of the same consumption good (A) so that we can put both wage curves on the same set of axes, as we have in Fig. (3.15). The question is which technique will be adopted when the wage rate changes? We reiterate that a preferable system is one that enables the payment of a higher wage at the same rate of profit, or allows the earning of a higher rate of profit at the same wage.

There is a system in use at a particular wage-profit rate, and the question arises as to whether an alternative system would be preferable given the existing cost circumstances. But the answer here is not always a straight forward matter as it can be argued that the preferred system depends on which of the two (α or β) happens to be in use. Suppose that at r_2 it is technique (α) that is in use with a corresponding w_2^α. Then we can calculate p_K^α as well as p_K^β using the existing distributive costs. There will be a difference due to the different physical inputs which, of course, leads to different prices for the consumption good. But say that it was the (β) technique that was in use with r_2 and a different wage w_2^β, then we can calculate p_K^α and p_K^β for r_2 and w_2^β, and we will get different values for the price of capital and the costs of the consumption good produced with the two alternative systems will also be different from what they were when technique (α) was in use. One can ask the question whether system (α) would be preferred under the conditions of r_2, w_2^β.

78

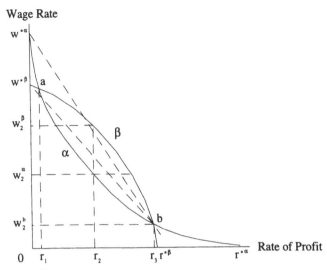

Figure 3.15

We can certainly imagine a situation where if (α) is in use with r_2, w_2^{α}, it is always going to be preferred to (β); and the conditions under which (β) is brought into play will find (β) preferable to an alternative technique. Thus from whatever system is in use there is no tendency to change. Or we might consider a situation such that from a particular wage-profit condition and technique an alternative system is always preferable; but when this alternative comes in with resulting changed prices then the other system becomes preferable and we would get an endless switching back and forth between systems. We can though rule out these possibilities as we relate to a realistic ordering between systems; as we find that a particular system is preferable over a range of wage rate-rate of profit conditions, and at the point where the economy is prompted to switch to an alternative technique it will be to one that permits the highest wage rate for the corresponding rate of profit.

In Fig. (3.15) we see this realistic ordering in terms of reswitching between our two systems. System (α) is preferred for rates of profit to r_1; for increasing rates of profit to r_3 it is system (β) that is the least cost and called into play, yet for rates of profit in-excess of r_3 to the maximum $r^{*\alpha}$ the economy switches back to the (α) system. At the switch or so-called corner point, the two systems are 'adjacent' or equally profitable at the given rate of profit. Our wage rate-rate of profit curve which can now be best referred to as the 'wage-frontier', i.e. that curve which traces the

79

relation between the wage and the rate of profit as the preferred system is adopted, is represented by the outside line $w^{*\alpha}abr^{*\alpha}$. Reswitching is clearly exposed in the light of both systems having unequal capital to labor ratios in both sectors.[11]

Note the tangencies drawn from point (b) to the wage curves which, as a result of our analysis of Fig. (14), tells us about the value of capital per unit of labor and about the net physical product resulting from the individual systems. We see that r_1 — with the rate of profit rising — producers switch to a system with a lower net product per worker $(w^{*\beta} < w^{*\alpha})$ and a lower value of capital per worker (the slope of the tangent to $w^{*\beta}$ being flatter than to $w^{*\alpha}$). This association, so far being in line with orthodox theory; but at r_3 — with the rate of profit still rising — the switch is to system (α) having a higher net product per worker and a higher value of capital per worker, these results being out of line with neoclassical doctrine. And what is very striking is that at higher rates of profit the economy switches back to a system which had already been in use at lower levels of (r).

To juxtapose what is happening, the reader should return to Fig. (12) where the design showed systems (different capital to labor ratios) changing continuously with the rate of profit. The traditional implication is that any change in (r) brings about a change in the technique of production so that one technique (and not the same one) is in use at each possible level of the rate of profit. This orthodoxy then produces our smooth curve associating negatively techniques with a higher capital to labor ratio and the rate of profit. But we have seen that there is no automatic rule regarding such an association. In addition to calling into question the relation between capital per worker in a physical sense and the rate of profit, we need also put to aside the neoclassical negative association between the rate of profit and the value of capital per worker. We observe that this can take on a positive relationship; what we have with this notion is the associated capital reversing phenomenon. There are some interesting considerations regarding capital reversing that we do not get into in this work. Certainly the value of capital can change in association with changes in the distribution of income corresponding to a single technique; this being the so-called 'price Wicksell effect' (recall the Joan Robinson critique). But there is also a 'real Wicksell effect' where we refer to a change in the value of capital associated with a change in the rate of profit that relates to a change in the technique of production; where both price and 'mechanization' effects come into play. And it is this latter effect that is involved for us in our discussion. The reader, wishing to move beyond our 'introductory' analyses can consult another work by this author where these effects are discussed in some detail.[12]

Let us at this point look back over the road travelled so far. The orthodox message instructs us to deduce income shares from the productivity curves of the associated factors and to this end constructed the relevant production functions. Thus we were led to Fig. (3.11) and Fig. (3.12) and the 'algebra' of the resulting wage curve via equations 54 - 56. To repeat the earlier observation: that from a point on the wage curve one can read the relation between the factor price ratio, the factor input ratio, and relative shares where this latter result is represented by elasticity at a point on the curve. For this apparatus to have been constructed one had (as we can appreciate all the more after our reswitching analysis) to have entered into the highest level of aggregation.

We therefore spoke in terms of an all-encompassing output that could be consumed or used as an input to reproduce itself: as well this 'capital' was able to re-constitute itself to work with greater or lesser amounts of labor and still maintain its identifiable physical quantity so that one can observe the results of changing the input of this same 'capital'. Thus to establish the productivity principle of income shares the neoclassicists had to boil down the reality of the diversity of capital and different categories of output into some metaphysical composite of capital (qualities of ectoplasm can serve this purpose) operating in a one-commodity world.

Well, this is not so bad. There is nothing wrong with trying to capture the complexity of reality by means of an allegorical tale. But it became more than a simplified way to explain the world; it was promulgated as a surrogate for an explanation of the rate of profit in a real world of heterogeneity of output produced by labor and heterogeneity of capital. And this was accomplished by way of general acceptance of a proposition so as to become a postulate. We can state this proposition as follows: If at any given wage rate (w') two techniques (say α and β) are equally profitable (at r'), then the technique that becomes more profitable at a wage rate greater than w' (at a rate of profit below r') is the one which entails greater value of capital per man. To this proposition the orthodoxy would add the capital-malleability theory assumption (that ectoplasm quality) so that there is no wastage of capital as the system changes from one technique to another having the capital stock always appropriate to the most profitable technique in use and fully employed. Any time a switchpoint is encountered the directional change of the magnitudes follows the postulate; but one can even eliminate switchpoints by assuming that as between any two techniques no matter how close one can always intersperse a third so that all techniques crowd together to yield infinite variation and yield that smooth curve relating changes in technique (the capital to labor ratio) and the rate of profit. In this way, the desired end result of inversely relating the rate of profit and the capital to labor ratio (as well as value of capital) is made to emerge. Thus the infinite technique one output case and the emerging results are extended to being a general feature of any economic system.

But the world of heterogeneity of output and input cannot in general be refocused to reveal the orthodox homogeneous universe. Joan Robinson saw through this straightaway by asking the question concerning the unit in which capital is measured. And since it must be a 'value' unit it will contain a rate of profit cost factor which supposedly was to be determined by changes in that very capital itself. What this meant is either a retreat to the homogeneous fantasy unit depicting capital, or the abandonment of the approach that read the rate of profit from the productivity curve of capital. And we were moved to redesign the production function and extract a different message. The previous discussion concerning reswitching reinforced our critical analysis of neoclassical doctrine from the vantage of dealing directly with a multi-sector system where each sector while using the same physical capital employs a different ratio of capital to labor. Where we compare two systems, we would reiterate that not only is the technique different in each sector of a system, but that each system uses different types of capital.

However, we do want to demonstrate a particular case where the properties emanating from the traditional function can also be generated from a world characterized by heterogeneous capital goods and fixed input proportions. As Professor Samuelson points out in the construction of what he labels the 'surrogate production function': "What I propose to do here is to show that a new concept, the surrogate production function, can provide some rationalization for the validity of the simple J. B. Clark parables which pretend there is a single thing called capital that can be put into a single production function and along with labor will produce total output".[13]

What we have are multiple systems of production each working with a particular 'type' of capital in fixed proportion with labor that will differ in each system. Each of the systems can produce a unit of consumption good or a unit of capital good, and identical though different proportions of inputs are used in the consumption and capital output sectors of each system.

We set out the rate of profit and wage rate equations that accompany the use of a particular technique of production — the (α) system. Thus:

$$\frac{L_\alpha}{K_\alpha}(w) = \frac{1}{K_\alpha} - r \tag{73}$$

and

$$w = \frac{1}{L_\alpha} - \frac{K_\alpha}{L_\alpha}(r) \tag{74}$$

The wage curve as expressed in (75) is seen in Fig. (3.16).

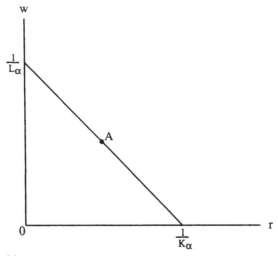

Figure 3.16

A point such as (A) will yield a particular income distribution and attendant employment level. We read from the wage curve that the elasticity of a change in the ratio of the wage rate to the rate of profit is the ratio of factor shares; and also that the slope of the curve is the aggregate capital to labor ratio associated with that process. By differentiating (74) we arrive at:

$$-\frac{dw}{dr} = \frac{K_\alpha}{L_\alpha} \tag{75}$$

83

giving us the same results as generated by equations (55) and (56) representing the traditional production function. Note again that a point on the wage curve shows a ratio of factor shares as given by the elasticity of the curve at that point; and for that given distribution, the technique that is in use is most profitable.

In Fig. (3.17) we find the (α) technique in use with a particular factor payment ratio at point (A). Now consider what happens when there is a reduction in the wage rate; the economy will switch over to the adoption of technique (β) which results in the highest rate of profit — a move to point (B).

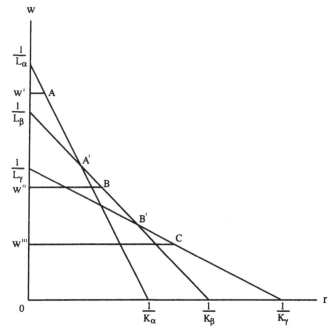

Figure 3.17

The intercepts of the (β) system tell us that when $w = 0$, $1/K_\beta > 1/K_\alpha$ so that $K_\beta < K_\alpha$, and the maximal wage when $r = 0$ is $1/L_\alpha > 1/L_\beta$ hence $L_\beta > L_\alpha$. We find the slope of the wage curve for the (β) technique less than that of the (α) technique, so that the lower wage associates with the use of a higher labor to capital ratio (a less mechanized system comes into play). A further fall in the wage to w''' will have the economy adopt the (γ) technique where $K_\gamma < K_\beta$

and $L_\gamma > L\beta$ so that a higher rate of profit (lower wage rate) is associated with yet a lower capital to labor ratio.

For any given wage, it is the technique curve furthest out that yields the highest rate of profit, so that the adjustment is to a different outermost curve. This yields a factor-price or wage curve frontier as defined by our three systems as $AA\,'BB\,'C$ with two switchpoints. But note there is no reswitching as no wage curve intersects more than once with another so that it cannot reappear along the frontier.

We have then the reinforcement of the traditional message of the negative association between the capital to labor ratio and the rate of profit extracted from what would appear as the real world of heterogeneous capital and fixed input proportions. But this confirmation, comforting as it may seem, is a very special case and cannot really be considered to validate the orthodox explanation of income shares. This 'rescue' holds only under the conditions where both the factor proportions and the magnitudes involved in these proportions are alike in the consumption and capital goods output. It is this which permits the collapse of the heterogeneous world into the aggregate production function as the two outputs are treated identically when considering the unified way of their production.

Should we propose a change whereby the magnitudes of the inputs differ, then matters do not turn out 'right'. What this leads to is:

$$w = \frac{1}{L_A^\alpha} - \frac{K_K^\alpha}{L_A^\alpha}(r) \tag{76}$$

While we do have a straight line relation, the slope of this line cannot be read to give the aggregate capital to labor ratio; hence the elasticity of the curve at a point cannot say anything about aggregate relative shares. We find:

$$-\frac{dw}{dr} = \frac{K_K^\alpha}{L_A^\alpha} \tag{77}$$

and

$$-\frac{rdw}{wdr} = \frac{rK_K}{wL_A}$$

which gives a ratio of profits in the capital goods sector to wages in the consumption sector.

At the end of these discussions we remain with the need to determine different supporting principles for the distribution of income. Certainly it is a dead-end to anchor an understanding of income shares within a productivity framework and orthodox production function mechanism. In Chapter 4 we begin a look at an alternative approach to the distributive shares of output.

NOTES

1. Similar to the neoclassical story as told by William H. Branson, *Macroeconomics*, Harper and Row, New York, 1989.

2. Joan Robinson, "The Production Function and the Theory of Capital", *The Review of Economic Studies*, 1953-54 #55, p. 81.

3. Ibid. p. 84.

4. Ibid. p. 82.

5. Ibid. p. 88.

6. G. C. Harcourt, *Cambridge Controversies in the Theory of Capital*, Cambridge University Press, 1972, p. 128.

7. Via the following manipulations, we divide (62) by (w) to obtain:

i) $$\frac{1}{w} = l_A + \frac{k_A p_K (r+d)}{w}$$

and re-arrange (63) to read:

ii) $$p_K - k_K p_K (r+d) = l_K w$$

leading to:

iii) $$\frac{p_K}{w} = \frac{l_K}{1 - k_K (r+d)}$$

Substituting (iii) into (i) gives:

iv) $$\frac{1}{w} = l_A + k_A [\frac{l_K}{1 - k_K (r+d)}]$$

leading to:

v) $$w = \frac{1 - k_K(r+d)}{l_A + (l_K k_A - l_A k_K)(r+d)}$$

8. Some of the manipulations go along this way:

We have:

i) $$p_K - k_K p_K(r+d) = l_K w$$

leading to:

ii) $$p_K = l_K \left[\frac{\dfrac{1 - k_K(r+d)}{l_A(l_K k_A - l_A k_K)r + d]}}{1 - k_K(r+d)} \right.$$

yielding:

iii) $$p_K = \frac{l_K}{l_A(l_K K_A - l_A k_K)r + d}$$

9. Equation 64, for the general case of $l_K k_A - l_A k_K \neq 0$, defines a rectangular hyperbola describing a function $y = c/x$. If we take $c > 0$, then as it increases y decreases without limit and approaches but never quite reaches zero. In our diagram (3.14) we have a rectangular hyperbola with asymptotes parallel to the (r) and (w) axis.

10. Along the lines of the model set out by P. Garagnani, Heterogeneous Capital, The Production Function and the Theory of Distribution," *Review of Economic Studies*, 1970, pp. 407-35.

11. See Garagnani, op. cit., for a look at the mathematics underlying such a wage-frontier.

12. Stanley Bober, *Modern Macroeconomics*, Croom Helm, London, 1988, Chapter 8. also G. C. Harcourt, *Cambridge Controversies in the Theory of Capital*, Cambridge University Press, 1973, Chapter 4.

13. Paul A. Samuelson, 'Parable and Realism in Capital Theory: The Surrogate Production Function,' The Review of Economic Studies, XXIX. Reprinted in the Collected Papers of Paul A. Samuelson, Edited by Joseph E. Stiglitz. MIT Press, Cambridge, Mass.

4 An alternative approach

Some basic thoughts

We begin by imprinting a different picture on our minds. The image we want to dispel is that of essentially identical 'factors' bringing resources to factor markets, and having them purchased by profit maximizing firms. The reward or payment to the factors is then the result of an exchange process within markets that are guided by marginalist considerations. In replacing the image we want first of all to eschew the anonymous non-descript term 'factors of production' and substitute as economic agents the particularity of capitalist and worker.

The capitalist's relation to the production process rests upon his ownership of the means of production; that is, the legal entitlement to the physical structures that make production possible and generates income. This agent receives income (which we label profits) as a right in conjunction with ownership of this income-bearing property. This payment is not an exchange for some contribution to the process of production; it does not imply an environment in which productivity is gauged and reward based on it. It is a reward related to one's holding of 'property'. This brings to mind a distinction made earlier in our critical discussion of the production function where we differentiated between capital as money and capital as a produced physical structure that gives rise to profits as money. While the reward to capital as money may be determined through some market arrangement, the reward to capital as a means of production in terms of profits as money is a payment for ownership as such. It is not, to reiterate, a payment based upon an exchange mechanism.

But what gives rise to this profit income claimed by capitalists? How do we account (justify) for its existence — is it something that comes out of the production process itself? To the question of where profits (economic profits) come from, neoclassicists would reply from a money viewpoint that it is a return on investment in excess of opportunity cost. The firm realizes costs (explicit and implicit) in carrying through production — with these costs being reckoned in factor markets — and a value of output in excess of these costs marks the appearance of profits. Thus profits represent a return on investment in excess of opportunity costs (i.e. in excess of that obtainable elsewhere). The appearance of such profits would then attract new producers to the source of these profits which by expanding supply and reducing prices would sooner or later eliminate this excess return and restore what is usually termed as long-run equilibrium, i.e. a condition where profits are equal to opportunity costs of 'purchasing' those explicit and implicit factors.

Thus the neoclassical explanation of profits in terms of market outcomes is the difference between the sale price of produced goods and the costs of input; and these profits can exist as a short-term deviation from perfect competition or be related to non-competitive structures. Its existence would be seen as the required reward for risk taking and innovation. But what this approach does is to mask what is happening 'inside' the production process to bring about this profit; for it tends to separate in our thinking the value of the quantity of goods produced from the method used in its production. Nor does it show how the disposal of this profit feeds back to production to allow the reproducibility or growth of the output.

The alternative approach begins with the idea that capitalist societies produce an economic surplus inherent in the production process itself, which can be defined as a quantity of goods greater in value than what is used up in the creation of the goods themselves. This surplus is, at first glance, entirely the property of the capitalist who (or through agents) has brought production into being by contributing the means of production that he owns. One needs to explain how this surplus is divided among groups or economic classes in society and how this division affects subsequent production levels.

Furthermore, we will see that relative prices of finished goods are not to be determined in a manner that would seem to present these prices as being separate from the 'conditions of production'. A change in the relative prices can be brought about by a change in the method of production and/or a change in the distribution of income; but in saying this we sequentially link prices of production as being determined by cost — as if we can measure costs independently of, and somehow prior to the price in question. But this kind of separation is operable for those goods which are not directly or indirectly required as inputs for the production of all other goods, which we label as 'non-basic' goods. However, most are 'basic' goods which means that they are directly/indirectly necessary to the production processes of all other goods; hence the price of these goods themselves play a role in determining their costs of production and the price of any one basic good cannot be determined in the absence of knowing the conditions of production and the prices of all other basic goods — there is a reciprocal relationship between prices of commodities and their costs of production. Thus we will need to view the economic system as a set of producing sectors linked to one another via an interdependent system of outputs and inputs. In order to determine the price of a good used as an input it is necessary to consider the entire system of technical relationships among all the producing sectors; and here we stress its own use in the production of all other goods and of itself.

Let us go back and see what would prompt this 'intertwining' view of the system. Adam Smith in his discussion of the component parts of the price of commodities observes that as soon as stock has accumulated in the hands of particular persons and land has become private property, the price commodities resolves itself into three parts and thus is arrived at by adding up that of profits, wages and rent. In talking about the corn commodity, Smith makes the observation that "One part pays the rent of the landlord, another pays the wages or maintenance of the laborers and laboring cattle employed in producing it, and the third pays the profit of the farmer. These three parts seem either immediately or ultimately to make up the whole price of corn".[1] A reading of this would seem to implicitly assume that these cost elements of the price are independent of each other so that a rise in the normal level of wages would produce a rise in prices generally. But we know from our analyses of the wage curve that a rise in the real wage would produce a reduction in profits and the impact on price would depend on the capital to labor ratio involved, so that some prices may rise while others may fall. Of course, the distributive variables are not independent of one another as Smith may have intimated. So that costs (in the broad sense of distributive variables plus other produced goods) should not be taken as somehow appearing prior to values, and in a simple way determining them.

Perhaps we can present the matter more directly with the following statement.[2]

If the costs of production of a commodity are reduced to wages, profits, rents and the price of the means of production, and then these means of production are decomposed into wages, profits, rents and the price of their means of production, and so on, it is impossible to arrive at a commodity whose costs of production consist solely of wages, profits and rents because, by definition, there exists no commodity which does not require at least one basic commodity for its production. There will then always be a 'residue', composed of the basic commodities of the system under consideration even if the value of this 'commodity residue' is made as small as possible through a sufficient number of stages of reduction.

Prices of commodities are not a simple result of a particular distributive composition of output, so that the analysis of price formation would have to be held distinct from that of income distribution. An understanding of prices of commodities and that of the distributive variables does not rest on the same explanatory principle.

One explains prices in terms of being in support of or corresponding to given levels of production. These levels emerge from capital investment in conjunction with the employment of labor under an existing technology; there will then come into being a set of prices which will make it possible for these activity levels to be maintained. We say this in the sense that these prices will feed back to the production system the required rate of profit (and wage costs) that maintains the necessary rate of capital accumulation to permit the reproducibility of this output. So that the set of relative prices should be handled in a subordinate way to the determination of production that requires a particular level of profits and investments. But a particular price being determined by the conditions of production in a particular sector is interrelated with the prices of all other sector outputs (all other 'conditions' as they bear on this sector's costs).

Thus prices in the non-neoclassical framework are referred to as 'prices of production; and an understanding of the economy would be sought through the interdependence of sectors via a production arrangement that presents the output of some sectors as the input of others. By the term 'conditions of production' we do mean a set of equations that link the different sectors via an interdependent system of outputs and inputs.

With these preliminary observations in tow, we proceed to illustrate an interdependent system of production which we will need for a later discussion of prices; thereafter we will examine the Ricardian model of distribution and production to provide some introductory analysis concerning production and the appearance of an economic surplus, and the sharing of the surplus among the economic classes and its effect on capital accumulation and the capacity to produce.

Consider a three-sector economy A, B and C, with the following production arrangements:

$$A_a p_a + B_a p_b + C_a p_c = A p_a$$

$$A_b p_a + B_b p_b + C_b p_c = B p_b \qquad (1)$$

$$A_c p_a + B_c p_b + C_c p_c = C p_c$$

where A is the production level of the sector, and A_a, B_a and C_a represent respectively the amount of each of the sector's outputs needed per unit (a) output of sector A, and p_a represents the price per unit of A output. This notation for sectors B and C are analogous.

We have in this simple case a system with no economic 'surplus' in that the value of the output produced is equal to that which is used up in production. Thus:

$$A_a + A_b + A_c = A$$

$$B_a + B_b + B_c = B \qquad (2)$$

$$C_a + C_b + C_c = C$$

Of course, at the end of the production period the different outputs end up in the hands of different producers, and if the aggregate level of output is to be maintained it is necessary that the outputs be distributed according to the left side of the system in (1) which requires a particular set of relative prices to exist. For example, the value of the output of the B sector enables the purchase of the required value of the A and C inputs which then leaves the B sector with a residual that goes to purchase labor at the existing wage as well as to 'purchase' its own output for its own production (which we can think of as an act of reinvestment). This residual is equal to that portion of each sector's output that is required as input towards the maintenance of its own production level. We do not use the term 'surplus' where 'investment' is normally related to a growing level of output; but even within this limited exposure (the wage rate and rate of profit are not overtly expressed here), we can see how prices stand in relation to one another as a reflection of the technical interdependence of sectors. It is via this approach that neo-Keynesians link up sectors, which is quite different from the neoclassical linkage via the interdependence of markets. The former attitude prompts understanding of value as it bears directly upon production and distribution.

We can then consider the notion of equilibrium prices as relating to those prices of production that permit the reproducibility of output; equilibrium is not to be thought of as reflecting the shorter term (day-to-day) market price wherein such prices deviate around those longer-term 'gravitational' prices of production. We will return to a discussion of pricing in greater detail but, as we mentioned, at this point we want to look at some basic relationships concerning distribution and production.

The Ricardian precursor

As a first step we would collapse our three sectors into one common model — let us say an economy consisting of one gigantic farm whose output is corn — that serves simultaneously as a wage good and 'circulating' capital (this is the famous corn model rationalization of Ricardo's arguments). Assume that the amount of land as well as its quality and technique of farming (i.e. the possibilities of intensive cultivation) are all prescribed. Corn is produced by applying alike doses of labor and 'capital' (actually we should think here in terms of an amalgam of labor and capital into a homogeneous input) to this given quantity of land with the production period lasting one year. At the beginning of the period investment consists of the wage advanced to labor (that of corn) so as to sustain itself through the production process, plus an amount of corn as seed. Thus the amount of 'advance', i.e. the capital stock, that initiates production had to be on hand and thus be someone's property before output is undertaken; and once it is invested it is all used up in the act of acquiring production over the one year period. All capital is thus circulating capital in this very simple approach; but if we want to also think in terms of agricultural tools then we can employ the trick of making believe that part of the corn advance transformed itself into hardened capital at the beginning and is then made to disappear at the end as though it had never been. Thus the whole of the investment — that portion of corn used as wage goods and consumed by labor, as well as the portion of corn used as seed and tools and 'consumed' by production — can be thought of as circulating.

At the end of the production period all of the output of corn reverts to the owners of capital as a reward or 'payment' for advancing (investing) their property, i.e. their corn holdings. But while all of the capital consists of the commodity output, not all of the output will be utilized as capital. And this brings us to the identity of the classes of people (not factors of production) in the production process.

We recognize the class of persons identified as landlords who own and provide the land and receive a rent payment, and that of the capitalists who provide the capital and organize production and receive payment in the form of profits, and there are workers who provide the labor and receive payment called wages. Now these payments comprise the distribution of the total production; but while the total production is entirely determined by the technical conditions inherent in the production process, its distribution is a complex affair determined by the interplay of technical and demographic factors. Yet the outcome of this distribution will itself greatly determine the level of production, as it influences the level of capitalists 'savings' — their corn holdings — that is to be advanced towards production.

Let us consider the determination of the rent payment which, as Ricardo stated, "is that portion of the produce of the earth which is paid to the landlords for the use of the original and indestructive power of the soil".[3] The consideration that determines the total output out of which rent is extracted is that this fixed element is composed of different pieces of land of varying fertility, and that successive applications of labor and seed to the same quality of land will see output being subject to diminishing returns. It is this technical property that makes rent a net gain to the landlord. We look at some numbers in table (4.1) so as to bring this clearly into focus; still keeping our discussion in physical terms, we then suppose that the 'cost' of a unit of labor is 140 bushels of corn.

A capitalist (farmer) on any grade of land will cultivate it more intensely by greater application of labor as long as the resulting output exceeds the cost of production. We note five lands (A - E) of varying fertility with the most fertile (A) taken up first; and as the economy expands there will be recourse to less fertile land that is available to be taken up freely when needed. Land in the Ricardian scheme is one of those natural endowment type resources that is specialized as to its use and fixed in supply. The land we are considering is used for crop (corn) production and cannot be used alternatively, say for animal grazing. Thus rent emerges from the productivity of land and does not contain an opportunity cost payment. This is a way of telling us that rent is not price determining (it is not a gauge of an alternative productive use that the value of the current output must at least be equal to) but that it is price determined — the higher the surplus the higher the rent payment. Thus rent emerges because the price of corn is high and not the reverse; and not to belabor the point we are saying that rent is not a cost that enters into the determination of price.

Table (4.1)

Total Product						
Time	Input	A	B	C	D	E
	0	0	0	0	0	0
1	1	180	170	160	150	140
2	2	350	330	310	290	
3	3	510	480	450		
4	4	660	620			
5	5	800				

Marginal Product						
Time	Input	A	B	C	D	E
1	1	180	170	160	150	140
2	2	170	160	150	140	
3	3	160	150	140		
4	4	150	140			
5	5	140				

Each grade of land will be intensively cultivated as long as the return to the additional dose of input exceeds its cost. For example, on the most fertile land (A) undertaken first, the initial input yields an output of 180 which creates a surplus of 40. A second dose yields an additional output of 170 and an additional surplus of 30. For the two units we have a surplus of 70 as a result of the productivity of land (A) for the given costs of production. This surplus becomes the rent payment to the individual who happens to have title to the land; in essence a reward to the fixed factor that happens to be there — it does not have to 'earn its way' to become an input.

98

Land (A) will be intensively cultivated up to five doses of input which will produce a total rent payment of 100 units of output. Thereafter the less fertile land (B) is taken up generating a smaller rent of 60 units up to the least fertile land (E) on which the rent is zero. Land (E) is considered at the extensive margin of cultivation; that is, being of that quality where the total output is equal to its cost.

Before commenting further on this element of distribution, it might be helpful to array the numbers in a somewhat different way in Table (4.2) so as to perhaps get a better read as to what is happening on any type land — say land (A).

Table (4.2)
Rent Determination

Input	Output	Avg. Product	Marg. Product	MC
0	0	0	0	140
1	180	180	180	140
2	350	175	170	140
3	510	170	160	140
4	660	165	150	140
5	800	160	140	140

For an input of say three doses the marginal product of 160 of which 140 goes as payment to the 'variable input', the payment to labor and the farmer, with the 20 remainder going to the rent payment. This shows that while the non-fixed contribution receives the marginal output, the fixed contribution receives the intramarginal surplus (i.e. the difference between the marginal product and the constant marginal cost) which sums to the rent payment of 100 units of output.

Rent, then, arises for two reasons: "If land is homogeneous, the limitation of supply creates scarcity rent. Rent is the difference between the product of all capital and labor and the product of the final dose at the intensive margin. When land differs in quality, the scarcity of acres gives rise to differential rents".[4] But however it may be, what has been said about this landed class in the process of economic development? They are considered as unproductive, to engage wholly in self-indulgence by spending their income on 'luxury goods', and not to put their wealth to work to further production and employment. Adam Smith characterized landlords as follows:[5]

Those who live by rent....are the only one of the three orders whose revenue costs them neither labor nor care, but comes to them, as it were, of its own accord, and independent of any plan or project of their own. That indolence, which is the natural effect of the ease and security of their situation, renders them too often not only ignorant but incapable of that application of mind which is necessary in order to foresee and understand the consequences of any public regulation.

Certainly an unequivocal, uncomplimentary statement.

We add 'economic content' to the term luxury goods by considering such goods as being produced by the system but which themselves do not enter directly or indirectly into the production of other goods. They do not form a part of that interdependent production and price mechanism that we spoke about earlier; and such goods must be handled within a multi-sector context. But for now we are in the one commodity framework where the output serves as both consumption good and as input for further production.

Let us return to the discussion in Chapter 1 where we considered scarce goods as being of the natural endowment type that while not produced nevertheless enter the production process, so that they are akin to goods of the production type that are not scarce in the Ricardian-classical sense. These latter goods are in the main the type that enter into the production process and are the object of Ricardo's investigation in his discussion of values. In order not to confuse matters concerning the goods that enter into production, he had all goods of the endowment type be represented by land at the extensive margin of cultivation so that it yields zero rent and is then no longer scarce. Of course, output of goods on land that is not at the margin would yield a rent, but if the rent is deducted before one determines prices it is as if the land was not scarce. For Ricardo the value of commodities was determined by the quality of producible input employed on the marginal piece of land — one which yield no rent. Thus as Pasinetti tells us, "The problems of scarcity had thereby been eliminated from the analysis, and Ricardo could carry on his inquiry into the commodities which he really wanted to investigate — the produced commodities which are by far the greatest part of goods which are the object of desire".[6] These goods, to reiterate, have positive prices, can enter the production process as produced means, but they are not considered 'scarce'.

We turn to the wage element of distribution. The classical (Ricardian) approach to production takes the inputs of 'capital' and labor in a fixed proportion relationship. There was thus no diminishing returns — marginal productivity basis for the division of the output-less rent — between wages and profits. Neo-Keynesians in consideration of the firm in modern capitalism have restructured the cost curves apparatus in that it eschews the neoclassical diminishing returns basis for an explanation of costs, and at a later point we will bring this out. Here in our one output model it is sufficient for us to see that there was no notion of holding constant the investment of corn (seed) capital while varying that of corn (wage) capital. Indeed Ricardo treated the whole of capital as consisting of total wages to workers, i.e. circulating capital; he avoided handling the variables of labor, land and capital by reducing labor and capital to one variable input.

Wages are then not related to labor's 'contribution' in the production process as reflected in the marginal product approach of neoclassicism. So that while we might talk about the magnitude of the rent being determined by the forces making for diminishing returns (the application of applying the one variable input to a fixed supply of land) there is no similar way to consider the reward to labor. At this point let us fast-forward out time frame and indicate that Keynes in the General Theory denied that the real wage is equal to the marginal disutility of the existing employment, and thereby negating the notion that labor can choose the real wage at which it will work. He did construct a theory of employment upon effective demand rather than upon the level of money wages. There are reasons other than the technicalities of the production function that would have us put aside a productivity explanation of wages and the apparatus that was constructed earlier in this chapter. Marginalist principles do not determine total wages or the amount of employment; but if so, what does?

Ricardo related the level of wages to the physiological (and we may add psychological) necessity of the working class to maintain and reproduce itself; it is a price 'required' by labor to sustain its availability to the production process. Looking at wages this way, he would have us see it as a payment that comes out of a previous period's production to maintain labor's availability for the current period — the wage is then not tied to current output and to any immediate contribution of labor. In Ricardian thinking the wage income is not a flow from current production (which is a small step from labor's current production activity) but a part of a division of an already accumulated output (i.e. capital stock).

Thus the wage would be determined by the scarcity of labor relative to its demand as given by the technology of production, and it is not linked to any 'productive contribution' in bringing about the existing output. The wage is considered as an 'advance' that sustains labor over the current production period. But the essential question is what determines the amount of advance and thereby the level of employment at the outset of a production period?

There exists a real wage (which we can reckon as a particular basket of goods) that Ricardo considers as the 'natural wage rate' (or natural price) which is taken as a long run notion, in that it works to maintain the labor force at some constant level over time. And this natural price can be expected at a point in time to differ from the market price of labor which results from, as Ricardo states, "the natural operation of the proportion of the supply to the demand; labor is dear when it is scarce and cheap when it is plentiful".[7] With regard to the natural price (not necessarily a strict subsistence price) perpetuating a particular size of the labor force Ricardo has the following to say:[8]

> It is when the market price of labor exceeds its natural price that the condition of the labourer is flourishing and happy, that he has in his power to command a greater proportion of the necessaries and enjoyments of life, and therefore to rear health and numerous family. When, however, by the encouragement which high wages gives to the increase of population, the number of labourers is increased, wages again fall to their natural price and indeed from a reaction sometimes fall below it.
>
> When the market price of labour is below its natural price, the condition of the labourers is most wretched: then poverty deprives them of those comforts which custom renders absolute necessaries. It is only after their privations have reduced their numbers, or the demand for labor has increased, that the market price of labour will rise to its natural price, and that the labourer will have the moderate comforts which the natural wage will afford.

The market wage will tend to conform to its natural rate but the market rate "may, in an improving society, for an indefinite period, be constantly above it". And we should also reckon that the natural wage will tend to drift upward with the 'progress' of society as customs and habits change, leading workers to expect a higher standard of living.

So the second of the distributive elements, the wage rate, is determined by institutional and social factors (we would say by non-economic conditions at least as compared to the marginalist technicalities), and the first rent element was determined by the output of the marginal land put into cultivation. This leaves us with the third element that of profits which accrues to the capitalist as the organizer of the production process. Profits are considered as a residual equal to the total product minus rent less the wage bill.

The total product at the end of a production period would depend on the amount of investment (advance undertaken by the capitalists) in working capital at the beginning of the production process given the technique of farming and quality of land. The level of this investment though is equal to the residual of a previous period (less capitalist consumption of corn) that is claimed by the capitalist as his property (his reward) for putting his savings into the process.

If we think for a moment in terms of a no-rent production scene, then profits emerge as total product minus the wage bill which is equal to the previous investment of the circulating capital. If we splice this investment into wage 'capital' and seed capital, then, given the wage rate, it is the productivity of the seed capital that influences the profit level. But the point is that we cannot get hold of the productivity of this 'seed-tool' as a result of holding other inputs constant — there is no marginal productivity basis for an explanation of profits. Indeed in this circumstance one might expect to see a constant rate of profit.

The determination of the rate of profit will be drawn from what happens to the distribution of income and production levels as the production process enlargens. We want to read this linkage from the Ricardian system; for this model can be seen as the precursor to the post-Keynesian alternative paradigm that represents a clear break with marginal economic theory and whose roots go to the classical tradition.

We consider again the bare one-sector model.[9] . Identifying the composite labor-capital input by (N), then:

$$Y_1 = f(N_1) \tag{3}$$

subject to the properties:

$$f'(N_1) > \overline{w} \tag{4}$$

telling us that when production gets underway initially on the best land, the economy will find a level of production in excess of the natural wage rate so as to yield the surplus necessary to continue production in the following period. As well production will be subject to:

$$f''(N_1) < 0 \qquad (5)$$

revealing decreasing marginal returns as greater levels of the input are committed to production due to the existing fertility and technique of farming that characterize the natural factor.

Of the total output the composite factor is paid the marginal product while the rent payment is equal to that intramarginal surplus; so that the total rent payment comes to:

$$R = f(N_1) - N_1 f'(N_1) \qquad (6)$$

And profit (P) residual is:

$$P_1 = f(N_1) - [f(N_1) - N_1 f'(N_1)] - N_1 w$$

$$= Y_1 - R - N_1 w \qquad (7)$$

The relative share of rent $(\dfrac{R}{Y})$ is:

$$\frac{R}{Y_1} = \frac{f(N_1) - N_1 f'(N_1)}{f(N_1)}$$

$$= 1 - \frac{N_1 f'(N_1)}{f(N_1)} \qquad (8)$$

We can express the last term in (8) as:

$$1 - \frac{f'(N_1)}{a_{N_1}} = 1 - \Sigma_N \qquad (9)$$

where a_N is the average product so that (Σ_N) is the elasticity of production with respect to changes in employment. There is an upward movement in the share of output going to rent as a result of (Σ_N) decreasing with the application of greater levels of (N).

Equations (7) and (8) can be illustrated along with that of relative shares within the expanding system by using Figs (4.1) and (4.2).

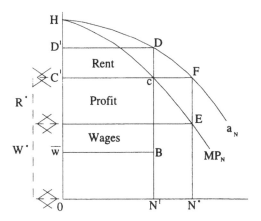

Figures 4.1

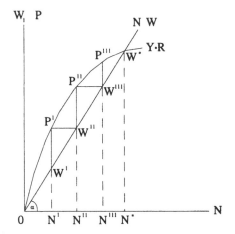

Figures 4.2

Before proceeding to the diagrams we consider again table (4.2) which allows us to calculate the total rent payment of 100 reflecting the increasing levels of rent on the intra-units of production with the application of greater amounts of employment. The remainder of output less rent constitutes profits plus wages; and while we cannot read profits directly, we do read total wages (Nw) as N times 140 and find that wages rise correspondingly with that of employment. However, output rises correspondingly less than employment and with rent levels increasing with employment, it becomes evident that the profit portion of that remainder

105

declines as employment and production enlarges. We note that with N = 5 output less rent is equal to total wages of 800. At this point there is no difference, after rent has been paid, between what has been advanced in wages and what remains at the end of the production period.

In Figure (1) for a level of employment ON' the total product is $f(N')$ equal to $ONN'D$. Then from equation (6) we read the rent level as $CDC'D'$. The natural wage is given as $(\overline{w})$ and towards which the market wage will tend; and assuming that is what is paid, total wages for $N'\overline{w}$ is $O\overline{w}N'B$. The profit residual is the rectangle $\overline{w}C'CB$. As we can discern, the greater the level of employment the higher the total rent payment; the move along $H\text{-}MP_N$ reveals an increasing intramarginal surplus. As well, increasing levels of employment mean higher total wages; and all this will go to reduce the profit share of production while increasing the share accruing to the landowner. But let us get into the system to see 'behaviorally' what is happening.

At the end of a production period with a level of employment ON', the capitalist realizes a residual profit level of $P'W'$; that is, a level of output minus rent that is greater than the advance of the circulating capital at the outset of the previous period. The output is specified as a function of the investment of previously accumulated capital, i.e. profits in physical units here, is a reflection (given the technique) of the amount of employment that this investment 'commands' at the market wage rate (w). It is the capitalists who are the entrepreneurs of the system; they represent the 'productive' class in that they organize production and devote their profits to the act of investment in order to accumulate still greater levels of profits. They were considered to be generally thrifty as compared to the profligate landowner; hence we can consider accumulated profits as essentially savings (they consume very little of their own corn production). It bears emphasizing that the demand for labor is determined by the level of accumulated capital.

Quite possibly an investment of $P'W'$ will induce a market wage rate above the natural rate $N'W'$ which means a smaller level of employment and, with given technology, a smaller level of output such that at the end of the production period the output less rent would be equal to the total wage bill; that is, wages would rise to $N''P''$ which effectively chokes off further investment. A counterclockwise movement of the wage line would need to be balanced by some change in technique of production so as to avoid negative effects on the rate of profit and on subsequent employment and output levels.

But this increase in labor's per capita standard of consumption cannot be, as Ricardo viewed the matter, anything more than a temporary gain. For over a longer period this gain prompts an increase in the numbers of the labor force so as to pressure the real wage rate back to its natural level. Professor Pasinetti in his works on the Ricardian system makes the point that "it is very impressive to notice how strongly Ricardo is convinced of the operation of this mechanism. To be precise, he always speaks of a process which will operate ultimately, but the emphasis on it is so strong that his analysis is always carried on as if the response is almost immediate".[10] Ricardo telescopes it all into the long term: in figure (2) an investment of $P'W'$ while it may temporarily increase the real wage while at the same time foster counterbalancing increases in the labor supply, so that we would consider a level of ON'' employment resulting from the investment of the circulating capital equal to $P'W'$.

The transformation of profits into capital is the essential force propelling the system forward; with the required accompanying increase in the labor force emerging as a by-product of capital accumulation. An explanation of the increase in the labor force was an important ingredient for an explanation of growth generally with the demographics responding to wage rate changes that itself was considered linked to the level of profits. It is interesting to note that in the 'short-term' a higher rate of profit is positively associated with a higher wage rate. We will at a later point consider this relationship more closely.

Getting back to the discussion we have that the employment of ON'' leads to profits of $P''W''$ which, upon investment causes employment to rise to ON'' and so on. But as we can observe the level of output less rent over the previous level of circulating capital investment is, beyond some point, becoming increasingly smaller. The economy is being moved towards the stationary state where the rate of profit is zero which calls a halt to any further accumulation of capital. For a level of employment of ON^* the output less rent is equal to the total advance at the outset; there is then no capability to bring about further increases in employment and production. Let us say again that due to the given technique of production and that of the quality of land, diminishing returns will characterize the application of new capital and labor to the 'fixed' factor with the resulting increase in rents over time, along with that of total wages, resulting in the consequent fall in the rate of profit. At ON^* the increase in output is insufficient to bring about a profit residual. For example, at a level of output characterized by employment ON'' the rate of profit will be:

$$r = \frac{P''N'' - W''N''}{W''N''}(100\%)$$

$$= (\frac{P''N''}{W''N''} - 1)100\% \tag{10}$$

and diagram (2) clearly shows the rate of profit declining with higher levels of production. We should make the point that the stationary state where the labor force and production do not change and which Ricardo believed would eventually come to pass, need not be taken at the extreme point of zero profits; but will be reached before then as reflective of a certain minimum rate of profit where capitalists lose any inducement to accumulate.

Yet it is not the stationary state as such that is of central interest to us, as much as an understanding of the interplay of economic factors that continuously wards off this 'end-point', that is, keeps the system on a growth trajectory over the long-term. We would need to consider the impact of technological change in terms of how it gets infused into the system and its impact on the distribution of income and thereby on the level of savings. As well, we would want to consider the outcome of conflict between capital and labor as it impacts on income distribution via its effect on the pricing policy of firms; and to reckon the rate of profit within the framework of economic growth and the behavior of different class constituencies of the economy. In general, the Ricardian model does open the door to growth analysis which, as we mentioned, is what non-neoclassical economics is essentially all about.

A point about this is that the act of accumulation increases the demand for labor and bids up the market wage; and if over the longer term labor translates its improved income situation into a higher permanent consumption standard, rather than have it prompt an increase in numbers, we get a higher natural wage which rotates the tan (α) line to the left. This does increase worker's welfare but at the expense of reducing profit levels and employment. A counterforce would have the economy subject to a stream of technical innovations that may prevent profit erosion as real income increases over time. Yet these technical changes may themselves have regative employment effects which then impact on profita via effective demand; and if profits falter so will savings and investment — and investment is the means through which technical change becomes imbued into the economy. There are certainly a number of factors to be analyzed and brought into 'balance' if we are to understand the economy's movement along a growth path. It would then behove us to go beyond the bare outline of the Ricardian system to see what further insights can be gleaned as prelude to recent analysis.

Let us extend the system to the existence of a second produced commodity (Y_2) considered as a 'luxury good' consumed by rent and that small portion of profits. Consider this commodity as gold which at any place and time requires the same quantity of labor per unit of its production (it is produced under constant return). This good will be the numeraire of the system; prices are expressed in terms of gold which serves as the monetary unit of the system. We would then add the simpler production function of gold to our equations:

$$Y_2 = \alpha(N_2)$$

and

$$f''(N_2) = 0 \qquad (11)$$

with (α) being the quantity of gold produced by one worker in one year (the production period being the same as that of the wage good). We add the following equations to complete the structure:

$$N = N_1 + N_2 \qquad (12)$$

$$W = Nw \qquad (13)$$

$$K = W \qquad (14)$$

(The capital stock is equal to the circulating capital wage bill into which we fold the capital-seed component.)

We describe the Ricardian system now in terms of value rather than physical units, with the prices of the respective sector's outputs being p_1 and p_2. Restating (7) as:

$$Y_1 - R = P + N_1 w \qquad (15)$$

and still thinking in physical terms, we are aware from our discussion of figure (2) that the residual after rent payment is a function of the level of employment. Let us assume the Y-R position at N'' and consider that $N'' = 10$ units of labor; if we assume that (α) of equation (11) is equal to one, then the output minus rent residual is valued at 10 units of gold. Thus the value of the total wage good production and obviously that of profits would be determined by the quantity of labor required in its production. Owing to the way we have expressed the monetary unit (in terms of the luxury commodity gold), the value of the output, after the rent payment, is equal to the number of workers employed. Thus:

$$p_1 Y_1 - p_1 R = p_1 (P + N_1 w) = N_1 \qquad (16)$$

Yet to see the relationship more explicitly, we state (16) as:

$$p_1 f(N_1) - p_1 [f(N_1) - N_1 f'(N_1)] = N_1 \qquad (17)$$

then:

$$p_1 = \frac{N_1}{f(N_1) - f(N_1 - N_1 f'(N_1))}$$

$$= \frac{1}{f'(N_1)} \qquad (18)$$

The value of the output in the corn sector is equal to the inverse of the productivity of labor employed. The price in the luxury sector is:

$$p_2 = \frac{N_2}{Y_2}$$

$$= \frac{1}{\alpha} \qquad (19)$$

Value is based on the cost of production as measured in terms of the quantity of labor employed, where this quantity translates into an equivalent amount of the monetary unit.

What we have worked out are separate explanations for value and for the distribution of the output. Let us reiterate the components of the latter,

$$\text{Rent} = p_1 R \qquad (20)$$

this portion being determined by the technical factors relating to the non-producible input and to labor. It is a deduction from the value of the total product and does not enter into the determination of value.

$$\text{Wage} = p_1 W \equiv p_1 N w \tag{21}$$

This being subject to those physiological and psychological factors that make for the natural wage over the long-term.

$$\text{Profit} = (N_1 + N_2)(1 - p_1 w) \tag{22}$$

Equation (22) results from the use of some foregoing equations. For profits in the corn sector (restating 7) we have:

$$P_1 = Y_1 - p_1 R - p_1 N_1 w \tag{23}$$

and profits in the luxury sector as:

$$P_2 = p_2 Y_2 - p_1 N_2 w \tag{24}$$

Aggregate profits are:

$$P = p_1 Y_1 - p_1 R - p_1 N_1 w + p_2 Y_2 - p_1 N_2 w \tag{25}$$

however:

$$p_1 Y_1 = N_1 + p_1 R$$

$$p_2 Y_2 = N_2$$

then:

$$P = N_1 + N_2 - p_1 w (N_1 + N_2) \tag{26}$$

$$= N_1 + N_2 (1 - p_1 w) \tag{27}$$

or

$$P = N(1 - p_1 w)$$

Equation (27) certainly expresses the possibility of 'conflict' between the economic classes as shown by the relations between profits and the real wage. Yet let us go on to explain some other results. We have the monetary usage rate (w_m) as:

$$w_m = p_1 w \tag{28}$$

which, via the substitution of (18) reads:

$$w_m = \frac{w}{f'(N_1)} \tag{29}$$

The rate of profit (r) is determined as:

$$r = \frac{N(1 - p_1 w)}{p_1 N w} = \frac{1}{p_1 w} - 1 \tag{30}$$

and by substitution for p_1 we get:

$$r = \frac{1}{\dfrac{w}{f'(N_1)} - 1} = \frac{f'(N_1)}{w} - 1 \tag{31}$$

To complete this Ricardian system we take:

$$w = \overline{w} \tag{32}$$

$$K = \overline{K} \tag{33}$$

$\overline{K}$ being the stock of capital at the outset of the production period

While we see separate explanations for value and distribution (it is a characteristic of post-Keynesian theory that distribution is not simply a facet of pricing theory), we still need a statement of expenditures so as to specify production. And again, in a departure from the neoclassical faceless factors of production, the composition of spending reflects the 'tasks' of the classes in the economy. Workers are assumed to spend all their income on 'necessities' (primitively speaking on corn) in their task to maintain their numbers and provide the labor, while capitalists carry on their obligation to invest and earn profits by 'saving' all, i.e. they consume all of their income on capital accumulation (again corn), while landlords are seen to spend all their rent on luxurious living; of course, this is a simplification, but necessary in that it clarifies the driving mechanism of the system. Capitalists do not save all — they do consume — and at a later point when we consider the modern extension of Ricardo we will see what impact this has on our results.

We have statements for the production of Y_1 and Y_2; and from what we have just assumed, all of Y_1 is consumed by the expenditure of workers and capitalists, which given the technical factors of production determines the level of output. We need only specify the demand factor for the output of the luxury good; and for that we have:

$$p_2 Y_2 = p_1 R \qquad (34)$$

where all prices are expressed in gold units. As Ricardo assumes Say's law, all income is spent; should the economy realize a lower rate of expansion its cause would then not be found in an insufficiency of demand in that capitalists 'hoard' part of their profits thus demanding to reduce their accumulation and thereby demand less labor and affecting levels of production.

The foregoing set of equations showed solutions for some relevant variables for an expanding economy driven essentially by the accumulation of capital towards the stationary society. Ricardo put little emphasis on technological change; he did acknowledge that such changes could delay the onset of the stationary condition but he did not build a mechanism to account for it in an ongoing way. Certainly he did not relate its presence to the pace of capital accumulation itself. As we can see from the diagrams depicting the system, the outcomes for variables such as employment, the rate of profit, the wage bill and the shares going to capital and labor will change with the accumulation of capital. If we take the derivative of the essential variables with respect to capital we get expressions for what is going on during the growth process. But first a statement representing capital accumulation itself. We can state:

$$\frac{dK}{dt} = \beta(\frac{1}{p_1} \cdot P) \qquad (35)$$

113

which can be expressed more clearly to reveal the driving forces by the substitution of equations (18) and (27). After some manipulation we arrive at:

$$\frac{dk}{dt} = \beta[N[f'(N_1) - w]] \tag{36}$$

The dynamic forces for growth are the intertwinnings of capital accumulation resulting from the realization of profit under the given technique $f'(N_1)$, and the growing labor force and resulting employment that responds to $w > \overline{w}$ stemming from the increased demand for labor engendered by the very increase in accumulation. Thus growth continues as long as $f'(N_1) > w$; with the stationary condition being given by:

$$w = \overline{w} > 0 \tag{37}$$

$$P = 0$$

The share of wages in total output will rise with every increase in employment. With a given real wage, the wage bill grows proportionately with an increase in employment; but output grows less than proportionately as employment increases in response to investment of profits. Overall, as long as the accumulation of capital goes on we see an increase in employment (N), the total wage (W), rent payments (R), the price of the wage good (p_1) and the market wage rate in money terms. However, with the given technology of production the rate of profit will fall as the economy is growing as will the relative share of profits in total output. In exact form with respect to capital we have:

$$\frac{dr}{dk} = \frac{f''(N_1)}{\overline{w}} \cdot \frac{dN_1}{dK} < 0 \tag{38}$$

from another angle [equation (30)] we note that when the price of the wage good rises profits will fall and the share accruing to labor will go up. We would end this 'mathematical look' at Ricardo by stating the equation that shows that the sign of dP/dt depends upon the size of K. Based on the profit equation (27) one obtains:

$$\frac{dP}{dk} = \frac{1}{f'(N_1)} \left[\frac{f'(N_1)}{\bar{w}} - 1 + K \cdot \frac{f''N_1}{f'(N_1)} \cdot \frac{dN_1}{dk} \right] \qquad (39)$$

At the beginning of the accumulation process when $K=0$, the third term in the bracket drops out and as $f'(N_1) \succ \bar{w}$ the change in profits will be positive as the capital stock increases. In the stationary condition where $f'(N_1) = \bar{w}$, the first two bracketed terms vanish and $dP/dk < 0$. In between these extremes there is obviously one level of capital stock where profits are at maximum, i.e. $dP/dk = 0$. Yet as we realize capitalists do not stop accumulating when profits are at their highest, but continue to accumulate as long as profits are positive. This reflects Ricardo's behavioral assumption that it is the capitalist's nature to accumulate and carry out his role providing there are profits to be transformed into capital.

There are some overall observations about this Ricardian story. Firstly, he presents a theory of value that is independent of a theory of distribution. The former is related to the technique of production; the value of output after payment of rent is equal to the numbers employed — it is a straightforward labor theory at least in its initial presentation. This follows from the stance that the price of labor is not determined from 'inside' the system as reflective of labor's contribution within the production process but is given from 'outside' by the physiological necessities of the time. Labor is not the non-descript neoclassical factor but a particular 'class input' requiring a particular wage rate $(\bar{w})$ to bring it into the production process. Any deviation of (w) from $(\bar{w})$ is to be considered as a short-term phenomenon and is not considered significant when considering the long-term growth pattern. And relatedly, the sector prices are dependent upon technical factors as we can see from equations (18) and (19).

Distribution theory is dependent on the interplay of technical, economic and physiological factors. Certainly it is not explained by the 'same mechanics' as, and thereby considered a facet of the theory of value. The particulars of distribution are found in our equation (20) and (27); whereas the value of our outputs depend, to reiterate, on technical factors, that is, on the quantity of labor required to produce them.

Secondly, we are made aware of the different roles played by the wage good and luxury good outputs; and it is the production function for the wage commodity that is of fundamental importance. The value for all variables except (p_2) depends upon the function $f(N_1)$ or its derivatives. For example, that of (p_1), the rate of profit in the system and the money wage rate are all independent of the conditions of production in the luxury good sector. It is only the price and output level of the luxury sector itself that depends on the constant technical (α) variable for their solutions. And this relegates the luxury output to what we previously referred to as the non-basic category in that it does not enter into the production of any other good.

As well we can relate the 'basic good' to output shares. Labor's share is:

$$\frac{W}{Y_1} = \frac{N\overline{w}}{f(N_1)}$$ (40)

then:

$$\frac{d(\frac{W}{Y_1})}{dN} = \frac{\overline{w}\cdot[f(N_1)-N_1 f'(N_1)]}{f(N_1)^2}$$ (41)

As long as rent is paid the whole term on the right side as positive and labor's share increases with increases in employment (again it is Y_1 which plays the role). Also, note its role in equation (88) which gives the rent share in output; and this will rise with the accumulation of capital and increases in output. With regard to the ratio of the profit share to the labor share we have:

$$\frac{ProfitShare}{LaborShare} = \frac{N}{p_1 W} - 1$$ (42)

telling us that as the price of the wage good rises the share of labor goes up (the profit share falls) [see equation (27)] with p_1 being determined by $f'(N_1)$.

The relation between the rate of profit and (p_1) can be seen directly from equation (30), which brings us to a different way to reckon the price of the wage good so as to relate it to how we structure price equations generally. We write:

$$p_1 = aw_m(1+r)^t$$ (43)

which is explainable in the light of the Ricardo model and adds an important consideration.

116

The capitalist advances wage-goods to labor, the money value of which constitutes the circulating money capital. Of course, the capitalist must earn profit on the value of this investment; hence the money flow upon the sale of the output will exceed the value of the advance to bring about the output. Thus the value of this circulating capital is the present value of the future income (the profits) discounted at the ruling rate of profit. With a given rate of profit, value is then determined not merely by the cost of production as measured by the quantity of labor employed, but also by the length of time of production. The longer the production period the greater the amount of advanced capital and the greater the profit return given the rate of profit.

From equation (43) we read that the value of the output is equal to the wage costs plus a rate of return on these costs which makes the rate of profit internal to a determination of value. But a glance at the rate of profit equation shows the value of the commodity being the determinable variable; that profits are determined by the difference between value and wages. Thus to know value one has to know the size of profit, and profit itself depends upon size of value.

There is nothing inherently wrong with this circularity of reasoning; it is reflective of that interdependence of sectors that we talked about early in this chapter. Yet Ricardo's model contains a theory of value which is taken as separate from the distribution of income; and while we accept that there are different theoretical constructions at work here, it is not to suggest that they do not affect each other and can be considered independently — though this would seem to be what Ricardo was thinking.

A question that arises is under what circumstances can we consider relative values being dependent on the conditions of production in a sequential way where we sort of add-up prior existing information to obtain values (where these 'technical factors' include elements of distribution). Yet it bears reiterating that Ricardo did not include distribution in these prior conditions; it has been suggested that he worked out a theory of profit before constructing a theory of value. Be that as it may, we can see a situation where relative values depend on 'technical factors of production' and where such values are unaffected by distributional changes; in this way, meeting the model's separation of the theory of value from that of distribution. Such a circumstance exists where both the wage good and luxury good sectors have the same time period of production. While we mentioned this earlier as a characteristic of the model, it is within the context of this value discussion that we can appreciate its full importance.

Consider the sector price equation as:

$$p_1 = aw_m(1+r)^t$$

$$p_2 = \alpha w_m(1+r)^t \qquad (44)$$

where a and α are the technical conditions, i.e. the numbers of labor employed, say 4 and 8 respectively, with a money wage of 2 and $r = .05$. Also that $t = t_2 = 2$ being the identical time periods of production. Then relative prices are:

$$\frac{p_1}{p_2} = \frac{8.4}{16.8} = \frac{1}{2} \qquad (45)$$

The luxury good is twice as expensive as the wage good and requires twice the capital of the wage good; so that at the ruling rate of profit the sector must earn twice the profit. And no change in the rate of profit and/or the wage rate will alter the price ratio. Recall that the value equations for the two sectors:

$$p_1 Y_1 - p_1 R = N_1$$

$$p_2 Y_2 = N_2 \qquad (46)$$

can also be written in terms of our price equations which we restate here:

$$p_1 = \frac{1}{f'(N_1)}, p_2 = \frac{1}{\alpha} \qquad (47)$$

Then the ratio of values can be seen as:

$$\frac{p_1}{p_2} = \frac{\alpha}{f'}(N_1) \qquad (48)$$

as the production of the luxury good operates with the constant (α), relative price will be determined by the productivity of labor in the wage good sector which is itself dependent on the amount of labor employed — on the (α) term in our value equations.

If we altered the situation somewhat to read $t_1=1, t_2=2$, the relative prices work out to:

$$\frac{p_1}{p_2} = \frac{1}{2.1} \tag{49}$$

or

$$\frac{p_2}{p_1} = \frac{\alpha w_m}{a w_m}(1.05)^{t_2-t_1} \tag{50}$$

Relative prices do not correspond to relative labor inputs, and a change in the distribution variable will affect relative prices though quantities of labor do not change. Thus we cannot talk in terms of relative prices reflecting the labor inputs unless we consider a most unreal circumstance of $t_1=t_2$, which causes the expression $(1+r)$ to disappear. But then we are back to what Adam Smith referred to as that "early and rude state" which is certainly not what Ricardo had in mind. As another example of this rude state, consider a two-sector economy producing 400 tons of wheat and 25 tons of iron. Let the value of the inputs at their wage costs be $200 and $250 respectively (the only form of income being wages). Since the value of the outputs will in each case be equal to the sum of the inputs at wage costs, the price of a ton of iron will be 20 times that of wheat which will reflect the technology that it takes 20 times as much labor to produce a ton of iron as it does that of wheat. Presuming a wage per man to be $5, we find that it takes 40 units of labor to produce the wheat output and 50 units of labor to produce the iron output; it takes 20 times as much labor to produce a ton of iron as is required to produce a ton of wheat. The price ratio of a unit of iron to that of wheat is $10.00/.50$ mirroring a labor ratio per unit of output of $5/.25$. Indeed when Ricardo looked at the complexity of a real economy, he found that the value of total output was dependent on the distribution of income between social classes, and that the profit share was dependent upon relative prices. He considered that the labor embodied theory of value, what has been considered as the classical law of value, had to be modified in the face of profits into a cost of production approach.

Ricardo was then aware of the interrelationship in the system reflective of the idea that a change in distribution will affect different sector values differently, according to their proportion of fixed capital to current labor employed. Yet he couched his whole approach in terms of a labor theory of value as if distributional factors were a separate issue. Perhaps he took this approach as a rough approximation of relative values, i.e. that relative prices were 'mainly' determined by relative quantities of labor. Though it has been considered that Ricardo's primary purpose was not to explain value but the laws governing distribution of the product and its impact on the growth process.

Let us construct a way, in Ricardian terms, to impart a degree of validity to his approach to relative prices and perhaps come to understand what he had in mind. Certainly Ricardo (or for that matter Marx) would not assert the naive proposition that commodities really do exchange in proportion to their labor content; in the reality of a capitalist society where the net product is shared between wages and profits, prices do not follow this simple rule.

Suppose an economy made up of three sectors, A, B, and C, where each sector will combine labor and the 'means of production' in different proportions. We can, relating to the Ricardian model, consider that this capital will in each sector be used up over the production period. At first we presume that capitalists as a class do not appear on the scene so that all of the value of the output minus that of capital replacement (the value of the used-up means of production) is absorbed by wages.[11] We see this in table (4.3).

Table (4.3)

Sector	Value of Used-up Capital	Wages	Price
A	800	200	1,000
B	600	400	1,000
C	200	800	1,000

The price of the output is equal to the wage bill where this bill includes the wage to direct labor and the 'wage to the production process', if you will, meaning the capital replacement necessary to carry on the level of production.

Suppose that a capitalist class now arrives who owns the means of production and will now draw profits from the value of the net product, i.e. they will share the value of the finished product minus the value of the consumed capital with labor. Suppose that profits rise from the previous zero share to 25% of the value of the capital; clearly wages will have to fall to 'accommodate' profits out of the net output, and say that they fall by 50% to yield the rate of profit. The price of such sector's output will comprise the value of the capital (assuming that it remains as in table 3), the wage bill and that of profits at a 25% rate. This circumstance is seen in table (4.4).

Table (4.4)

Sector	Value of Used-up Capital	Wages	Profits	Prices
A	800	100	200	1,000
B	600	200	150	950
C	200	400	50	650

Using the cost of production equation we have:

$$p_A = 100 + 800(1.25) = 1100$$

$$p_B = 200 + 600(1.25) = 950 \tag{51}$$

$$p_C = 400 + 200(1.25) = 650$$

Certainly prices would have to change from their original condition in the light of the change in distributional condition.

Should the price of the output of sector A remain unchanged (at 1000), it would not be able to pay wages at the given rate while at the same time be earning profits at the prevailing 25%. Indeed, after the payment of wages of 100 the sector would earn profits of 100 amounting to 12.5% on the value of its means of production. At the original price one would

121

consider sector (A) as being in 'deficit' with regard to securing receipts to earn the going rate of profit.

On the other hand, sectors (B) and (C) would, at the original price, reveal themselves to be in 'surplus' in that they are able to obtain receipts that is more than sufficient to pay wages at the ongoing rate and realize the prevailing rate of profit. For example, in the (B) sector when wages go down by one-half, profits are earned at a 33-1/3% rate.

It is clear that in order to relate to the change in distribution, relative prices would change from their original standing, as a result of the difference in the proportion in which inputs are combined in each — if they are all going to realize the prevailing rate of profit. Now one can imagine the construction of a fourth sector whose input proportions are an amalgam of the three emerging as a sort of 'borderline sector' between the deficit and surplus, such that a reduction in the wage would permit the prevailing payment of profit without having to alter its price; there would then be no change in the price of this sector's output relative to any other product. But the simpler approach, and one which probably shows what Ricardo was thinking about, is to construct three sectors where the proportions of input are the same in each case; and we see that their relative prices remain unaffected when profits come upon the scene.

Consider this condition for sectors A, B and C in table (4.5).

Table (4.5)

Sector	Value of Used-up Capital	Wages	Price
A	400	800	1,200
B	300	600	900
C	200	400	600

When wages take up all of the net product, the prices of each of the sectors will stand in relation to each other in the ratio of, let us say, A:B and B:C as 4:3:2. With wages falling by one-half and the profit rate at 23%, we find prices of:

$$p_A = 400 + 400(1.25) = 900$$

$$p_B = 300 + 300(1.25) = 675 \qquad (52)$$

$$p_C = 200 + 200(1.25) = 450$$

And they still relate to one another in the ratio of 4:3:2. What we are seeing with the price equations in (52) reflects what we previously referred to as the situation of equal time periods of production as the latter implies the same technology in each of the sectors.

It is in this sense that Ricardo puts forth a labor theory of relative values; but with the clear understanding that to the degree that sectors differ in input proportion, a fall in the wage (a change in distribution) will increase the price where the ratio of labor to capital is low, and decrease the price in sectors with a relatively high proportion of labor. Looking back at equation (42) we can see why Ricardo needed to grapple with the value problem, though it was probably not the main thrust of his thinking. We see that if the price of the wage good (corn) goes up, the share of profits fall, and it is out of profits that the 'advance' comes to propel the system. Pricing is tied up with distribution and growth, but how is one to account for the change in the price?

The problem was to be able to identify changes in relative prices attributable to changes in 'method of production' from those price changes caused by alterations in the distribution of income. Ricardo would have liked to consider technical factors, i.e. the quantity of labor required for production, as an overall or unambiguous measure of value. Yet if one is to read relative values from labor proportions, one would have to take these proportions as uniform for all sectors. But if we read relative price changes from distribution changes, then there are differences in sector production methods; but if this is so, then price changes could emerge from different changes in sector input proportions as well as from changes in distribution or some simultaneous changes in both areas. Ricardo may have wanted an unchangeable store of value with his embodied labor theory, and as such he wanted too much from such an approach. The labor theory cannot be that invariable measure of value, i.e. a yardstick that is itself unchangeable to changes in the wage rate or rate of profit, except in the circumstance that Ricardo himself would have considered most unlikely.

Nevertheless, his search for such an invariable measure of relative values pointed up the need to deal with 'pricing mechanics' in setting forth the long-term movement of the system. Much of what troubled Ricardo was addressed over one hundred later by Pierro Sraffa, and we will introduce some Sraffian economics later on; indeed Sraffa has been referred to as a "rehabilitator of classical economics" and a "Ricardo in modern dress".[12]

Yet having mentioned Sraffa, let us call attention to two problems that would have confronted Ricardo as we glean his thoughts via tables (4.3)-(4.5) and for which Sraffa provided solutions. With regard to table (4.4), it would seem that we have some clear-cut rules about what happens to prices when wages fall; it certainly looks as if the price in sector (c) would fall. But this result assumes that the fall in the wage had no effect on the value of the means of production. Yet the wage change alters the value of capital as an 'end-product' in the period before, just as it impacts on the value of the current end-product with this value of capital as an input. What if these means of product were produced in a sector such as (A) where the proportion of labor is relatively low, then the price of capital would rise when wages fall with the possibility that the price of sector C's output would increase rather than decrease. An understanding of the movement in the relative price of any two products when there is a change in distribution requires a knowledge of the interrelationships of all the producing sectors; not only of the proportions of inputs of the immediate sectors, but also a knowledge of the proportions by which the 'means' in these sectors were themselves produced and then knowing the proportion by which the means of production of the period before were produced, and beyond this. This type of interrelationship was beyond Ricardo's analysis, but it was brought to the fore by Sraffa in constructing what we referred to as the 'borderline' sector.

Another issue is the assumption that when the wage went down by one-half, profits rose to pay an arbitrary chosen rate of 25%. But just how far profits will in fact go up for a particular wage reduction was worked out in an interesting formulation by Sraffa, making use of his borderline sector construction. We will return to these developments.

We have stressed that what is at the heart of the difference between the conventional (neoclassical) and post-Keynesian (neo-Ricardian) approaches is the latter's concern with an understanding of the growth of the economy over the long term. That at the core is the historical growth process of the economy. The Ricardo model serves well as the precursor to modern growth discussions and the understanding of those 'balances' necessary to explain the secular development. Ricardo did bring to light how growth is tied in with the activity of particular classes of people in society, with how distribution of the output relates to these activities and its impact on economic growth, and that one has to account for technological change and how it can effect growth via the way this change is so-to-speak 'distributed' between these economic classes. And while Ricardo may not have spoken with equal perceptiveness on all of these as well as other issues, his framework provides the right launching pad from which to arrive at modern economic thinking.

NOTES

1. Adam Smith, *The Wealth of Nations*. Clarendon Press, Oxford, Second Edition, p. 52.

2. A. Rancaglia, *Sraffa and the Theory of Prices*. John Wiley, New York, 1978, p. 9.

3. David Ricardo, *The Principles of Political Economy and Taxation*, Everyman's Library Edition, 1957, p. 33.

4. Mark Blaug, *Economic Theory in Retrospect*, Cambridge University Press, London, 1985, p. 82.

5. Smith, op. cit., p. 265.

6. Luigi L. Pasinetti, *Structural Change & Economic Growth*, Cambridge University Press, London, 1981, p. 7.

7. Ricardo, op. cit., p. 53.

8. Ibid., p. 53.

9. In the modelling of Ricardo's thinking, we are guided by such works as L. Pasinetti, *Growth and Income Distribution*, Cambridge University Press, London, 1974, also M. Morishima, *Ricardo's Economics*, Cambridge University Press, London, 1989.

10. Pasinetti, op. cit.

11. Our discussion is based on the illuminating example by Ronald L. Meek, "Mr. Sraff's Rehabilitation of Classical Economics," *Scottish Journal of Political Economy*, 1961, Vol. VIII.

12. Ibid.

5   Introduction to Growth Analysis

Beginning mechanics

We propose the post-Keynesian approach as a different conceptual framework for understanding how the economy works. It is one which meshes various elements (both micro and macro) derived from a non-neoclassical basis into a supportive structure to help explain the two significant dynamic movements of the economic system as an aggregate — the cyclical fluctuations and the trend line (the growth path) of the exponential type. The latter circumstance is one where the change in the output variable, for example, per unit of time is continuously increasing. The exponential (nonlinear) trend function is given by:

$$Y = ab^t \tag{1}$$

which yields a constant ratio of increase per unit of time (t = 1, 2, 3 . . .) on the condition of $b > 1, a > 0$. This differing from a linear trend function where the amount of change per unit of time is constant.

Over the long historical course of the economy, one clearly observes recurrent non-periodic cyclical fluctuations of a 'short' period that in recent time (since World War II) has averaged about 60 months in duration, encompassing nine such 'business cycles'. While at any point in time the economy is in a stage of the shorter-term movement, it is clear that a trend reading of this non-periodic cyclical motion reveals a state of economic growth. The historical development of a capitalist society is one of economic progress marked by pronounced cyclical 'irregularities'. The attempt to explain these movements and to clarify the relationship between them contrasts with the neoclassical equilibrium approach to economic understanding; and contrasts as well with the Keynesian model in the General Theory where the focus is one equilibrium position where the economy comes to rest. The usual mode of analysis is for the economy to be modeled as coming to a state of rest, i.e. to a fixed level of activity, if left undisturbed; but in the type of dynamic model which is the basis of post-Keynesian analysis, the economy will continue to change indefinitely. What a disturbance does is to propel the system onto a different path of movement, which is different than jolting the system out of a state of equilibrium.

This author has argued that the main thrust of post-Keynesian modeling is an occupation with the long-term movement (in keeping with the Ricardian attitude). If one can identify and mesh the economic magnitudes that maintain the state of 'growth equilibrium', then the fluctuation would seem to emerge largely as a result of failure of policy and/or institutional arrangements. It is though of little value to debate which of these changes should be looked upon as 'basic', but to treat them as complimentary and to understand the behavior of the economic variables that are integral to both and relate each to the other. As Alfred Eichner pointed out: "To understand the actual historical course the economy takes, a course marked by pronounced cyclical movements, it is necessary to compliment the long-period analysis with a short-period analysis. The two need to be carried out cojointly — the short-period analysis because it allows deviations from the warranted growth rate and the long-period analysis because these deviations can be explained only in reference to what they are deviations from".[1] In our look at models which set out a hypothetical path of steady growth, the 'warranted' notion will be clarified. Our consideration of such economic factors such as income distribution, savings functions, the setting of prices, the behavior of consumption expenditures, the role of money and the like — all drawn from a non-neoclassical setting — will generally occur within the process of capital accumulation and the secular growth movement.

The post-Keynesian scene in terms of the type of analysis that occupied economic thinking after Keynes, dealt with models of continuous movement. To appreciate this changeover from the 'equilibrium core' we might begin with Keynes himself. Certainly he was in the tradition of Ricardo and Marx in that his design was to construct an apparatus that deals with the whole economic system; the behavior at the macro level has an integrity of its own, it is more than an extrapolation of observed behavior at the micro level (but that is as far as the relationship goes). Keynes had, I would say, a specific intent which is mirrored in the design of his model. His purpose was to explain (perhaps apologize for) and preserve a system that, at the time, seemed to be on the verge of collapse stemming from its own internal behavior. His method consisted first in explaining why the economy was being trapped in the state of difficulty that it was in (which over time would wear away its institutions), and then to propose actions that would propel the system out of its severe state of unemployment and return it to prosperity (to some level that was previously achieved). His method consisted in investigating equilibrium conditions; to understand the forces that maintain the economy in a particular state, and the mechanics required to move the economy to a different equilibrium state. The framework, then, is one of comparative macro-statics, in that the movement of the system is one of a sequence of 'still-pictures' where the corresponding values of the aggregate relate to different values of sub-aggregates which, at least at first glance, are taken as independent data. And as the economy is caused to move from one level of activity to another, its institutions and form remain largely intact. Keynes was quite aware of the cyclical nature of the economy, but it seemed from the vantage point at the time he was writing that society was mired in an intractable state of under full-employment from which it would not begin to expand for a long time; and while it would eventually do so, the political and social damage in the interim would be too high. So he did not frame his analysis in terms of movement be it cyclical or otherwise; but assumed that, if left undisturbed, the system would remain 'trapped' and hence need prodding to move to another rest state. His concern was not with the development of the economy over time, but with the problems that seemed to enmesh the economy at a particular period of time. Given Keynes' concern, his approach then in terms of equilibrium mechanics similar to neoclassical economics would serve well. And he was able to give clear, definite and extremely powerful prescriptions of what to do to overcome slump conditions. This made him the most influential economist of our time.

The basic ingredient of his prescription dealt with the principle of effective demand and the analytical tool devised to highlight the connection between changes in demand and its impact on the aggregate system. This 'multiplier' tool presented a powerful argument; and it became clear that there was no necessity for the increase in demand to come from private investment which, in any event, may not be forthcoming in sufficient strength due to the circumstances of a low marginal efficiency of capital and the liquidity condition of the economy. Any autonomous increase in demand would generate the same multiplier effects as that of investment; indeed the lingering effect of this was the impact of government expenditures via deficit spending on the net addition to effective demand. Though in the formal analysis of the General Theory it was business

129

investment and not public spending that played the critical role. Be that as it may, let us set out the multiplier in its lagged version as the appropriate lead-in to systems of continuous movement. This view of the multiplier shows how the actual level of savings adjusts over time to a predetermined level of investment via changes in income.

We have the lagged consumption function (omitting the usual constant terms):

$$C_t = C'Y_{t-1} \tag{2}$$

with the relation:

$$Y_t = C_t + I_t \tag{3}$$

where I_t is determined exogenously. We illustrate this mechanism with table (1) where $C_t = .5Y_{t-1}$. Assume the economy is given 'life' with the onset of investment spending of 100 which thereafter remains at this level. How does the system respond to this injection? What is the magnitude of the response; and perhaps more interestingly, what can be said about the nature of the change? Is the change even-spaced through time, or does the system experience the greatest change early on with subsequent responses becoming smaller and smaller, or does the greatest change come at the end of the adjustment process? Indeed, it is only via the lagged multiplier version that one can determine this.

We see that the increase in income in each period is the result of the increase in consumption; and this increase in consumption expenditures can itself be traced back to the original impulse in investment spending. Thus the increase in consumption in the second period is:

$$\Delta_2 C = C'I \tag{4}$$

And that of the third and fourth periods are:

$$\Delta_3 C = C'^2 I \tag{5}$$

$$\Delta_4 C = C'^3 I \tag{6}$$

and so forth. The change in the level of income becomes:

130

$$\Delta_1 Y = I = 100 \tag{7}$$

$$\Delta_2 Y = C'I = 50 \tag{8}$$

$$\Delta_3 Y = C'^2 I = 25 \tag{9}$$

etc. The total increase in income from $t=0$ to $t=n$ is $\Delta Y = Y_n - Y_o$ then:

$$\Delta Y = \Delta_1 Y + \Delta_2 Y + \Delta_3 Y \ldots$$

$$= \Delta_1 I + C'I + C'^2 I + C^\beta I \ldots. \tag{10}$$

$$I(1 + C' + C'^2 + C^\beta \ldots C^{m-1} \tag{11}$$

Table (5.1)
The Lagged Multiplier

PERIOD	ΔI	I	Y	ΔY	C	S	ΔS
0			0				
1	100	100	100	+ 100			
2		100	150	+ 50	50	50	+ 50
3		100	175	+ 25	75	75	+ 25
4		100	187.5	+ 12.5	87.5	87.5	+ 12.5
5		100	193.7	+ 6.2	93.7	93.7	+ 6.2
6		100	196.8	+ 3.1	96.8	96.8	+ 3.1
7		100	198.4	+ 1.6	98.4	98.4	+ 1.6
8		100	199.2	+ .8	99.2	99.2	+ .8
∞		100	200	200	100	100	0

With the use of the equation for the sum of a geometric progression we have:

$$\Delta Y = \frac{1 - C^{m-1}}{1 - C} \tag{12}$$

131

$$\Delta \frac{Y}{n \to \bowtie} = \frac{1}{1-C'}(I) \qquad (13)$$

The increase in income does not go on indefinitely but tends to a finite limit as $n \to \infty$ since $c' < 1$.

What we observe in this lagged sequential approach is the inner workings of the comparative static instantaneous multiplier where the total income change is obtained immediately. But in the above exercise the total change will be arrived at asymptotically; thus the greatest response occurs early on in the process.

Another way to get at the sequence of change is (from the observation that $t = 0$, $Y = 0$) to write for $t = 1$:

$$Y_1 = C_1 + I$$

$$= C' Y_o + I = .5Y_o + 100 = 100 \qquad (14)$$

then

$$Y_1 = Y_o + I \qquad (15)$$

for $t = 2$:

$$Y_2 = C_2 + I$$

$$= C' Y_1 + I = .5Y_1 + 100 = 150$$

then

$$= Y_o + C'I + I \qquad (16)$$

The value for Y_3 is:

$$Y_3 = Y_o + C'^2 I + C'I + I = 175 \qquad (17)$$

and for $t = 4$:

$$Y_4 = Y_o + C'^3 I + C'^2 I + C'I = 187.5 \qquad (18)$$

etc.

At every step of the process the actual level of savings cannot be determined in the absence of current consumption which is itself dependent on previous income; hence current or actual savings will be less than it otherwise would be should consumption be forthcoming out of current income which would be the case when the multiplier has been worked out, i.e. when the total change in income has been achieved. We can refer to this latter savings level as 'proper savings' that is equal to the predetermined level of investment. Actual savings is:

$$S_t = Y_{t-1} - C_t \qquad (19)$$

Thus the increase in income between successive periods is equal to the difference between proper and actual savings.[2] The process is illustrated in Fig. (5.1).

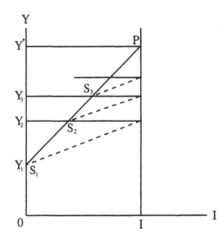

Figure 5.1

In the absence of the lagged effect, the increase in investment to I would immediately raise the level of income from 0 to PI; the instantaneous adjustment means $Y^* = C^* + I$ and that $S^* = Y^* - C^* = I$ so that actual savings equal to proper savings equal to investment. In the sequence approach, the increases in income are read as 0 to Y_1, Y_1 to Y_2, Y_2 to Y_3 and so on, with the changes in savings read off the S_1S line. In period one, after the change investment is equal to I and remains stable. However, savings being lagged is dependent upon income in period zero and is therefore equal to zero; investment exceeds savings by the distance S_1I. In period two, savings being dependent on income in period one increases to Y_2S_2; this increase in actual savings narrows the difference between investment and savings to S_2I. In successive steps of the adjustment process, actual savings increases as it asymptotically approaches its proper savings level where it is equal to investment. Thus for increases in investment it is proper savings that exceeds actual savings.

This lagged mechanism has been used in business cycle discussions to explain the behavior of consumer expenditures as a retarding force to the amplitude of the cycle; certainly over the initial stages of the contraction phase. In the reverse situation when investment falls, the effect of the consumption lag is to slow the decline. The level of proper savings is below actual as the system adjusts downward, i.e. current levels of income will be higher than the corresponding equilibrium income associated with the lower investment expenditures.

The multiplier mechanism in its lagged or instantaneous form was not put forth by Keynes in relation to business cycle analysis; it was rooted in the static very short-term nature of his analysis. The thrust was to restore full-employment within the time frame of an 'immediate horizon', that is to establish the condition of full employment for a given level of productive capacity. The Keynesian approach did not envisage a rate of growth in capacity and output (demand) over time; the concern was not with carrying the cyclical peak employment condition continuously forward. This vision lent itself to consider employment as a function of demand as such; and thereby concentrating on the demand-generating aspect of investment and on the non-spending aspect of saving, taking the state of supply, that is, the state of capacity as given.

While the level of investment expenditures plays the critical role in creating effective demand and temporarily increasing employment, it would not necessarily maintain full employment over time or correct persistent unemployment — the increase in demand per se is not the issue. And this was seen as a shortcoming of Keynes' analysis, for what seemed to be overlooked was the simultaneous capacity (supply) creating aspect of the very investment that is creating this income. "Once the new capacity that the investment made possible were to come on line, it might well lead to a situation in which aggregate supply capacity exceeded aggregate demand, thereby discouraging further investment and producing a slump in business activity which would, in turn, cause unemployment to rise".[3] Thus one should treat employment as a function of the relation between demand growth and that of productive capacity, and not per se as being determined by the growth in income. Yet the Keynesian effort dealt with policies needed to restore a full-employment regime and not with maintaining such a condition over the long term; and considering the time in which he wrote, this was a very plausible vision. One can then assume capacity as given and concentrate on increasing demand which by absorbing this capacity restores desirable employment levels. It is, to reiterate, a (static) short run analysis where the length of the 'run' is not a reflection of the change in supply capability.

Turning to a longer time frame of analysis would unhinge the system from a static position and set it into some design of continuous motion; and this involves activity in net investment and capacity growth which brings to the fore the 'acceleration principle' as an expression of the behavior of entrepreneurs in the attempt to specify an investment function. There does not however seem to be a generally used form of the investment equation as contrasted to, say, the commonly found consumption function. It would then be best to begin by identifying the more obvious variables that bear upon the investment decision and construct the investment-acceleration relationship up to the level needed for the analysis.

In its simple form an investment function would tell us that the induced change in the capital stock, i.e. net investment, is a function of the expected change in the level of output given an aggregate capital to output ratio that is usually assumed to remain constant over the cyclical movement of the economy. This approach is based on the notion that realized output is equal to anticipated output; this condition of continuous realized expectations makes for an investment statement that does not contain the existing capital stock as a variable bearing on net investment. There will be an acceleration impact on the change in gross investment flowing from the change in output, the magnitude of the impact being determined by the value of the capital/output ratio. This simple accelerator vision can be set out as:

$$K_t = \alpha Y_t \tag{20}$$

$$I_{net} = K_t - K_{t-1}$$

$$= \alpha Y_t - \alpha Y_{t-1} \tag{21}$$

$$= \alpha(\Delta Y_t)$$

and

$$I_{gross} = \alpha \Delta Y_t + \text{depreciation}$$

This supposes that the capital stock is always in correct proportion to the realized level of output, so that it is the change in output that drives the change in the stock of capital.

An interesting point is that the accelerator principle does not work as well during the contraction phase of the cycle as it does during the expansion, even if we were to assume that the economy confronts the turning points of the cycle with a level of capital on hand that corresponds to the level of existing output. A downsizing of capacity being largely determined by 'technical factors' cannot as easily be tuned to declines in output as can an increase in capacity when the economy turns up. But we do not want to get sidetracked here; and again make the point that in the Keynesian scheme of things the level of investment did not add to capacity so that the increase in demand would simply absorb the existing capital and there was no issue of a supply problem as the economy was propelled upwards. A problem which, if it were to appear, could result in 'internal' investment decisions that might retard or halt the expansion process.

The capacity issue does not enter the Keynesian investment explanation (his purpose was not to deal with the role of investment as a cyclical causing activity); nor does it enter our investment explanation as given by the statements in (21). But this latter explanation removes the investment decision as an essential causal feature for the cyclical movement in the economy. There is sufficient evidence of the high magnitude of change in investment expenditures over the business cycle — all the more so over the contraction phase — that is explainable by the acceleration principle. And it is this accelerated response that in turn magnifies future changes in output itself. This kind of interplay cannot emerge when investment expenditures are related to an exogenous change in output, which is like saying that it is tied to an estimate of future output that is taken 'out of the blue' and always turns out right. Thus the simple version as seen in (21), while it may explain the principle (we can show gross changes at rates greater than changes in the level of output) is anchored in unreal assumptions and cannot serve, in conjunction with the multiplier, to illuminate the cyclical movement.

We see this in the following way. Taking the consumption function from the lagged multiplier display and the investment relationship of equation (21) as expressions of the aggregate behavior of consumers and entrepreneurs (giving endogenous relations) we have:

$$C_t = bY_{t-1} \tag{22}$$

$$I_t = \alpha(\Delta Y_t) \tag{23}$$

$$Y_t \equiv C_t + I_t \tag{24}$$

which yields:

$$Y_t = \frac{b-\alpha}{1-\alpha}(Y_{t-1}) \tag{25}$$

As long as (b) and (α) are positive equation (25) cannot generate a business cycle. The model simply reduces to the form:

$$Y_t = x(Y_{t-1}) \tag{26}$$

Should the system deviate from its static position, it will return to it if $x < 1$ and continually diverge when $x > 1$. There is no internal mechanism that triggers a continuous regular movement; no cycle can occur within a first-order difference system.

To move away from equilibrium we would need a different expression of an investment equation (indeed the multiplier is not needed to cause the cycle, and the higher the marginal propensity to consume the less likely to occurrence). A different lag structure and form of the accelerator results if we base expenditures on the likelihood that expectations will not turn right. One would need to adjust investment to account for the different between predicted and actual output which means that the level of capital stock becomes a variable in the investment equation. This would lead to a flexible capital to output ratio which implies that output changes will not be the sole driving force for investment expenditures. The approach is to reckon entrepreneurial behavior as a result of 'looking back' as well as 'looking forward'.

Consider table (5.2) where, without becoming enmeshed in expectations analysis, we simply presume that expected sales or output (Y^e) is equal to realized sales of the last period. The capital to output ratio is .25.

The expected output in $t = 2$ is 6000 which, given the constant replacement number and the fact that the capital on hand is what one desires to have, will yield a gross investment equal to replacement of 200. But expectations turn out wrong and realized output is 8000 with the desired capital and investment numbers in parenthesis. In $t = 3$, expected

137

output (Y^c) will be 8000 requiring the capital be adjusted equal to .25 the difference between actual and expected output in t = 2, or what comes to the same result it will be equal to .25 the different between actual output in t = 2 and actual output in t = 1 (since the expected output in t = 2 is the actual output in t = 1). We assume a full adjustment between the level of capital one desires to have (K^*) and the level of capital that one does have.

Table (5.2)

t	Y	Replacement	Req'd Capital K*	I net	I gross
1	6000	200	1500	—	200
2	e= 6000	200	1500	—	200
	(8000)	200	(2000)	(500)	(700)
3		200	2000	500	700

The form of the accelerator is now:

$$K_t^* = \alpha(Y_{t-1}) \tag{27}$$

$$I_{net(t)} = \alpha(\Delta Y_{t-1}) \tag{28}$$

with

$$I_{gross(t)} = \alpha \Delta Y_{t-1} + D \tag{29}$$

D = replacement investment

Though we should state that the lag involved in this less naive form of the acceleration principle might also be partially due to delays in ordering and production; but essentially, to reiterate, it is presumed that businessmen do not know what their output will be during any given time period so that they base this year's capital requirements on last year's output — and this year's capital needs will involve a capital adjustment process. That is to say, will involve a change in net investment to reflect the misjudgment concerning expected sales of the last year.

This investment equation together with our other endogenous relation of the lagged consumption function yields a second order lagged system that is capable of producing periodic fluctuations and sets the foundation for steady growth. Thus:

$$C_t = b(Y_{t-1}) \tag{30}$$

$$I_t = \alpha(\Delta Y_{t-1}) \tag{31}$$

$$G = \overline{G} = 1 \tag{32}$$

and:

$$Y_t = (b+\alpha)Y_{t-1} - \alpha Y_{t-2} + G \tag{33}$$

Professor Samuelson in his path-breaking article on the interactions between the multiplier and the accelerator arrives at such a second-order difference equation by lagging the consumption function and then proposing investment as:

$$I_t = \alpha(\Delta C_t) \tag{34}$$

And this leads to:

$$Y_t = \alpha(1+b)Y_{t-1} - b\alpha(Y_{t-2}) + 1 \tag{35}$$

Professor Hicks in his *Contribution to the Theory of the Trade Cycle*[4] proposed a similar model to which he appended a long-term exogenous growth factor to investment spending as well as making investment directly related to a one-period lag change in output.

What these models have in common is a mechanism to unhinge an understanding of the economy from its static equilibrium framework; although the acceleration principle in the cast of the above investment equation is too rigid and in reality does not give us a very good tool in the analysis of investment. Before putting forth a revised more general form of the accelerator we look at the time paths for the level of output once it leaves its static position; the shape of the paths will depend on the values for (b) and (α). Overall, the greater the value of the investment coefficient, the more likely the occurrence of the cycle of greater and greater amplitude for reasonable values of the (b) coefficient, the greater the value of (b) the less the likelihood that cycles occur at all unless we assume 'high' values for (α). For example, if we imagine (b) in the .8 or .9 range, we would need (α) to be 2 or greater to produce cycles that approximate reality — cycles that are not damped nor reveal constant amplitudes. As (α) increases the cycles reveal greater amplitudes; with the economy taking off onto a nonoscillatory explosive growth path for such values as $b=.8$ and $\alpha=3$. These paths appear in Fig. (5.2) where each can be represented by a difference equation with its appropriate solution indicating the nature of the movement.

We are no longer in a Keynesian comparative-static mode where the system needs primarily to be jolted by exogenous forces to turn from one cyclical phase to another. The economy should be seen as a self-generating cyclical mechanism that may also be able, under appropriate conditions, to generate and maintain a secular growth pattern. And in all of this we leave far behind the equilibrium notion of the neo-classical economics. Yet before we move further along in this dynamic world it would be worthwhile to introduce a further modification of the investment function and underlying acceleration principle so as to provide a more realistic basis for a continuously changing economic situation.

It is reasonable to propose that the level of the capital stock be overtly included in the investment equation as a determinant factor. To the degree of past mistakes in sales projections, the existing stock will reflect an excess or insufficiency of the capital level relative to projected output; and all the more should the expected output itself will be influenced by the previous misjudgment. We would expect that the capital/output ratio would be modified in the face of this circumstance and thereby influence investment spending. The basis for this is that the estimates of the ratio (α) obtained from an investment function such as $I=\alpha\Delta Y+\beta$ is less than the yearly value of the aggregate capital to output ratio. Studies showed the latter being approximately 2.5, while the former was less than one. The point is that the ratio of net investment to the change in output shows up as invariably less than the existing ratio of capital stock to output. Of course, this difference between an 'average' and a 'change' would not exist should expectations always turn out right — that naive investment function. But we cannot presume that the capital stock in any period is at an appropriate level, so that the stock at the end of a period as well as the flow of output expected during a following period have bearing on investment expenditures.

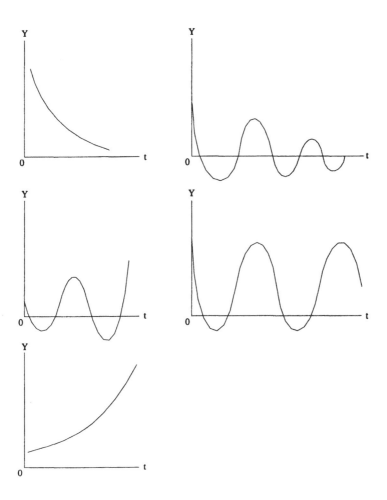

Figure 5.2

A net investment equation incorporating these thoughts can be structured as:

$$I_{net_t} = \alpha(1-\lambda)Y_t - (1-\lambda)K_{t-1} \qquad (36)$$

which is based on the idea that it is more sensible to presume that the capital stock is proportioned to some weighted average of previous output instead of being related to output of the immediate past period. Clearly some of these past outputs will have fallen short of expectations. If we add a depreciation term that assumes replacement as proportioned to the capital stock of the last period, we have $D=d(K_{t-1})$, with a gross investment equation as:

$$I_{gross} = \alpha(1-\lambda)Y_t - (1-\lambda)K_{t-1} + dK_{t-1}$$

$$= \alpha(1-\lambda)Y_t - (1-\lambda-d)K_{t-1} \qquad (37)$$

Note that the lambda term (λ) acts as a reducing agent on the (α) ratio as a reflection of the influence of the existing level of capital. In a world of always correct predictions, we would have $\lambda=0$ reverting to the simple accelerator where the capital stock is always at the appropriate levels with gross investment being determined by output flows plus depreciation. That is:

$$I_{gross} = \alpha\Delta Y_t + Depreciation \qquad (38)$$

Evans refers to the accelerator inherent in equation (34) as the 'flexible accelerator'. And this approach seems to remedy the inconsistency obtained with the simple accelerator where, to reiterate, we find different values for the (α) term obtained from $K=\alpha(Y)$ and $I=\alpha(\Delta Y)$. As Evans points out:[5]

> This inconsistency is easily remedied with the flexible accelerator, for the marginal coefficient of the unlagged term is now $\alpha(1-\lambda)$ instead of α. Since λ is probably between 0.8 and 0.9, $\alpha(1-\lambda)$ will be only 1/5 to 1/10 the size of the average K/Y ratio. As shown later this agrees with a wide range of empirical results.

In the usual explanation of the accelerator, it is used as a means to demonstrate the sensitivity of investment expenditures to changes in output as compared to consumption spending, and why investment spending is to be considered as the cycle producing factor. Thus we find that increases in output will cause greater than proportionate increases in investment, and that investment will decline in response to a slowdown in the rate of expansion of output — it does not require that output actually be falling. And in the contraction phase, the upturn in investment spending is in response to a slowdown in the rate of economic decline. Generally, investment orders and contracts tend to lead the business cycle turns. But this story about how changes in output produce accelerated changes in investment expenditures is based on the assumption (not always made explicit) that the system arrives at the cycled turns with the capital stock appropriate realized levels of output — the simple accelerator notion.

However, the flexible accelerator tells us that net investment may continue to rise during a period when output is rising at a declining rate. The negative effect of an increase in the capital stock may take a while in developing before it outweighs the positive effect of higher output levels, as compared to the simple case where it shows up right away. It is not the level of output per se that matters, but of output relative to an existing level of capital that is essential. And this brings in the experience with previous expectations.

Thus with given expectations investment change will be guided by the difference between the capital stock on hand and the level of the stock one desires to have on hand relative to the projected change in output. We then add another ingredient to the investment equation by writing:

$$I_{net} = \mu desiredK_t^* - ActualK_{t-1} \qquad (39)$$

$$\text{where } K_t^* = \alpha Y_t$$

The μ-term is the fraction of the capital gap that is to be filled; and if we assume as is normally the case, that $\mu = 1$ we have:

$$I_{net} = \mu \alpha Y_t - \mu K_{t-1} \qquad (40)$$

and I guess

$$= \mu \alpha Y_t - \mu K_{t-1} + dK_{t-1}$$

143

$$= \mu \alpha Y_t - (\mu - d) K_{t-1} \tag{41}$$

which relates to the flexible accelerator version of equation (37) by making $(1-\lambda)=\mu$.

The accelerator principle in its different versions — depending on how one structures the net investment equation — is an essential ingredient in models that construct hypothetical paths of steady growth. This is the framework that post-Keynesians would utilize to set out those structural economic magnitudes that underpin a growth movement, and thereby attempt to understand the long-term experience of capitalist economics.

There are two approaches to the construction of balanced growth paths. One would be to set out the assumptions and associated equations that produce the desired result, but where the path is related to the externally given limitations of the system. That is, the path, is not a purely endogenously 'manufactured' movement where the variables are self-contained, but relies on prescribed attributes such as the growth of technological change and that of the labor force to give the 'natural' productive capability of the system and the associated growth path. The original work in this direction were the Harrod-Domar models which do not incorporate a feedback mechanism from the growth experience itself to these external data; but these models have been elaborated upon. We also mention the basic neoclassical growth model that relates the growth path to the 'external' movements of the labor force and technological changes.

A second approach relies on the purely endogenous interplay of the multiplier and accelerator which, as we have seen, is helpful in understanding the forces behind economic fluctuations; but which has also been shown capable of producing a path of steady growth. This means that the economy, if left to itself, does not require 'external conditions' to set up and maintain the growth trajectory. Now such a path is not such a hypothetical construction to which one relates the proper behavior of economic variables in order to maintain the movement. The 'normal' activity of consumers and businessmen can of itself produce steady growth which means that the economy is not necessarily limited to the reality of the cyclical experience. It was thought that a system if left to purely endogenous forces could only produce periodic fluctuations. But whether the system can get into a position from which stable growth would flow is questionable. Both of these approaches are theoretical constructions through which we can appreciate the economic behavior that sustains a growth path and learn something about the deviations from such an underlying movement.

Before we construct these models, we want as yet a further 'rephrasing' of the net investment equation. We find the equation:

$$I_{net} = \alpha Y_{t-1} - (1 - \lambda) K_{t-1} \tag{42}$$

Should $\lambda = 1$ then the level of capital has no bearing on net investment, implying that capacity is always at the desired level relative to output. Then:

$$K_{t-1} = \alpha Y_{t-2} \tag{43}$$

$$K_t = \alpha Y_{t-1} \tag{44}$$

giving the simple accelerator principle that makes all of net investment depend on the rate of change of income;

$$I_t = \alpha(\Delta Y_{t-1}) \tag{45}$$

which we arrived at earlier. To make the matter read simpler we can write $(1 - \lambda) = \beta$.

$$I_{net} = \alpha Y_{t-1} = \beta K_{t-1} \tag{46}$$

and should $\beta = 1$ then $\lambda = 0$. Equation (46) is akin to (36) where the β term is reflective of how investment is spread over previous outputs when the capital stock differs from the quantity that is desired.

An endogenous growth model

Focusing initially on the purely endogenous model we make use of the following system.

$$Y_t = C_t + I_t \tag{47a}$$

$$C_t = aY_{t-1} \tag{47b}$$

$$I_t = \alpha Y_{t-1} - \beta K_{t-1} \tag{47c}$$

$$K_t = K_{t-1} + I_t \tag{47d}$$

If we substitute (47c) and (47b) in (47a), we obtain:

$$Y_t = (a+\alpha)Y_{t-1} - \beta K_{t-1} \tag{48}$$

Similarly, by substituting (47c) in (47d) we get:

$$K_t = \alpha Y_{t-1} + (1-\beta)K_{t-1} \tag{49}$$

With equations (48) and (49) we have a model which will generate a sequence of values for income and the capital stock from any set of initial values for these variables. If such values were given at $t=0$ and put into the system for Y_{t-1} and K_{t-1}, the equations can then be used to calculate the respective values for $t=1$ with the process being repeated and so on. Recalling our previous discussion about difference systems, equations (48) and (49) are first order systems so that a displacement of these variables from their stationary state values cannot produce cyclical sequences. But we see singular directional change so that one can extract a growth path for capital stock which gets underway when investment exceeds depreciation, i.e. when it departs its stationary condition of net investment equals zero. And income grows when investment exceeds savings that results from the lagged consumption function.

From equations (48) and (49) we write:

$$\frac{Y_t - Y_{t-1}}{Y_{t-1}} = (a+\alpha) - \beta \frac{K_{t-1}}{Y_{t-1}} - 1 \tag{50}$$

$$= (a+\alpha-1) - \beta \frac{K_{t-1}}{Y_{t-1}}$$

$$\frac{K_t - K_{t-1}}{K_{t-1}} = \alpha \frac{Y_{t-1}}{K_{t-1}} - 1 + 1 - \beta \tag{51}$$

$$= \alpha \frac{Y_{t-1}}{K_{t-1}} - \beta$$

Expressing the proportional rates for income and capital as G_y and G_k respectively, and (v) for the capital/output ratio, the growth equations can be restated simply as:

$$G_y = (a + \alpha - 1) - \beta v \tag{50a}$$

$$G_k = \alpha \frac{1}{v} - \beta \tag{51a}$$

If the system is said to be experiencing steady growth, i.e. to be in a steady-state condition, all the variables are growing at the same constant rate so that the ratio between these variables remain constant. Such a state of affairs is sometimes referred to as a balanced-growth path. Thus the growth in income with its attendant demand would be equal to that of capital with its accompanying capacity.

Both growth equations are linear functions of the capital/output ratio or its reciprocal, so that the two rates of growth will remain constant if (v) remains constant. The point is that if one can identify a capital to output ratio at which output grows at the same pace as capital, then output can be shown to grow steadily. Equations (50) and (51) are represented graphically on a single diagram with the rates of growth on the vertical and the capital/output ratio on the horizontal axis. The rate of growth of income is a straight line with an ordinate (vertical axis) intercept at $(a + \alpha - 1)$ with a negative slope of $-\beta$. The growth of capital is a hyperbolic function of (v) with the curve, as portrayed by Duesenberry,[6] asymptotically coinciding with both axis as in Fig. (5.3).

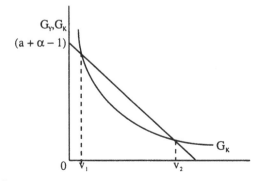

Figure 5.3

147

However, as Pasinetti tells us,[7] these diagrams are not totally descriptive of the growth equations. Regarding G_k, Duesenberry always represents it as if its asymptotes were the abscises and the ordinate, but his diagrams are not correct. One of the asymptotes is a straight line parallel to the abscissa (the horizontal axis) as determined by the distance (β) as in Fig. (5.4).

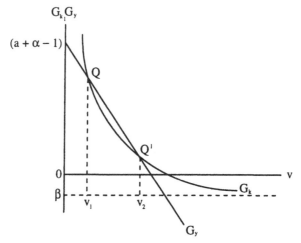

Figure 5.4

Aside from the technical point differentiating these diagrams we find two points of intersection represented by v_1 and v_2 at which the proportional rates of growth in income and capital are equal. And of these two positions it is (v_2) which is unstable; for even if we were to suppose that the system arrived there by chance, it would immediately diverge from there if it were displaced. The intersection at point (Q) represents stable equilibrium in that once this state is established it will correct itself in the event of a displacement. For example, if in a particular period the system revealed a capital to output ratio to the right of (v_1), then output would grow at a greater rate than capital reducing the ratio until Q is reached. Interestingly enough, if (v) lies to the right of Q', then G_k and G_v both decline with the ratio increasing; but at some point the excess of capital may lead to capital de-accumulation (negative net investment) though one can suppose some lower level to the attendant fall in income coming from autonomous investment factor. Eventually income will start to rise resulting in positive capital growth.

So the rates of growth in income and output will change from period to period unless the system finds itself in either the (v_1) or (v_2) positions — with (v_1) being one of stable equilibrium. But how are these points arrived at? The issue of the existence of steady growth is central; can we presume that the economy will find a (v_1) position based on its endogenous behavioral equations? And if so, does the steady growth in income necessarily carry with it the continuous presence of full employment? Or is it a matter of the capital to output ratio being determined for the economy by technological considerations, and the problem is to understand the behavior of the constituencies of the system that will maintain full capacity (and full employment) output through time given particular parameters that reflect this behavior. Here we are considering such variables as the savings to income ratio and the growth rate of investment; indeed the investment change emerges as the solution to the maintenance of the growth path. And if the economy departs from the steady growth path, is there a mechanism for correction, or is the departure self-sustaining? These matters will come to be analyzed as we formulate our basic growth models.

We return to the endogenous nature of fig. (4) to see how a position such as (v_1) is arrived at. The point Duesenberry makes is that this constant ratio of capital to output is not technically given; the ratio is changeable and is simply "the result of the cumulative effects of investment on the capital stock and of investment and consumption on income".[8] Starting from a point to the left of (v_1), the capital to output ratio will increase as a reflection of a decline in the growth of capital that is less than the decline in income. Capital growth deteriorates as a proportion of income because the existing capital stock represents a growing excess capacity which lowers profits per unit of capital and thereby investment as a proportion of output causing the capital stock to grow at a slower pace. A realized rate of growth in output that is below expectations affects investment via the (β) parameter in the form of the acceleration equation that includes the capital stock as a determinant of investment expenditures. But this behavior via the multiplier principal impacts negatively on the growth of income and demand. The increases in the capital to output ratio then represents a 'defeat' of the economy's attempt to bring capacity growth in line with the realized growth in income. The time-lag with which new investment adapts to changes in income is more immediate than adaptations of consumption spending, thus a slowdown in economic growth quickly triggers the accelerator response that overwhelms the positive impetus from a lagged consumption response, resulting in the magnified slowdown in income growth. In the move from a low to a higher ratio of capital to output, both the rate of growth of income and that of capital decline.

If the ratio lies to the left of Q', the rate of income growth exceeds that of capital as both capital and income over time asymptotically approach the particular ratio represented by (v_1). But what is happening in this interval? The level of the capital stock is found to be less than desired given realized income which will cause the rate of investment to accelerate driven by the need to correct capital stock levels in conjunction with anticipated levels of output. This investment response will cause increases in output and demand which thwarts the very attempt to maintain 'correct' capital levels, and the capital to output ratio continues to fall. But as the expansion continues the pace of advance of income tends to diminish; so that at some point the change in investment will bring forth a rate of growth of demand that justifies the rate of increase in the capital stock which is the (v_1) position of the capital to output ratio. From this point on investment growth and thereby additions to the capital stock will proceed at pace with the increase in income generated by that very investment change. Let us consider the interval from (v_2) to (v_1) as an accelerated movement through an expansion phase of the business cycle to the points where the growth of the economy takes on the relatively subdued pace of a steady advance.

Should the fall in income carry the ratio to the right of Q' the economy is thrown into severe cyclical contraction. Capital growth will turn negative as replacement investment becomes zero; in effect, the accelerator stops functioning and income is no longer declining due to a fall in investment expenditures. The pace with which the capital stock can be diminished is now divorced from the fall in demand, though it probably can be hurried through changes in tax laws that can accelerate the process of obsoleting capital. But the point here is that income will not increase until the deaccumulation has been carried to the point where the remaining stock is deemed insufficient relative to the existing low level of income. In other words until a point where (v) falls sufficiently to a position to the left of (v_2) and growth is again possible.

From this view we can imagine the economy growing steadily with a (v_2) ratio, and then falls off the path; the economy will take a long time in righting itself (if at all) and we can consider the capital to output ratios to the right of (v_1) is representing an unstable range of the economy. In this range, even if the level of income demand returns to its approximate level before the decline the system would still be carrying the burden of an excessive capital stock.

150

Should growth be carried on with a ratio at (v_1) and the system experiences a 'shock' that causes income to fall, the economy will be displaced from the growth path and the capital to output ratio will rise. However, should the ratio remain within the (v_1) to (v_2) range then, after the stock has been absorbed, income will begin to grow again in a manner that will cause the ratio to fall to the point where steady growth is again possible. What we see is that "when the conditions for an endogenous steady growth are satisfied, the system is capable of absorbing external 'shocks' in the sense that it tends to reproduce its equilibrium proportions whenever it is displaced from them, provided that the displacement does not upset the system beyond a certain critical value, which is represented in our case by a ratio of capital to income equal to (v_2) ".[9]

Our consideration of the possibilities of steady growth come out of a set of endogenously related equations containing the multiplier and accelerator parameters that were normally used to demonstrate the business cycle as an internally generated movement. Certainly there was a range of values for the parameters which produces steady growth, though these values were considered by some economists to fall outside of what might be reasonably expected. It is this range that is the basis for the endogenous growth model, and the cycle then emerges as the result of occurrences that displaces the system beyond the stability range of the capital to output ratios.

We can identify two cases where steady growth may be prevented. One is if the system begins with a ratio higher than (v_2) and the other is when the parameters are such that the growth curves do not intersect. Regarding these possibilities Duesenberry makes the following observations:[10]

If the parameters of the system lie outside certain boundaries, sustained growth will be impossible. Given appropriate initial conditions, income may grow at first, but the rate of capital accumulation will exceed the rate of growth of income. The resulting increase in the ratio of capital to income will reduce investment and the rate of income growth will decline until it becomes negative. There may be an eventual recovery, but not until a long period of capital decumulation.

Furthermore:

. . . But even if the parameters of the system are such as to make growth possible, income will not actually grow unless the initial values of the variables are appropriate. If initially the ratio of capital to

151

income exceeds a certain figure, capital will grow faster than income and a depression will ensue so the economy will not experience growth either because it is incapable of doing so, or because it starts from the wrong initial condition.

It is the state where growth is not possible that has been used to explain the regularity of business cycles. As we have said, the use of the equations (47a-47d) has been primarily to demonstrate the presence of cycles. We can extract from these equations a dynamic system that produces cycles of different amplitudes depending on the values of the parameters. From equations (48) and (49) we obtain:

$$Y_t = (a + \alpha + 1 - \beta)Y_{t-1} - (a + \alpha - a\beta)Y_{t-2} \tag{52}$$

The cycle emerges because the values of the parameters yield equations (50) and (51) that do not intersect each other and thereby produce the gyrating changes in (Y).

We have a framework which tells us that given the right conditions the economy is capable of steady growth. Yet we are left with some unease. The growth state emerges from the response mechanics inherent in the multiplier-accelerator equations that reveal a systematic interaction between the capital stock, the level of investment, income and savings. The level of income and capital stock determines the level of demand and savings as well as that of investment for the next period. Investment in this following period depends on the level of demand relative to the capital stock, i.e. capacity, on hand. This investment will in turn determine the change in income and the capital stock for the following period after that which then reveals the level of demand (and savings) and capital stock that in turn governs investment and so on. And if matters remain in balance, investment will be equal to generated savings, giving rise to an increase in the capital stock that will be absorbed by the increase in demand flowing from the investment itself. The idea, as we have seen, is to appreciate a situation where the growth rate of capital and the capacity represented be equal to the growth of income and demand.

But there are exogenous factors (external data) which would impact on this growth scenario and which must be taken account of. Here we think of technological change which via its impact on employment and demand will affect investment; the pace of such changes must be factored in to the growth process. As well one has to consider changes in the population (labor force) which along with the state of technology will limit the growth in output. Furthermore, one has to account for the distribution of income between profits and wages along the growth path in order to get a realistic handle on the growth of savings, and this will bring into consideration the pricing policies of firms in relation to labor union activity in determining wage rates. These factors must be brought into correct alignment in support of those broad behavioral equations of a purely endogenous growth model.

The basic neoclassical model

We take a step to relating these 'outside' elements to the growth condition with a look at a one-sector growth model that is based on the neoclassical mechanics of production and distribution. [11] In chapter (3) we analyzed this traditional approach and subjected it to some critical analyses, and concluded that we would need to take an alternative track in order to gain a realistic understanding of these matters. It may seem somewhat odd that we should now want to examine a growth model that makes use of the neoclassical 'well-behaved' production function and which treats income distribution as determined by factor output elasticities, i.e. that relative shares are essentially to be read from the mechanics of production. That is, to recall a point, that the profit rate, for example, is simply the slope of the per capita production function.

It is though worthwhile to proceed with this, by now, standard piece of equipment; in order to appreciate how this neoclassical apparatus explains the existence of a capital to labor ratio and through this a capital to output ratio, and how it accounts for the stability of the growth condition. The model also speaks of how the system can move from one trend growth path to another. So we will pick up the discussion from the first section of chapter (3) and view the neoclassical structure as one way to explain steady growth; thereafter, as we proceed to /replace and modify these neoclassical tools (relating in part to the second section of chapter 3), we will come upon alternative, more realistic means with which to comprehend the long-term pattern of the economy.

The setting for the model is an idealized extreme aggregative economy that produces a single all-purpose commodity. Thus output serves as a consumption good, and that portion of the output that is not consumed, i.e. saved, is automatically invested and increases the capital stock. No distinction need be made between those who save and those who invest, and there is no need to work up separate behavioral equations for investment and savings. Desired savings are always realized and investment intentions are always in harmony with desired savings. All savings accumulated by households is absorbed by firms for accumulation of capital.

Furthermore, our single output when treated as capital is perfectly malleable; it can be squeezed up or down to operate with greater or lesser amounts of labor. Thus capital can be instantaneously transferred from a production process reflecting one level of the capital to labor ratio to another appropriate to a different capital intensity. Taking the single good as numeraire, there is no possible change in the price of output, so we can speak unambiguously of the system's real output.

The technical possibilities of production of this one good world creation are represented by a continuous constant return to scale production function that was discussed in chapter (3). In addition, the model presumes that the labor force grows at a constant relative rate independent of the other economic variables.

We set all this out in exact form. The exogenous growth of the labor force (L):

$$L = nL$$

and

$$L_T = L_0 e^{nt} \tag{53}$$

Assuming that the capital stock does not depreciate we can write:

$$K = I \tag{54}$$

or

$$K = s(Y) \tag{55}$$

With the given savings coefficient the change in the capital stock becomes a function of the level of output:

$$\frac{dK}{dt} = I_t = s(Y_t) \tag{56}$$

The model employs the usual neoclassical production function with constant returns to scale, capital and labor substitutability and diminishing

154

marginal productivities. Repeating here some of the characteristics that were talked about earlier, we have:

$$ZY = F(ZK, ZL) \qquad (57)$$

If K and L are doubled $(Z=2)$, then output will also double. This allows the expression of the function on a per capita basis. If we let $Z = 1/L$, we have:

$$y = \frac{Y}{L} = F(\frac{K}{L}, 1) = f(\frac{K}{L}) = f(k) \qquad (58)$$

giving output per capita as a function of capital per capita. Increasing the scale of operations by increasing capital and labor proportionately will have no impact on output per man. There is no gain from increasing capital and labor as long as the (k) is the same because of the constant returns assumption. However, the marginal productivity to increasing the capital to labor ratio is positive but diminishing; this is the standard stuff that we can write as:

$$f'(k) > 0, f''(k) < 0 \qquad (59)$$

An example of a function embodying these characteristics is the widely used Cobb-Douglas function (equation 32 of chapter 3) which we restate:

$$Q = AK^{\alpha}L^{\beta} \qquad (60)$$

which can be put on a per capita basis as:

$$y = \frac{Y}{L} = \frac{AK^{\alpha}L^{\beta}}{L} = \frac{AK^{\alpha}}{L^{\alpha}} = A(k)^{\alpha} \qquad (61)$$

as

$$\beta = 1 - \alpha$$

And, as we are now aware, these exponents are the output elasticities of capital and labor which when factor payments are equal their marginal product reveals the relative shares of profits and wages in output.

155

The face for this production format is seen in Figure (5.5) which is a simpler version of Figure 3.9.

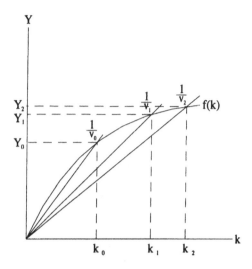

Figure 5.5

Each point on the function determines a ratio of output to capital:

$$\frac{y}{k} = \frac{\dfrac{Y}{L}}{\dfrac{K}{L}} = \frac{Y}{K} = \frac{1}{v} \tag{62}$$

Then a line drawn from the origin to a point on the function reveals the slope of the function at that point as given by the inverse of the capital to output ratio (v). At point k_o we find the ratio Y_o/K_o or $1/v_o$; an increase to k_1 results in a smaller proportionate increase to k_1 causing a greater increase in the capital to output ratio. Thus the move to k_2 reveals that $1/v_1 < 1/v_o$. Again the point to keep in mind is that the production mechanics assume diminishing returns to increases in the capital to labor ratio.

Once the savings ratio is known we immediately determine the composition of demand as between that part of output to be consumed and that part to be set aside for capital accumulation. The growth rate of capital is then known, and the growth rate of the labor force is given exogenously. Thus at a point in time with specified endowments of capital and labor, the level of output is determined from which future factor growth and that of output follows, and so on. Thus from any starting point, that is, from a specified capital to labor ratio, we should be able to follow a particular growth path. Let us first consider the steady growth condition as reflected in what has been termed "the fundamental equation of neoclassical economic growth" and then look at the stability characteristics of this outcome.

The division of the level of output on a per capita basis is:

$$y = f(k) = \frac{C}{L} + \frac{I}{L} \tag{63}$$

and

$$I = s(Y) = \dot{K} \tag{64}$$

The proportionate rate of growth of the capital to labor ratio is equal to the proportionate rate of growth of capital minus that of labor. Thus:

$$\hat{k} \equiv \frac{\dot{k}}{k} = \frac{\dot{K}}{K} - \frac{\dot{L}}{L} \tag{65}$$

$$= \frac{\dot{K}}{K} - n$$

Multiplying (65) through by $k = \dfrac{K}{L}$ gives:

$$\dot{k} = \frac{K}{L} \cdot \frac{\dot{K}}{K} - \frac{K}{L} \cdot \frac{\dot{L}}{L} \tag{66}$$

$$= \frac{\dot{K}}{L} - kn \tag{67}$$

and

$$\frac{\dot{K}}{L} = \dot{k} + kn \tag{68}$$

Now relating to the division of output and substituting into (65) we find:

$$y = f(k) = \frac{C}{L} + \dot{k} + nk \qquad (69)$$

then

$$\frac{S}{L} \equiv \frac{s(Y)}{L} \equiv sf(k) \qquad (70)$$

and

$$sf(k) = \dot{k} + nk \qquad (71)$$

so

$$\dot{k} = sf(k) - nk \qquad (72)$$

with the proportionate rate of growth in the capital to labor ratio being:

$$\hat{k} = \frac{sf(k)}{k} - n \qquad (73)$$

We can arrive at equation (73) directly by noting:

$$\hat{k} = \frac{\dfrac{dk}{dt}}{dt} = \frac{\dfrac{dK}{dt}}{K} - \frac{\dfrac{dL}{dt}}{L} \qquad (74)$$

then:

$$\hat{k} = \frac{s(Y)}{K} - n \qquad (75)$$

which in per capita terms:

$$\hat{k} = \frac{s(y)}{k} - n \qquad (76)$$

$$= \frac{sf(k)}{k} - n \qquad (77)$$

158

What these fundamental equations tell us is that the change in the ratio (or the proportionate rate of growth of the ratio) is given in terms of the ratio (k) itself. There is then a particular level of the capital to labor ratio that results in a zero change of the ratio; and given the constant returns to scale assumption results in a constant capital to output ratio.

Before diagramming this equilibrium growth condition it would be helpful to consider again the ingredients of equation (72). The $sf(k)$ gives us the level of savings for the savings ratio as a function of (k); and we might immediately feel some unease here at both constancy and aggregateness of this savings relationship. The (nk) term reveals the amount of investment (i.e. savings) that would be needed to equip the new entrants to the labor force with the same 'tool power' as the existing labor force. This is the 'capital widening' notion that has the capital stock accumulate at a pace to match, and hence absorb, the expanding labor force. The (k) term is the amount of investment that would be forthcoming in excess of (nk) and causes capital to be accumulated at a rate that results in an increase to the capital to labor ratio; what is normally referred to as 'capital deepening'.

Rearranging ((72) shows:

$$sf(k)=nk+\dot{k} \tag{78}$$

And steady growth implying the constancy of the capital to output ratio means that $\dot{k}=0$; so that there is a particular (k) and hence output per capita that brings forth a level of savings that maintains that existing capital to labor ratio.

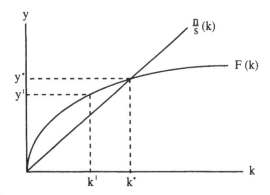

Figure 5.6

159

We see this in Fig. (5.6) with the steady growth outcome given in terms of (y) and (k).

There is a ray through the origin with slope n/s where all points on the line indicate the level of investment (savings) necessary to maintain capital widening for the corresponding (k). From (72) or (77) we have:

$$s(y)=nk \qquad (79)$$

$$y=\frac{n}{s}(k)$$

The level of savings that will be forthcoming for a given savings ratio is a function of output via the corresponding (k) and can be read off the $f(k)$ line. Where the two lines intersect we have a level of savings such that its investment will maintain the existing capital to labor ratio at k^* and $\dot{k}=0$.

Thus the steady growth condition is one where:

$$\frac{sf(k^*)}{k^*}=n \qquad (80)$$

or

$$y^*=f(k^*)=\frac{n}{s}(k^*) \qquad (81)$$

This (k^*) position gives us the equivalence of the (v_1) outcome of the purely endogenous growth model. Yet here the result is in terms of expressed production conditions — output is growing steadily due to a particular factor input ratio. Since in this neoclassical world we can read relative income shares from a point on the production function then steady growth implies that demand will grow at a pace which justifies past capital accumulation. The acceleration principle inherent in the investment equation of the endogenous model operates 'normally' and decisions are taken to maintain the existing growth in the capital stock and the associated capital to output ratio.

While the endogenous model does not seem to take into account those 'outside' factors that limit the system such as the growth of the labor force, they are present by implication in the investment and consumption relationships. On the other hand, the neoclassical growth model certainly relates to businessmen behavior, but it is not clearly marked. When we

160

say that firms stand ready to absorb all savings volunteered by households, it seems to be a totally passive response and in no need of an active investment demand function. But this passive behavior is a reflection of a response that is justified by a level of consumption that brings investment demand (i.e. investment needs) in line with available savings — there is an investment function lurking behind the scene. It is off stage because the neoclassical model puts at the center the mechanistic interplay between production and relative income shares and hence demand read off the production function. Yet, as we discussed in Chapter 3, it is questionable whether the traditional production function can be used to provide this information.

Nevertheless, we consider neoclassical stability of the growth position starting from a point to the left of k^* which we label k', y', then for the given savings parameter, the system will be accumulating capital at a rate in excess of that needed to keep constant the capital to labor ratio. Investment per unit of labor is increasing as we find:

$$sf(k) > nk$$

or

$$\frac{sf(k)}{k} > n \qquad (82)$$

and

$$s(\frac{Y}{K}) > n$$

Whatever expression we want to use, what we have is an unsustainable pace of capital growth. The increased growth rate of capacity brings with it a lower then proportionate increase in output and demand. The higher level of capital stock begins to exercise an increasing negative impact on investment decisions compared to the positive influence of the increase in output. This would come through to us via an investment demand function, but in the neoclassical passive investment approach it is accounted for by the aggregate diminishing returns nature of the production function which results in the smaller pace of increase in (y) and the subsequent reduced rate of accumulation.

The surplus of investment by which, to reiterate, we mean a rate in excess of the growth of the labor force, will over time be reduced to a pace that can be justified by the increase in output; and that occurs when it is equal to the growth rate in the labor force itself.

Reverse reasoning holds from a point such as k'' where we have:

$$sf(k) < nk \qquad (83)$$

At this level of output per capita the amount of investment generated by $s(Y)$ is insufficient to equip the growing labor force with the existing capital to labor ratio. This condition is telling us that there is excess capital on hand as a reflection of a too low a level of output; and this will lead to a reduction in the pace of accumulation. But this reduction in the growth of capital while reducing the capital to labor ratio will cause output per capita to fall less than proportionately. There will be a lower level of (y) that will produce a level of demand per capita such as to 'motivate' a rate of capital growth equal to that of the labor force — k will stop falling.

Thus from whatever the initial (k) and capital to output ratio happens to be, the economy is pictured over time as converging to the steady (balanced) growth condition. The vehicle for this convergence is the changing (y) along the production function given the savings propensity and the growth of the labor force. Variations in the capital to output ratio is at the core of neoclassical growth stability. Let us also reiterate that the long-term growth outcome is that of the growth of the labor force, and is not, as would seem the commonplace notion, dependent upon the rate of savings.

This stability characteristic is seen in the so called 'phase diagram' of Fig. (5.7).

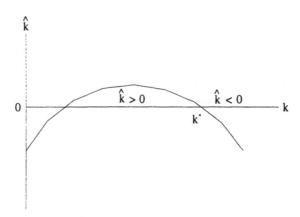

Figure 5.7

If the savings ratio does not determine the steady-growth rate, it does effect the level of the path upon which the economy is proceeding. In other words, an increase in the savings rate can serve as the shift instrument propelling the economy to a position of a higher equilibrium capital to labor ratio and output per unit of labor. Consider that at k there is an increase in the savings ratio to s' and that the authorities initiate policies that stimulate investment spending to compensate for this exogenous decline in consumption. Investment will be increasing at a rate in excess of the labor force, and the ray through the origin attained smaller slope as we now find:

$$\frac{n}{s'}(k) < f(k) \tag{84}$$

This happening is quite positive as it results in a deepening of capital and an increase in output per unit of labor. However, this higher pace of capital accumulation is not sustainable due to the eventual slackening of the increase in demand that itself relates to the diminishing rate of increase in output — again the technicalities of the production function holds sway. The system approaches the position where the growth rate of that higher level of capital stock moderates to a sustainable pace which is one equal to that of the labor force. Of course, capital deepening has been achieved, output per unit can now proceed as before but at a higher level. Demand increases in line with the increase in the labor force and reflects the higher level of output per capita (we will need a higher level of output to support the now higher level of capital).

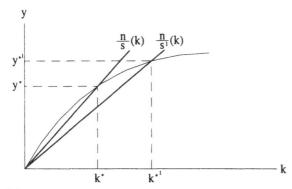

Figure 5.8a

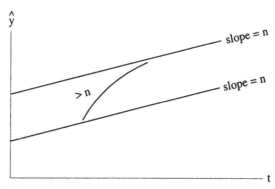

Figure 5.8b

We see this change from one level of the growth path to another in Figures (5.8a) and (5.8b).

What the system is doing is supplying more capital of an existing technology, and in the sense similar to the usual diminishing returns type of an example, we have more input supplied to a relatively fixed factor which itself results in a reduction in the rate of increase of output and the profitability of the existing higher rate of accumulation. As long as the rate of capital growth exceeds that of the labor force, it will engender conditions leading to the reduction in the rate of accumulation itself. At some point the rate of capital growth will fall back to the sustainable pace; and it will thereafter continue at this rate but from a higher level — the (k) and output per capita will be permanently higher.

This scenario does require, to say the least, some suspension of belief; we do draw attention to the malleability assumption mentioned at the outset of the description of this model. At $k^{*'}$ we have a greater level of capital per unit of labor than at k^*; and it is the same 'type' of capital in both cases and there is no unused capital. There is something here that easily fits different input proportion without losing its identifiable characteristic (in this sense we are in the Ricardian corn model). Yet in laying out this neoclassical analysis one must be cautious against slipping into a state of mind that would relate the observations of the model to the world of heterogeneous output. The neoclassical model cannot act as a surrogate for an explanation of growth and distribution in a world where commodities are produced by labor and capital goods and where output and input are heterogeneous goods.

And still another point that stretches the imagination is being able to increase the rate of accumulation without realizing technological change.

Is it likely that the system will be adding to its capital stock machines that are a replica of what it already has? Or is it more likely that capital accumulation is the vehicle by which technological change permeates the system, and that it becomes unreal to separate the two. Before considering how this model incorporates this other 'exogenous' factor, we reiterate the point that for the given steady-state condition the system exhibits stable relative income shares that can be read from such a point on our well-behaved production function. This result is drawn from the mechanics of neoclassical distribution that were discussed in Chapter 3 and which we illustrate in Fig. (5.9).

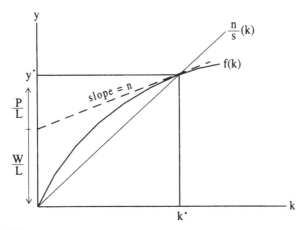

Figure 5.9

Recalling that:

$$r = f'(k) \tag{85}$$

$$w = f(k) - kf'(k) \tag{86}$$

then for wages per man we have:

$$\frac{W}{L} = w = \frac{Y}{L} - \frac{K}{L} \cdot \frac{P}{K} \tag{87}$$

$$= \frac{Y}{L} - \frac{P}{L}$$

or

$$y - rk \qquad (88)$$

Then:

$$y = w + rk \qquad (89)$$

which, upon multiplication by (L) gives the division of total output into wages and profits. So:

$$Y = W + P \qquad (90)$$

In Fig. (5.9) we have $(K/L)^*$ and $(Y/L)^*$, and:

$$P/L = K/L \cdot P/K \qquad (91)$$

$$= K/L \cdot r$$

where (r) is given by the slope of the production function at the point k^*, y^*. The graphical representation of P/L is given by the difference between $(Y/L)^*$ and the intercept of the tangent to the production function with slope (r). The y-axis intercept of the tangent drawn to the function at k^* yields profit per man which, upon deduction from output per man, results in wages per man. Thus once the economy reaches the steady growth condition as given by y^*, k^*, it will generate constancy in the distribution of output.

Next we consider how the basic neoclassical model incorporates a second supposed externally given limitation to the growth of output, that of technological change (the first being the growth of the labor supply). But first let us consider those 'stylized facts' of the historical development of capitalist economies. It has been suggested that the long-run relations between the growth of labor, capital, and output and the behavior of relative income shares shows evidence that: [12]

   a) The growth of real output tends to be about the same as the stock of capital goods, so that the ratio of capital to output has remained fairly constant showing no systematic trend.

166

b) The stock of real capital grows at a generally constant rate exceeding the growth of the labor input. Thus capital per man grows at a steady rate over long periods of time. As well, output per unit of labor shows more or less a steady rate of increase over the long run. Since output is the result of labor input and output per unit of labor, then the rate of growth of output is the sum of the rates of growth of the labor input and the productivity of labor.

c) The rate of profit is fairly constant over the long-term.

d) The relative shares of capital and labor in output is generally unchanged, i.e. there is a constant relative distribution of output between wages and profits.

Regarding the distribution of income we might take a look at some recent numbers; and in table (5.3) we have wages and salaries as a percentage of national income designated by the column (W/Y) and also the sum of proprietor's income non-farm and corporate profits as a percentage of income under the heading (P/Y). Over the years between 1975 and 1991 we find an overall constancy of the wage share. The profit share does evidence a downward drift from its high in the latter 1970s but other than the particular decline attributable to the recession in 1981, the ratio shows stability throughout the decade of the 1980s.

Considering that we are trying to understand the characteristics of an economy as it resides within a steady growth environment (which we take as an acceptable proxy for the long-term behavior of the system), then this neoclassical model would seem to offer a viable explanation. The model seems then to serve well as a parable, as it generates conclusions that are in line with the observed facts of the real world, providing it can incorporate the characteristic of technological change and innovation that is an ongoing reality of an expanding economy. The stylized facts tell us that while capital and output both grow at the same rate, it is at a faster rate than that of the labor force. Thus the constancy of relative income shares must be explained within the context of:

$$\frac{\dot{K}}{K} = \frac{\dot{Y}}{Y} > \frac{\dot{L}}{L} = n \tag{92}$$

Table (5.3)
Income Distribution

YEAR	$\dfrac{W}{Y}$	$\dfrac{P}{Y}$
1975	.63	.17
1976	.62	.18
1977	.61	.19
1978	.61	.19
1979	.61	.18
1980	.63	.15
1981	.62	.14
1982	.63	.12
1983	.62	.14
1984	.60	.16
1985	.61	.16
1986	.61	.15
1987	.61	.16
1988	.61	.16
1989	.61	.16
1990	.61	.15
1991	.62	.15

Again we reiterate the point that the model without technical change produces the result that along the growth path output and capital will grow at the same rate as the labor force, i.e.:

$$\frac{\dot{K}}{K} = \frac{\dot{Y}}{Y} = n \qquad (93)$$

Yet the reality is that of statement (92); and this difference is reconciled with the introduction of technical progress that simultaneously accounts for the constancy of relative shares. The model incorporates such progress in

168

the form of an exogenously determined rate of increase in the productivity of labor designated by the λ term, and we have this progress being absorbed by all of the labor force; those already employed with existing capital and those coming into employment with nearly accumulated capital.

To illustrate what we mean consider Fig. (10) where we have the standard isoquant allowing output ($Y=1$) by a variety of input propositions. Suppose a shift of the isoquant by a factor of 1/2 in the direction of the K-axes (that is, parallel to the labor axes). Then in a comparison of the new 'technique' with the original, the system is now able to produce the same amount of output using the same amount of capital, but only half as much labor. But this is formally the same as if the labor force has increased in size; or to put the matter a different way, the 'effective' labor services provided by each physical unit of labor has increased by a factor of two. Thus we redefine the labor force as the effective labor force including not only the number of workers but also the element of productivity improvement due to the technological change. Labor is not only measured in terms of the number of hands, but also in terms of each pair of hands representing an efficiency unit.

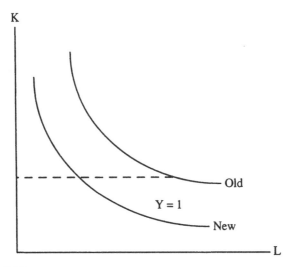

Figure 5.10

We have the growth of the labor force on nominal terms (n), but as well the growth of the labor force in terms of efficiency units (or that of effective manhours). The growth of this effective labor force (E) is represented by:

$$E_t = L_o e^{e^{(\lambda+n)t}} \tag{94}$$

and it is this representation of the labor force which is incorporated into the production function. Note that the ratio of effective labor force to the labor force itself grows at the rate equal to that of labor productivity (λ). So that given (n) we have effective labor as $E_t = L_t e^{\lambda t}$.

Newly acquired capital brings with it an increase in labor productivity on the part of those engaged with it; however, this particular characteristic of the new capital is assumed to be capable of being passed on to all existing operating capital so that all of the labor force absorbs this progress equally. We are dealing with a technical progress that is labor-augmenting in the aggregate, as a reflection of that 'malleability assumption' again that here supposes all of the capital stock to transform itself into the type capital embodying the latest technology, so that the capital stock is always alike capital. With this in mind we write:

$$y = \frac{Y}{E} = f(\frac{K}{Le^{\lambda t}}) = f(k) \tag{95}$$

with the rate of change in the capital to output ratio being:

$$k = \frac{s(y)}{k} - (n+\lambda) \tag{96}$$

The equilibrium growth condition is given by:

$$y^* = \frac{n+\lambda}{s}(k^*) \tag{97}$$

Note that the y^* of (97) exceeds that of (81) due to the inclusion of the (λ) factor in the production function. The increase in the ratio of capital per unit of 'natural' labor causes output to grow at the same rate as that of capital. The tendency to diminishing returns due to the capital stock growing at a rate in excess of the labor force is offset by the increase in the productivity of labor at the (λ) rate. The steady growth condition is characterized by the equality of K and Y and both exceed L by (λ) — all this in keeping with those stylized facts.

There remains to elaborate on income distribution within this context of technological progress which will bring us to some discussion of the 'neutrality' of such progress. The rate of profit in the conventional fashion is equal to the slope of the production function which in this context is:

$$r=\frac{dy}{dk}=Le^{\lambda t}f'(\frac{1}{Le^{\lambda t}})\cdot f'(\frac{K}{Le^{\lambda t}})=f'(k) \tag{98}$$

The wage rate in its neoclassical determination is given by the marginal productivity of labor which, as a result of stating the production function:

$$Y=Le^{\lambda t}f(k) \tag{99}$$

and differentiating (Y) with respect to (L) yields:[13]

$$w=e^{\lambda t}[f(k)-k\cdot f'(k)] \tag{100}$$

The wage rate rises at a rate equal to the increase in labor productivity. And we would suspect constant relative shares to be maintained after the introduction of technical progress as before.

With the rate of profit generally constant, total profits rise at a pace set by the growth of the capital stock which is equal to the growth of labor productivity; thus:

$$K=Ke^{\lambda t} \tag{101}$$

It is the pace of capital accumulation that is the conveyor of the rate of technological change. So both capital and output grow at a pace which exceeds that of the labor force by the (λ) factor with the total growth rate being $(n+\lambda)$.

The wage rate is growing at the same (λ) rate which tells us that the wage bill growth exceeds that of the labor force in an alike manner. Thus profits and wages are both rising at a pace which exceeds that of the labor force by the (λ) factor — with the total growth rate of both variables equal to $(n+\lambda)$. Both the ratios of K/L and Y/L are growing at the (λ) rate. We are simply saying that the growth in the ratio of the wage rate to the rate

171

of profit is balancing that of capital stock to labor input, so that relative shares remain unchanged.

The notion of neutrality or non-neutrality of a technical change describes, in one respect, what happens to relative income shares subsequent to the change. In our discussion, the change impacts on the productivity of labor but leaves unaffected the marginal productivity of capital; we can then say that given the productivity of capital such change will be neutral thereby leaving relative income shares constant, if the higher ratio of capital to output resulting in the same rate of profit as prior to the change also causes the ratio of output to capital to remain unchanged. This notion of neutrality is called "Harrod neutrality" (we will shortly encounter this name again); and it is telling us that, with the constant returns to scale assumption, this change allows output and capital to have a common growth rate because it results in capital and effective labor growing at the same rate. So the characteristics of this neutrality are the constancies of the ratio of income shares, the rate of return to capital and the capital to labor ratio properly defined. Fig. (5.11) illustrates this change.

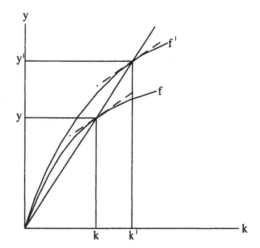

Figure 5.11

The production function can now be stated as:

$$Y = F[K, A(t)L] \tag{102}$$

with the index of progress (A) prefixed to the L component; thus in the productive process technical change and increases in the labor force can be substituted for each other. In Fig. (5.11) we note a deepening of capital, but this deepening disappears, so to speak, when the technology causes more 'working ability' per worker to emerge. The slope of the line through the origin is the ratio of output to capital, and this ratio is constant. There is no change in the productivity of capital as shown by the parallel slope of the tangents at f and f'. We do reiterate that this labor-augmenting technical change is considered 'disembodied' in that it changes the efficiency of all of labor regardless whether they enter the work force before or after the innovation.

We would also want to consider another facet of neutrality normally presented within the neoclassical framework and labelled 'Hicks neutrality'. This concept of neutrality requires that given the amount of capital and labor the effect of a technical change will leave unchanged the relative income shares of the factors. The increase in maximum output for a given capital to labor ratio may be attributable to improvements in organization which increases the productivity of capital and labor and/or it may be the result of 'learning by experience'. But the point is that 'technical progress' (like manna from heaven) distributes itself without bias over all capital and labor in use leaving unchanged the ratio of the marginal product of capital to that of labor and thereby unchanged the marginal rate of substitution between them. Hence if progress over time is equally capital and labor augmenting, then we can picture the production function itself shifting upward as a function of time. The function can now be represented as:

$$Y = A(t)f(K,L) \qquad (103)$$

where (A) is an index of technical change. Figure (5.12) shows us Hicks neutrality.

There is a production function (F) relating output per capita to capital per capita, and the function (F') is derived from (F) by showing the change in (y) for a given capital to labor ratio. There is no change in the ratio of the respective factor marginal productivity and thereby no change in the ratio of the rate of profit to the wage rate. The constancy of the ratio of income shares is given by the distance OR.

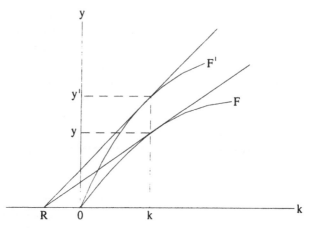

Figure 5.12

However, we do remind ourselves that it is Harrod neutrality of technical change that brings the basic neoclassical model into line with those stylized facts of history. When the rate of capital accumulation and technical change are raising productivity at a steady rate, then to maintain balance, the real wage rate must be rising at the same rate and thereby maintaining relative income shares. Steady growth requires not only that technical change be neutral, but also that the rate of capital accumulation be constant, and that the real wage rise at the required rate. When real wages fail to rise appropriately, demand fails to expand in line with supply and the system may face a condition of underconsumption causing the economy to fall off the steady growth path.

We can define neutrality as a condition of innovation or technical change in that it does not reduce the relative share of labor. But it is possible for the rate of accumulation to carry innovations that have a strong capital-using (labor-saving) bias such that the relative share of labor becomes lower after the technical change. To maintain a constant rate of profit would now require real wages to rise in smaller proportion than net output; but to make up for this the system would require a higher flow of gross investment if it is to avoid unemployment and maintain adequate levels of demand.

Let us not pursue this neutrality matter any further at this point for we do not want to stray too far from the intent of this chapter. In this neoclassical growth model we have a second design to account for the long-term developments of the economy. It does account for the 'external data' of labor force growth and technological changes, but in a rather 'mechanistic' way that hides the endogenous relations expressing the behavior of consumers and entrepreneurs. And while this growth model may be intellectually satisfying, it is built upon a foundation of a constant return to scale production function, capital and labor substitutability, diminishing marginal productivities, savings being a constant fraction of output, and income shares as read from the production function. Yet it is this entire edifice that, as we have seen, has been called into question. Thus while the model sends the right message — it does explain the stylized facts of growth — the messenger needs restructuring in the light of recent theoretical developments.

The dynamics of Harrod-Domar

We can consider the Harrod-Domar growth models as taking their point of departure the Keynesian short-run static equilibrium, and formulating the circumstances that maintains full-employment of a growing labor force and growing capital stock through time.[14] The essential Keynes concentrated on the income-creating character of investment which, considering the state of economic conditions at the time much of the theory of employment was formulated, was quite understandable. There was a need to restore full employment within the time frame of an 'immediate horizon'; that is to say, to raise national income to the levels needed to employ existing capital and labor resources. It was not a matter of envisioning the growth of output over time to accommodate the growth of resources. This vision naturally led to the consideration of employment as a function of demand, i.e. national income, and to look upon investment as the 'income creator' and solution to the employment problem. To reiterate, one determines the level of involvement required to increase the level of income to the point of absorbing existing resources. Thus the emphasis on the demand generating aspect of investment and the non-spending aspect of saving, taking the conditions of supply as given. And it is this attitude of taking the capital stock and the capacity of the system as given that marks the short-term (cyclical) analytical framework (re-emphasizing a point made early on in this chapter).

Since net investment is the process of expanding the capital stock, it appears anomalous to speak of investment at the same time as one speaks of a constant stock of capital.

175

However, in dealing with certain problems in which investment is involved, if one assumes the short-run to be short enough, the assumption of a constant stock of capital may be justified. It might be asserted, for instance, that it takes some time for investment to take effect in the sense of enlarging the capital stock. In particular is this acceptable if the stock of capital is very large to begin with, so that small changes in its size may temporarily be ignored.[15]

Yet sooner or later the assumption of a fixed stock must be dropped when discussing the effects of investment, and the analysis must reckon with the two-sided nature of investment; that while it is an income creating act, it is as well a capacity (supply)-creating act. And as Joan Robinson points out,

> Keynes hardly ever peered over the edge of the short period to see the effect of investment in making additions to the stock of production equipment.[16]

When we do peer over we are struck by the fact that for investment decisions to remain positive, the addition to capacity resulting from past decisions must be utilized. Output has to expand proportionate to the stock of capital if the negative effects of idle capacity are to be avoided. The savings-investment static equality will not do — at least for very long. We can see this straight away though it will be brought out clearly in the analysis of the models. Any particular level of income can be maintained over time in association with a constant level of investment. But as this investment continues, the capital stock and output capacity enlarges while the equilibrium income remains unchanged. The result is a growth in excess capacity that will cause investment to fall below savings leading to a fall in equilibrium income. The system will not be able to sustain the existing level of employment and income; either the equilibrium level of income must rise to absorb the growth in capacity originating with the given rate of investment or it will decline.

This growth in income via the multiplier apparatus originates in the induced entrepreneurial investment decisions motivated by the realized change in output via the acceleration principle; this in turn propels output growth which again triggers the accelerator and so on (behavior patterns are explicit). The Harrod-Domar models combine the multiplier and accelerator to determine the required rate of income growth (not the level of income) that assures the equality of planned savings and investment and the full-utilization of a continually growing output capacity.

These models define a path of steady state taking into consideration the externally given possibilities of the economy and determine the conditions which the economic magnitudes must satisfy to adhere to that path. This growth movement is derived in the context of a production model. We posit an economy with a fixed coefficient technology; that is, a production process which requires fixed amounts of labor and capital per unit of output. This approach may be considered a realistic step in the redesign of the neoclassical model; it will allow for a restructuring of the cost curves of the firm and thereby a modern analysis of pricing. This will come later on; now we want to see the operation of this production function in setting out a growth path.

Suppose one unit of output requires b units of labor and v units of capital, the production function can then be written as:

$$Y = \min[\frac{1}{v}(K), \frac{1}{b}(L)] \tag{104}$$

which produces the L-shaped functions of Fig. (5.13).

Under constant returns to scale these production isoquants are replicas of each other; the isoquant for output Y_2 being a radial magnification by a factor of 2 of the isoquant $Y=1$. We have right-angled relationships with corners along a ray from the origin with a slope v/b.

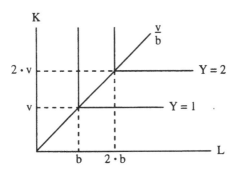

Figure 5.13

Suppose at a point in time we have some fixed amounts of labor and capital $(\overline{L}, \overline{K})$ and a level of output Y_1. The amount of labor and capital

177

employed will be Y_1b and Y_2v respectively, and if all available resources are to be employed, then output level Y_1 is equal to K/v and L/b. That is:

$$Y_1v=\overline{K}, Y_1b=\overline{L} \tag{105}$$

$$Y_1=\frac{\overline{K}}{v}=\frac{\overline{L}}{b} \tag{106}$$

and

$$\frac{\overline{K}}{\overline{L}}=\frac{v}{b} \tag{107}$$

Using some numbers: presume that the coefficient ratio is 4 units of labor and 2 'units' of capital per unit of output, with production being 4 units of output. We find:

$$\frac{\overline{L}}{\overline{K}}=\frac{4(4)}{2(4)}=\frac{16}{8}=\frac{2}{1} \tag{108}$$

and

$$\overline{L}\cdot v=\overline{K}\cdot b$$

$$\overline{L}=\frac{b}{v}(\overline{K}) \tag{109}$$

$$=\frac{4}{2}(8)=16$$

Thus if the capital stock is given at a level of 8 units then the maximum level of employment that this can give rise to is 16 units of labor stemming from the technology inherent in the system (assuming that all capital is fully employed). Clearly any labor supplied in excess of 16 units will be unemployed, or to see this in another way, unemployment results if $K/L < v/b$. Similarly:

$$\overline{K} = \frac{v}{b}(\overline{L}) \qquad (110)$$

$$= \frac{2}{4}(16) = 8$$

A capital stock in excess of 8 units, i.e. a condition of $K/L > v/b$ will result in unemployed capital and no investment.

Equilibrium with full employment of both factors requires, to repeat, that:

$$\frac{\overline{K}}{v} = \frac{\overline{L}}{b}$$

or

$$\frac{8}{2} = \frac{16}{4} \qquad (111)$$

Should we find $\overline{K}/v > \overline{L}/b$ such that $10/2 > 16/4$, there is an excess supply of 2 units of capital, and the level of output would be determined by the ratio of the labor supply to the labor coefficient, that is, by the smaller of the two ratios $(Y = \overline{L}/b)$. Capital will be employed up to the full-utilization of the labor force. Perhaps a more realistic vision would be a situation where $\overline{K}/v < \overline{L}/b$ such that $6/2 < 16/4$. Here we find an insufficient level of capital stock to fully employ the existing labor force (there is an excess supply of 4 units of labor). The upper limit to the level of output is determined by the smaller ratio, i.e. $\overline{K}/v$; the demand for labor is determined by the level of capital stock employed. In this scenario there is no recourse to alleviating this unemployment by changing the input mix since the coefficients are bound by the prevailing technology. The solution would seem either to increase the capital stock and/or to reduce the growth of the labor force. Keeping the nature of this production function in mind, we can now deal with the particulars of the models. First, Harrod.

There is the assumption of an unlagged savings function which gives the aggregate net savings of the economy at time (t) as a function of the level of income during that time period. Thus:

$$S_t = s(Y_t), 0 < s < 1 \qquad (112)$$

179

where (s) represents the constant marginal propensity equal to that of the average propensity to save. The system plans to and does save a particular proportion of its output every time period — Harrod assumes that savings intentions are always realized. The question is whether the economy will plan a level of investment expenditures sufficient to absorb the available savings? What indeed determines the level of intended investment?

To say that savings intentions are realized is to say that expected incomes are realized since actual savings will differ from intended savings should income turn out different from expectations. Now by definition, and in the most aggregative view:

$$S = Y - C = I \qquad (113)$$

that is, actual savings equals realized (actual) investment. But the 'dynamics' comes into play when we realize that intended investment may not be equal to intended savings. Assuming this is the situation, then investment plans and savings intentions cannot both be realized. Since Harrod assumes that savings plans (savings ex ante) are realized (equal to savings ex post) then it is investment intentions that go awry. As actual investment always equals actual savings, then the difference between intended savings and intended investments must be reflected in the condition that actual investment exceeds or falls below investment plans. The system has levels of investment that are unintentional which must reflect the condition that levels of income differ from expectations.

Should intended savings exceed intended investment the level of income will fall below expected income and actual investment will exceed investment ex ante by the amount of the unintentional 'investment' in inventory accumulation. And in reverse reasoning, investment ex post will be less than planned investment by the degree of inventory disinvestment and the system will find that it has not produced enough.

We can appreciate the essential role of planned investment. Given the assumption that the economy plans to save a particular proportion of output, what are the circumstances that motivate a level of planned investment so as to 'absorb' the available savings and thereby reflect the equality of planned and realized investment and a level of income that justifies the investment expenditure. What is the mechanism at work that causes the level of income to change in line with expectations? This brings us to Harrod's investment equation and his assumption concerning the acceleration principle.

There are two related interpretations of Harrod's investment function. Being that the function is of the fixed coefficient type, it depicts a technical relationship indicating the additional capital needed if the system is to bring about a certain change in output. Assuming that the average and marginal capital to output ratios are equal, we have:

$$\frac{K}{Y} = \frac{\dot{K}}{\dot{Y}} = v \qquad (114)$$

In this case the (v) is simply the measured increase in the capital stock divided by the measured increase in income. It shows an association between a change in output and that of capital, and is therefore the result of a past behavioral action effecting intended investments.

And it is entrepreneurial behavior that propels the economy, so we need another 'behavioral interpretation' of investment in terms of how businessmen will respond to a realized level of output. What change in the capital stock (and associated change in output) is required so that at the end of the period businessmen will be satisfied that they have corrected the right amount? If the system is satisfied with the level of investment undertaken in the past in the light of realized demand, then what is the guide determining current investment such that a future level of capital will be appropriate in terms of a future level of demand?

We see this second interpretation of investment as a 'response mechanism' that will, via the fixed coefficient premise, result in a particular change to the level of output. The question here is what is this investment response based upon such that the investment that is entered into is equal to an amount that the system would have wanted to undertake? This brings us to Harrod's premise concerning the acceleration principle which supposes that the entrepreneur's desire to undertake investment depends on the rate at which output is increasing; i.e., that intended investment is a constant proportion v_r (giving us the response coefficient) of the amount by which output in the current period exceeds that of the previous period. We have:

$$I_t = v_r(Y_t - Y_{t-1}) \qquad (115)$$

There are two related elements at work here. One is that the savings (realized investment) is a fixed proportion of the level of income, the other states that desired investment (investment ex ante) varies in constant proportion with the rate of increase in income. It follows that given income and realized investment, the economy will be satisfied with that level of investment only if the realized change in income and demand results in the system wanting to have invested as much as was actually invested. And if this is so, and here we come to another underlying premise, entrepreneurs based on the response coefficient will undertake a further level of investment that results in a repetition of the realized growth in output, such that the subsequent investment ex-post equal to the higher level of savings is again appropriate in the light of the higher level of demand. There is a rate of growth of output which will satisfy entrepreneurs that they have invested the correct amount; and upon realizing this they will undertake investment expenditures that will result in a continuation of the existing correct growth rate.

Again we might want to look at our two coefficients (v) and (v_r). The former is the technical relation given by the production assumption and tells us the increase in output for a given increase in investment expenditures; the later tells us what the increase in investment needs to be in order to bring about a particular increase in output. But they are the same in the state of growth equilibrium where the realized growth rate of output is precisely the rate that the system wants to see in the future. Let us have an illustration of this and the definition of some growth rates.

A realized growth rate between Y_t and Y_{t-1} can be stated as Y_t/Y_{t-1} and a comparison made between this rate and that of a previous period Y_{t-1}/Y_{t-2} in the form:

$$\frac{Y_t}{Y_{t-1}} = \frac{Y_{t-1}}{Y_{t-2}} + f(U_t) \tag{116}$$

where the term $f(U_t)$ is negatively related to U_t itself. We let U_t represent the state of investment and production relative to demand in the previous period. Then:

$$U_t = Y_{t-1} - D_{t-1}$$

and

$$f(U_t) \underset{>}{\overset{<}{=}} 0 \text{ as } U_t \underset{<}{\overset{>}{=}} 0 \tag{117}$$

and we find that the current growth will exceed that of the previous period should the system find it is 'suffering' an unintentional disaccumulation of inventories reflecting the condition that in the previous period it had not invested enough. Should $U_t > 0$ then the economy finds that it has produced too much, and will take steps to cause the current growth rate to be less than the previous realized rate. Intended investment will be less than intended savings indicating the presence of unintended or excess investment.

We restate equation (116) to easily see this in terms of a specific rate. So:

$$\frac{Y_t}{Y_{t-1}} = \frac{Y_{t-1}}{Y_{t-2}} \cdot \frac{D_{t-1}}{Y_{t-1}} \tag{118}$$

where $D_{t-1} = C_{t-1} + I_{t-1}$. If $U_t > 0$, then $D_{t-1}/Y_{t-1} < 1$ and the growth rate in (t) will fall short of that realized in period $(t-1)$. For the demand equations we have (using the behavior coefficient for investment):

$$C_t = bY_t \tag{119}$$

$$I_t = v_r(Y_t - Y_{t-1}) \tag{120}$$

Substituting these 'demands' in equation (118) yields:

$$\frac{Y_t}{Y_{t-1}} = b + v_r(\frac{Y_{t-1}}{Y_{t-2}}) - v_r \tag{121}$$

Given values for b and v_r there will be a particular realized rate of growth that induces a level of investment demand that brings about a future rate of growth equal to the realized rate.

Supposing $b = .85$ and $v_r = 2.15$ then:

$$\frac{Y_t}{Y_{t-1}} = 3(\frac{Y_{t-1}}{Y_{t-2}}) - 2.15 \tag{122}$$

should:

$$\frac{Y_{t-1}}{Y_{t-2}} = 1.075 \tag{123}$$

then:

$$\frac{Y_t}{Y_{t-1}} = 1.075 \tag{124}$$

The 7.5% rate is the growth equilibrium rate because at all points it reflects the correct working out of past expectations, thereby motivating an investment response that sustains the realized growth experience. The level of past investment is always appropriate in terms of realized demand so that we can write:

$$bY_t + v_r(Y_t - Y_{t-1}) = Y_t \tag{125}$$

$$Y_t(b - 1 + v_r) = v_r Y_{t-1} \tag{126}$$

and

$$\frac{Y_t}{Y_{t-1}} = \frac{v_r}{b - 1 + v_r} = 1.075 \tag{127}$$

We emphasize that the (v_r) term is a behavior coefficient telling us how entrepreneurs will react to a change in output and this response must result in a particular further change in output and demand if one is not to be disappointed with the investment undertaken. Of course, the (v_r) will have a determinable value which must be equal to the specific technical coefficient (v). The induced investment must be equal to the amount that the capital coefficient tells us is needed to increase income by the required amount.

If producers are to be satisfied with the increase in output the rise in demand must be sufficient to absorb it. Only when this happens can entrepreneurs be said to have correctly anticipated the change in demand, so that the investment they have undertaken is what they would have wanted to undertake.

In terms of demand (D) — simply stated — we have:

$$Y = C + I = D \tag{128}$$

and

184

$$\Delta Y = \frac{\Delta I}{1-b} = \Delta D \qquad (129)$$

The change in demand is a proportional function of the change in investment, and we want the particular growth rate for investment such that the growth in demand will justify the rate of change in output stemming from the change in investment.

Then, in terms of the capital coefficient:

$$\frac{Y}{K} = \frac{\Delta Y}{\Delta K} \qquad (130)$$

$$\Delta Y = \Delta K(\frac{Y}{K}) = \frac{\Delta K}{v} \qquad (131)$$

Relating (129) and (130) we find:

$$\Delta Y = \frac{\Delta I}{s} \qquad (132)$$

so

$$\frac{\Delta I}{I} = \frac{s}{v} \qquad (133)$$

Similarly:

$$v\Delta Y = \Delta K = s(Y) \qquad (134)$$

and

$$\frac{Y}{Y} \equiv \frac{\Delta Y}{Y} = s/v = G \qquad (135)$$

The proper growth rate of investment that leads to a growth in output such that demand expectations are satisfied is one that is equal to s/v. Given our parameter values the equilibrium growth rate is .075.

Thus we have the 'fundamental equation' (135) as a truism in that investment ex post is equal to ex post savings, with (G) the actual or realized growth rate. That is:

as:

$$v = \frac{I}{\Delta Y} \tag{136}$$

then

$$\frac{\Delta Y}{Y} v = s \tag{137}$$

and

$$\frac{\Delta Y}{Y} \cdot \frac{I}{\Delta Y} = s \tag{138}$$

So

$$\frac{I}{Y} = \frac{S}{Y} \tag{139}$$

Defining (v) in the technical coefficient sense means getting the accounting identities and a realized growth rate that necessarily equals (s/v). Working matters another way we find:

$$I = v(Y_t - Y_{t-1}) \tag{140}$$

$$S = s(Y_t) \tag{141}$$

then:

$$s(Y_t) = v(Y_t - Y_{t-1}) \tag{142}$$

$$G = \frac{Y_t - Y_{t-1}}{Y_t} = s/v \tag{143}$$

But the obvious is not what Harrod intended to convey; to give insight as to what supports the growth path and to impart theoretical content to equation (143) we want to define (v) as (v_r). This latter relationship is, as we pointed out, 'behavioral' in that it conveys an expression for

186

entrepreneurs' requirements for investment given the growth of income and will result in a further output growth that leaves the 'system' in a state that it has invested the right amount. Along the growth path it is the behaviorally induced investment that is continually adjusted to savings. Now we state:

$$\frac{Y}{Y} = G_w = s/v_r \qquad (144)$$

Here we do not have a truism but an expression of the rate of growth of output that justifies entrepreneurs' past investment decisions. We consider such a rate as the warranted growth rate (G_w); and along the steady-stated path $G = G_w$ so that:

$$Gv = s = G_w v_r \qquad (145)$$

That is, that the actual growth rate is equal to the expected rate on which investment decisions are based. In Harrod's words, describing the G_w, "that overall rate of advance which, if executed, will leave entrepreneurs in a state of mind in which they will be prepared to carry on a similar advance".[17] Since the investment that was undertaken was validated by the realized growth in demand, producers will anticipate a similar advance in the following period and will execute investment decisions that will indeed perpetuate the existing growth rate. And this will happen when entrepreneurs desire to invest the amount that is being invested in the sense of being equal to realized savings.

This is telling us that the higher the level of income the more will be invested, and thus the greater the pace of increase in income necessary to validate the greater investment. So the higher the income the faster income must grow, but the faster income grows the higher will tomorrow's income be. We can restate equation (143) as:

$$\frac{s}{v}(Y_t) = Y_t - Y_{t-1} \qquad (146)$$

and with s/v a constant the change in income $(Y_t - Y_{t-1})$ is a constant multiple of Y_t. So that as income grows so must the pace of increase — though at a constant geometric rate of increase through time. Equation (146) can be translated into a first-order difference equation as:

187

$$Y_t = \frac{v}{v-s}(Y_{t-1}) \qquad (147)$$

which tells us how income must behave from period to period — it gives the warranted course of income. This type of equation has a 'solution' in that given initial conditions it enables us to determine the warranted level of income for any future period.

What we are then considering along the path where $G = G_w$ is a continuous circumstance where investors' expectations come to be realized, which means a rate of growth that maintains full employment of the capital. But this need not necessarily imply full employment of an expanding labor force; the economy can move along a warranted path with growing involuntary unemployment. Professor Harrod then sets forth another growth rate which he calls the natural growth rate (G_n); this is defined as that rate of growth which, in the presence of full employment, is 'allowed' by the growth of the labor force and the rate of technological progress. We can consider this rate of advance as maximally sustainable and is, to reiterate, the rate of growth required for the full employment of a growing labor supply; as distinct from the G_w which is required to absorb into production the additions to productive capacity provided by each period's net investment.

We can determine the proper growth of output that will maintain full employment almost straight out of production function in equation (104). The level of output which full utilizes a given labor supply and productive capacity is given by (to repeat equation 106):

$$Y = \frac{\overline{K}}{v} = \frac{\overline{L}}{b} \qquad (148)$$

so that output must be equal to $\overline{L}/b$ with the ratio of labor to output being fixed at (b). Then to maintain the full employment condition output would have to grow at the same rate as the labor force whose growth is exogenously prescribed at an (n) rate (the same symbol used for Harrod's natural growth rate but they are not always the same). Of course, given the constancy of the input coefficients capital would have to grow at that particular rate which maintains the capital to output ratio and which 'structurally' absorbs the growing labor force — this being our warranted rate. So at first glance we can write:

$$G = s/v = G_w = n = G_n \qquad (149)$$

But a realized growth rate that is considered natural would have to do more; not only must it absorb a growing labor supply but a supply of increasing productivity of what we previously considered as 'Harrod-neutral' and which we presumed to grow at an (λ) rate per unit of time. This replaces a growing labor force with that of effective labor (E) which goes into our production function as:

$$Y = \min[\frac{1}{v}(K), \frac{1}{b}(E)] \qquad (150)$$

To maintain full employment output must grow at the same pace as effective labor input, so that:

$$\frac{\dot{Y}}{Y} = n + \lambda = G_n \qquad (151)$$

Indeed, Harrod makes the point, "of my two growth rates (referring to the G_w and G_n) it is the natural rate that is to be regarded as the welfare optimum."[18]

Thus G_n is a ceiling growth rate whose capital requirements and determined by the combined rates of growth in the labor force and technology. For example, if we assume a 2% growth in the labor supply and a 2.5% growth in output per unit of labor, then the growth in output would need to be 4.5%. Assuming our capital to output ratio of 2.15, the rate of capital accumulation required to result in this maximum rate is about 9.7% of the national income. But this rate of capital accumulation is, to reiterate, not necessarily the same as the requirements associated with maintaining the full capacity of the growing stock itself.

It seems reasonable to presume that the economy will not 'normally' strike the required balance that results in $G_w = G_n$. The elements of $s, v, n + \lambda$ are, in this context, considered to be independently determined so that their correct alignment would indeed be fortuitous. Joan Robinson in her path-breaking work *The Accumulation of Capital* refers to the condition of equation (149) as a "golden age" (thus indicating that it represents a mythical state of affairs not likely to obtain in any actual economy). As she defines this age, it is one "with a desired rate of accumulation equal to the possible rate, compounded of the rate of growth of population and of output per head, starting near full employment and a composition of the stock of plant appropriate to the desired rate of accumulation, near full employment is maintained".[19] If we say that the growth in the labor force and the rate of technical progress is given by 'nature' then there is a warranted growth rate appropriate to these conditions.

There are some questions one can ask of the steady growth character of the model. One is a question of existence. Given the structure of the model and the values of the parameters (those outside conditions) is there a set of reasonable values of the variables that will permit the economy to grow at a steady pace? Secondly, there is a question of stability. If the economy encounters conditions that dislodge it from the growth path, or if it is assumed initially off of it, is the reaction one which will return the system to the steady state path, or is it one which causes further deviations from it? And should an equilibrium growth solution exist, then one can ask a question about the stability of the value of the variables that underpin it. For example, how is the level of the capital to output ratio affected by changes in the rate of technical progress? As Joan Robinson points out, the assumption of a given by nature rate of technological change "is not a very enlightening way of looking at the matter, for technical progress is not a natural phenomenon, and there is no limit to human ingenuity".[20]

We can relate to a scenario that would 'internally' cause the economy to become more inventive. Assume a reduction in the growth of the labor supply or a speeding up of the pace of capital accumulation so as to result in a scarcity of labor driving up wage rates. This would, in all likelihood, call forth more labor-saving inventions and cause a more rapid diffusion of those already in existence which increases the productivity of labor all the faster. What is the impact of the subsequent faster increase in the real wage on the ability of the economy to generate the required rate of accumulation? And on the capital to output ratio itself? We will need to weave together a "fabric of balances" among variables if the economy is to sustain steady expansion.

Yet if the system is inherently unstable, then we can identify two related, though logically separable, obstacles to steady growth. One is that the G_w may be unequal to the G_n which, if over time causes the actual growth rate to fall below the warranted rate, will only worsen matters. One can think of the condition $G = G_w < G_n$ as a dynamic version of Keynesian under-employment equilibrium notion. But is such a condition itself sustainable? Secondly, one can consider a situation where the warranted rate is itself unstable even without reference to the G_n. So that if $G < G_w$ is telling us that income is not rising fast enough to warrant investment the system will have overproduced, and this will lead to actions (by reducing the G_w) that will cause the insufficiency of demand to worsen. If the economy does not grow fast enough, and it is unstable, it will find itself with an ever-growing overproduction and in a state of economic contraction and growing unemployment. While both of these obstacles combine to generate unemployment, they are logically separate difficulties.

Before a closer examination of the stability problem we introduce the Domar model which is another version by which we can carry the Keynesian static analysis into the long term, and which expresses a somewhat different formulation of the steady-state path. Domar's analysis brings to the forefront the growing capacity resulting from net investment; that is he would have us overtly recognize the capacity creating effect as well as the income creating effect.

The Keynesian 'static' system treats employment as a function of the level of income (demand), and a full-employment income level is attained and maintained when the economy is persuaded to invest sufficiently, and then holds the equilibrium condition of planned investment equal to planned savings. Assume a full employment income level of $200 billion with an aggregate savings function of $s=.25$. Should investment be equal to 50 billion, the economy will then maintain the existing income level as there will be no unintended change in inventory levels. Yet this investment which creates a demand sufficient to absorb existing capacity should at the same time be expected to cause that capacity to enlarge. Unless we suppose that this investment is totally for replacement (net investment being zero); but even if this were so we would have to add the unlikely proviso that the replacement capital is an exact replica of what it is replacing — technological progress completely shuts down. Hence the continued existence of the $200 billion income level will show up as representing a state of insufficient demand with resulting Keynesian employment effects. The full employment level of income at a point in time is not the same level of income at a later point in time even if we were to assume a constant labor force. We must conclude that the existence of full employment requires that investment and income be growing through time (this seems all the more obvious when we consider the growth of the labor force itself). Of course, from the Keynesian view the aim is to use investment to restore a particular level of output. Domar observes that . . . "the standard Keynesian system does not provide the tools for deriving the equilibrium rate of growth. Growth is entirely absent from it because it is not concerned with changes in productive capacity. For Keynes investment is so simply an instrument for generating income".[21]

Now to the model, beginning with the supply side. Investment is proceeding as $I_t = s(Y_t)$ and let the notation (σ) stand for the portion of the dollar amount invested that represents the addition to the productive capability of the economy. To some degree the operation of the new capital will obsolete existing capital, hence the economy's ability to increase output is given by σI. Thus the (σ) notation should be read as a productivity ratio that is the reciprocal of the technical capital coefficient. That is:

$$\sigma \equiv \frac{\Delta Y}{\Delta K} \equiv \frac{\Delta Y}{I} \qquad (152)$$

where ΔK is synonymous with net investment.

Whether the economy will increase output by the full extent of its ability depends on the growth of demand. We should then read the (σ) term as representing the potential increase in aggregate output made possible by the increase in the capital stock, taking into consideration the increase in other inputs (essentially labor) necessary to go along with the increase in capital in order to produce under existing techniques of production. The sense of the Domar model is to determine that particular rate of income growth that will result in the system's actual output being equal to its productive potential. We emphasize that the above identity looks like but it is not the marginal productivity of capital, that is a partial derivative concept — other inputs are not held constant.

Instead of holding other inputs constant, as we do in calculating the marginal product of capital, the calculation of (σ) allows for whatever increases in other inputs are necessary to accompany an increase in capital in order to produce with prevailing techniques of production. In short, underlying the concept of the productivity ratio is the assumption of a constant capital-output and capital-labor ratios.[22]

Domar refers to this productivity ratio as the potential social average investment productivity which he represents as:

$$\sigma = \frac{\dfrac{dP}{dt}}{I} \qquad (153)$$

And makes the point that it would be more correct to say that (σ) refers to an increase in capacity accompanying rather than caused by investment and he emphasizes that the magnitude of (σ) very much depends on technological progress. So that we begin the analysis with the understanding that:

$$\frac{dP}{dt} = \sigma I \qquad (154)$$

Note that given (σ) this increase in potential productivity is a function of I and not of dI/d_t; whether the change to positive or negative, the increase in net product is always positive as long as (I) and (σ) are positive. But whether or not this potential increase in production results in a larger income depends on the behavior of aggregate spending. What the economy wants to avoid is to have this productive potential turn up as excess capacity.

Turning to the expenditure side of the 'equation' we determine the change in the level of aggregate demand, based on the straightaway multiplier, as:

$$\Delta Y = \frac{1}{s}(\Delta I) \qquad (155)$$

Now assuming that prior to this change in investment, the level of output then in existence was sufficient to employ the existing capacity implying that the system's output is equal to its maximum potential, then in order to maintain this condition the growth in demand must be equal to the growth of productive capacity stemming from this very same increase in investment. This relationship gives Domar's fundamental equation. We have:

$$\frac{1}{s}(\Delta I) = \sigma I \qquad (156)$$

which upon multiplying by (s) and dividing by (I) yields:

$$\frac{\Delta I}{I} = \sigma s \qquad (157)$$

Equation (157) tells us what the rate of investment must be if the economy is to generate a rate of growth of output (demand) to fully employ the level of productive capacity. In other words, to cause actual output to rise as fast as potential output thereby avoiding excess capacity which would depress future investment and employment causing the economy to fall off the steady growth path. In Domar's words ". . . the maintenance of a continuous state of full employment requires that investment and income grow at a constant annual relative (or compound interest) rate equal to the product of the propensity to save and the average (to put it briefly) productivity of investment".[23]

Table (5.4)

Year	Capital Stock	Potential output (Y)	Actual output (Y)	Consumption	Investment
PANEL A					
1	400	100	100	88	12
2	412	103	103	90.64	12.36
3	424.36	106.09	106.09	93.36	12.73
4	437.09				
PANEL B					
1	400	100	100	88	12
2	412	103	100	88	12
3	424	106	100	88	12
4	436				
PANEL C					
1	400	100	100	88	12
2	412	103	102.3	90.12	12
3	424.28	105.45	104.69	92.12	12.5
4	436.85				

The essential point is that a growing economy requires that investment itself be continuously growing, and we are determining that rate of investment growth that results in a steady growth for the aggregate system. As Domar tells it, "It is not sufficient, in Keynesian terms, that savings of yesterday be invested today, or as it is often xpressed, that investment offset savings. A mere absence of hoarding will not do".[24] This is made clear with the numerical examples in table (5.4).

We assume a savings propensity of .12 and a productivity ratio of .25 so that one dollar of net investment creates .25 of additional productive capacity. Now begin with year 1 in panel A where the economy is in Keynesian short-term equilibrium. The level of investment of 12 in period 1 enlarges the capital stock and causes productive capacity to grow by 3 which increases the economy's potential output to a level of 103 in period 2. In order for this potential to be realized as actual output in period 2 (so as not to appear as excess capacity) investment in period 2 will have to grow by an amount equal to σs so as to bring about the required growth in actual output (demand).

Utilizing equation (156) we can have:

$$\frac{1}{.12}(x) = .25(12) \qquad (158)$$
$$x = .36$$

Investment will have to increase by .36 which is at a growth rate of .03. This results in actual output increasing by 3 which absorbs the additional capacity and reflects a rate of growth of output of .03 equal to the growth in the economy's potential.

But the correct level of investment in period 2, equal to savings, increases the capital stock and enlarges capacity by 3.09 (.25 x 12.36); this requires that investment itself grow by .03 to 12.73 resulting in the proper growth in demand to absorb the growth in capacity, and so forth. The upshot of all this is that a steadily growing system requires that investment be growing at some appropriate rate; so, to reiterate, investment in a given period must always exceed the savings of the previous period.

This is brought out in panel B where we find that maintaining the Keynesian equilibrium will result in a growing unused productive capacity. A given level of investment that may be appropriate at one point in time is certainly not appropriate over time. This growing unused capacity will eventually cause investment to fall below yesterday's savings leading to a fall in actual output. Unless investment and output are continuously increasing, they will decrease; the system cannot be expected to maintain a zero growth in investment.

In period C we note that too slow a growth rate (.024) results as well in a growing disparity between capacity and output. It is not only a matter of increasing the level of investment, but of investment growing at the proper rate.

The full-capacity growth rate of output varies directly with σ and s. Given the productivity ratio σ, the larger the proportion of the national output that is saved the larger is the increase in productive capacity generated by this investment; and hence the greater must be the increase in demand, via a greater growth in investment, to avoid idle capacity. Similarly, given s, the larger σ, the greater the increase in capacity stemming from a given level of investment; and so the greater must be the rise in investment to generate the required increase in national output to justify the previous investment.

We realize that if the incremental capacity resulting from investment is to be used, then national income must increase by the same amount. But this increase in income can only come about through an increase in investment. Now the greater σ the greater the increased capacity accompanying a given amount of net investment; therefore in order to assure the full utilization of the increased capital originating with a given amount of net investment, it is necessary to bring about a still greater amount of investment. As Domar makes the point, "If sufficient investment is not forthcoming today, unemployment will be here today. But if enough is invested today, still more will be needed tomorrow".[25] Because the 'enough today' requires higher levels of investment and income tomorrow; the higher the level of investment at a point in time, the greater must be the increase in investment and income at a point thereafter. And this reads very similar to our view of the Harrod growth trajectory. Certainly the two models can be reconciled as they both approach the problem of balanced growth from the standpoint of investment.

Domar's concern is with the capacity effect of investment, and therefore with determining the rate of growth of investment (and income) that prevents this effect from inhibiting steady growth. But there is nothing in the analysis that talks to us about the actual behavior of investment; we know what the proper amount of it must be but not what determines it. From this view Domar's approach can be said to run in terms of exogenous investment, whereas Harrod's model does provide us with an investment-demand (behavior) equation. Indeed Harrod's approach can be expressed by the question, at what rate must the economy grow so as to motivate entrepreneurs to bring about that particular increase in investment that maintains the existing growth rate? As compared to the question Domar poses, which is, how rapidly must investment grow in order for full capacity output to be maintained?

The demand side for both models is clear enough stemming from the multiplier which gives the growth in national income or aggregate demand; but the output or supply consideration is not as explicitly stated for Harrod as it is for Domar. Harrod's (v_r) is the amount of induced new investment needed to produce an extra unit of output — it is the capital coefficient with no explicit reference to the productivity of capital. But, as we pointed out, Domar's σ term is the reciprocal of this coefficient telling us directly the possible output resulting from a unit of investment, so $\sigma = 1/v_r$. Both models are looking at the same phenomenon with Harrod's approach giving explicit reference to the acceleration principle and hence building in an investment explanation. Both models are formally identical as:

$$\frac{\Delta I}{I} = s\sigma = s/v_r = \frac{\Delta Y}{Y} \tag{159}$$

We can say that Harrod's necessary level of induced investment results in a rate of growth of output that utilizes Domar's increasing productive capacity. Or that Domar's changing capacity is the result of Harrod's investment behavior equation. Both are concerned with the long-term problem of meshing the capacity and creating income generating aspects of investment.

What we come away from these particular models, and a study of growth theory in general, is an understanding of the balances that must be struck if the economy is to maintain a steady growth path. But we are not explaining an existing condition; the likelihood of experiencing the golden age is quite nil. We will find the economy off such a path; and what we will perhaps be able to discern is what changes need to be undertaken in the appropriate variables to steer the economy towards the proper growth rate.

Using some earlier relationships we can sort of see the reality of matters along the following lines. The best of all worlds is where:

$$G = G_w = s/v_r = G_n = n + \lambda \tag{160}$$

But as we mentioned, these variables are, at least at first glance, given independent of each other; and while they do determine a growth process they are not seen to be influenced by the process itself. Thus we could find:

$$s/v < n + \lambda \tag{161}$$

with increasing unemployment of labor. Clearly the economy needs to grow faster; but is there sufficient response within the system to bring this about? For example, is there an effect from this unemployment to the savings ratio or to the rate of technological change? Note that with (161) the warranted rate is sustainable over time but with increasing 'social cost'.

Alternatively the economy might reveal:

$$s/v > n + \lambda \tag{162}$$

Excess capital will develop driving down the rate of profit and discouraging investment. The economy will quickly be driven off the equilibrium growth path.

These models have been considered too rigid in that they do not provide for flexibility in the variables. Should $s/v = n + \lambda$ then all is well; but if this is not the case, there seems no way to self-correct the problem. In this sense the Harrod-Domar models can be said to present the growth path as one of a 'knife-edge' equilibrium; the system is conceived to be in precarious balance, if jolted it loses its footing entirely. But there has been some discussion concerning this knife-edge term.

A somewhat different attitude is to consider this edge term as relating to a unique existence. Given the independent nature of the savings ratio and the stability of (v_r), there exists only one warranted growth rate; and the problem then lies with the actual growth rate. There is one value of increasing output, given s, that allows G_w to occur. Now in terms of G_n, there is a particular required savings ratio that will allow a rate of investment that utilizes the expanding labor force and technical advances. The problem here is the uniqueness of the savings ratio that allows the natural growth rate to exist at all. The knife-edge from this view relates to the existence of a particular value, as distinct from the problem of falling off the path.

If we do not realize the unique values, we will not be on the path as there is no stability from which to depart; or if all attainable growth rates are steady rates then there is also no reason to talk in terms of stability. However we want to view the 'edge', whether one of unique existence or reflecting the problem of falling way (instability), Harrod's primary purpose was "to show that there is nothing inherent in the system to guarantee that it will reach any stable growth path (much less the natural rate of growth), and that if by chance or good guidance it did reach such a path, that there is nothing inherent in that path to make it persist".[26]

It behoves us then to look at the instability characteristic of the Harrod-Domar dynamics, before considering proposals that may relieve the over-determined nature of these models, and thereby bring us to some recent developments in economic thinking.

Let us plunge right in by assuming that income does not grow rapidly enough to justify the level of investment. From Domar's view the level of productive capacity is now excess, and from Harrod's view the investment that was undertaken was not what entrepreneurs would have wanted to undertake — we find $G < G_w$. What we have is situation of overproduction which becomes cumulatively worse; the economy will be ensnared in a paradoxical situation in that if it does not increase output rapidly enough it will be found to have produced too much.

This state of pessimism will lead to a curtailment of the rate of growth of investment which requires a smaller increase in output and demand to justify it; but this will not happen. The economy does not stabilize at this lower level of investment, the smaller investment change will result in demand increasing less rapidly than the relative decline in output to be sold, causing as yet the lower investment level to be excessive and resulting in a growth rate that is all the more so below the warranted rate. The point is that demand can be expected to increase even less rapidly than output when output is growing less rapidly than warranted. This flows from the Harrodian behavioral equation which tells us that if $G_w > G$ then $v > v_r$: entrepreneurs will find that the increase in the capital stock that actually occurs is greater than they require given the growth of income. The response to this situation is to reduce investment further, which forces the actual growth rate further below the warranted rate and actually increasing the difference between the desired and actual level of productive capacity. If entrepreneurs are inclined to bring about a reduction in output every time they find a state of overproduction, then such a condition which is reflective of $G < G_w$, must result in a cumulative fall in production. The seriousness of this instability is not only that a divergence of G from G_w will not correct itself, but will lead to an increasingly greater departure from the required line of advance. Once the economy becomes unhinged because it is not growing fast enough, its rate of growth increasingly declines, and it may be very difficult to get it back on track.

Let us consider an example of this from our illustration of the Harrod warranted path. Repeating equation (127) we see:

$$\frac{Y_t}{Y_{t-1}} = \frac{v_r}{b-1+v_r} = 1.075 \qquad (163)$$

199

which is a case of $G = G_w$ and the working out of expectations — and it is on this growth rate that entrepreneurs undertake investment. But suppose plans are not realized and the actual growth rate turns out to be 6%, that is, $Y_t = 106, Y_{t-1} = 100$. Then with (163) we find:

$$\frac{Y_{t-1}}{Y_t} = 3(\frac{106}{100}) - 2.15 \tag{164}$$

$$= 1.03$$

with the level of output in Y_{t+1} being:

$$Y_{t+1} = 106(1.03) = 109.18 \tag{165}$$

And further along:

$$\frac{Y_{t+2}}{Y_{t+1}} = 3(\frac{109.18}{106}) - 2.15 \tag{166}$$

$$= .94$$

$$Y_{t+2} = 109.18(.94) = 102.6 \tag{167}$$

In this rather extreme example, once the economy leaves the equilibrium path it plunges quickly to the point of an absolute fall in output.

Considering an upward displacement we can presume that businessmen increase the rate of accumulation which brings with it a rate of growth in output in excess of that warranted by the previous rate of investment. But while this increases the quantity sold, it will increase demand even more and so the result will be underproduction. Entrepreneurs are dissatisfied in a positive sense; their optimism in the face of their being able to sell more than they have produced will cause entrepreneurs to want to invest even more, thereby sending the actual rate further above the warranted and widening the discrepancy between actual and desired productive capacity. The required capital to output ratio (v_r) exceeds the actual ratio (v) and the attempt to increase it drives it further below its warranted rate value. Thus we have the other paradox in that the economy finds itself having produced too little as a result of having increased production too rapidly.

It would seem that what is meant by the terms 'warranted' and 'instability', i.e. the centrifugal forces surrounding the path, are clear enough; but this is not completely the case as different interpretations have sprung up concerning this stability problem. We want to linger somewhat longer around these notions; for, as we mentioned, much of recent developments in economics can be understood in terms of 'mechanics' that would tend to reduce the centrifugal forces and maintain the economy near its sustainable growth path.

A point which comes to mind is that if the economy can be depicted as proceeding smoothly with growing unemployment, can it not also be seen doing so with, say, a growing capital redundancy? Why must the system retrench and set up the cumulative decline every time there is overproduction? If one defines the G_w as simply a rate of advance which, if adhered to, will be maintained, then one can imagine maintaining the same rate of investment growth and excess capacity. And if the actual rate of growth in demand were suddenly to increase it would reduce the redundancy and not necessarily motivate the system to invest even more. On the other hand, if there is a growing capital shortage along the warranted path, then a rate of growth of output below it would lessen (or perhaps eliminate) the shortage but would not in and of itself be cause for a cumulative downward movement. If the warranted rate is to be reckoned as unstable, then it has to be defined in terms of something more than a constant rate of growth; it needs the added stipulation that the warranted path is one upon which expectations turn out correctly so that entrepreneurs are content with the policy they are pursuing. The fact of redundancy or shortage of capital mirrors expectations that have not turned out and hence businessmen will want to change their current investment policies which trigger the movement away from the warranted growth path. Entrepreneurs are not presumed to want to maintain existing investment and output policies in the face of mistaken expectations.

Making use of our illustration for the Harrod model we know that expectations are realized if they are based on a growth rate of 7%. The investment action then undertaken and the actual income generated will in fact cause income to grow by 7%. But if policies are undertaken based on an expected growth rate of, say, 9% (because that has been realized), then the actual growth rate will turn out to be greater, say, 11%. Now based on this expected growth entrepreneurs enter into investment decisions only to find that realization exceeds expectations by even a greater disparity and so on.

We have made reference to both a maintainable growth rate if adhered to, and one which reflects entrepreneurial satisfaction in our discussion of the G_w and its instability characteristic. Now we want to reinforce the idea that the former is an insufficient definition if the path is surrounded by centrifugal forces; for the path to be adhered to the 'representive' entrepreneur must be satisfied with his policies. Instability forces show up when plans are going awry.

This brings up an instructive different approach to this 'instability theorem'.[27] Restating some terms let:

$$K = \text{capital stock on hand}$$
$$Y = \text{net income (or output)}$$
$$v = \text{capital to output ratio}$$
$$s = \text{proportion of income saved}$$

Required capital is vY and:

$$Z = vY - K \tag{168}$$

with $Z > 0$ defining a capital shortage ($Z < 0$ means capital redundancy). The absolute change in the state of (Z) is expressed as:

$$DZ = vDY - DK$$

as

$$DK = sY = \dot{K} \tag{169}$$

then

$$G_K = \frac{sY}{K} = \frac{\dot{K}}{K}$$

And we will be able to express the change in the state of shortage or redundancy of capital in terms of the rate of growth of capital itself. Dividing equation (168) by (K) we find:

$$\frac{Z}{K} = \frac{vY}{K} - 1 = \frac{\dfrac{sY}{K} - s/v}{s/v} \tag{170}$$

202

Statement (170) allows the expression of (Z) in terms of the capital stock with the ratio (s/v) immediately taking on the characteristic of a warranted rate of growth of income. Clearly if capital grows faster than (s/v) then $Z/K>0$ and capital is in short supply. It is only when capital and income are growing at the (s/v) rate can capital requirements be continuously fulfilled.

Perhaps more interestingly we can reckon the centrifugal forces, i.e. the change in (Z), in terms of the change in income. Taking the change in (Z) and dividing through by (Y) yields:

$$\frac{DZ}{Y} = \frac{vDY}{Y} - \frac{sY}{Y}$$

$$= G_Y v - s \tag{171}$$

Should $G_Y v - s > 0$, then $DZ > 0$ as $G_Y > s/v$; in this condition there will be a growing capital shortage or a declining capital redundancy. And in the event of $G_Y v - s < 0$, then $DZ < 0$ with either the excessiveness of capital increasing or the capital shortage declining as $G_Y < s/v$.

But these connections are made to work with an assumption about entrepreneurial behavior. In the case of $DZ > 0$ capital requirements are outstripping the rate of capital accumulation and the assumed response is to increase the rate of investment; that is, to meet the capital shortage by increasing capital outlays more than in proportion to the previous increase. Yet, as we have pointed out, this action to eliminate a capital shortage is self-defeating as it causes the shortage to grow. The attempt to do away with underproduction causes underproduction to increase; and entrepreneurs seeing that they can sell more than they produce are buoyed by their optimism to the point of further increasing the rate of output and so on. In a reverse sequence when $DZ < 0$, the redundancy of capital persuades entrepreneurs to increase their outlays less than in proportion to the previous increases. So, to summarize, if income is growing faster than the warranted rate, the rate of growth will increase and the capital shortage only get worse. And if income is growing more slowly, the rate of advance will continuously decline and the capital excessive state worsen with income eventually declining.

But is the entrepreneurial response dependent as it is on recent experience in realized growth sufficient cause for instability, as seems to be the case; or is it because the decisions are operating with another not too obvious assumption. Rose argues the position that "this dependence is not destabilizing on its own, but becomes so when it is made to operate in conjunction with a time interval between investment decisions and capital outlays".[28] Let us consider how lags enter into the matter.

Certainly, as we have stated, the change in the rate of growth of investment, that is, in the build-up of capacity, is related to the change in the degree of capital excess or reduced via the change in the growth of income. So that:

$$DG_I \underset{<}{\overset{>}{-}} 0 \text{ as } DZ \underset{<}{\overset{>}{-}} 0 \qquad (172)$$

Although Rose relates this change in the growth rate of capital to the state of capital redundancy, say, as a proportion of realized income. Thus:

$$DG_I = \psi(\frac{DZ}{Y}) \qquad (173)$$

then

$$DG_I = \psi(vG_Y - s)$$

(where ψ represents the proportion of the capital discrepancy to be adjusted)

In the best of conditions along the equilibrium path the availability of output stemming from the growth rate of capital accumulation is equal to the rate of increase in output and demand determined by the investment multiplier. Thus:

$$DG_I = DG_Y$$

and

$$DG_Y = \psi(DvG_Y - s) \qquad (174)$$

There is a particular rate of growth of income equal to s/v which, if the economy were initially growing at that rate, it would adhere to it. At every point on the path demand is equal to supply.

Now suppose that realized growth is other than warranted which in period (t) results in a realized difference between equipment and capacity on hand and what is required on the basis of current experience. What this does is effect planned expenditures in (t) with the impact of this in terms of actual outlays coming in $(t+1)$. Thus the 'demand problem' realized in (t) cannot be addressed by altering income and spending in that period which were determined by decisions taken in $(t-1)$. And as the instability thesis tells us, the change in orders (planned expenditures) placed in (t) will only magnify the problem in $(t+1)$. Implicit in the centrifugal forces surrounding the path is a time interval between the investment decision and the expenditures determining the change in demand. One cannot adjust demand — within the same time frame that one sees a capital requirement problem — or can one?

Can the analysis be thought of differently so that when confronted, for example, with a capital shortage, the system will exhibit a lower than warranted growth rate rather than have such a realized rate be reflecting of a capital redundancy. The rationale here is that the presence of a capital shortage will motivate entrepreneurs to undertake a level of investment and hence bring about a level of output (Y) in excess of what they require as judged by the immediate realized growth in output (DY). Planned investment is determined by both the immediate experience of the change in demand as well as by past decisions. It is current events as well as past events that influence planned capital outlays; which means in this case that the growth in output (DY/Y) will be low relative to the warranted rate as a consequence of intentions to eliminate the capital shortage. This differing, of course, from the usual approach where a rate of growth below the warranted rate is a sign of a growing capital surplus and the failed attempt to eliminate it; indeed the surplus becomes magnified.

Before any further comment, let us work this out. We have planned investment (Ip) as:

$$Ip = vDY + \psi Z \qquad (175)$$

where $\psi = 1$ entrepreneurs are fully adjusting their capital stock so as to result in $Z=0$. That is, to reiterate, if there is a capital shortage the rate of growth in planned outlays will be greater than governed by the immediate past increase in output in proportion to the degree of the capital deficiency. As $Ip = sY$ then:

$$vDY = sY = \psi Z \qquad (176)$$

and using (169) yields:

$$DZ + \psi Z = 0$$

or

$$(D + \psi)Z = 0 \tag{177}$$

We know $Z=0$ entails $DZ=0$ and this is reflective of $G_y = s/v$.

But the interesting point concerns the nature of the system when it is growing at an unwarranted rate. We pose this situation of $Z \neq 0$ as:

$$\frac{DZ}{Z} = -\psi < 0 \tag{178}$$

Should $Z > 0$ (a capital shortage) it follows that $DZ < 0$; and $Z < 0$ (capital redundancy) as $DZ > 0$. A shortage or surplus of capital tends to be eliminated not enhanced. With the use of equation (171) we observe that $DZ > 0$ reflects a condition of $G_y > s/v$, and $DZ < 0$ is one of $G_y < s/v$. It follows that a less than warranted rate is indicative of a capital shortage and a growth rate in excess of warranted is reflective of a capital redundancy with the inherent tendency for these capital conditions to be eliminated. "Here is, perhaps, the most striking contrast with Harrod's model — the forces at work at either side of the warranted path are centripetal".[29]

Consider again a state of capital shortage that results in orders placed (i.e. planned investment outlays) in excess of the experience of the realized growth in output which is used as the basis for predicting future needs. And these outlays are dispensed almost immediately after the placing of the order. Why need we envision a 'period lag' or a significant interval between placing orders and the commencement of work and thereby the creation of income and demand. Furthermore, entrepreneurs want to minimize any delay in bringing additional capacity on hand in recognition that investment projects take time to complete. If we accept a narrowing of the interval between the decision to increase the growth of investment and such increase in capacity coming on line, then demand will not exceed supply (or will do so for a short interval) and the system will generally be able to adjust the capital stock within the same time frame as the need to do so. This whole approach shows up 'technically' as a reduction in the rate of growth below warranted, i.e. below what it would be if there were no capital shortage. Yet this does not strain credibility; if the economy is growing too rapidly would we not want to take steps to reduce the capital shortage; that is, bring about a lower growth rate of output as capacity grows.

Harrod's response to this is that the experience at a point in time informs the entrepreneur where he is (relative to the warranted condition); and his reaction to this occurs in the following period. He rejects the notion that the entrepreneur can adjust the capital stock to required levels within the same time frame. Be that as it may, we do not pursue this matter more than we have; certainly there are different interpretations of the stability problem.

In this chapter we have introduced some fundamental growth models with differing characteristics. Subsequently we use this growth venue to examine recent (non-neoclassical) developments in economic thinking.

NOTES

1. Alfred S. Eichner, *Toward a New Economics*, M.E. Sharpe, Armonk, New York, 1985, p. 117.

2. See the more involved mechanics in J. R. Hicks, *Trade Cycle*, Oxford University Press, New York, 1951.

3. Eichner, op. cit., p. 115.

4. Hicks, Ibid.

5. Michael K. Evans, *Macroeconomic Activity*, Harper & Row, New York, 1969, p. 84.

6. James S. Duesenberry, *Business Cycles and Economic Growth*, McGraw-Hill, New York, 1958, p. 205.

7. Luigi L. Pasinetti, *Growth and Income Distribution*, Cambridge University Press, London, 1974, p. 57.

8. Duesenberry, op. cit., p. 206.

9. Pasinetti, op. cit., p. 65.

10. Duesenberry, op. cit., p. 236.

11. The standard references are R. M. Solow, "A Contribution to the Theory of Economic Growth", *Quarterly Journal of a Economics*, LXX (Feb. 1956). Also T. W. Swan, "Economic Growth and Capital Accumulation", *Economic Record*, XXXII, Nov. 1956; and H. G. Johnson, "The Neoclassical One-Sector Growth Model", *Economics*, August 1966. Explications may be found in E. Burmeister and R. Dobell, *Mathematical Theories of Economic Growth*, Macmillan, New York, 1970, and S. Bober, *Modern Macroeconomics*, Croom-Helm, London, 1988.

12. See Nicholas Kaldor, "A Model of Economic Growth", *Economic Journal*, Dec. 1957; "Economic Growth and Capital Accumulation"

in the *Theory of Capital*, F. Lutz, D. C. Hague (eds), Macmillan, London, 1961.

13. We find:

$$w = [L_e^{\lambda t} f'(\frac{K^{\lambda t}}{L_e}) \cdot (-\frac{K}{L_e^{\lambda t}} \cdot \frac{L}{L}) + e^{\lambda t} f(k)]$$

$$= e^{\lambda t} f'(k) \cdot (-k) + e^{\lambda t} f(k)$$

$$w = e^{\lambda t} [f(k) - k \cdot f'(k)]$$

14. Harrod's writings are many, but essentially: R. F. Harrod, *Towards a Dynamic Economics*, Macmillan, London, 1948. Also, Harrod, "Themes in Dynamic Theory", *Economic Journal*, Sept. 1963. In addition, Evsey D. Domar, *Essays in the Theory of Economic Growth*, Oxford University Press, 1957, especially essays III and IV. Discussions about these models can be found in H. G. Jones' *An Introduction to Modern Theories of Economic Growth*, McGraw-Hill, New York, 1976. Also, William J. Baumol, *Economic Dynamics*, Macmillan, New York, 1951. More recently, S. Bober, *Pricing & Growth*, M. E. Sharpe, 1992.

15. D. Hamberg, *Economic Growth and Instability*, W. W. Norton, New York, 1956, p. 23

16. Joan Robinson, *What are the Questions? And Other Essays*, M. E. Sharpe, Armonk, New York, 1980, p. 80.

17. Harrod, *Towards*, (op. cit.), p. 82.

18. Harrod, "Domar and Dynamic Economics", *Economic Journal*, September 1959.

19. Joan Robinson, *The Accumulation of Capital*, Richard D. Irwin, 1956, p. 99.

20. Robinson, op. cit., (Essays), p. 52.

21. Domar, op. cit., (Essays), p. 72.

22. D. Hamberg, *Models of Economic Growth*, Harper and Row, 1971, p. 5.

23. Domar, op. cit., p. 93.

24. Ibid., p. 92.

25. Ibid., p. 101.

26. J. A. Kreyel, *Rate of Profit, Distribution and Growth*, Aldine, New York, 1971, p. 112.

27. As put forth by H. Rose, "The Philosophy of Warranted Growth", *Economic Journal*, 6/59.

28. Ibid., p. 39.

29. Ibid.

6 The role of prices and their formation

Introduction

As we talked about in the very first chapter, the core of economic analysis for post-Keynesians is the reproducibility and growth of the material output of society. The conceptual framework for this approach, as we reiterate, is that of a society which produces a surplus; that is, an excess of commodities produced over the quantities of the same commodities required for their production. It is within such a context that we will come to understand the role of relative prices which, when established, must satisfy the conditions for the system to maintain a particular growth path. They must be such as to cover production costs while at the same time resulting in the proper distribution of the surplus within the economic classes of society so as to result in the required investment that underpins the movement of the economy.

This book mirrors a fundamentally different approach from that of neoclassicism or marginalist theory. And with regard to our immediate concern we will be dealing with an objective determination of value drawn from the physical costs of production, and not with a subjective based approach drawn from utility maps of consumers. One explains prices in terms of man's activities and relations as a producer, and not in terms of a framework emphasizing man as a consumer. Relative prices are to be viewed as ratios linked to the process of production and not to be interpreted as indicators of relative scarcity — scarcity is no longer the basic theme of what economics is about.

It will be helpful here to re-emphasize some points made in Chapter 3 concerning an explanation of distributive shares in the economy. The post-Keynesian attitude is to consider capital and labor as items of production that enter into a particular process of production in which they are held as owners of income-bearing property. This emphasis would have us consider income as a payment to those who hold such rights in accordance with the extent of their holdings. Labor receives wages in 'exchange' for work, but the level of the wage is the outcome of 'conflict' with that of property holdings as it reflects the current technology and institutional arrangements. The post-Keynesian approach brings this ongoing conflict between capital and labor to the foreground and finds relative prices dependent on the outcome of this relationship. In general we will be dealing with a theory of distribution that is grounded in the property arrangements inherent in the production process.

The neoclassical system smothers this distributive conflict by talking in terms of non-descript factors or households (rather than social classes) that sell their services in a market setting, thereby creating an analogy between the product and input markets with the same principles operating in both. Since neoclassical theory established equilibrium values for the distributive variables, it was possible to disregard any conflict between them; for their existed a 'natural' solution that implied optimality. This conventional approach postulated an essentially harmonious relationship between productive inputs that is most simply expressed in the marginal productivity theory associated with the aggregate production function. But post-Keynesian analysis rejects this entire model and eschews the notion that input rewards are to be understood as a facet of price theory (neoclassical price theory) generally.

For the post-Keynesian approach the factor 'payment' is related to the existence of the surplus and one's position in the process that brings the surplus into being. While for neoclassicists payment is determined in a market that is not directly connected (at least one does not overtly make a connection) to the way production is organized; one describes the players in this market as merely buyers and sellers.

Our discussion of the Ricardian growth model certainly illuminated a link between the capitalist's share of the output and the role played in production. In this chapter we will extend this approach to modern times and be more explicit concerning how relative prices fit into maintaining the growth path. This will require a different (non-neoclassical) understanding of how prices are determined.

The intellectual antecedents of the post-Keynesian paradigm is to be found in classical political economy and given most vivid expression in the models of Ricardo and Marx. So we begin by setting out what we might consider as the general classical model to arrive at those Ricardian relative prices; here we will consider matters that were not explicitly brought out in our previous discussion of Ricardo.

A General Classical Model

Productive economic activity was conceived by the classicists as a circular or repetitive process that is to be analyzed through a 'period analysis' approach. And this way of looking at matters was largely dictated by the capital concept itself. As we understand from the Ricardo model, capital is to be thought of, at least initially, as a putty-like resource that can be readily allocated either to wage goods or to machine goods (i.e. the corn model). At the beginning of the cycle or period of production, this 'capital' or requisite produced commodity is in the hands of and at the disposal of capitalists or producing firms. In classical thinking the capitalist class owns all the capital stock at the beginning of the production period and owns all the economy's output at the end of the period.

At the outset of the production period the capital stock is disposed of via its division into the means of subsistence for the labor force, that is, the wages fund; and into the tools of production, i.e. machinery. We want to see this 'fund' as that portion of the capital stock which consists of advances to labor to tide them over the period of production. This brings up an interesting point concerning what is involved in the wage payment if such payments are being paid in advance (as classical economists presume) and thereby come out of capital, or in arrears, i.e. at the end of the productive period, and thus come out of revenue. Should wages come at the end, so that payment to labor comes after the purchase of labor, the wage will contain an element of interest. This interest payment can be seen in two ways.

We can suppose that the worker is lending his labor to the capitalist; he is postponing his wage claim thereby allowing the capitalist to keep his capital for a longer period, and would require a compensation for this delay. This supposes that the wage payment includes an interest over and above subsistence as a matter of payment arrangements in the economy, and permits savings on the part of labor. This interest factor is all the more telling if we presume that the wage is pegged at subsistence, as was the classical presumption; then arrears payment must presume that labor borrows what is needed for the interim period, and at the end of production the actual wage payment would have to include the interest to be repaid. However we look at it the wage payment would be influenced by the length of time of the production period. It was the classical sense that both labor and capital enter the production process together at the very outset and that wages actually be paid at the time labor is performed, so that it was a logical approach to have wages advanced out of capital. This fits in with Marx's notion of labor's complete dependency as labor is presumed not to own any capital. He tells us: "The labour-process turned into the process by which the capitalist consumes labor power, exhibits two characteristic phenomena. First, the labourer works under the control of the capitalist to whom his labour belongs....Secondly, the product is the property of the capitalist and not that of the labourer, its immediate producer".[1] We will comment again on the placement of the wage payment when discussing the Sraffian model. But now let us not stray from the main contours of the classical model.

Classical economists assumed a fixed ratio of labor to machinery which was regarded as short term technological parameter of the system. Additions to the capital stock — presumed fully utilized — would necessarily imply an increased demand for machinery and labor [in the Ricardo corn (physical capital) story demand for labor is related to the 'investment' of capital in terms of tools and advances which, given the subsistence wage, automatically determined the level of employment]. What we have is a joint demand function for capital and labor that results in a long-term equilibrium outcome in the input markets.

In this context of this analysis we have (α) as the ratio of labor to machines (in previous discussions this was our $1/v$). The demand for labor resulting from the production technology is:

$$L^D = \alpha K^D \tag{1}$$

The supply of machine goods is specified as:

$$K^S = f(p) \tag{2}$$

where (p) is the money price of machines deflated by the price of wage (consumer) goods. We have the price of capital in terms of wage goods. The classicists assumed that the price of capital goods would fall over the long term relative to that of wage goods. The assumption was that of increasing productive power of labor in manufacturing (in the least we would have constant returns), while in agriculture and mining the tendency was for diminishing returns. Thus the expectations for $f'(p) < 0$.

Now a given amount of investment, that is, demand for capital, translates into a particular supply of capital in use and an associated level of demand for labor, i.e. employment. In money terms we have:

$$K = w\alpha K + \bar{p}K \qquad (3)$$

where $(\bar{p})$ is the equilibrium price of machines and (w) is the real wage rate. This gives us a labor demand curve by rearranging terms in equation (3) and using (1) as:[2]

$$L^D = \frac{K}{w + \dfrac{\bar{p}}{\alpha}} \qquad (4)$$

A lower real wage rate and/or an increase in capital accumulation increases the demand for labor, and this increase in capital comes from the higher 'surplus' at the end of the period of production.

The labor supply is taken as a function of the subsistence real wage which over the longer term is presumed to trend upwards. But in any particular state of the system, as we recall from the Ricardian model, there exists a given real wage which may be considered as the 'natural price of labor'. Certainly with the accumulations of capital the demand for labor may drive the market wage above its natural level; but given the population's response to short-term wage increases, this difference in wage rates will be temporary in nature with the market wage returning to its natural level. Thus:

$$L^S = n(w) \qquad (5)$$

But there is a unique demand for labor associated with equilibrium in the capital goods market (both for the production of wage goods and machine goods). Hence equilibrium in the labor market implies a level of investment that results in a market wage equal to the natural real wage, so that:

$$L^S = L^D \qquad (6)$$

"Since all points on the labor demand schedule are associated with equilibrium in the machine-goods market, equilibrium in the labor market necessarily implies general equilibrium".[3] A bit more clarification may be in order for equation (3). What we have is a division of the capitalist's accumulation in money terms between the purchase of 'tools' and the purchase of labor. The purchase of labor is at a real wage implying a certain level of wage goods. Again we might think of the Ricardian capitalist dividing his accumulation between wage goods plus seed (the circulating capital) and machines with a fixed ratio of labor to capital. In the Ricardo corn model the trick is to have part of the corn advance to change itself into tools at the beginning of production, and then, is made to disappear at the end so that it is 'consumed' similar to corn that is used as wage goods.

What we are talking about takes place at the outset of the production period where commodities (the output of the previous period) are put to use either as means of production or as means of subsistence. And the system does operate to assure the full utilization of the capital stock, i.e. that no part of the stock is removed from productive employment. When production activity is over, the exchange period (the other 'activity') then begins. At the end of the production period, in the system as a whole, there exists a surplus consisting of the excess of the output over the total advances which, assuming subsistence wages accrues to the capitalist class as profits.[4]

Let us be a little more explicit about this surplus notion. The net product, that is, total output less replacement of capital, is the surplus of the economy and the source of its savings. When we look at this surplus as income we propose that it all accrues to the capitalist as profits; and when considered as an expenditure the surplus will in part be 'consumed' productively to yield output via the employment of labor and augmentation of capital, and a portion will be consumed unproductively by the employment of unproductive labor (in terms of furthering material output) and expenditure for capitalist consumption (classicists looked upon this as acting to receive immediate enjoyment). Savings is considered as that portion of the surplus that is not consumed unproductively and is invested either directly in one's own enterprise or given to the loanable funds market where it is borrowed for debt-financed investment or to finance unproductive expenditures. All investment originates in savings, but not all savings is investment unless we presume away unproductive consumption. In our discussions in this chapter we will do just that keeping clear the idea of the surplus and investment and its relationship to prices in the economy. We mention as an aside that the classical theory of interest revolves around its role in affecting 'abstinence', that is, influencing the behavior regarding abstaining from the unproductive use of one's resources.

It is in the period of exchange that the distribution of the total output takes place. At the end of production each producing unit (i.e. capitalist) has at its disposal the particular commodity which it produces. Before starting another production period, it needs to acquire the other requisite commodities for its own production through the market mechanics by 'exchanging' part of its own output for the production of the producing units.

The capitalist sells all of his particular output, the revenue of which is used to replace the capital used up in the previous production period, and additionally to augment the capital stock to enable an expansion of production as well as to engage in capitalist consumption and employment of non-productive labor. Recall that the firm realizes a surplus in physical production over the previous advance which in the reality of revenue terms converts to profits, enabling the firm to expand production. But this expansion would require additional employment at the market wage rate as well as additional machines in some fixed proportion, so the capitalist for the given size of the surplus will seek out the technologically correct input mix. And assuming that the market wage is at subsistence, the workers would then not partake of the surplus. Of course, in the reality of workers not getting paid in kind (as occurs in the corn model), they similarly acquire their means of subsistence in the market from the wage good producers which are thereby able to recover the money they advanced to the workers as wages.

At the outset of the period of exchange production is emerging from firms that place their output on the market. We bear in mind that capitalists produce in order to place it all for sale; this aggregate output is:

$$Q_i^S \quad (\text{where } i=1....n) \tag{7}$$

and generates a sales revenue of:

$$R = \sum_1^n p_i Q_i^S \tag{8}$$

The output of the ith commodity is Q_i^S with its price p_i in terms of the wage good which we take as numeraire. This revenue received by the firm generates an equal level of spending or demand for commodities, so:

$$R = \sum_1^n p_i Q_i^D \qquad (9)$$

This spending enables the firm to replace the previous production period's consumption of circulating capital and depreciated fixed capital as well as to increase the categories of capital stock. And at the end of the period of exchange the system evidences the equality of:

$$\sum_1^n p_i Q_i^D = \sum_1^n p_i Q_i^S \qquad (10)$$

It is in this period of exchange that relative prices are determined and the system is readied for the next production period. In the classical vision the dominant capitalist class owns the total commodity output at the beginning of the exchange and still owns it all at the end. What happens in the interim is an exchange of this output among capitalists in order to permit them to reconstitute and augment the capital stock in preparation for subsequent production.

From a production viewpoint, general equilibrium exists when the given supply of commodities which constitutes the total capital stock is equated with the total joint demand for machinery and circulating capital, i.e. raw materials and wage goods. Now disaggregating to the individual firm this means that the revenue from the sale of its output allows it to cover costs of production in the sense to replenish used-up capital, and also provides a surplus as profit in proportion to the capital employed which is equal to the prevailing rate of profit in the economy as a whole. This firm will, in the following activity period, be able to expand production by an amount equal to the profit realized in the current period of exchange. The actual price realized by the firm then equates to what has been considered as its 'natural' or 'necessary' price which, to reiterate, is one that enables it to earn a rate of profit that conforms to what is earned throughout the economy. Should this firm be representative then all firms are earning the same rate of return and all are augmenting their capital stock at the same rate. The economy at large is expanding at a rate reflective of the uniform rate of expansion by all firms. The point here is that the division of the total output between producing units (being the outcome of the next production period) is unchanged mirroring the constancy of the division of the capital stock.

Classical economists used this condition as the criterion for identifying an optimum set of relative prices. And we emphasize that this uniform profit principle derives from the pattern of capital allocation in the system overall, which itself reflects a pattern of relative prices in the circumstance of no change in relative demand between outputs or in technologically induced changes in sector productivity rates. Certainly changes along these lines will cause changes in relative prices and rates of profit resulting in a reallocation of the total capital stock.

This natural set of optimum exchange ratios (or relative prices) can be referred to as 'prices of production' that are determined on the basis of 'physical' costs of production; and in this way one sees the role of prices within the context of the reproducibility of output rather than a means of identifying relative scarcity of commodities. For the classicists and modern-day classicists scarcity is simply a prerequisite of a good whose price is based on costs. Thus Ricardo's generalized cost of production concept in which goods exchange with one another according to the relative quantities of inputs in their production; though we will want to consider some clarification about his approach in this matter.

This natural set of relative prices has been looked upon as 'gravitational prices' in that the actual price determined during the exchange period may be expected to deviate temporarily from the corresponding long-term price outcome. But this circumstance will trigger a movement of capital and production that alters supply to eventually return the price to its natural level and restore the balance to the rate of profit. Regarding the deviation of the actual price level, Ricardo had this to say:

> In making labour the foundation of the value of commodities, and the comparative quantity of labour which is necessary to their production, the rule which determines the respective quantities of goods which shall be given in exchange for each other, we must not be supposed to deny the accidental and temporary deviation of the actual or market price of commodities from this their primary and natural price.
>
> In the ordinary course of events, there is no commodity which continues for any length of time to be supplied precisely in that degree of abundance which the wants and wishes of mankind require, and therefore there is none which is not subject to accidental and temporary variations in price.[5]

To see what is clearly involved in this variation, we analyze Ricardo's two-sector model with regard to determining relative prices and provide further insight to our previous discussion of Ricardo.

His two sectors are agriculture and manufacturing (what we considered before as the 'luxury good sector), with the former seen as the 'lead' sector in that its own rate of profit sets the rate of return on capital for the manufacturing sector, i.e. for the whole economy. We can think of the input to these sectors in terms of a 'composite' factor of capital to labor in the technologically given correct mix which is assured to be the same for both sectors. So we have the aggregate capital stock packaged with the correct amount of labor divided between agriculture (K_a) and manufacturing (K_m); with the output in agriculture subject to diminishing returns and that of manufacturing subject to constant returns.

The profit in the agricultural sector is equal to the product of the additional input of this composite factor minus the amount of the output that has, one can say, been consumed in its production which is essentially equal to the depreciation factor plus the wage to labor. We represent these 'costs' by an (x) term so that we have the surplus (P) in this sector as:

$$P_a = f'(K_a) - x \tag{11}$$

All elements in this sector are expressed in terms of agricultural (corn) output, hence the money rate of profit and the physical (corn) rate of profit are equal. An increase in the price of corn means, to the same degree, an increase in the price of inputs. An existing market price of corn implies a production level equal to the subsistence requirements of the population resulting from the allocation of a quantity of composite factors. This automatically determines the rate of profit which can be read from the production relationship; and it is this rate which is the pervading rate for the entire economy. The fixed capital portion of this input involves conjuring up somewhat of a trick whereby part of the corn advance transforms itself into machinery that is made in total or in part to disappear at the end of the production period to be reconstituted anew.

But conditions are somewhat different in the manufacturing (cloth) sector where we have a constant marginal product and where the inputs and outputs are different physical commodities. The cloth sector uses corn as the composite input to produce cloth so that an equality of the rate of profit for the two sectors implies a relation between the price of cloth and the price of corn; with the former expressed in terms of corn which is taken as numeraire. Thus we have profit in the manufacturing sector as:

$$P_m = p_m f'_m(K_m) - x \tag{12}$$

And equilibrium in the allocation of capital requires that the money rate of profit earned on capital be the same in both sectors, that is:

$$r_a = r_m \qquad (13)$$

If the corn rate of profit falls, the price of cloth in terms of corn must fall to prevent cloth from being more profitable to produce than wheat. And as we want to make clear, it is this movement in prices that prompts a reallocation of the capital stock and a readjustment in the rate of return. Note that in a generalized two-sector model all prices are expressed in units of corn, so that the money rate of return in manufacturing can be translated into corn unit terms and be equal to the corn unit rate of return in agriculture which itself depends on the given production relationship for corn. So the rate of return in the Ricardian two-sector model is determined in the same way as it would be in his one-sector corn model.

But let us consider a more realistic scenario where we have the agricultural sector with its 'gravitational' or 'regulating' rate of profit and two manufacturing sectors (i) and (ii). A way to appreciate the central position of the agricultural sector in Ricardo's thinking is that its output is set to produce the level of subsistence for the population; that is, it is set equal to demand as determined by those psychological and other factors operating at a point in time. Thus its market price will be equal to its natural price given the magnitude of the capital stock and the prevailing technology. And once we know the production level and the required input, we can read the rate of profit from the production function; and it is a rate reflective of a level of output which maintains the labor that is, after all, central to the output for the whole system. Now a particular manufacturing sector may find its rate of profit exceeding or below that of the agricultural sector which, to reiterate, is stipulated to be the pervasive rate of profit for the whole economy. This difference in the rate of return is a function of the amount of capital employed in the particular manufacturing sector and thus in its level of production relative to the demand for its output; and this discrepancy shows up in terms of the sector's actual (market) price being different than its natural price. Again, this difference in price results in the sector's rate of profit diverging from that of the 'lead' agricultural sector.

If the divergence in the rate of profit is positive, say for sector (i), it speaks of the actual price being above the natural price and that of an expanding market. This condition attracts capital from other manufacturing sectors in search of a higher rate of return resulting in increased production levels and a diminution of the difference between market and natural prices. Perhaps it would be good to recall that the natural price is one that covers cost of production and the realization of the pervading rate of profit; it is a price given for the existing production technology. Hence the changes in profitability that we are considering stem from demand induced changes in market prices and not as a result of changes in productivity rates.

The scenario is reversed for a sector, say sector ii, whose actual price is below the natural price, so that the rate of profit falls below the overall rate as a reflection of a declining market for its product. Capital is diverted from this sector or line of production; production declines and the rate of profit, as a result of the upward movement in selling prices, approaches the sector's natural rate.

Overall, when a sector's market price exceeds its natural price, the sector will attract capital and expand; and when the market price is below the natural price, capital exists and the sector contracts. Price changes reallocate the capital stock to equalize profit rates; that is, in Ricardo's thinking when sector rates of profit are identical to the established rates in the agricultural sector, Ricardo's own words make for interesting reading here:

> Suppose now that a change of fashion should increase the demand for silks and lessen that for woolens; their natural price, the quantity of labour necessary for their production, would continue unaltered, but the market price of silk would rise and that of woolens would fall; and consequently the profits of the silk manufacturer would be below the general and adjusted rate of profits. Not only the profits, but the wages of the workmen, would be affected in these employments. This increased demand for silk would, however, soon be supplied by the transference of capital and labour from the woolen to the silk manufacture; when the market prices of silks and woolens would again approach their natural prices and then the usual profits would be obtained by the respective manufacturers of those commodities.[6]

It is then the desire, which every capitalist has, of diverting his funds from a less to a more profitable employment that prevents the market price of commodities from continuing for any length of time much above or much below their natural price. It is this competition which so adjusts the changeable value of commodities that, after paying the wages for the labor necessary to their production, and all other expenses required to put the capital employed in its original state of efficiency, the remaining value or surplus will in each trade be in proportion to the value of the capital employed.

Putting Ricardo's words into equational form we can write:

$$p_i - p_i^* = e_i(K_i) \tag{14}$$

$$r_i - r_a = g_i(p_i - p_i^*) \tag{15}$$

$$\Delta K_i = u_i(r_i - r_a) \tag{16}$$

where P_i^* = natural price; r_i, r_a = the rate of profit respectively, in the i and agricultural sectors.

Equation (15) tells that the divergence in price leads to a disequilibrium rate of profit that, in turn, via equation (16), adjusts the capital stock. The economy is in general balance when the rate of profit is identical throughout, implying that the market price and natural price are the same in all sectors.

We have an understanding about the long-term behavior of relative prices, and can appreciate referring to them as 'prices of production' in that they are a unique set of exchange values that bring about an overall rate of profit and a uniform rate of advance. What the 'simple' classical model conveys is that the rate of growth tomorrow results from the investment of today's surplus which itself is determined by today's prices given the production process and the determinants of the distribution of the output. Output, distribution and prices are all interrelated in an understanding of economic growth; investment is a primary determinant not only of output and employment but also of the distribution of the output. We recall in our discussion of the Ricardo model that the change in profits will be positive as the capital stock and thereby investment increases.

Yet there is an element of circularity in these relationships that we would need to unravel. Prices themselves are tied-up with the distribution of the surplus product between wages and profits, while the surplus itself cannot be measured without first knowing the prices of the commodities that compose it. Furthermore, there is the awareness that changes in relative prices may also occur due to changes in methods of production as well as to changes in the distribution of output. Is there a clear measure of value that can be used to identify relative price changes due to both of these causal disturbances? And if there is no single such unambiguous measure of value, then we are faced with two different problems. One is to come up with a standard that allows us to identify changes in the value of goods due to technological changes which will lead to changes in relative prices; the second is to design a way to distinguish such changes in relative prices from those caused by changes in the distribution of income.

We touched upon these value matters towards the end of our discussion of the Ricardo model in Chapter 4; and what we will do here is to elaborate somewhat and propose a solution to these value problems. This will bring us to a look at some Sraffian economics — Pierro Sraffa being considered perhaps the most influential modern-day classicist — and, as we mentioned, a Ricardo in modern dress.[7]

The Sraffian approach

A basic feature of Sraffa's work was that one can understand the core properties of an economy such as the determination of prices, the emergence of surplus, and the reproducibility of the system, without having to make any assumptions about the constancy or variability of returns. With Sraffa we are in an economy where production continues exactly the same way from period to period; and if there are no alterations in the production process, we need no assumptions about 'returns'. This is not far removed from classical economics where the concern with these central properties was based on the assumption that under given technological conditions returns to scale to the system as a whole would be constant, and the proportions with which the different inputs were used in any particular sector is constant. But, as we indicated, Sraffa makes no assumptions about returns; the matter is irrelevant since production is carried on in the same way without any changes in factor proportions or in scale. Yet in drawing out the inherent properties of an economy reproducing itself of a given size, Sraffa opens the door to an understanding of those 'balances' characteristic of an economy whose size is expanding over time.

His concern with prices as prices of production relates prices to levels of output and not to variations in costs associated with variations in production. In his early works Sraffa launched what has been considered as an answerable critique of the neoclassical construction of equilibrium prices under conditions of pure competition. While we will not get into a detailed look at his writings in this area, it will be helpful to refer to the principal points of his objection to the Marshallian theory of price determination.

The matter of returns

Sraffa was critical of the Marshallian theory of the firm by questioning the theoretical laws of decreasing and increasing returns as a basis for a theory of value. Marshall's theory assumes that variable returns predominate as opposed to classical theory which implies universal constant returns. It is not that classical thinkers (Ricardo) did not recognize the operation of variability of returns, but they reckoned their application to a broader area of analyses than an underpinning of the firm's supply curve and thereby an instrument for determining prices within a partial equilibrium analysis. We recall that the conventional price outcome from the inter-section of the demand and supply curves is subject to the conditions of perfect competition and 'coeteris paribus', i.e. independence of the conditions of production of the good in question from those of all other industries. Sraffa makes clear that one adopt the laws of variability of returns as espoused by the classicists to construct a single law of nonproportional returns, and use it in the area of price theory to functionally relate costs and quality produced. In this way, of course, neoclassicists come up with a law of supply in individual markets that would be coordinated with the law of demand. Sraffa tells us that:

> We are disposed to accept the laws of return as a matter of course, because we have before our eyes the great and indisputable services rendered by them when performing their ancient function, we often neglect to ask ourselves whether the old barrels are still able to hold the new wine.[8]

In the original intent the law of diminishing returns was associated with the issue of rent and its foundation was with reference to land. The question was what happens to output as a whole when labor and capital increases and land remains fixed. The affect is not related to the output of a single commodity in isolation, but to the whole of production into which the totality of the singular factor (land) enters which gives rise to diminishing returns. We are considering the emergence of rent at the intensive margin of cultivation where there is a uniform supply of the fixed input and rent arises from the scarcity of this resource in an aggregate sense. The law of diminishing returns in classical analysis belongs, as Joan Robinson puts it, "to the department of output as a whole";[9] and it was proper usage of the law to explain an element of the distribution of the total output. But what does a law designed for the analysis of rent have to do with using supply price of a particular commodity, and how was it taken up to serve such a purpose?

Well, in a very simple way, all that was necessary was to generalize from the particular case of land to all situations where there is an input of a constant quantity, and the firm in question uses a considerable if not the entire amount of this fixed input. Under this condition an increase in output will result in a more intense use of the 'fixed' resource and we can expect to associate such usage with diminishing productivity. But what is more likely the case, and all the more so when considering the behavior of a single firm or sector as in the partial neoclassical analysis, is that a marginal increase in production will be met by drawing doses of this required input from other firms rather than by the firm intensifying its own use of it. We can reasonably suppose that the single industry employs only a small part of this constant resource, so that one cannot look at the single industry and talk as if one were looking at the economy as a whole. But if this is so, then one is not likely to encounter the presence of diminishing returns and the basis for the upward sloping cost curve of the firm loses validity taking with it a piece of the foundation for the neoclassical theory of prices.

When discussing the operation of this law of returns, the professor illustrates the matter with an agricultural example, or talks about injecting labor into a plant with given capital all the while perhaps thinking about the agricultural case. And at the end a statement could be made that this assumes, heroically, that one can indeed inject these doses of labor; and before any examples are put forth one hurriedly moves on to the cost-curve constructions.

What happens to costs (factor prices) in an industry upon an increase in demand depends on how distinct its production process is from industries in general. If it employs the constant factor in greater proportion than 'generally', i.e. if it uses a considerable part of the resource; or if the resource can be increased at more than proportional cost, then we will see a more intense utilization of the factor and an increase in its cost — and we have the upward sloping supply curve. But if a particular industry employs factors in the same proportion as they are 'released' by other industries as a result of changes in demand then the increase in output in the particular industry is produced under constant costs with no change in relative prices. Indeed the whole diminishing returns theory comes into play around cases where the industry employs a rare factor such as a special skill or a particular mineral so that one must make more intense use of it, or that if it can be siphoned away it has to be by far greater amounts than its use generally. But these circumstances are too particular to propose a general application of the law in support of the upward sloping supply curve and the determination of prices. So what has happened in the construction of the supply curve is a form of make-believe that the firm or industry in question is like the aggregate system exclusively employing all of a factor of given limited supply with the classical diminishing returns outcome.

But there is another difficulty even if the firm does not employ all of the factor. Certainly in the competitive environment the firm can purchase all of the input it requires without affecting its price; but then this counters the increasing cost basis for the supply curve. Yet if this firm causes the price of the factor to go up in response to its increased demand then we are no longer in the competitive situation. It seems we have to maintain the make believe of a single firm or industry employing the whole of a fixed input. The law of diminishing returns as used in the micro sense to underpin the firm's supply is an example of a mis-application.

Regarding that other law of increasing returns this too represents a case of misapplication. In classical political economy this law was associated with the division of labor that was seen as cause and consequence of economic growth, it had to do with overall economic progress. Whatever cost changes occurred were understood within a broader context than the individual firm or industry in question. The law was not designed to reckon the result of change in the scale of operations of producing units in isolation.

Conventionally speaking, the question is how much can output expand if all inputs were increased simultaneously by the same percent? And under increasing returns to scale a doubling, for example, of inputs results in a more than doubling of output. In order to maintain the competitive nature of the industry in this circumstance, the reduction in the firm's unit costs must depend on external economies; that is, economies that are realized when the entire industry is expanding this way. In other words, such returns must be seen as internal to the industry but external to individual firms within the industry.

The result that each firm is becoming more efficient as the industry's output is expanding, which could be the result of entry of more firms, means we are considering a kind of interdependence between the firms comprising the industry. But this immediately removes the 'coeteris paribus' aspect of the consideration of the particular firm's long-run supply curve, if not that of the industry itself. In the consideration of external economics, Marshall himself did not consider them to be confined to a single industry; he makes the point that "the economies of production on a large scale can seldom be allocated exactly to any one industry: they are in great measure attached to groups, often large groups, of correlated industries".[10] This is telling us that the long-term price outcome of a particular commodity cannot be determined independent of the production conditions of other commodities in different industries. But the neoclassical analysis in constructing the equilibrium conditions of particular commodities does exactly that as a reflection of their 'partial approach'. Sraffa makes the point that the assumption of coeteris paribus becomes illegitimate when, "a variation in the quantity produced by the industry under consideration sets up a force which acts directly, not merely upon its own costs, but also upon the costs of other industries; in such a case the conditions of the particular equilibrium which it was intended to isolate are upset and it is no longer possible without contradiction to neglect collateral effects".[11] It is reasonable to suppose that in the overwhelming majority of cases the application of external economics falls into this circumstance. Again, the point is that the presence of external economics are traceable to interrelated changes in all industries rather than to an increase in the scale of production in any one industry — it seems we have to abandon partial equilibrium analysis or perfect competition or perhaps both. There is nothing about increasing returns that can be related to the neoclassical (Marshallian) long-term supply curve that does not violate its own conditions for the existence of the curve.

To base an understanding of prices on variability of returns, i.e. diminishing returns determining the nature of the supply curve in the short term and increasing returns exercising its influence in the long term, leads one in Sraffa's view to a dead end of understanding; the supply curve in either framework is not solidly based. Sraffa initially considered accepting the classical approach of constant returns (here the scale of output makes no difference to input proportions) as a basis for his analysis of prices. Interestingly enough, Marshall considered this case to be highly improbable, so he took the variability approach which in Sraffa's critique led to insurmountable difficulties for his analysis. Sraffa was then left with these alternatives to construct a theory of prices. As Roncoglia in his work on Sraffa tells us:

First to attribute general importance to the case of constant returns; second, the recognition of the general interrelations among the costs of production of various industries and the analysis of these interrelations by means of a system of general economic equilibrium; third, to abandon completely the assumption of perfect competition, basing the analysis of prices on the elements of imperfection that we always present in reality.[12]

Sraffa did acknowledge the existence of a link between costs and quantity produced via the constant returns assumption, but argued that this relationship cannot be fully analyzed in the context of partial equilibria; thus constant returns can only serve as a first step toward the formation of a theory of prices. A full understanding must include the mechanics of interdependence of sectors, and this is necessary regardless of the degree of competitiveness in the economy. So Sraffa's approach was to construct a theory of prices based on a system of general equilibrium without any assumption on returns. His concern was with those 'prices of production' that relate to the activity levels of production. These prices are long-term equilibrium (steady-state path) prices that have their basis in the conditions of production and the distribution of the output between wages and profits. Sraffa's analysis reflects the abandonment of the concept of prices as determined the supply and demand curves and thereby the whole marginalist underpinning for partial or general equilibrium; clearly what is also to be jettisoned is the notion of the simultaneous determination of prices and quantities. There are two problems that of output and price determination that are to be treated separately with Sraffa's work concentrating on the latter. Perhaps a last thought on the returns matter; if one 'needed' to think in terms of a supply and demand equilibrium to understand price determination, then thinking in terms of constant returns might be a mental aid in grasping Sraffa's work. But Sraffa makes no such assumption, and he sought to understand the nature of the economy along lines different from the traditional schemes of analysis.

A subsistence economy

Sraffa begins with a simple model of a 'subsistence' economy in which there are two commodities produced, let us say corn and iron, and in which the output of each of these commodities is equal to the amount of that good required as input to the two productive processes of the economy. In other words we have a system in which the total amount of each output which goes into the productive process is the same as the total amount produced. Thus:[13]

$$280t \text{ corn} + 12t \text{ iron} \rightarrow 400t \text{ corn} \qquad (17)$$
$$120t \text{ corn} + 8t \text{ iron} \rightarrow 20t \text{ iron}$$

We have the corn sector producing 400 tons (t) of corn requiring as input 280t of its own output to be used as 'seed' plus the wage advance to sustain labor, and given the technology, 12t of iron. In a similar way, we set out what is required for the annual production of 20 tons of iron. If we add the amounts of corn and iron used as inputs we see that the sum is equal to the amounts that are produced at the end of the year. In this sense the economy is one of subsistence in that no production process yields a surplus of output over the amount of it required as input.

The different products at the production period end up in the hands of different producers. If the production process is to continue at the same level it is necessary that the commodities be distributed between the sectors according to the left side of the equations in (17). The corn sector will 'set aside' 280 tons of its output for production in the following period, it will then have to sell 120 tons of corn at a price that will enable it to purchase 12 tons of iron. Likewise the iron sector will need to realize proceeds from the sale of 12 tons of iron that enables it to purchase 120 tons of corn as input for the following production period. If production is to continue at the same level from year to year a particular set of relative prices must exist; prices must be such that 120 tons of corn can be exchanged for 12 tons of iron. The price of a ton of iron must be 10 times the price of a ton of wheat. The message at this point is that in a system of subsistence production there is a unique set of exchange values which makes possible the repetitiveness of production; and such values are determined directly and solely on the basis of the methods of production.

We generalize this model to n-sectors with the following notation (reinforcing our discussion in the early pages of Chapter 4 concerning the technical interdependence of sectors). The outputs of sectors a...n are A,B...N. The inputs are A_a the amount of product (a) used in its own production, with B_a being the amount of output B used in the production of product (a) etc. The price of a unit of output of (a) is p_a and that of (b)p_b etc. We set up the following equations:

$$A_a p_a + B_a p_b + c_a p_c \ldots N_a p_n = A p_a$$

$$A_b p_a + B_b p_b + c_b p_c \ldots N_b p_n = B p_b \qquad (18)$$

$$\bullet$$
$$\bullet$$
$$\bullet$$

$$A_n p_a + B_n p_b + C_n p_c \ldots N_n p_n = N p_n$$

And as the system reproduces itself without surplus, then:

$$A_a + A_b + Ac \ldots A_n = A$$

$$B_a + B_b + B_c \ldots B_n = B \qquad (19)$$

$$\bullet$$
$$\bullet$$
$$\bullet$$

$$N_a + N_b + N_c \ldots N_n = N$$

In the system of equations (18) we have (n) production processes and (n) unknown prices. But if we take one commodity as the standard of value — say good (a) — and set the price equal to a unity we can determine the price of all the other goods in terms of commodity (a) reducing the unknowns to $n-1$ equations. If we set the exchange value $P_a = 1$ (making it the numeraire of the system), all other prices are determined.

We can best demonstrate this with our less general two-sector system. From (17) we find:

$$280 p_c + 12 p_i = 400 p_c$$

$$120 p_c + 8 p_i = 20 p_i \qquad (20)$$

$$c = \text{corn}, \quad i = \text{iron}$$

Setting the exchange value $P_c = 1$ gives:

$$280 + 12 p_i = 400$$

$$p_i = 10 \qquad (21)$$

231

and:

$$280+12(10)=400$$

$$120+8(10)=20(10)=200 \qquad (22)$$

And in a similar manner one can determine the prices of all the commodities produced in the system of (n) commodities.

Even within the confines of the rather unrealistic case we can see that these prices of production ($p_c= 1, p_i= 10$) are determined independent of any simultaneous determination of production levels and, importantly, interdependent of any marginal variations of neoclassical thinking. To reiterate, the question is, given the activity levels of the economy, what set of relative values must exist to allow the economy to reproduce itself at that level? There is no presumption that these long-term (if you will) prices of production will be encountered on a day-to-day basis in the economy. We hesitate to use the term 'day-to-day market' because market implies certain institutional arrangements that could rob the analysis of all reality. In the absence of an explicit analysis of short-term ('effective') prices, Sraffa did not venture any relationship between the day-to-day prices and the prices of production. He concentrates on the determinants of the latter and their relation to the uniform rate of profit as a long-term equilibrium characteristic of the economy. But now let us move to a more realistic framework.

A surplus economy

In this model one of the sectors produces a surplus above the amount of its output required as input in the processes of the system. At first we see this as a physical surplus, thus we have an economy with the following production relations:

$$
\begin{array}{lll}
280\text{t corn} + & 12\text{t iron} \rightarrow & 575\text{t corn} \qquad (23)\\
\underline{120\text{t}}\ \text{corn} + & \underline{8\text{t}}\ \text{iron} \rightarrow & 20\text{t iron}\\
400 & 20 &
\end{array}
$$

We point out that in this model and in that of subsistence the wage of labor does not show up explicitly in the analysis. The understanding is that the wage is treated ('advanced') as part of the value of the iron and corn input at a subsistence level. Labor is seen here as equal to material input, giving us a system akin to that of Marx. Labor is considered as an instrument that helps to create the surplus but does share in it; the entire value of the surplus of 175t of corn will be available for distribution in the form of profit.

If we restate the subsistence system of (18) — for two sectors — as:

$$(A_a - A)p_a + B_d p_b = 0$$

$$A_b p_a + (B_b - B)p_b = 0$$

that is:

$$280 - 400 + 12(10) = 0 \tag{24}$$

$$120 + 80 - 200 = 0$$

(where A = corn sector; B = iron sector)

Thus the value of the output in each sector is entirely consumed by the 'purchase' of the inputs required to reproduce the respective outputs. The introduction of a surplus clearly negates the equations in (24) as the relationships in (19) no longer hold. What we find is:

$$280p_c + 12p_i < 575p_c$$

$$120p_c + 8p_i = 20p_c \tag{25}$$

We need to incorporate the surplus (profit) of the corn sector into the total economy so as to result in an 'equilibrium' condition similar to that of (24). This is done by Sraffa introducing a uniform rate of profit in the economy which results from a simultaneous determination of a particular set of relative prices (notice the similarity to those Ricardian prices in the general classical model). Prices must be such so as to allow the replacement of all inputs (so the system can reproduce itself) as well as to allow profits on the value of these inputs to be earned at the same rate in both sectors. We obtain the relative prices that fulfill these conditions by setting-up the production equations in price terms (including the 'price' obtained on the advance of capital) in the following familiar way.

$$(280p_c+12p_i)(1+r)=575p_c$$

$$(120p_c+8p_i)(1+r)=20p_i \qquad (26)$$

Taking the price of a ton of corn equal to one, then this set of non-linear equations yields:

$$p_i=15$$

$$r=.25 \qquad (27)$$

$$p_c=1 \text{ (by assumption)}$$

Prices which make one ton of corn exchange for 15 tons of iron bring about uniform rate of profit of 25 per cent.

Putting these results into (26) and appreciating the outcomes via (24) we have:

$$[280+12(15)]+.25[280+12(15)]=575$$

$$[120+8(15)]+.25[120+8(15)]=20(15)=300$$

and:

$$(A_a-A)p_a+B_a p_b+P=0 \qquad (28)$$

$$280-575+180+115=0$$

$$A_b p_a+(B_b-B)p_b+P=0$$

$$120+120-300+60=0$$

The corn sector produces a value of output of 575 of which 280 is spent for 'internal' replacement and 295 to purchase the requisite 12 tons of iron valued at 180. This leaves a profit of 115 and a rate of profit of:

$$\frac{115}{280+180}=.25 \qquad (29)$$

Similar reasoning for the iron sector finds a rate of profit of:

$$\frac{60}{120+120} = .25 \qquad (30)$$

What we come away with from this model is that in the circumstance where the wage consists of the necessary means of production and enters the process as any other input, the profit (claimed entirely by the capitalist) is determined simultaneously and through the same mechanism that determines relative prices. An essential concern would be how the system determines the day-to-day prices and their relation to those prices of production. We get a sense that prices are tied in with the distribution of the output which itself has great bearing on the system's ability to reproduce itself at the same level or at some steady pace of increase. This relationship will become even more evident when we extend this surplus model one step further into reality.

But the model as it stands now confronts us with the question of what happens to the surplus? If we assume that the profit does not get turned back to the productive processes so that the sector's output levels remain unaltered, we can then account for a third sector producing a 'luxury good' that is purchased by capitalists with their profits. This is a good that does not enter into the production process of the corn and iron sectors, but would be an input in the production of itself. We can think of a three-sector model consisting of iron, corn and a luxury good (u); all three use corn and iron as inputs and the profits of all three are expended on the output of the third. Setting this up we have:

$$(A_a p_a + B_a p_b)(1+r) = A p_a$$

$$(B_a p_b + B_b p_b)(1+r) = B p_b \qquad (31)$$

$$(A_u p_a + B_u p_b + U_u p_u)(1+r) = U p_u$$

The prices of the (a) and (b) sectors, i.e. corn and iron, are independent of the existence of the luxury good. However, the price of this (u) sector will be influenced by the prices of p_a and p_b. The reason for the passive nature of the u-good in that it does not influence the price structure of the overall economy is that it enters only into the production of the final consumption good; and Sraffa refers to this type of commodity as a non-basic good. As distinct from what Sraffa refers to as a basic commodity which enters, no matter how directly or indirectly, into the production process of every other commodity including itself. There is some interesting commentary concerning Sraffa's conception of basic and non-basic goods and its relation to a similar kind of distinction made by the classicists, but this is best handled after we take Sraffa's analysis to its next stage.

A shared surplus economy

Up to this point labor need not have appeared explicitly in the price equations; it was treated as any other material input. That is, it was paid for at a subsistence wage in terms of an advance of an amount of corn and iron; the products which workers needed to survive are inputs in the production process and the labor costs could be folded into the costs of these inputs. But now we presume that labor shares in the surplus product, so that the wage can be seen as consisting of two parts; one being that constant portion of subsistence and a second being a part of profits. The latter portion is variable not only because of the variability of profits, but would also reflect labor's negotiating strength to command a larger or smaller share of profits. Thus labor's cost as reflecting the profit share cannot be seen as part of the other inputs, but must be treated as an additional explicit cost. It is as if this part of the wage represents some additional 'phantom' input.

If we maintain this two-sides version of the wage and as labor is needed as input for every output, then purchases out of the subsistence wage portion would consist of basic goods; what classical economists thought of as 'necessaries' or wage goods. Since necessaries then enter into the reproduction of labor, they enter into the output of every commodity and their conditions of production would influence the entire system of relative prices. Goods reflecting expenditures out of the surplus share would be considered 'luxuries' or non-necessaries that may have a correspondence to Sraffa's non-basic goods. Yet the distinction put forth by the classicists as between necessary and non-necessary or between wage goods and luxury goods was a distinction based on the direct use of a particular good in final consumption, and is thus a rather arbitrary classification. Furthermore, relating this distinction to consumer goods and producer goods does not help matters since some goods may be used for both consumption purposes and as a means of production.

Sraffa abandons the arbitrariness of such distractions which is based on how the wage is used and on the treatment of the wage into fixed and variable portions. Sraffa's terminology is linked to how the good is used in the productive processes of the system; his distinction has a technological basis to it. To reiterate, if the good enters directly or indirectly into the production of all goods it is considered a basic good, if it does not then it is non-basic. Indeed, in the shared surplus model Sraffa does away, at least overtly, with the split-side view of the wage and makes the entire wage variable as part of profits (it is then not immediately evident what goods enter only as wage goods). This means that in setting up the relative price equations the amount of labor employed in each process has to be represented explicitly replacing the corresponding quantities of subsistence goods, and the wage rate becomes a variable in the analysis. Furthermore, the wage cannot now be treated as an advance (where it was reckoned as part of the material input) since there is no way of knowing what goods are to be advanced; so the wage is to be considered as a payment at the end of the production period, and labor acquires what it considers as its subsistence out of the surplus that it attains. Thus considering the wage in total as a variable emphasizes the point that labor and capitalists share the profits which, in turn, opens matters up to the influence of labor unions in determining what part of profits remain with the capitalists and thereby the level of savings in the system. But let us not get too far ahead of ourselves, as we are simply pointing to further discussions. Right now we want to turn to the price equations of this shared surplus approach.

We formulate the general system as reflected in the following two process models.

$$(A_a p_a + B_a p_b)(1+r) + wL_a = Ap_a$$

$$(A_b p_a + B_b p_b)(1+r) + wL_b = Bp_b \tag{32}$$

and

$$L_a + L_b = 1$$

In this manner the net income of the system is related to the usual definition of national income which we put here as income earned in the form of profits and wages. Thus we can view (32) as:

$$[A - (A_a + A_b)]p_a + [B - (B_a + B_b)]p_b = 1 \tag{33}$$

The value of output minus that part of it which is used to reconstitute the material input is the national income (which we can set equal to unity) that constitutes the surplus to be distributed between capital and labor. With equations (32) and (33) we have three equations and four unknowns in the two prices, the wage (w) and the rate of profit (r).

We have here one degree of freedom, in that if we stipulate the value of one variable the value of the others is determined. For example, if we know the wage rate and given the technology of production and thereby relative prices, we know the portion of the surplus accruing to the capitalist and thus the rate of profit. The overall point is that if labor shares in the surplus then relative prices and one of the distributive variables (the wage rate or the rate profit) are simultaneously determined given the other distributive variable and the technology of production. What Sraffa does is to assign successive values to the wage from one to zero in order to show what happens to relative prices and the rate of profit. To reiterate, from a different angle, we see that relative prices are determined by the technology of production and the manner in which the surplus is divided, i.e. by the distribution of the national income. Glancing back to a comparison with the second of Sraffa's models, there the profit constitutes the entire surplus and is determined solely by and along with the determination of relative prices.

Let us put Sraffa's shared surplus model into 'play' and see where it all leads to. At once extreme all of the net product goes to wages which in effect reverts the discussion to Sraffa's subsistence model, except that labor appears overtly in the value equations rather than being represented by quantities of commodities. Here all income is wages and all costs ultimately reduce to wage costs. Assuming a uniform wage rate the value of the output will simply reflect the amount of labor directly and indirectly embodied in its production; so that price ratios will be equal to labor employed ratios. Within the context of the Ricardian analysis in Chapter 4 we looked at this particular circumstance referring to it as the classical law of value. Now we consider this in terms of the value equation in (32).

Consider the following economy:

$$2C + 2I + .75L \rightarrow 8C$$

$$2C + 5I + .25L \rightarrow 8I \qquad (34)$$

The gross production of the economy consists of 8 units of corn and 8 units of iron with its net output being 4 of corn and 1 of iron. It is the value of this net product, i.e. the national income that is subject to distribution between labor and capital.

Writing (34) in terms of our value equations we find:

$$(2p_c+2p_i)(1+r)+.75w=8p_c$$

$$(2p_c+5p_i)(1+r)+.25w=8p_i \qquad (35)$$

The value of the net product is set equal to 1 (it is used as numeraire) and becomes the standard of value to express prices. Thus:

$$4p_c+1p_i=1 \qquad (36)$$

Now we want to solve for relative prices when all of the net product is absorbed by wages so that $r=0$. Then restating (35) we have:

$$(2p_c+2p_i)+.75=8p_c$$

$$(2p_c+5p_i)+.25=8p_i \qquad (37)$$

and using (36) to solve for prices in terms of the net product gives:

$$p_i=1-4p_c \qquad (38)$$

Substituting into the first equation in (37) yields:

$$[2p_c+2(1-4p_c)]+.75=8p_c$$

$$p_c=.196 \qquad (39)$$

with the solution for p_i being:

$$[2(.196)+5p_i]+.25=8p_i$$

$$p_i=.214 \qquad (40)$$

The value of the gross product is:

$$8(.196)+8(.214)=3.28 \qquad (41)$$

with a price ratio of:

$$\frac{p_c}{p_i} = \frac{.196}{.214} = .916 \qquad (42)$$

We arrived at our price ratio from the equations in (35) by the assumption that all of the surplus is claimed by labor. Now this is somewhat different than that 'early and rude' state of society envisioned by the classicists when they promulgated the law of value whereby price ratios are equal to embodied labor ratios; in that state there is no profit to be claimed. To relate to this rude state let us modify our equations slightly to read:

$$2C + 2I \rightarrow 8C$$

$$2C + 5I \rightarrow 8I \qquad (43)$$

and

$$2p_c + 2p_i = 8p_i$$

$$2p_c + 5p_i = 8p_i \qquad (44)$$

And we have the following story. We find a two-sector economy producing 8C and 8I, and let the sum of the inputs at wage cost be \$4 for C and \$7 for I. Since the value of the end product will be equal to the sum of its inputs, we will find that the price of a unit of iron will be 1.75 times the price of a unit of corn. Taking the wage equal to \$1 means that 4 units of labor are required to produce 8 units of corn and 7 units of labor go to produce 8 units of iron. Then on a per unit output basis we have an embodied labor ratio of iron to corn as:

$$\frac{.875}{.5} = 1.75 \qquad (45)$$

Our value ratios are:

$$4 = 8p_c \qquad (46)$$

$$7 = 8p_i$$

and the price ratio of a unit of iron to that of corn is clearly equal to that of embodied labor of 1.75 to 1. In the equations of (44) we have an equal number of equations and unknown variables without having to stipulate one of the independent variables as equal to zero as was done for the equations in (35) and (36).

Certainly the classicists were aware that this law of value is at best a very rough approximation of relative prices, and does not really provide an explanation when capitalists come onto the scene and the value of output gives rise to a surplus. The simple and direct relationship of price ratios being equal to embodied labor ratios would be subject to important modifications; and "Sraffa like his predecessors now goes on to consider the nature and causes of these modifications".[14] Now, relative prices will change when there is a change in the relations between the rate of profit and the wage rate; and the key to the movement in these prices lies in the difference in the proportions in which labor and the 'means of production' are combined in the various productive processes. We mentioned this matter of relative price changes in the discussion on Ricardo in chapter 4, and we want to pick up on this again within the modern context of the Sraffian value equations.

To show the impact of a distributional change let us take the extreme opposite case from that of the system in (37) and presume that labor does not at all share in the surplus. Thus for the given technology the profits accruing to the capitalists are at maximum with the rate of profit being .333 (we will see how this maximum rate of profit is determined).[15]

With the use of our 'cost of production' equations we now find:

$$(2p_c + 2p_i)(1.333) = 8p_c$$

$$(2p_c + 5p_i)(1.333) = 8p_i \tag{47}$$

$$4p_c + p_i = 1 \tag{48}$$

In considering $w = 0, r = .333$, we have reduced matters to two equations in two unknowns, that of p_c and p_i. Going about obtaining the sector prices via expressing in terms of the net product, we write the value equations as:

$$[2p_c + 2(1 - 4p_c)](1.333) = 8p_c \tag{49}$$

$$p_c = .166$$

and

$$[2(1.66)+5p_i](1.333)=8p_i \qquad (50)$$

$$p_I=.333$$

And we have a value of gross output of:

$$8(.166)+8(.333)=4 \qquad (51)$$

Note the changes in relative prices upon a change in the distribution of income from an extreme of $w=1$ to one of $w=0$. In the former situation, we found a price ratio of .916, and in the latter situation we have:

$$\frac{P_c}{p_i}=\frac{.166}{.333}=.498 \qquad (52)$$

In stating the extremes of $w=0, r=1/3$ and $w=1, r=0$, we are pointing up the existence of a systematic inverse relationship between the distributive variable showing all possible combinations of a non-negative wage rate and a non-negative rate of profit. One exhibits this relationship on what we have considered as a wage curve or wage-profit curve; this curve was instrumental in the reswitching discussion in Chapter 3 as part of our critique of neoclassical distribution theory. So we have that relative prices will change upon a change in the distribution of income as a result of differences in the production technique of the two sectors. If the techniques, i.e. input proportions, were the same then relative prices would not change from their previous levels as we showed in an example in Chapter 4. But relative prices would also change as a result of a change in input proportions for given values of the distributive variables. Indeed, Ricardo emphasized that not only were relative prices determined by relative amounts of embodied labor, but what was perhaps more significant was the changes in relative prices were mainly determined by changes in relative quantities of embodied labor. For Ricardo this labor embodied standard constituted a uniform standard with respect to changes in the techniques of production. Yet an awareness of the combination of forces that can alter relative prices brings us to a look at that special Sraffian device, the standard commodity, which was put forth to solve what may be considered as the 'Ricardian problem'. This will give a better understanding of the relationship between prices and distribution and also show us how we arrive at that maximum rate of profit.

That 'invariable measure' and standard commodity

What Ricardo tried to come up with was a uniform measure of value capable of identifying and measuring those changes in relative prices due to changes in technology from those due to changes in profits and wages. We have two different problems here: one is to be able to identify those commodities whose values change due to a change in relative prices caused by a change in input proportions. The second is to separate such changes in relative prices from those caused by changes in income distribution. Ricardo proposed has embodied labor measure of value to serve both purposes, and as a result tried to make this measure serve too many different purposes.

Certainly we can identify those price changes due to changes in technique of which embodied labor may serve as an adequate representation. Ricardo's labor measure works well because it represents an absolute value of an input, and a change in this value between two commodities would show up as an alike change in their relative prices for given values of the wage rate and rate of profit. But with input proportions differing in the various productive processes how are we able to determine whether relative price changes are attributable to distributional or technical changes? Of course, if input proportions were alike then technique changes cannot be the determining agent, and distributional changes would have no impact; and if they differ relative price changes can be attributable to one or both causal factors. Let us say again that if factor proportions are uniform relative prices would reflect existing productive technologies; but with factor proportions (embodied labor) changing there is no way to attribute price changes per se to this cause. For Ricardo to have stressed this link between labor ratios and relative prices, he must have relegated distributional changes to a lower order of importance.

Yet there is a further consideration concerning the impact of distributional changes that we touched upon towards the end of Chapter 4, and would be helpful to revisit at this point. The result of a fall in the wage rate (increase in the rate of profit) could put some sectors into what we referred to as a state of deficit in that they could not pay wages and also earn the higher rate of profit from current receipts; while others may end up in a state of surplus in that they earn receipts more than necessary to realize profits at the prevailing rate. Since the rate of profit must be the same, and we assume no alteration of the technique of production, then relative prices will change simply because the input proportions in the various sectors are different. As our example indicated in Chapter 4, the sector with a low proportion of labor to capital would be in deficit and its price would rise when wages fell; and the sector with a high proportion would be in surplus so that its price would fall when the wage rate declines. In our example where the wage rate dropped from 1 to 0, the corn sector price fell from .196 to .166 with an input ratio of labor to means of production of .18 to 1, while the iron sector price increases from .214 to .333 for an input ratio of .03 to 1.

However we have to reckon that sectors contain products from other sectors as raw material, i.e. as means of production; then the sector which uses fewer workers such as the iron sector or that of sector (A) in our example in Chapter 4, need not be placed at a disadvantage, that is, be put into deficit with its price increasing. Quite possibly it could be obtaining its input from sectors whose processes use a high enough proportion of labor so that their output price falls as a consequence of a wage decline; then the sector using these inputs might actually find the price of its output falling when wages decline (it would be put into surplus). Thus we have to know considerably more than the productive processes of say any two sectors to determine what will happen to their relative prices as a result of a change in wages. To pick up on Sraffa's words here, the relative prices would depend "not only on the proportions of labor to means of production by which they are respectively produced, but also on the proportions by which those means have themselves been produced, and also on the proportions by which the means of those means of production have been produced, and so on".[16] Clearly relative prices would follow the Ricardian dictate, for example, that sectors with high labor ratios would find their prices falling when wages fall, should all sectors down the line which contribute to its production directly or indirectly, have the same input ratio.

These considerations bring us to the Sraffian standard commodity which provides a solution to that second problem if we use this 'commodity' as the standard of measure. What is the nature of this commodity, how does it come into existence, and how does it help our understanding of the change in relative prices? First of all, it is one that represents what we called the borderline sector; that is a sector where a change in the wage allows the payment of profits at the general rate without having to alter the price of the sector's output. So a reduction in the wage would be exactly balanced by an increase in profits (there being no change in the technique of production); the sector stands neither in deficit or surplus as a result of a change in the distributive variables. But for this to be the case we must further suppose that the 'capital' input in this borderline sector was itself produced with the same technique of production, i.e. with the same labor to means of production ratio, as the borderline sector's output. And the same assumption holds as we go back down the line. Since the output at any one stage becomes the input to the next higher stage, and as the value of output is not changing, then in this standard commodity we have an output whose value will not change relative to the value of its own means of production. Thus we can say that the ratio of the value of its net product to that of its means of production would always remain unaltered when wages change. Now if we can imagine an economy consisting of a non-basic good and several basic goods that directly or indirectly feed into its production, then unless all these sectors are prescribed as outlined above relative prices will vary when distribution changes.

Again, the important point to keep in mind is that there would be nothing in the technique of production of the standard commodity that would make its price change when wages rise or fall. Though it is not that relative prices will not change; it is that such fluctuations will occur because of the particulars of the production processes of other commodities being compared with the standard commodity, and not because of the particulars of the latter.

Now the interesting question is where can such a standard commodity be found; for it is highly unlikely that a sector fulfilling the required conditions will actually exist in the economy. And Sraffa answers that such a standard sector can be constructed out of a mixture of sectors that actually do exist in the economy; the standard commodity emerges as a composite output distilled from the actual economy since it is an output that stands, so to speak, in the middle of an array of sectors that to one side have the characteristic of being deficit sectors while on the other are those in surplus. The construction of this composite sector requires the application of appropriate multipliers to the actual sectors such that the product has the property that the ratio between the outputs of it is the same as the ratio of it that is used as inputs. Keeping matters in physical terms we construct a standard sector from our actual system in equation (34) by applying the multipliers of .8 to the corn sector and 1.6 to the iron sector. Restating the actual system we have:

$$2C+2I+.75L\rightarrow8C$$

$$2C+5I+.25L\rightarrow8I \tag{53}$$

Applying the multipliers:

$$.8(2C)+.8(2I)+.8(.75L)=.8(8C)$$

$$1.6(2C)+1.6(5I)+1.6(.25L)=1.6(8I) \tag{54}$$

yields:

$$1.6C+1.6I+.6L=6.4C$$

$$3.2C+8I+.4L=12.8I \tag{55}$$

with the composite sector as :

$$4.8C+9.6I+L=6.4C+12.8I \tag{56}$$

Thus we have a composite system whose conditions of production are shown in (55) and which produces the outputs of corn and iron in the ratio of 1 corn to 2 iron. And, as we can see, this sector employs these outputs in the same proportion as they are produced.

The net output of this standard system, following the reasoning we used for the real economy, forms the surplus or national income which will be distributed between capital and labor; and we express the wage in terms of this standard net product. This surplus in physical terms is:

$$(6.4C+12.8I)-(4.8C+9.6I)=1.6C+3.2I \tag{57}$$

Now if we presume that all of the surplus goes to capital we come up with the maximum rate of profits for our imaginary standard system. Thus:

$$\frac{1.6C+3.2I}{4.8C+9.6I}=\frac{4.8}{14.4}=.333 \tag{58}$$

Note that in (58) the commodities in the numerator and the denominator are made up of the same goods and combined in the same proportions; thus, regardless of the relative prices of corn and iron, the ratio would remain unchanged. Whether stated in price (money) terms or in commodity (physical) terms the ratio in (58) remains the same, then by comparison to the actual economy where a change in wages subsequently alters values we find in the composite commodity one whose value remains invariant to a change in the distributive variables.

Using this standard sector we can set up a variation in the rate of profit that is proportional to the variation in the wage for the given technology of production. And while we read this relationship from the 'imaginary' standard construction it can be applied to the actual system as well. Indeed we can now see where the maximum rate of profit comes from that we used in the actual economy equations of (41) and (50) to solve for actual relative prices in the circumstance where labor does not share in the surplus at all. We write this relationship between the rate of profit and the wage as:

$$r = R(1-w)$$

or

$$\frac{r}{R} = \frac{1-w}{1} \qquad (59)$$

$R =$ maximum rate of profit

Then setting the wage in terms of the standard net product, and assuming that no part of it goes to labor ($w=0$), we arrive at $r=R=.333$.

Suppose that the wage rate increases to .25, we then calculate the actual rate of profit as:

$$r = .333(1-.25)$$

$$= .25 \qquad (60)$$

And we see actual rate of profit as being .75 of the maximum rate as:

$$\frac{r}{.333} = \frac{1-.25}{1} = .75 \qquad (61)$$

247

But looking at this through the eyes of ratio (58), the rate of profit of .25 results from three-fourths of the net product or the standard system going to capital. Let us write this out:

$$\frac{1.2C + 2.4I}{4.8C + 9.6I} = \frac{3.6}{14.4} = .25 \qquad (62)$$

And if the wage increases again to .50 we obtain a rate of profit of seventeen percent. Thus for every .25 increase in the wage we get a .08 drop in the rate of profit; or, for every .01 increase in the wage rate we get a .0034 drop in the rate of profit.

We use this rate of profit wage rate relationship and apply it to the actual economy (equations 53) to see what happens to actual prices when these prices are solved for using the standard net product as numeraire. Since we express the distributive variables in terms of this net product, then the subsequent price determination must be expressed the same way. There is no problem in taking expression (59) into the real world, for the real (actual) system is the basis for the standard system. As Sraffa tells us, "it consists of the same basic equations as the standard system only in different proportions; so that once the wage is given, the rate of profit is determined for both systems regardless of the proportions of the equations in either one of them."[17] The rate of profit for the real system as a whole becomes known once we determine the (R) and the (w) from the standard system. Let us consider some examples.

Taking the case of $w = .25$ and $r = .25$ we first solve for the price of iron in terms of our numeraire. So:

$$1.6p_c + 3.2p_i = 1 \qquad (63)$$

$$p_i = .31 - .5p_c \qquad (64)$$

and using the distributive relationship and the actual system to determine prices, we have:

$$[2p_c + 2(.31 - .5p_c)](1.25) + .75(.25) = 8p_c$$

$$p_c = .142 \qquad (65)$$

The price of the iron output can be determined directly as:

$$p_i = .31 - .5(.142)$$

$$= .24 \tag{66}$$

and

$$1.6(.142 + 3.2(.24) = 1 \tag{67}$$

To see this another way, if we know prices and the wage expressed in terms of the standard net product, we can solve for that overall rate of profit for the actual system which will be the same as determined by the standard expression of (59). Thus:

$$[2(.142) + 5(.24)](1 + r) + .25(.25) = 8(.24)$$

$$r = .25 \tag{68}$$

For a different distributive combination of $w = .30, r = .17$, we find prices of:

$$[2p_c + 2(.31 - .5p_c)](1.17) + .75(.50) = 8p_c$$

$$p_c = .161 \tag{69}$$

and

$$p_i = .23 \tag{70}$$

Thus in the actual economy relative prices will change when the wage rate is altered as we find:

$$\frac{p_c}{p_i} = \frac{.142}{.24} = .59 \text{ when } w = .25$$

$$\frac{p_c}{p_i} = \frac{.161}{.23} = .7 \text{ when } w = .50 \tag{71}$$

We compare this to the 'invariance' of our standard commodity that has a value of gross output of 4, independent of what prices are used and hence of the change in the distributive variables. And the matter to be distributed, i.e. the standard net product, is unaffected by price changes having a value of 1.

To reiterate the observation concerning the 'Ricardo problem'; the standard commodity is unchanged with regard to income distribution, so that a change in relative prices as a result of distributive changes shows up as a change in value of the other good. The value of the standard commodity will, however, change when there is a change in the technique of production; a change in relative prices shows up as a price change generally.

We do not continue our analysis of Sraffian economics beyond these discussions, though he does use his relationship between the distributive variables to elucidate other theoretical problems. One direction is to obtain relative prices by transforming the entire production process into dated labor terms which serves as a powerful critique of the neoclassical theory of capital and its relation to distribution. Sraffa's work here is a further supportive plank for the reswitching phenomenon (considered in Chapter 3) that does not allow us to go from a productivity curve that is reflective of different quantities of capital to a relation between wages and profits — the concept of 'capital' cannot be used to explain the distribution of income.

Our concern in this chapter is with understanding the determination of relative prices in their existence as those long-term prices of production that relate the system's capability to reproduce itself. And we take note as a result of Sraffa's work that in the reality of an economy producing a surplus, these prices are determined by conditions of production and by the manner in which the surplus is distributed between wages and profits. There is no demand side in Sraffa's pricing analysis; if there exists technical coefficients for the production of single outputs per sector (we are not looking at cases of joint production) and if the wage is uniform in the economy there is no need (indeed there is no place) for demand functions in price determination. Sraffa makes no reference at all to 'market' or 'day-to-day' prices, but concentrates on the determination of those Ricardian 'normal' prices whose equilibrium level is dictated by the inter-sector uniformity of the profit rate. And there is, within the context of steady-state growth, a particular distribution of income that connects to a level of savings so as to result in the desirable growth rate, as will be discussed in the following chapter.

Yet the day-to-day prices are what we experience; and there is no reason to presume that they are at any time equal to the 'normal' or long-run equilibrium prices, in the same sense that we do not presume the system to be in a steady-growth configuration much less one equal to its natural rate. The relative price picture in the short term or, as the classicists would say, during the exchange period, reflects the non-uniformity of the rate of profit which influences the allocation of capital and the composition in the following production period while simultaneously altering the distributive allocation. So we look upon these normal relative prices and values of the distributive variables as gravitational theoretical constructs, leaving us with the task of determining prices on the day-to-day basis which is really asking about the influences on the rate of profit.

One can suppose that Sraffa understood well enough the imprecise nature of the determination of short-run prices and the problem of relating them to those prices of production. In Chapter 2 we elaborated somewhat on why the demand curve with its underlying utilitarian theory of consumption is incapable of providing a basis for the 'competitive' explanation of prices and we also discussed the invalidity of the Marshallian construct of the supply curve (we reiterate that in Sraffa the whole discussion of price determination is independent of the neoclassical marginal variation). Abandoning the competitive model leaves us with the elements of imperfection, i.e. degrees of monopoly, as the well spring for short-term prices that reflect the interdependence of these large producing units. We can look at Sraffa's prices of production as reference points to understand the day-to-day prices in a similar way that the golden-age growth construction serves as benchmark with which to gauge an existing growth experience.

The setting of prices

Price setting in our non-neoclassical post-Keynesian world is based essentially on two realities. One is the production function of the fixed input coefficient variety which we have been talking about all along, and secondly is the size of the producing unit itself which is anything but a small powerless player in a highly impersonal environment. Regarding the production function we have not only a set of technical coefficients, but we would also presume that the right-angled function represents the least cost per unit technology at the time the production facility was constructed. It is not a matter of the lowest cost per unit of output being a function of a particular level of output; it is always at least cost for any level of output in the utilization of a particular plant or a production line. The fixed set of input coefficients is represented by the quantity of labor hours and associated raw materials inputs required to keep the production line in operation; and these inputs will not change as a proportion of the level of output coming off the production line. Thinking for a moment in terms of a single operating line, the firm can shut down or start up the production line in varying degrees as it responds to demand changes (if not shutting it down totally or running it fully) without incurring any significant increase in its average variable costs and hence in marginal costs. The level of output that represents the full running of the line and thereby the full capacity use of the plant is the result of the technology designed into the facility at the time of its construction or modernization. The firm will have an associated level of overhead or fixed costs which will be reduced on a per unit basis as these costs are spread over a larger volume of output when the production line is more fully operative.

But let us consider a firm having many plants or production lines at its disposal which represent its productive capacity; it can then vary its output over the short term, i.e. in response to business cycle conditions, by starting up or shutting down entire production lines (or plants) with essentially constant marginal costs, and all the more so if we reckon these plants as being duplicates of one another in that they are all of the same technology. Yet it can do this because it is to be expected that as a matter of policy these 'large' firms will always maintain a degree of reserve capacity likely consisting of plants with built-in older technology requiring a greater amount of variable costs. Presumably these older 'vintage' plants would have been the first to be shut down during a downturn in demand; but they do afford the firm the opportunity to quickly take advantage of an upturn in business, perhaps effectively closing off the opportunity of new firms entering the industry to take up the unsatisfied demand that might otherwise arise. In bringing this vintage capacity on line the firm will experience some increase in average variable or direct costs; but this will in all likelihood be overbalanced by the continued decline in overhead costs per unit, so that overall we can expect to see a constant decline in average total costs as more capacity becomes operative. Again, it is important to keep in mind that each productive unit, i.e. each plant, embodies in the form of its fixed set of input coefficients, the least cost technology of its time.

An additional point here is that the firm will accumulate inventories when sales are below output rather than engage in price cutting. This provides a further means to respond quickly to a sales upturn; it is generally a matter of policy for the firm to use inventories to bridge the gap between sales and production as a first response before activating an additional production line. We have another reason why increases in demand will not, at least over the short horizon, translate into higher costs and hence higher prices given the values of the wage rate and the rate of profit. But even if the firm does activate additional capacity it will not be subject to pressure on the cost side as unit variable costs do not depend on the degree of capacity utilization.

Generally prices will then remain unchanged given the values of the distributive variables and the techniques of production; which brings up the need to understand the response mechanism on the part of the firm when faced with changes in the wage rate, and when confronted with the longer term need to add to its capacity so as to keep pace with its projected secular growth in sales.

We talk about a 'firm' and about a 'price policy' which puts us in a world apart from the usual neoclassical environment where we envision many small individually owned enterprises; and where it is easy to think in terms of the lone entrepreneur's decision maker concerned essentially with the objective of profit maximization or loss minimization with his decisions having no impact beyond his immediate world. We recognize this pure competitive model is usually placed first in the line of models purporting to explain the real world and which is considered as the 'ideal' or 'norm' against which industrial structures can be compared and evaluated. However, the post-Keynesian attitude in its micro dealings is to start with 'what is' if it is to provide a realistic useful model of firm behavior. And what exists and is predominant in the economy are large corporate structures most likely multinational in scope and where decisions flow from an organizational set-up rather than from an individual — and where decisions have ramifications beyond the firm itself. These decisions involve more than what to produce and what price to charge; they involve the perhaps more important determination of how much to invest and how best to finance that investment. Indeed the decision regarding what price to set is more closely tied to the investment decision than to how much to produce. Furthermore, it is through the ability to set and to change prices that the decision of the firm affects the real wage, and thereby the amount of real resources devoted to current consumption, so that the system has the resources available to support the capital accumulation in line with the investment plans of firms. This is another way of stressing that the results of the pricing decision must be understood in terms of the broader impact on accumulation of capital and growth.

The term used to designate this firm in the real microanalysis is the "megacorp"; and it would be helpful to set out some of the goals of such an organization to appreciate how different matters are from the firm of conventional neoclassical analysis. A primary goal of the corporation is the expansion of its operations at the highest possible growth rate as measured by cash flow and/or volume of sales; and as well to meet a target rate of return on investment. To bring this about it will strive to maintain its existing market share in those product lines (industries) where sales are growing at a pace at least equal to that of the overall economy, and to leave or reduce those lines on which the sales growth is insufficient or where the rate of profit is below that set for the firm in general. Decisions are made through a managerial hierarchy, and they deal with setting a target rate of return, the investment projects to be included in the annual capital budget, the setting of prices, changes in the amount of external debt and the annual additions (if any) to payouts such as dividends, salaries and wages. And as the megacorp considers these matters, we reiterate that it is looking at multiple plants or production lines in the output of each of the products it is engaged in. Its plants are situated in various parts of the country if not globally so that its decisions have wide impact; and its costs, as it varies the operation of these production lines, can be significantly effected due to the variability of the technology in its multiple operations. Thus in looking at the world as it is, one has to reckon that the decisions taken at the 'firm' level regarding such matters as investment, pricing and production levels will have a major impact on the economy as a whole.

There is another characteristic that should be mentioned that further differentiates this organization from what is normally thought of as the firm; and that is considerable separation of control or management from ownership, with the former depending on the executive position within the hierarchy rather than on equity holdings. We are accustomed to think in terms of a profit-maximizing strategy as the objective of the firm; and while the shareholders fare best under this strategy, the managers may have other objectives such as growth of the organization. The growth rate chosen by managers may not be what the shareholders would most desire with the result of lowering the market value of the shares of the firm. For example, management may decide to increase capacity and to finance this essentially from internally generated funds by paying out less dividends than the owners would like with the result of lowering the firm's valuation ratio, that is, the value of the shares to that of the assets of the firm. And this 'pay-out' ratio, that of dividends to profits, will then have an impact on aggregate savings. But we do not want to get too far afield here; we want to conceptualize the producing unit in a far different way than the firm in the usual mode of neoclassical analysis. In general then what we have is an economy which, in Sraffian terms, we want to conceive of as set of interdependent sectors predominantly oligopolistic in nature; we need to get away from a thought process based on large numbers of enterprises competing in atomistic markets.

The firm can set and maintain a price over time that is consistent with its objectives. It is a price that results from applying a certain margin or mark-up above average costs of production calculated to yield profits at the ruling rate on the capital invested, so that prices in each of the sectors are seller-determined rather than the firms being 'price takers' in the jargon of the usual competitive setting. The organization can be expected to maintain the markup over a period of time that it views as a short-term pricing period which can be considered as a span over which the firm maintains its productive capacity. If within this time frame average costs increase, prices will change by applying the existing markup to the higher costs to arrive at a new list price, thereby maintaining the average cash flow deemed necessary. Over this decision period which it will be helpful to think of in terms of a business cycle, prices are generally determined by average costs which depend essentially on what is happening to unit labor costs which in turn reflect the growth in money wages relative to that of output per worker. Also, some raw material prices are a factor and these will depend on commodity prices (those Sraffian basic goods) and the production technology reflecting the interdependence of the megacorp.

Over the longer term, going beyond any one business cycle, the consideration is a change in the set price resulting from a decision to alter the markup in order to generate investment funds to construct new capacity, owing to the increase in the size of the market reflecting the secular growth in output per capita. Indeed, it is the secular growth in real income that, because of its impact on aggregate demand provides the essential thrust for the firm's expansion. One of the objectives of the organization is not to lose market share over time. The decision in the light of this consideration concerns what change, if any, in the size of the markup is optimal; for the setting of the markup will depend on the demand for these investment funds relative to the cost of generating them internally rather than externally, i.e. borrowing.

What are some of the costs of raising the required funds internally? There is the need to consider the possible long term loss of sales as determined by the price elasticity of demand — what we can term as the substitution effect. In addition one must consider the likelihood of attracting new firms or having existing firms emulating the product as the margin increases, with the loss of hard-earned market share — the megacorp must be aware of the 'entry' factor. And thirdly there is the possibility of triggering government intervention if the firm excessively stretches the margin above costs. These three types of costs should the megacorp decide to increase the size of the markup can be converted into an implicit interest rate; each cost can then be related to a discount formula that will yield the long-term expected reduction in cash flow. The smaller the implicit interest rate the greater the gain via internally generating funds relative to external borrowing. The organization comes up with a supply curve for internally generated funds that is compared with the demand for these funds based on the expected rate of return on the various projects in the capital budget.[18]

In general, over the short run, the assumption is that of a rather stable markup with the list price affected by the change in average costs; in the longer period the markup itself is variable as determined by the requirements for additional investment funds. An expected rate of capacity utilization is a basis for estimating unit costs upon which the margin is figured to generate the cash flow. However, should the utilization rate increase it may very well prompt higher levels of planned investment which itself can be expected to result in a higher markup.

The pricing equation for this cost-plus approach will contain a markup (m) that may be viewed as the excess of price over unit variable (prime) costs which yields an average cash flow sufficient to cover overhead costs and result in a profit per unit of output. The (m) is simply seen as a proportion of unit prime costs. Thus:

$$mu = p - u$$

or

$$m = \frac{p - u}{u} \tag{72}$$

$$
\begin{aligned}
m &= \text{markup} \\
u &= \text{unit prime cost} \\
p &= \text{the firm's price}
\end{aligned}
$$

The share of gross profits in the price is a reflection of the markup which is a proxy for what is at times referred to as the gross profit margin; indeed the former can be written as a function of the latter. A simple example will do. Suppose we have unit prime costs of 10.00 and a gross profit margin of 5%, the selling price reflecting this margin will read:

$$p = 1.05(10.00)$$

$$= 10.50 \qquad (73)$$

The share of gross profits is 5%, and the greater this share the greater the percentage markup on costs or that of the profit margin. We have the share of profits (θ) as:

$$\theta = \frac{m}{1+m}$$

so

$$m = \theta + \theta m \qquad (74)$$

or

$$m = \frac{\theta}{1-\theta}$$

$$= \frac{.05}{.95} = .05$$

A variation of the pricing mechanism, and one that may be more recognizable, is to place the markup on the full costs per unit (direct plus overhead cost). We have:

$$p = (1 + m')C \qquad (75)$$

Yet the full cost (C) pricing equation cannot be specified unless we designate the level of output since unit costs will vary with production levels. There have been various suggestions as to what level of output should be put into the equation. One suggestion is to base costs on expected levels of output perhaps equal to the immediate past level which, for given direct unit costs, will have prices fall up to a full capacity output; if expectations carry production beyond this point higher prices will in all likelihood result via a higher markup. With this approach prices would change as a function of expected output levels, but the tie-in here is certainly far removed from neoclassical reasoning. Another suggestion is to presume — perhaps as a first approximation — that firms are operating at their notion of full capacity (implying a certain reserve capacity) and have prices essentially depend on unit labor costs.

However we may want to consider the pricing equation, the ability of the organization to set and maintain the markup depends on what Kalecki refers to as the "degree of monopoly".[19] It is a term which can be used to group those influences that comprise the implicit rate factor which plays on the firm's markup policy. We will look at some particulars of Kalecki's work dealing with his price equation and the connection between price setting and income distribution (this latter connection to be studied in the following chapter). But at this point we illustrate the post-Keynesian description of the firm's price and cost curves in Fig. (6.1).

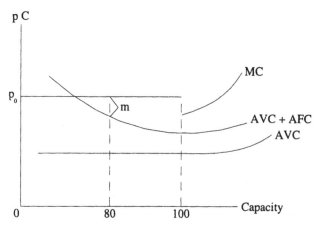

Figure 6.1

What we called the gross profit margin resulting from a markup that sets the price at p_o with 'full' (80%) capacity operating, is the difference between p_o and the direct costs per unit. A net profit margin would emerge if we consider the markup being placed on the full costs per unit; so that the price per unit or the average cash flow (AFC) is equal to the full costs per unit plus the markup on those costs.

With Fig. (6.1) we can see that an important decision of the organization is whether to shift the price line; and as we indicated that would depend on whether or not there has been an increase in the costs of production since the last price review. As Eichner points out, "it can be assumed that, at the very least, the firms in the industry will attempt to offset any rise in costs by an upward shift in the price line in order to preserve the existing markups".[20] But there is always the possibility of increasing the markup, certainly in response, as we made mention, to the longer range considerations of additions to productive capacity; but perhaps as well, in response to cost changes. The essential question is whether the existing markup, let us say the profit margin, is the proper one to have been set for existing conditions, and if increases are to be considered what change in the markup would be optimal? This question is a proper lead-in to the Kalecki pricing equation which overtly tries to account for the relative power of the organization in setting prices. What Kalecki tries to do is to capture the interdependence of firms in the pricing decision and in the same equation account for the particular influence of any singular firm.

To take account of this Kalecki tells us that:

> In fixing the price the firm takes into consideration its average prime costs and the prices of other firms producing similar products. The firm must make sure that the price does not become too high in relation to prices of other firms, for this would drastically reduce sales, and that the price does not become too low in relation to its average prime cost, for this would drastically reduce the profit margin. Thus, when the price p is determined by the firm in relation to unit prime costs u, care it taken that the ratio p to the weighted average price of all firms $\bar{p}$ does not become too high.[21]

These considerations are set out in his equation of:

$$p = ku + n\bar{p} \tag{76}$$

where k and n are positive coefficients of $k > 1$ and $n < 1$. The markup on prime costs using this equation is:

$$m = \frac{p-u}{u} = \frac{ku - u + n\bar{p}}{u}$$

$$= k - 1 + \frac{n\bar{p}}{u} \tag{77}$$

259

The values of the two parameters (k) and (n) reflect Kalecki's degree of monopoly for the individual firm, and he combines these into a single measure $k/1-n$.

Suppose a firm that produces a substantial share of a sector's output decides to increase its markup on unit prime costs. The higher markup and resulting price by this firm greatly influences the average price $(\bar{p})$ for the aggregate sector's output; and the other firms not wanting to be out of step with the average price, which in essence is with that of the lead firm, will adopt the same pricing policy. The firm in question has a degree of monopoly allowing it to confidently raise price by increasing the markup — its (k) parameter is appropriably greater than one. A 'follower' firm would exist with a smaller (k) and larger n (though less than one) and hence with lesser tendency to raise its price via markup changes in any given situation.

We are assuming no price collusion among the megacorps; it is then more likely for a firm to raise its price if other firms follow its actions which stem from a sort of automatic response on the part of other firms to the average sector price. But the other firms may follow (and thus seem to possess a smaller degree of monopoly) for reasons of fearing to start a price war, or because they have a similar view of the profit potential of the higher markup. It is too simple to say that "the other firms will be pushed in the same direction because their price formation depends on the average price".[22] Again, while the leader greatly influences the average price, its price is not the average price nor is that of any other singular firm; the degree of monopoly in this sense is a reflection of the firm's ability to influence the average price — indeed Kalecki deduces that (n) must be less than one from the observation that should a firm's price be equal to the average price equation (76) then:

$$p=ku+np \tag{78}$$

and (n) must be less than unity for the firm to possess some arbitrary power in marking up its units costs.

But this does not have to be the case. What if the sectors, whether by covert agreement or precedent, had a distinct price leader price/follower situation. All firms maintain the price set by the leader which makes all prices equal to the average price resulting in $n=1$ and reducing (k) to zero — the firm has no power to independently set its profit margin. The ratio of income to prime costs for a follower would be equal to the ratio of the existing sector price to its unit prime costs. Of course, for the price leader the (n) parameter is zero since it determines the average price, and the question now is what factors is this particular firm considering in determining the markup and what it considers an appropriate rate of return on its capital. There are complications in trying to stipulate an exact formulation of pricing within oligopolistic structures; one can bring in a degree of product differentiation which may then allow the follower to depart from the leader price by some acceptable difference. Perhaps the best way to appreciate Kalecki's "degree of monopoly" term is not via its application to the individual firm acting independently, but to relate it to the industry as a whole where firms are interdependently situated, as the ability of the industry to protect the rate of profit of its established firms.

Overall, prices in the economy are generally arrived at by marking up unit prime costs and, as we indicated, we may consider these markups as stable in the face of changes in demand as it impacts on plant utilization over a range of output.

These prices are what we previously considered as those day-to-day prices and it bears emphasizing that they are not 'clearing' prices in the sense of intending to equate supply with demand; they are cost based intending to yield a certain rate of return. We have relative prices at a point in time that are akin to those long-run classical natural prices determined by costs of production. It is not a matter of the 'market' price (it is more appropriate to use the term short-term) deviating from the natural price; there is no difference between these terms when we think of the natural price as one that maintains a particular rate of profit under existing technical and demand conditions. The market price is now the determined markup price set by the seller to yield a profit which is believed desirable given the productive capacity on hand and an expected 'normal' range of output.

We can now see how demand fits into the picture; and it does play a part in the 'strategic' role of causing a shift in resources between sectors and not as an instrumental to cause prices to adjust so as to clear markets. And this is due to the observation that, in general, fluctuations in demand do not play a direct role in price determination. Should a change in demand cause the megacorp to see the need to increase capacity, it may very well increase its selling price via a higher markup so as to generate the required funds to finance the project. In this way, the set price and higher profits reflect future need; and we can say that the 'market' price exceeds the previously considered natural price (i.e. that previous market price that provided a particular level of profits) which will draw additional capacity to the sector. This additional capacity in response to the higher profit rate is, of course, not drawn in the form of new firms entering the sector, but in the form of existing firms 'enlarging' themselves (which could at these higher prices mean the reopening of high cost based capacity).

The story is similar to the classical relationship between the short-term market price and the long-term natural price reflective of the continuous changes in demand and rates of profit between sectors. The classicists were clear about the stability of relative prices over the longer term as being reflective of stability of demand patterns and the uniform profit principle. Well, in a modern context we can conceive of a long-term set of relative sector prices reflective of mark-up patterns that yield uniform rates of profit; the image being is of an economy progressing with demand patterns and cost conditions as given parameters. The reader may want to revisit Chapter 2 to recall the forces that are indeed constantly changing these patterns of demand, and so the continuous reality of changing markup-determined prices. Though, to reiterate, the demand change is to be thought of as a longer term capacity adjustment phenomenon.

NOTES

1. Karl Marx, *Capital*, The Modern Library Edition, p. 206.

2. Dividing equation (3) by (α) yields:

$$K = \alpha K w + \frac{\alpha \bar{K} \bar{p}}{\alpha}$$

or

$$K = L^D w + \frac{L^D \bar{p}}{\alpha}$$

and

$$L^D = \frac{K}{w + \dfrac{\bar{p}}{\alpha}}$$

3. Robert V. Eagly, *The Structure of Classical Economic Theory*, Oxford University Press, London, 1974, p. 39.

4. In the analysis of the determination of prices, land was relegated by the classicists to a position of secondary importance. The Ricardian theories of rent in fact eliminated rent completely from a determination of prices; thus we are going to assume that all of the surplus goes to the capitalist, and we are then concerned with a single 'dominating' class in society.

5. David Ricardo, *The Principle of Political Economy*, E. P. Dutton, New York (reprinted 1957), p. 48.

6. Ibid., p. 50.

7. The essential reference being Piero Sraffa, *Production of Commodities by Means of Commodities*, Cambridge University Press, Cambridge, 1960.

8. Sraffa, "The Laws of Return Under Competitive Conditions," *Economic Journal*, 1926, XXXVI. Reprinted in *Readings in Price Theory*, Allen and Unwin, London, 1953, p. 182.

9. Joan Robinson, "Rising Supply Price," *Economics*, Vol. VIII, 1947. Reprinted in *Readings* (Ibid.), p. 223.

10. Alfred Marshall, *Industry and Trade*, 1919, p. 188, as quoted in A. Roncoglia, Sraffa and the Theory of Prices, John Wiley, New York, 1978.

11. Sraffa, "The Laws of Return Under Competitive Conditions," op. cit., p. 184.

12. Alessandro Roncoglia, *Sraffa and the Theory of Prices*, John Wiley, New York, 1978, p. 12.

13. We use the numbers set out by Ronald L. Meek, "Mr. Sraffa's Rehabilitation of Classical Economics," *Scottish Journal of Political Economy*, 1961, VIII.

14. Ibid.

15. With this example we are in effect back to the second of Sraffa's cases with wages being part of the material input, but with the general rate of profit being overtly expressed as part of the value of output.

16. Sraffa, *Production of Commodities*, op. cit., p. 15.

17. Ibid., p. 23.

18. For more detail, see the discussions in Alfred S. Eichner, *Toward a New Economics*, M. E. Sharpe, Armonk, New York, 1985. also the analysis in Stanley Bober, *Pricing and Growth*, M. E. Sharpe, Armonk, New York, 1992.

19. See M. Kalecki, *Theory of Economic Dynamics*, Rinehart, New York, 1954. Also, "The Class Struggle and the Distribution of Income", *Kyklos*, Vol. 24. an expository analysis is to be found in Bober, op. cit.

20. Eichner, op. cit., p. 37.

21. Kalecki, *Theory*, p. 12.

22. A. Asimakopulos, "A Kaleckian Theory of Income Distribution," *Canadian Journal of Economics*, 8.

7 An overall view

Introduction

We now pull together our analyses to forge a somewhat unified picture of the driving forces of the growing economy. First to reiterate a point: Post-Keynesians view the constituencies of the system in terms of class relations with regard to the essential task performed by each classification. We begin by drawing out the link between the distribution of income and the 'activity' of the economic class (a very much Ricardian-Marxian view). It is not the isolated economic agent that is the principle variable of post-Keynesian analysis.

Let us consider the determination of profits in a simple model of a closed economy and excluding a government sector and tax considerations or, if we assume that they exist, we would take them to be very negligible. The GNP will thus be equal to the sum of consumption and gross investment (in fixed capital and inventories); with the value of this product, i.e. the national income, divided between workers and capitalists. The former income consisting of wages and salaries, and the latter being gross profits which includes depreciation, undistributed profits, dividends, interest and rent. This gives us a balance sheet of the GNP in which we distinguish between workers' consumption and capitalists' consumption.

$$\text{GNP} = \text{Gross profits} + \text{Wages and Salaries}$$
$$\text{GNP} = \text{Gross investment} + \text{capitalists' consumption} \quad (1)$$
$$+ \text{Workers' consumption}$$

Assuming that workers do no saving, then wages and salaries are equal to workers' consumption and gross profits are equal to capitalists expenditures consisting of capitalists' consumption and gross investment. So:

$$P = K_C + I \tag{2}$$

P = Gross profits

K_C = Capitalists' consumption

I = Gross Investment

And Kalecki, whose analysis we are following, then asks a question concerning the significance of equation (2). "Does it mean that profits in a given period determine capitalists' consumption and investment or the reverse of this?".[1] We see a relation between what capitalists do (their essential task being the accumulation of capital and investment) and what they earn, but which is the driving force? The answer depends on which side of equation (2) is directly subject to the decision of capitalists. Certainly capitalists (and here we really mean the megacorp) can decide to invest more in any period than the preceding one which will then determine profits, but they cannot initially decide to earn more profits. It is the spending decision that determines profits and not vice versa. Again, if workers spend all of their income, then their wages must be equal to the value of workers' consumption goods produced. And this means that the income of the other class of persons, i.e. capitalists, will be equal to the value of goods purchased by them which essentially is that of investment goods, in keeping with their role in the system.

By increasing the amount spent on investment capitalists will raise the level of national income, but they will also increase their share of this higher level of output. Yet even if capitalists consume their income (profit) rather than invest it, they would still cause their income to be equal to the value of the goods purchased by them. The profit of the capitalist is maintained independently of how they exercise their spending; this thought is summed up by the Kaleckian adage that capitalists get what they spend while workers spend what they get. But we will need to modify this rather extreme but useful first approximation.

For more clarification, we can break this aggregative relationship into a three sector look. We postulate a sector (1) producing capital goods, a sector (2) producing consumption (luxury) goods of capitalists, and a sector (3) producing workers' consumption goods. The sector (3) will sell a value of its output equal to all of the workers' income in all three sectors; thus we can picture sector (3) as selling a portion of its production equal to its payment of wages, with the remainder being sold to the workers in sectors (1) and (2), so that this remainder constitutes the gross profit of sector (3) equal to the wages paid in the other two sectors. Thus total profits will be equal to the wages in (1) and (2) plus the sum of profits in these sectors; but this latter sum is equal to the value of capitalist goods sales in sectors (1) and (2) minus their wages which make up the profit of sector (3). So that given wages total profits become equal to the value of production of sectors (1) and (2).

Furthermore, should we presume that the distribution between profits and wages is given for the entire system, then we have a relation between the output in (3) and total employment and production in the capital goods sectors. Employment in the workers' sector will be increased to the point of being equal to the wages of sectors (1) and (2); or as Kalecki puts it, "....employment and production of department III will be pushed up to the point where the surplus of this production over what the workers of this department buy with their wages is equal to the wages of department I and II".[2] Thus the 'activity' of the capitalist class essentially that of sector (1) determines total employment as well as profits.

We can presume that capitalists' expenditures in a particular period are influenced by past decisions that determined the level of profits in the preceding period; but past profits are not the sole determinant of current spending for if this were so then profits would be unchanged from period to period. The fact that profits fluctuate in time clearly attests to the fact that capitalists in general in a particular period do not spend exactly what they have earned in the preceding one. Certainly past investment spending will not be a good indication of such expenditures in the current period if in the past such a decision let to an unintended disaccumulation of inventories; the fact of actual sales exceeding expected sales may prompt the firm to undertake current expenditures in excess of past earnings; and the reverse holds as well.

Given that profits are determined by the value of capitalists' spending, then it is workers' income that is likely determined by the institutional setting within which the bargaining (conflict) between labor and capital takes place, as well as the 'degree of monopoly' which reflects the overall mark-up price-setting capability that feeds back to the system in terms of the share of profits in output and subsequent capitalists' expenditures. Thus the spending on the part of capitalists as it impacts on employment cojointly with the bargaining outcome between employers and labor determine wages and thereby workers' consumption which together with the activity of the capitalist class give us the level of the national output and employment. What we are getting at is the determination of a real wage rate that gives a particular level of employment and output (given the methods of production); and profits out of this level of output will be equal to the level of capitalists' investment and consumption spending.

269

Let us collapse our depiction of the system into two sectors, with one producing all the consumption goods and the other the investment goods; and then, in a Sraffian manner, relate the flow of income and goods between them. This will make it easier to see the two related phenomena that need to be tracked simultaneously if we are to realistically understand the economy. Given a level of capital goods output we determine a level of employment in this sector and as a residual level of employment in the consumption goods sector. Then with given employment and the technical conditions of production (i.e. those interconnecting inputs) we determine aggregate output. The output in the consumption goods sector will be equal to the wage bill in both sectors. Thus the value of sales in this sector will exceed its wage costs by the amount equal to the wage bill in the capital goods sector; this difference is the profit (gross profits here being the difference between income and labor costs) which provides the funds this sector needs to purchase the capital goods for production.

The investment goods sector will 'purchase' a value of its own output equal to its own level of profits which is equal to the sale of capital goods to the consumption sector minus its own labor costs. Hence the total profits in both sectors must be equal to the value of capital goods produced and sold (capitalists' expenditures) while the real value of wages must equal the amount of wage goods produced. This scenario reflecting the extreme case where capitalists save and invest all and workers consume all. But what this does is highlight the relationship that the division of the national income between profit and wage shares is mirrored in the division of the national output between consumption and investment goods — these must be tracked simultaneously.

Thus a higher proportion of investment goods in total output will reflect a higher share of profits in total income relative to that of wages. A desirable growth rate of the economy with regard, say, to its impact on employment, will require a particular rate of investment which we now see as necessitating a particular 'allotment' of output going to consumption goods production and a level of wages in the national income. The level of profits in both sectors (both goods being produced under the megacorp set-up) result from the mark-up policies of firms; and it is via this capability that real wages are adjusted to 'release' the level of profits to sustain the required capital accumulation and aggregate employment levels. We reiterate the point made earlier that it is the activity of the capitalist class that determines total employment and profits. Our whole thinking here assumes, of course, a negligible government sector in the economy.

Employment is determined by technical conditions and the level of investment expenditures which are essentially influenced by past earnings that are themselves greatly the result of the control over prices. So we have a relationship running from the ability to determine prices which, when combined with the level of investment and consumption expenditures will then give total incomes which, for given wages, will give capitalists profits. Thus the post-Keynesian (Kaleckian) analysis emphasizes the reality of the influence of prices on investment and, as we will point up more concretely, the influence of prices on savings; since savings, at least under the assumptions of our discussion to this point, flow from profits. As gross profits are equal to capitalists consumption and investment expenditures, then by deducting consumption from both sides we have savings equal to gross investments. This approach does embody the 'traditional' Keynesian savings-investment equality, but savings are seen as specifically accruing to profits as a result of changes in the rate of investment. The reality is to run the line of reasoning from investment to profits (as the real wage is concomitantly determined) to savings and then again to expenditures and output and employment. This brings to the fore the elements of income distribution and the role of economic classes upon which one bases a realistic understanding of the driving forces of the system. These elements are not explicitly considered in the usual mode of thinking that runs from expenditures to output.

The following diagram presents this distributional approach.

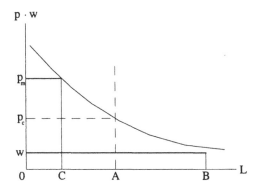

Figure 7.1

On the vertical we have prices and wages and on the horizontal axis total employment in the consumption and investment goods sectors. The full-

271

capacity operation and related employment level in the consumption goods sector is given by OA (production is carried on under modern conditions of constant marginal costs up to capacity). Investment in real terms is given for both sectors which results in a particular level of output in the capital goods sector and associated level of employment AB. It is the full-capacity operation of the consumption sector that determines employment not only in its own sector but as well in the capital goods sector (given the conditions of production and interrelatedness of sectors).

Now consider a competitively determined price (p_c) that results in a real wage rate such that demand and output in the consumption goods sector is carried to the capacity level. At this level the consumption sector is absorbing the output of the capital sector; for the determined level of employment in the capital sector, the profits in the consumption sector will be equal to the consumption expenditure on the part of workers in the capital sector (the assumption that workers spend all they earn). For a level of employment in the consumption sector, this sector will recover its costs as a result of expenditures on the part of its workers. We find a profit curve PP that reveals the level of profits in the consumption sector equal to $(w \cdot AB)$; i.e. equal to the level of employment in the capital sector times the money wage. But this profit level is the result of a real wage that results in OA employment of the labor force and associated AB employment in the capital goods sector. Profits in the capital sector is equal to the sale of capital goods minus its own labor costs which constitutes the consumption sector profits and hence the latter's expenditures on capital goods.

However, if, as in the real world, we generally are looking at administered prices, we find a price (p_m) and a lower real wage. The result is a lower level of production and employment in the consumption sector (employment falls from OA to OC). Profit levels in the consumption sector remain unchanged due to the higher amount of profit per worker (that of wp_m) for a smaller level of employment. Thus the higher mark-up price maintains the same level of expenditures and profits in the face of a decline in demand. But the smaller level of consumption goods output translates into a smaller level of employment in the capital sector as a result of a smaller capital expenditure in real terms due to excess capacity in the final goods sector. Whether a reduction in the real wage transfers an increased profit level to the capitalist and results, perhaps, in a higher level of investment, depends to a degree on the impact of this reduction on employment and demand. In any event, we come to appreciate the connection between the flow of income in a distributive

272

sense and the flow of output between 'types' of goods which relates to the price policy of firms and resulting real wage. It is via the pricing policy that real wages are adjusted to release the level of resources necessary to sustain a 'desirable' rate of capital accumulation. Thus we have the instrumental micro-considerations for the realism of post-Keynesian macroeconomics.

Further analysis - the Kaldor Model[3]

The connection to levels of investment from the real wage comes via the distribution of income through savings. We now set up a savings function that links savings to categories of income and respective savings propensities; and as a first look presume that these categories of income (profit and wages) flow to particular categories of people — hence workers receive no part of profits. Thus:

$$S = S_W + S_P = s_W(W) + s_p(P) \tag{3}$$

and

$$Y = W + P \tag{4}$$

$$S = s_W(Y - P) + s_p(P) \tag{5}$$

$$= (s_p - s_W)P + s_W(Y) \tag{6}$$

Where: S_W is the total savings from the wage bill, and S_P the total savings from profits. s_W and s_p are the respective marginal (= average) propensities to save. Also the assumption $1 > s_p > s_W > 0$.

From (6) we first obtain a savings ratio as:

$$\frac{S}{Y} = (s_p - s_W)\frac{P}{Y} + s_W \tag{7}$$

assuming the extreme Kaleckian case of 'classical thriftiness' where the propensity to save capitalists is equal to unity, serves to highlight their essential role as accumulators of capital. Thus the relation between investment $(= S)$ and profits becomes:

273

$$I = s_P(P) \qquad (8)$$

$$P = \frac{1}{s_P}(I) \qquad (9)$$

And with $s_P = 1$ we have:

$$P = I \qquad (10)$$

which gives us the distributional result of Kalecki's analysis that capitalists get what they spend — and here equal to their investment expenditures. But capitalists do spend a portion of their profit income on consumption goods ($s_P < 1$) which increases the level of profits in the consumption goods sector, a portion of which comes back to the capital sector; total profits being equal to the total value of capitalists' expenditures for both consumption and capital goods. A look at equation (9) reveals ($1/s_P$) to be a multiplier relating profits to investment; the lower the (s_P) the greater the multiplier and the level of profits. Recalling equation (2) we read that gross profits are equal to gross investment plus capitalist consumption. One can, from equation (2), state this relation as:

$$\frac{K_C + I}{P} \equiv 1 - s_P \qquad (11)$$

We want to arrive at the important distributive results from the less restrictive framework of equations 3 - 6. Using equation (6) and relating to the Keynesian savings-investment equality we have:

$$I = (s_P - s_W)P + s_W(Y) \qquad (12)$$

which, upon dividing through by (Y) yields:

$$\frac{P}{Y} = \frac{1}{s_P - s_W}\left(\frac{I}{Y}\right) - \frac{s_W}{s_P - s_W} \qquad (13)$$

The level of profits, as distinct from the ratio of profits to income, can be obtained from (5) as:

$$I = s_W(Y - P) + s_P(P) \qquad (14)$$

then:

$$P(s_P - s_W) = I - s_W(Y) \tag{15}$$

$$P = \frac{1}{s_P - s_W}(I) - \frac{s_W}{s_P - s_W}(Y) \tag{16}$$

from which one comes to (13) via division by (Y).

What is Keynesian about these outcomes is the independent and active role of investment; what is not Keynesian is that the static point-in-time equality of investment and savings is now accounted for by a particular distribution of income that yields the appropriate level of savings to accommodate the investment expenditure — one should no longer relate savings to a notion of aggregate income. Should we presume $s_W = 0$, then it is the level of profits that is strategic implying the existence of a real wage rate reflective of a related 'pricing policy'. But while this may not be overtly Keynesian, it is very much 'traditional', taking us back to the classicals who tied the growth of the economy to the role of different classes of people in society.

And, as we have mentioned, post-Keynesians tie their analyses to classical roots, so their essential framework is the movement of the economy over time, i.e. economic growth. One can then begin with a 'dynamization' of Keynes into a moving equilibrium mode of which the Harrod-Domar models of balanced growth served as good beginning examples but 'incomplete' in the light of later analysis. They served to refocus attention back to the long-term, and of necessity offered an explanation (certainly Harrod) for the change in the level of investment itself drawn from the behavior of the economy. We could use the Harrod-Domar approach as basis for 'factoring-in' some of the recent developments and thereby try to get a more complete picture of the various balances needed to maintain growth equilibrium.

While we are interested in structuring the long-term movement of the economy, the actual course of events is marked by the shorter-term cyclical change. Post-Keynesians would hold that while both types of movement are integrated and need to be looked at co-jointly, it is the underlying growth explanation that is paramount. Indeed one is to reckon the business cycle as a deviation from the growth path; we first have to understand the balances that maintain the steady-state condition (as a reasonable approximation of the trend experience) so that we can appreciate what can throw the system off the track and produce the cycle.

But central to the entire approach is that both the secular trend and the fluctuations around the trend can be explained by the same capital accumulation process.

This brings us back to the H-D models where we made the point that it would be quite fortuitous for the economy to be growing at its natural rate since the variables of the propensity to save, the capital to output ratio and the growth of the labor force are given to the system and seemingly independently determined. That is, that:

$$G_w = n = \frac{s}{v} \tag{17}$$

would rule other than by a 'happy accident'.

But in fact there is interdependence here: that the level of savings is connected to the distribution of income which is related to pricing policy and the technique of production which then has bearing on the capital to output ratio. This awareness now offers a solution to the 'bleakness' of the Harrodian 'razor-edge' condition that was discussed in Chapter 5.

We recall from the Harrod analysis that characteristic of the system along the steady-state path is the constancy of the capital to output ratio so we write:

$$G_K = s/v = n \tag{18}$$

as a way to express that desirable growth state. With a little manipulation we can relate the condition of (18) to our distributive savings function. So:

$$s = G_K v \tag{19}$$

and with the savings investment equilibrium we have:

$$s = \frac{S}{Y} = \frac{I}{Y} = G_K v \tag{20}$$

Now taking the extreme Kaldor (Kalecki) formulation that savings are equal to aggregate profits, then:

$$\frac{P}{Y} = \frac{I}{Y} = G_K v$$

$$= G_K(\frac{K}{Y}) \tag{21}$$

And (18) can be seen as:

$$G_K = \frac{\dfrac{P}{Y}}{v} \tag{22}$$

Upon estimating the growth in investment necessary to have the economy grow at the 'natural' rate, we can then bring about the required savings ratio to finance it by changing the profit share. It is not a matter of an accidental alignment of the variables in equation (18), but of an institutional arrangement that yields a value of the savings ratio required to have the economy grow at the full-employment rate. We are aware that the desirable combination of the profit ratio and that of investment to output requires a particular level of the real wage reflecting the 'price policy' of firms and the wage conflict outcome. It is the megacorp firms with their overall impact on the economy that are the prime initiators of investment expenditures based, in one respect, on profit expectations; and it is this spending that determines the change in profits from which the increase in savings comes. Therefore, for a given level of (n) one can reconcile the warranted growth rate of output by choosing the appropriate investment ratio; but what is perhaps more daunting is bringing about a social framework that motivates the undertaking. One could take the requisite investment ratio as an independent variable and construct a link between it and the distribution of income with the rate of growth resulting from this relationship.

The maintenance of economic growth at the natural rate, however, involves more than an independently given ratio of investment to output that is accommodated by a proper level of savings; the rate of growth of capital must be conditioned by the circumstance that the capacity to employ labor should grow at the same rate as the labor supply. One would then need to relate the growth of the capital stock to the growth of technological change; since the latter influences the growth of the labor supply while the former is the prime source that absorbs the supply. With technological change present in the system the growth of the labor supply can be more than that of the labor force. There is more embodied in the natural growth path of the economy than meets the eye with the Harrod formulations.

We obtain a fuller appreciation of the distributive, technological and other considerations as related to the steady-state path by an analysis of the Kaldor growth model; and we reiterate the notion that steady-state is used as an appealing approximation for the long-term reality. Kaldor's theory describes a way in which full-employment may be maintained (and initially we will see this as a point-in-time outcome) in the presence of changes in the investment and savings ratio, with different propensities to save out of profits and wages and with flexible distributive shares. The Kaldor mechanics emphasizes the role of the impact of changes in distribution on the equality of savings and investment. Kaldor considered his approach as 'Keynesian', though he makes the point that "Keynes, as far as I know, was never interested in the problem of distribution as such. One may nevertheless christen a particular theory of distribution as Keynesian if it can be shown to be an application of the specifically Keynesian apparatus of thought and if evidence can be adduced that at some stage in the development of his ideas, Keynes came near to formulating such a theory".[4] Kaldor refers to Keynes' *Treatise on Money* where Keynes came close to formulating a distributive theory and where Keynes regarded capitalists' income as being the result of their expenditure decisions and not the other way around — similar to the work of Kalecki.

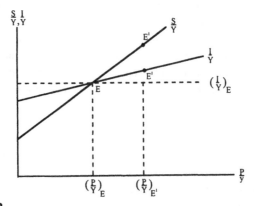

Figure 7.2

In Fig. (7.2) we see the savings and investment ratios plotted against the profit share, and where the stability of equilibrium depends on the effect

278

of a change in the level of output on its distribution. The level of profits at point (E) has to be such as to induce a rate of investment that equates to the rate of savings forthcoming at that particular distribution of income. Fig. (7.2) reveals a different nature of the operation of the accelerator-multiplier mechanism.

The ratio of savings to real output is given by equation (7) which we restate here:

$$\frac{S}{Y} = (s_P - s_W)\frac{P}{Y} + s_W \tag{23}$$

with the Keynesian equality:

$$\frac{I}{Y} = (s_P - s_W)\frac{P}{Y} + s_W \tag{24}$$

However, from the Kaleckian perspective we know to see the equation (24) as:

$$(s_P - s_W)\frac{P}{Y} = \frac{I}{Y} - s_W \tag{25}$$

$$\frac{P}{Y} = \frac{1}{s_P - s_W}(\frac{I}{Y}) - \frac{s_W}{s_P - s_W} \tag{26}$$

Given the wage earners' and capitalists' different propensities to consume, the profit share depends on the ratio of investment to output. It is important to reiterate that the level of profit may be considered as one of several variables inducing a level of capitalists expenditures, it is, therefore, as such, not the determining agent of those expenditures; whereas capitalists spending does determine the level of profits (given the respective savings propensities). We should be clear about what we are looking at in equations (24) and (26).

The next step it seems would be to put through a reasonably specified investment function; and the attempt to do this has been characterized as reminiscent of the search for a 'will-o-the-wisp', yet Kaldor may have close to the essence of the determination of investment expenditures by focusing on two related factors. One is the immediate past experience regarding demand and output expectations which is reflected in the degree of current capacity usage and hence the state of the existing capital to

279

output ratio. And this state will be an influential factor in the determination of desired additional capital in the following period and thereby current investment. There is an expectation of a level of demand in time t; and if we were to assume that capacity utilization in time t is equal to expectations (so that the capital stock in t is equal to the desired stock in $t-1$) then investment in t will be determined, in one respect, by the capital to output ratio in t. Assuming that the expected level of output in t is equal to realized output in $t-1$, then the desired level of capital stock at time t will be a coefficient (α') of the realized level of output in $t-1$. Hence we have a statement for the stock of capital in t as:

$$K_t = \alpha'(Y_{t-1}) \tag{27}$$

In particular, the change in the capital stock from $t-1$ to t is determined by the level of investment in $t-1$ which, to repeat, is governed by the desired capital in t which is itself influenced by the existing capital to output ratio in $t-1$. Assuming that this current ratio is a desired ratio, indicating the correct working out of past expectations, then the stock of capital in t will stand in some relation to realized output in the period before.

Aside from the need to adjust or maintain the capital stock as a determinant of investment, there is also the influence of the rate of profit earned on existing capital in $t-1$. Here we could presume that a higher than expected rate of return would favor still higher expectations as well as provide a greater pool of funds for internal financing of investment. This could induce a greater investment change than would result from the capacity adjusting factor (i.e. output expectations) as such. In modelling investment behavior Kaldor conceives of the rate of capital accumulation as a function of the expected rate of profit, and the current degree of capacity utilization. While these influences are not unrelated, Kaldor postulates the utilization factor as an independent variable to be thought of as not exerting its influence via its impact on the rate of profit — perhaps as a means of highlighting the effect of the acceleration principle. Changes in profits will result from the power of the firm to charge higher prices in relation to costs, and also merely result from variations in the degree of capacity utilization. We then have the influences of income distribution and effective demand on the level of investment; with the former (the profit share) being a function of the mark-up, but not being solely determined by it. The profit share will also vary with short-term fluctuations in the level of output.

Turning to Kaldor's investment structure which can be read to incorporate these influences, thought they may appear somewhat blurred, we find the level of the capital stock in t as:

$$K_t = \alpha'(Y_{t-1}) + \beta'(r_{t-1})Y_{t-1} \tag{28}$$

Stating the levels of capital in terms of looking ahead from t to $t+1$, we have investment in t as:

$$I_t = K_{t-1} - K_t$$

$$= [\alpha' + \beta'(r_t)]Y_t - [\alpha' + \beta'(r_{t-1})]Y_{t-1} \tag{29}$$

$$= \alpha'(Y_t - Y_{t-1}) + \beta' r_t(Y_t) - \beta' r_{t-1}(Y_{t-1}) \tag{30}$$

$$= (Y_t - Y_{t-1})[\alpha' + \beta'(r_{t-1})] + \beta'(r_t - r_{t-1})Y_t \tag{31}$$

$$\alpha' > 0, \beta' > 0$$

Starting from an arbitrary point in time t, there exists a level of capital stock K_t that is a heritage of the past; and assuming a state of full-employment, we can also take as given a level of income and demand which the labor force produces with this level of capital. Assuming that the stock of capital on hand is appropriate to expected output; we can write this state via division of (28) by Y_{t-1} and realizing (27), as:

$$\frac{K_t}{Y_{t-1}} = \alpha' + \beta'(r_{t-1}) \tag{32}$$

And the ratio of investment in (t) to realized income in (t) is then stated as:

$$\frac{I_t}{Y_t} = \frac{Y_t - Y_{t-1}}{Y_t} \cdot \frac{K_t}{Y_{t-1}} + \beta'(r_t - r_{t-1}) \tag{33}$$

but:

281

$$\frac{Y_t-Y_{t-1}}{Y_t}\cdot\frac{K_t}{Y_{t-1}}=\frac{Y_t-Y_{t-1}}{Y_{t-1}}\cdot\frac{K_t}{Y_t} \qquad (34)$$

So we can write equation (33) in terms of an appropriate expression for the rate of growth as:

$$\frac{I_t}{Y_t}=\frac{Y_t-Y_{t-1}}{Y_{t-1}}\cdot\frac{K_t}{Y_t}+\beta'(r_t-r_{t-1}) \qquad (35)$$

Equation (35) reads that the rate of investment in period (t) as a proportion of income in that period "equals the rate of growth of income over the previous period multiplied by the capital/output ratio of the current period plus a term depending on a change in the rate of profit over the previous period".[5] So we have an investment function which makes investment partly a function of the change in output and partly of the change in the rate of profit; and this function can be restated as:

$$\frac{I_t}{Y_t}=[\frac{Y_t-Y_{t-1}}{Y_{t-1}}\cdot\frac{K}{Y}-\beta'r_{t-1}]+\beta'r_t \qquad (36)$$

We relate this investment ratio to that of the savings ratio of equation (7) which we restate here:

$$\frac{S_t}{Y_t}=s_W+(s_P-s_W)\frac{P_t}{Y_t} \qquad (37)$$

With equations (36) and (37) we determine both the distribution and the proportion of income saved and invested at a point in time.

Let us take another look at Fig. (7.2). There is a particular distribution of income that gives rise to a level of savings equal to investment forthcoming at that distribution. The stability of this particular investment ratio comes through variations in the relation between prices and costs. Assume a higher profit share in income at E'; here we find that the investment plans (though higher than at point E) will fall short of the available savings. We have a condition of an insufficiency of demand necessary to sustain the level of output and employment resulting from the E' investment ratio. If the response is a reduction in prices relative to wages, then this reduces profit margins that induces a lower rate of investment and also results in a lower savings ratio. The discrepancy between investment and savings is eliminated through the consequential fall in profits as this fall operates on the level of economic activity. What we find in the upward sloping savings and investment functions is the workings of an 'accelerator-multiplier' mechanism; the accelerator coming into play via a change in investment in response to a change in the profit ratio, with this investment change via the multiplier impacting on the aggregate level of activity. The assumption being that matters would work in the usual Keynesian fashion; that a change in planned investment in response to a distributional change would cause economic activity to move in the same direction.

On the left-side of E' we find a distribution of income such that the level of investment exceeds the corresponding level of savings. Demand conditions are such that prices will rise in relation to costs with the consequent increase in profit margins. As we can observe, this induces an increase in the investment ratio that is less than that of savings thereby reducing the further tendency towards higher profit shares. Point E is a stable condition given that the slope of the S/Y function exceeds that of I/Y which implies that:

$$s_P - s_W > \beta'(\frac{Y}{K}) \tag{38}$$

telling us that starting from a point to the left of E the rise in prices and profits cannot be cumulative. If we had the condition of $s_P < s_W$, then a fall in prices resulting in a fall in profits will cause a further fall in demand generating a still further fall in prices and profits and so on.[6]

It bears repeating that we are talking about the stability in the distribution of a level of income, and it is that stability that renders the level of economic activity itself as one of 'equilibrium'. And it matters not whether the level of activity represented by point E is a point-in-time full-employment one or not, on the latter case stability involves Keynesian (effective demand) as well as distributional consideration whereas, in the former, we are dealing with a distribution theory and not with variations in output and employment. Kaldor's approach is to consider the stability outcome of point E as a full-employment condition. There is the assumption of an existing investment to output ratio such as to produce a level of effective demand that fully absorbs a constant labor force at a point in time. The maintenance of this outcome is the result of conditions that adjust the profit ratio to suit the existing level of output and thereby adjust savings to the appropriate investment level. It is the horizontal I/Y line in conjunction with the upward sloping savings ratio that yields the short-term result; and it is quite clear that the distribution of income is the strategic factor. Thus the profit share, the rate of profit and the real wage may all be considered as functions of I/Y which in turn is determined independently of them.

It can perhaps be argued that the main thrust was to structure the conditions of the system's natural growth rate; so that it would be best to begin from a state of full-employment and consider how this state can be maintained in the face of a growing labor force and technological change. But, as a reinforcing argument, perhaps Kaldor suspected that a movement to a full-employment E point may not be achievable via Keynesian forces, that a change in income as well as in its distribution (which is implied in the upward sloping I/Y line) would not result in a change in the level of real economic activity and employment — indeed that the Keynesian multiplier may not work. Thus we have Fig. (7.2) where the equilibrium point seems approachable via a movement along both functions; yet the assumption is that point E (presumed one of full-employment) is not internally generated, but is 'given' to the system in conjunction with the appropriate investment to output ratio that appears invariant to changes in the savings propensities. Kaldor's uncertainty about the effectiveness of the Keynesian tool to increase employment has, as we will see, much to do with the behavior of prices in the face of output changes. Here we will have another occasion to appreciate how macro results cannot be fully reckoned without an awareness of 'micro-foundations' — in essence how prices are determined in the real economy. Let us go through some of this analysis as it bears on the short-run outcome before finally coming to the long-run growth model.

Within the post-Keynesian revision of the megacorp world and mark-up pricing (described in Chapter 6) we could posit that an increase in the investment to output ratio reflects the longer-term consideration to increase capacity and thereby requiring a higher mark-up to generate the necessary finance. Thus we can relate the price level to planned investment expenditures.

$$p = \lambda I \tag{39}$$

A higher rate of investment results in a higher level of gross income and employment and also a higher share of profits in income by increasing prices relative to money wages. Yet prices can increase as a result of higher wage rates; that is, where the higher price results from applying an existing mark-up to a higher unit labor cost in order to maintain the existing cash flow. But if we assume the money wage as given in any short period,

$$w_m = \overline{w}_m \tag{40}$$

then the higher price reflects the 'degree of monopoly' (recalling Kalecki's term) and the firm's longer term needs.

Thus an increase in the investment ratio will see an increase in money profits; however, before we can structure an equation linking profits to investment expenditures that are essentially internally financed, we need a wage bill statement. The simplest way to get at this is to take employment as a function of real output, where the parameter (l) is the constant labor input per unit of output. Thus:

$$L = l(Y) \tag{41}$$

and with the wage rate given we have the wage bill as:

$$W = \overline{w}_m l(Y) \tag{42}$$

Money profits are:

$$P_m = pY - \overline{w}_m L = (\lambda I - \overline{w}_m l) Y \tag{43}$$

To reiterate, higher money profits stem from the increase in the investment ratio that causes both an increase in aggregate demand and prices.

We incorporate our savings function with the extreme assumption of $s_w = 0$, so that money savings (S_m) become:

$$S_m = s_p P_m = s_p (\lambda I - \overline{w}_m l) Y \tag{44}$$

The equilibrium output condition is one where money savings is equal to the value of investment:

$$S_m = pI$$

or

$$s_p(\lambda I - \overline{wl})Y = \lambda I^2 \qquad (45)$$

So that the corresponding level of output (not necessarily one of full employment) is:

$$Y_e = \frac{1}{s_p(\lambda I - \overline{w_m l})Y}(\lambda I^2) \qquad (46)$$

There is a general price level as a consequence of the level of investment which results in a level of profits such that the corresponding level of savings is equal to that of investment expenditures. What is implied is that the higher price level goes along with an increase in aggregate activity, and this results in higher profit levels through which the requisite savings level is generated. But perhaps more fundamentally we read the equilibrium state of (46) in terms of there being a particular balance between money profits and wages such that at the given price level, the real consumption and investment expenditures support the equilibrium level of real output and employment; thus:

$$\frac{W}{p} + \frac{S_m}{p} = I + C \qquad (47)$$

These considerations through the use of equation (46) may give us an insight to Kaldor's uncertainty regarding the change of aggregate activity in response to a change in real investment expenditures; the Keynesian response of both variables moving in the same direction may not hold. If we start from an output level to the left of point E, the system may not be able to attain this full-employment position via the sequence of distributional and activity changes. We want to understand the possibility that:

$$\frac{Y_e}{\Delta I} \lessgtr 0 \qquad (48)$$

real income may in fact fall upon an increase in real investment expenditures.

This could happen if the increase in savings exceeds the increase in investment expenditures that follows a change in the profit ratio. The increase in aggregate demand is insufficient to sustain the higher investment ratio due to the decline in real consumption expenditures that more than compensates for the increase in real investment. The system generates too high a profit ratio; prices have been pushed up excessively relative to money-wage rates, so that investment generates more savings than it requires which, can be seen as having brought about a too low real wage rate. Starting then from a level of economic activity below that of equilibrium, the 'normal' distributive and activity sequence may not move the economy to equilibrium, and if it does there is no reason to presume that the equilibrium condition need be one of full employment. But matters would work out as is normally expected if:

$$\Delta pI > \Delta S_m \qquad (49)$$

which implies that as planned investment expenditures increase, the economy maintains the supportive distribution between profits and wages reflecting a constrained increase in prices as economic activity increases.

We can state this with a bit more precision.[7] Corresponding to each level of investment is a value of this investment $pI(=\lambda I^2)$, so the relation between an increase in investment and that of its value is:

$$\frac{d\lambda I^2}{dI} = 2\lambda I \qquad (50)$$

and

$$d\lambda I^2 = 2\lambda I dI \qquad (51)$$

Related to each level of investment is a savings function with a slope of $s_p(\lambda I - \overline{w_m}l)$; though savings come out of profits, they can be plotted against output via the positive relation between the profit ratio and output. The savings coefficient is weighted by the share of profits in income which is itself influenced by the value of investment. From (44) we have:

$$\frac{dS_m}{dI} = s_p \lambda Y \qquad (52)$$

and

$$dS_m = s_p \lambda Y dI \qquad (53)$$

287

This gives the change in money savings for a given level of real output as investment changes; what we have in this context is that the increase in investment has been canceled out by the decline in planned consumption implying too great an increase in the general price level.

We do want that (Y) increase as (I) increases, i.e. that the increase in savings reflect higher profit levels that go along with greater levels of activity and employment; and for this we need that:

$$\frac{dpI}{dI} > \frac{dS_m}{dI} \tag{54}$$

i.e. $\quad 2\lambda I dI > s_p \lambda Y dI \tag{55}$

or

$$2(I/Y) > s_p \tag{56}$$

But there is nothing inevitable about this outcome. The point is, that with s_p as given, the upward movement in output and employment would depend on the behavior of prices to bring about a 'constrained' increase in the profit share.

It is probably due to this uncertainty that Kaldor chooses to begin with the economy in a short-term state of full-employment; hence, an increase in the investment ratio will not affect employment and output, but it will increase prices and profit margins. This results in a compensatory decline in real consumption with no change in real output — investment generates its appropriate level of savings through flexible profit margins thereby keeping the system stable at full-employment. Since in this scenario changes in investment have no effect on real output levels, then we can take an investment ratio that yields full-employment at (E) in Fig. (7.2) as given and go from there to the long-term. If we relate full-employment to reasonable full-capacity output, then increases in demand via higher investment levels will cause firms to put through higher mark-ups in contemplating the need to add to capacity; while this in the immediate term will increase profits, it will also reduce real wages with its negative impact on real consumption. Under a state of full-employment we can say that the level of prices relative to wages is determined by demand, but only in so far as demand changes impacts on the firm's pricing policy with regard to its long-term financing needs. The mark-up is not to be thought of as explained by short-term demand conditions as emphasized by orthodox pricing models. This could suggest another reason for Kaldor's short-term stance, since flexible profit margins are supposed to be reflective of price changes.

Be that as it may, what is being proposed with an independent ratio of investment to output at full-employment is a different way to reckon the multiplier tool. Here the multiplier is being applied to a relation between prices and wages on the assumption that the level of output and employment are given, rather than the accustomed Keynesian way where the multiplier is applied to a determination of the level of employment on the assumption that the relation between prices and wages is given (but in the usual expositions this proviso is seldom mentioned). Kaldor makes the telling observation, "The reason why the multiplier-analysis has not been developed as a distribution theory is precisely because it was invented for the purpose of an employment theory — to explain why an economic system can remain in equilibrium in a state of under-employment (or of a general under-utilization of resources) where the classical properties of scarcity-economics are inapplicable".[8] Though our feeling in this book is that the inapplicability of scarcity is not as much due to under-employment as it is to the impact of technology change and the diminishment of the notion of fixed resources.

Yet the system's stability at full-employment (i.e. the multiplier-distribution attitude) is itself subject to certain restrictions. The obvious one that we spoke of previously is:

$$s_p \neq s_W \tag{57}$$

$$s_p \succ s_W$$

which prevents cumulative departures in prices and the profit share. Aside from the slopes of the savings and investment functions there is the restriction that the short-term profit ratio determined by the model cannot fall below that level where capitalists lose their incentive to invest; with regard to the megacorp we can think in terms of not realizing that minimum rate of return necessary to remain in a particular line of output. Kaldor refers to this minimum rate as the "risk premium rate" (r^{*}); thus:

$$\frac{P}{Y} = \frac{P}{vY} \geq r^{*} \tag{58}$$

In the event, say, of an unintended inventory accumulation and with capitalists at or near the (r^*) rate, then it is quite likely that the demand problem would be met with a reduction in output and employment; the excess savings would not be reduced via a reduction in prices and profits. It is not profits that bear the brunt of securing the equality of savings and investment but that of income and employment to the point of generating the lower level of sufficient savings. And this, of course, violates a basic premise of our discussion.

There is the further restriction that the real wage be above some minimum (w^*) that we can equate to a 'subsistence' wage bill. This means that the prices can be increased and the equilibrium profit ratio be attained while maintaining the viability of the system — in reality labor could acquiesce to or not be in a strong position to defend against an erosion of the real wage. This restriction can be set out as:

$$\frac{W}{L} \geq w^*$$

$$\frac{P}{Y} \leq \frac{Y - w^*L}{Y} \tag{59}$$

The equilibrium profit ratio will not be greater than the surplus available after payment of the subsistence wage bill. Certainly if it were in less demand conditions would dictate an increase in the price level through which the system extracts the appropriate amount of savings. Given the full-employment level of income there is a maximum acceptable profit ratio that can be extracted from it.

As we turn to the long-run, we are considering a structure that maintains the point-in-time full-employment condition on a continuum through time. This means that the economy is correctly adapting to external forces such as the growth of population and the labor force and the continuous presence of technological change, though it can be argued that the latter factor should not be considered as 'given' to the economy. It is worthwhile here to reiterate some earlier thoughts involved with our discussion of growth models. Post-Keynesian theory is primarily concerned with explaining the long-term historical process of capitalist economics. And the most telling process is one that produces an uneven (cyclical) expansion of the economy over time. While it is true that the reality is the periodic cyclical experience, this process has given rise to a secular growth pattern. Our occupation with steady-state models is a way to capture the relationships that adheres the economy to the long-term growth track — as we have experienced with the analysis of the Harrod-Domar models. However, these models though clearly setting the right frame of mind, do not shed sufficient light on the secular trend as we can now appreciate from our awareness of the pricing and distribution elements as ingredients underpinning the growth process. Kaldor's long-period model opens the way to incorporate these elements and to consider other features of a regularly growing economy. We can perhaps view a cyclical contraction as an 'interruption' of the growth process traceable to a misalignment of these elements.

With an existing working population (and assuming full-employment), the proportionate rate of growth in real output would be read as the rate of increase in output per head which involves some learning-by-doing (skill improvement) or technological breakthrough (which may have a spill-back impact on employment); but with the labor force increasing the growth in real output is traceable to both the higher output per capita as well as the proportionate change in the labor force. Let us consider how we would relate technological change as an ongoing process within a growing economy.

Technological progress manifests itself in the long-term rise in output per worker, and it ultimately rests upon the growth of technical knowledge. This knowledge must be transferred to the productive process in order for it to show up as 'progress'; and this occurs when this knowledge is incorporated in the capital with which labor is employed. Considering additions to knowledge as an ongoing process, then the 'type' of capital is always changing; thus whenever new plant and equipment is being added to the existing stock it embodies knowledge that is different than what was housed in the older capital at the time of its coming on-line. Even if we were to think of a non-growth structure where gross investment is equal to replacement of capital, and here it is best to think of pieces of particular equipment rather than an 'amount of capital' (we do not want to get enmeshed here in the problem of measurement of capital that was discussed in Chapter 3), it is not likely that the new equipment is an exact replica of what it is replacing. It is reasonable to think of a modern society as one where knowledge is always expanding setting-up, so to speak, a warehouse of ideas, and the rate at which these ideas can be absorbed is itself limited by the rate at which capital is being accumulated. In general, output per worker can be expected to increase as investment proceeds apace provided that the economy generates the demand for the increased output.

291

We have a further argument for discarding the traditional production function (aside from the measurement issue) in that from the technical change aspect it is not right to talk in terms of an aggregative change in the capital to labor ratio. The ratio may be altered and per capita output increased in the newest productive process reflecting the latest addition to capacity, but this does not as a rule alter the productive relationships of older on-going processes. The knowledge embodied in the newest process cannot be passed back; technical change does not, as the saying goes, fall like manna from heaven, spreading itself evenly over the economy. Realistically one has to deal with the operation of a heterogeneous capital stock from the viewpoint of embodied technology; there are at a point in time different types of plants in use embodying different input ratios. We will want to relate this reality to the full-employment growth path.

Before going to the Kaldor model of the long-run and see how he handles the production function, we want to briefly revisit some of our discussion in the growth chapter concerning technical change. The Hicks neutral stance in the light of the above remarks leaves much to be desired. Recall that here we have a concept of neutrality such that technical progress leaves unchanged the existing input ratio and factor shares as it leads to an increase in output per unit of labor. This is reflective of a very limited view of 'progress'; one that emerges as we pointed out, as the result of an organizational change or in all likelihood as a result of becoming better at the job with time. The unit of labor using the machine becomes more adept and the 'bugs' within the machine itself get ironed out with greater use. And the assumption given the homogeneous nature of the production function is that this notion of progress will, with time, happen all over — it is like manna effecting all employed labor and capital. So we must consider the Hicksian approach a very introductory way to get hold of technical change, and in any event this kind of presentation is out of line with some long-term historical facts of economically advanced societies.

These facts (to reiterate, rising capital to labor and output to labor ratios, a rising real wage and a constant relative distribution of output between wages and profits) were, at least conceptually, addressed with what we depicted as Harrod technical change. Here the production function shifts upwards in conjunction with an increase in the 'machines' to labor ratio [see Fig. (5.11) in Chapter 5]. But the technical change which is housed in the capital reveals itself, or is accounted by, an increase in the productivity of labor. And to go further, this increased capability of labor is 'disembodied' within the labor force; that is, it affects the existing labor as well as new entrants presumably working with the latest additions to the

292

capital stock. In essence, the technical change incorporated in the most recent investment can be passed back to be absorbed by all existing operating capital resulting in an overall rate of advance in labor productivity. In this conceptualization all capital is treated as 'alike capital' and for that matter so is the labor force. There is no need to consider different facilities that at the same time embody different technologies. The meshing of the constant capital to output ratio with the growth in capital intensity poses no problem when we adjust the labor force in terms of efficiency units, it is as if the labor force in natural units were itself growing. Then the 'deepening' of capital disappears, the capital to effective labor force ratio is constant and the relative income shares of the two factors are unchanged. Again keeping in mind, that it is not the productivity of capital that is reckoned to be enhanced; it is that given the return to capital relative shares are unchanged (Harrod neutrality).

This Harrod-type approach to technical change while a step in the right direction in attempting to mirror some economic realities (we considered it somewhat of a rescue of the neoclassical model), itself falls prey to the general unreality of the malleability of capital — at least in the original version of his ideas, this was amended in a later model. Now how does Kaldor treat this matter?

Early on Kaldor realized the artificiality of attempting to put through a production function in a given state of knowledge with its usual configuration, as a separate notion from a shift of the function attributable to technical progress. The two phenomena of a rate of capital accumulation and the introduction of new knowledge are, as we mentioned, interdependent. It is not as if technical change is superimposed on the system; its presence is related to the growth of the economy itself. A society where new knowledge is not forthcoming or is developing very slowly will evidence a lack of incentive to increase the pace of capital accumulation; yet this very slow accumulation will deaccelerate the development of new knowledge and the introduction of technical change — but let us think of this dependency in a forward flow way. The point here is that the rate at which the society can absorb technical change is tied to its ability to accumulate capital. And the lack of ability certainly in 'primitive' societies may simply result from the reluctance to part with traditional ways of doing things.

Kaldor calls his production function a "technical progress function" which intertwines capital accumulation and technical progress, both working to increase output per worker as a function of the growth of capital per worker. But as we can observe in Fig. (7.3), the relationship

293

is drawn to reflect a diminishing rate of increase to the growth in productivity.

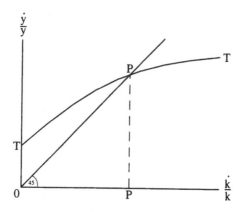

Figure 7.3

Yet over a range of experience we would expect to find an exuberant rate of increase in the growth of productivity relative to the percentage increase in capital per worker which is a testament to the pace of flow of new ideas permeating the economy. Looking again at our investment function (35) we would find in a position to the right of (P) a need to increase the rate of accumulation and thereby additions to capacity in the light of the rate of increase in demand (which could translate into a higher mark-up), reinforced by an increase in the rate of return predominantly driven by the reduction in costs. But whether this is so would depend on what is happening to wage rates as the economy is absorbing the unemployed as well as additions to the work force. One can think of the move to a point (P) as a rather long duration of a cyclical expansion phase that is witnessing an interdependent relation between the ratio of investment to output and the rate of profit glued together, if you will, by technological change.

The configuration of TT in Fig. (7.3) appears like traditional approach which has a basis in a diminishing returns application to a 'factor' input, but this is not what we are dealing with here. As capital intensity increases it is not the same aggregate notion of capital that is increasing. The 'nature' of the capital is always changing; but the pace of the flow of ideas to the production process (and thereby the different capital) may slow with the concomitant deterioration in the growth of output per worker. But why should the slowdown occur? What is needed for a society to continue to be a wellspring of research and new ideas? But it is more than simply creating new knowledge; what the system would want to foster is the continuous readiness to adopt this knowledge as new techniques of production. There are I would think more questions than answers in this area of motivation. Now as Kaldor tells us . . ."clearly the more capital is increased the more labor-saving techniques can be adopted though there is likely to be some maximum beyond which the rate of growth in productivity could not be raised however fast capital is being accumulated. Hence the TT curve is likely to be convex upwards and flattening out altogether beyond a certain point".[9]

Let us then conceive of that point (P) in Fig. (7.3) as one where the society has exhausted its new ideas or its willingness to create new capital, i.e. to adopt new ideas, so that additional accumulation increases the stock as a replica of what came before. Output growth per worker is no longer driven by technological change so that its growth will keep a pace with that of capital accumulation which will be of a sufficient rate to absorb the new entrants to the labor force. The economy maintains a state of full employment with a given capital to output ratio and constant rate of profit. Of course, underpinning this 'equilibrium state' is a distribution of income such that given the savings propensities the system extracts the savings necessary to maintain the appropriate investment to output ratio, and this support in turn presumes the existence of a particular mark-up policy and real wage rate. It is from this full-employment state which we can see as the co-dependency of points (E) and (P) in Fig. (7.2) and (7.3) respectively that Kaldor sets out the balances required to maintain this equilibrium condition through time, i.e. he works out the face of the economy in the long-term in a way that carries the Harrod heritage further along.

So the Kaldor exposition of the growth path is based on the hypothesis of full employment which, if we look again at Fig. (7.2), presumed an independently determined investment to output ratio. But as Kaldor developed his steady-growth analysis he gave up on this approach, fully realizing that while entrepreneurs determine the volume of investment, the ratio of investment to output depends on the operation of the multiplier and thereby on matters that are not all controlled by investors. The 'Kaldor of the growth model' does not take the rate of capital accumulation as an independent variable as was the case of the earlier 'Kaldor of the theories of distribution'. But now let us get to the basic growth model.

Starting from the position of point-in-time full employment at point (P) we find that the increase in productivity will result in an increase in output equal to that of the rate of capital accumulation. This point on the progress function is:

$$\frac{Y_{t-1}-Y_t}{Y_t}=\alpha''+\beta''\frac{(K_{t+1}-K_t)}{K_t}$$

$$= \alpha''+\beta''(\frac{I_t}{K_t}) \qquad (60)$$

Of course, with a given labor force the increase in output per worker is that of the increase in aggregate output which is, to repeat, equal to that of capital. The whole increase in output is driven by the degree of capital intensity operating with a particular level of technology. We can restate (60) as:

$$G=\alpha''+\beta''(G)$$

$$= \frac{\alpha''}{1-\beta''} \qquad (61)$$

(G being the usual symbol for the growth rate of output with α'' and β'' being the technical parameters of the progress function)

It would appear that the growth rates of capital and output — again which keeps the constant labor force fully employed — can simply be read from the progress function, i.e. would depend on the coefficients in equation (61). But there is more to the story; for the rate of capital accumulation must itself relate to the savings (distribution) and investment functions. The ratio of investment to output and the rate of growth of capital are not to be taken as exogenously given.

We restate our investment to output equation (35) as:

$$\frac{I_t}{Y_t}=G.\frac{K_t}{Y_t} \qquad (62)$$

The constancy of the rate of return removes one of the driving forces altering the size of the capital stock, thus, at a point in time, having it restricted to the given labor force. The Keynesian equality at full-employment (Y_f) is:

$$\frac{S}{Y_F} = \frac{I}{Y_F} \qquad (63)$$

which as a result of inserting the distributional savings function (37) yields a profit ratio and a rate of profit. Thus:

$$S_W + (S_P - S_W)\frac{P}{Y_F} = G(\frac{K}{Y_F}) \qquad (64)$$

and:

$$\frac{P}{Y_F} = \frac{G(\frac{K}{Y_F}) - S_W}{S_P - S_W} \qquad (65)$$

and

$$r = \frac{P}{K} = \frac{G - S_W(\frac{Y_F}{K})}{S_P - S_W} \qquad (66)$$

Taking the extreme stance that all savings comes out of profits (neglecting workers' savings and capital consumption) then the earnings of 'capitalists', i.e. profits, must be equal to the sum of investment expenditures — we recall Kalecki's point that capitalists get what they spend. This simplifies the distributional and rate of return equations to:

$$\frac{P}{Y_F} = \frac{1}{S_P}[G(\frac{K}{Y_F})] \qquad (67)$$

$$\frac{P}{K} = \frac{1}{S_P}[G] \qquad (68)$$

and with $S_P = 1$:

$$\frac{P}{Y_F} = G(\frac{K}{Y_F})$$ (69)

$$r = \frac{P}{K} = G$$ (70)

At the heart of Keynesian thinking is that investment is determined independently of current savings (it had to come from 'outside' via fiscal policy); there was no causality between them. But now we see that there is clear causality which makes more meaningful that accustomed 'mantra' that savings be equal to investment. The decisions concerning investment, i.e. capital accumulation, determines not only the level of income but also its distribution which in turn determines the level of savings. Thus, within reason, investment generates the level of savings that it requires.

The determinants of investment are, of course, at center stage, and with Kaldor's equation we do obtain some insight. Kalecki's exposition which we looked at early on in this chapter was very helpful; and it bears repeating his point that "although profits in the preceding period are one of the important determinants of capitalists' consumption and investment, capitalists in general do not decide to consume and invest in a given period what they have earned in the preceding one. This explains why profits are not stationary, but fluctuate in time".[10] Yet in our position of full employment with a constant working population, profits are a stationary proportion of output reflecting a particular investment ratio; so that 'businesses' are responding to, or their investment behavior is being motivated by, a particular condition. If we look at equation (62) it is the existing rate of growth that is the motivating force; and this growth rate reflects the economy's productive capability as governed by the size of the labor force and the technology in place. The given pace of technological change is mirrored in the constancy of the capital to output ratio; so that it is essentially the productivity of the fully-employed labor force which determines the output and investment levels.

The full-employment condition at a point-in-time portrays a system tuned to an exogenously given limit. And let us again say what this means; we are talking about the ability to maintain the proper ratio of profits to income and thereby the ability to finance the requisite level of investment. Put the matter as:

$$\frac{I}{Y_F} = S_P(\frac{P}{Y_F}) = \frac{S}{Y_F}$$ (71)

which makes it clear that savings can be made flexible to accommodate the natural growth rate of the system. The characteristics of equilibrium, with a constant labor force, will be those of an economy constantly adopting to a 'growing limit' as reflected in the size of the labor force and the pace of technological change inherent in the rate of change in investment; though the system maintains a constant ratio of investment to output with a constant rate of return (the economy is not to be motivated to invest at a greater rate than its sustainable output capability). At this point we can go back to our Harrodian growth model with the economy proceeding at its natural rate, but now with the added realism of distributional and pricing consideration thrown into the pot. Thus, within certain limits, there will exist a ratio of profits to income ensuring that the overall propensity to save is what is required to equate the warranted rate of growth ($G_w=S/V$ — using the symbols of our Harrod discussion) to the natural rate of growth G_n stating matters again so that we are sure of the growth framework we have:

$$S = \frac{S}{Y_F} = G_n v \tag{72}$$

and

$$\frac{P}{Y_F} = \frac{1}{S_P}[G_n v] \tag{73}$$

as

$$S = S_P P$$

Hence an economy that is progressing along a natural growth path cannot have a proportion of income saved be lower than $G_n v$ which means that the share of profits cannot be lower than that given by (67) or (72) if it is to realize the required growth in investment. As well, the profit share cannot be higher than $1/S_P[G_n-v]$ for if this were so we are saying that the system is evidencing excessive savings, bringing us to the problem of a lack of effective demand with consequent excess capacity and a reduction in the growth rate. This brings us again to Kaldor's distributional discussion as seen in Fig. (7.2). Should the real wage balance go awry in that profits are increasing too rapidly (say that the system has the tendency

299

to realize the result of any increase in productivity almost totally in the form of a lower wage bill) the system may generate a shortfall in effective demand. The way then to preserve full employment in the long-run is to have wages rise. We sense, and correctly so, the difficulty of striking the economic and accompanying societal balances needed to maintain a requisite rate of economic growth.

Before going on to modify aspects of this Kaldor distributional growth model so as to bring out further realities in this framework of post-Keynesian thinking, it would behoove us to clarify what may appear as a paradoxical technical point. As we observe, the rate of profit in this natural growth configuration depends upon that rate of growth and on the division of profit income between consumption and savings; and in the condition of what has been labeled as the 'superclassical' savings function with $S_P=1, S_W=0$ the rate of profit equals the rate of growth itself. So this rate of return on capital appears independent of the ratio of profits to income and thus of the capital to output ratio, which, itself, is a reflectin of the existing technological change and one ingredient in the formation of the natural rate. What is the rationale of the rate of profit coming out independent of everything else?

The answer rests on capitalists' behavior. If we assume that all profits are invested (with profits being the sole source of savings), then the rate of profit is equal to the rate of growth of capital which itself equals the rate of growth of output. Then the rate of profit in this extreme case can be seen as identical with the growth rate of the economy. To reiterate, it is not that the rate of return on capital is truly independent of the forces making for the constant capital to output ratio; it is that if all of profit income was given to accumulation, the rate of return would be determined by this rate of growth in investment spending which would then be instrumental in determining, and in the steady growth position, be equal to, the rate of the economy's advance.

If we change behavior and consider that some part of profit income is spent on consumption, then the profit share will be higher (the higher the reciprocal of the propensity to save) and the rate of profit would exceed the rate of growth. But this places us at some point to the left of the steady growth outcome, with the economy now converging to the growth equilibrium point with a different spending scheme. In this circumstance we have shifted the equilibrium growth path to a higher level reflecting a higher level of consumption spending and a higher profit ratio that, so to speak, compensates for the lower savings behavior in order to provide the required rate of accumulation of capital.

Speaking about behavior changes, what is perhaps more meaningful is to presume $S_w > 0$; this is a realistic and essential modification that we need to consider in some detail, though we can say something at this point. Picking up from equation (72) we would write:

$$\frac{S}{Y} = S_w \frac{W}{Y} + S_P \frac{P}{Y} = G_n v \qquad (74)$$

The savings ratio cannot be considered as a constant (as we are aware) but a weighted average of the savings propensities with the weights being the shares of profits and wages in the national income. Then as a variation of the profit ratio equation (65) we have:

$$\frac{P}{Y} = \frac{G_n v - S_w \dfrac{W}{Y}}{S_P} \qquad (75)$$

It is clear that an increase in S_w will reduce the profit share while a decrease in the savings propensity on the part of the capitalists will increase it. We have the seemingly paradoxical result that workers as a 'class of people' can increase their share of the national income only by spending less while capitalists as a group increase their share by spending more (as Kalecki instructed). There exists then a correct distribution of income between profits and wages which produces the proper savings ratio that permits growth at the natural rate. Of course the advent of $S_w > 0$ is not to change society in so far as obliterating the existence and essential purpose of the capitalist class; we cannot assume that wage earners save enough to make:

$$S_w \frac{W}{Y} = G_n v \qquad (76)$$

which upon inserting into (75) gives

$$\frac{P}{Y} = 0 \text{ and } \frac{W}{Y} = 1 \qquad (77)$$

so that the dual savings contribution that supports the required investment ratio operates on the provision that:

$$S_W \prec S_P \prec G_n v$$

or $\qquad\qquad\qquad\qquad\qquad\qquad\qquad\qquad\qquad$ (78)

$$S_W = G_n v - S_P$$

Another way to see what is to be avoided is to place the assumption $S_W = I/Y$ into our earlier distributive equation (13). Then:

$$\frac{P}{Y} = \frac{\dfrac{I}{Y}}{S_P - \dfrac{I}{Y}} - \frac{\dfrac{I}{Y}}{S_P - \dfrac{I}{Y}} = 0 \qquad\qquad (79)$$

The idea of the two class constituency with their essential raison d'etre comes to an end; the class of people under the tent of labor do all the accumulation and end up owning all the wealth.

We do need to look at the growth framework again with positive workers' savings — as we said this is clearly a necessary modification. Yet before moving on to this we would like to consider an additional point. We could directly relate the savings function to the capital to 'effective labor' ratio thus again stress the relationship between the rate of accumulation and that of technological change.

We restate the distributive savings ratio (7) as:

$$S \equiv \frac{S}{Y} = s_W + (s_P - s_W)\frac{rK}{Y}$$

$$= s_W + (s_P - s_W)rv \qquad\qquad (80)$$

The growth in the capital to effective labor (E) is:

$$\frac{\dot{k}}{k} = \hat{k} = \frac{s(y)}{k} = \frac{sf(k)}{k} - n + \lambda \qquad\qquad (81)$$

using the symbols from our discussion of the Harrod model where (n) is the rate of growth of labor in natural units and (λ) is the rate of growth in productivity.

The capital accumulation side of equation (81) looks as if we are using the standard neoclassical production function; but it is not to be read this way. It is to be seen as a move on the progress function with the movement being supported by the growth in the profit ratio. Thus we substitute the savings ratio into the expression for the $(\hat{k})$:

$$\hat{k} = [s_W \frac{y}{k} + (s_P - s_W) r v] \frac{y}{k} - (n + \lambda)$$

or (82)

$$\hat{k} = s_W \frac{y}{k} + (s_P - s_W) r - (n + \lambda)$$

and on the steady growth path we find $\hat{k}=0$. With the assumption of $s_W = 0$, we have:

$$s_p(r) = (n + \lambda)$$ (83)

And the growth of capital per worker is equal to that of output per worker, which we see upon dividing (83) by the growth of the labor force.

$$\frac{s_P(r)}{n} = \lambda$$ (84)

But under the circumstance of

$$\frac{s_P(r)}{n} \prec \lambda$$ (85)

output per capita and profits rates will be increasing thus stimulating higher rates of accumulation to exploit the possible stream of inventions and in doing so eventually reach the point where the growth of capital and output are equal. But it bears reiterating that the move to the equality of (84) is not the result of the traditional diminishing returns concept, but has to do with the pace of the development and exploitation of new ideas that may itself be related to the growth in the rate of return. The point is that there is a particular capital to labor ratio that yields the appropriate savings ratio and output to capital ratio that sustains a steady-growth path. What we have done in this little exercise is to see how the Kaldor distributional approach could be related to the neoclassical growth model which certainly comes through equation (81); and by removing the constancy and aggregateness of the savings function we impart some degree of realism to the neoclassical argument.

Another point to keep in mind is that when we maintain savings out of the two categories of income (with savings propensities differing), the relationship between the rate of growth and the rate of profit depends on income distribution as well as on technology which comes through the capital to output ratio as seen, say, in equation (66). And we would suppose that is a realistic relationship since the state of technology and resulting output per worker will effect income distribution depending on how this increase in productivity is allocated between labor and capital. But whatever the apportionment, both savings propensities determine aggregate savings and the subsequent rate of accumulation. The profit-growth relationship would be independent of technology only in the special but popular case where $s_w=0, s_p=1$ (what we referred to as the 'superclassical' savings function). Either all of the result of technological change goes to profits which there yields the rate of profit equal the rate of growth condition; technical methods of production do not matter, whatever the technology, it is the level of profits that determine the growth of the economy (there is no apportionment to concern us). With the superclassical function any rate of growth will find its appropriate rate of profit to sustain it — there is a two-sidedness to this approach, if you explain one you determine the other. But as we mentioned previously, there is no clear causality in this "extreme" picture.

However, as we know, backing away from this position would have the rate of growth depend upon the proportion of profits being saved. What we have is an interrelated causality; given the rate of growth the rate of profit is determined by the propensity to save out of profits which itself is the underpinning element determining the rate of accumulation and economic growth. And if we back up further, we confront $s_w>0$ and how this might impact on the growth path via the effect on the rate of return on capital and possible influence on the distribution of income between profits and wages.

We should note at this point that the Kaldor approach of connecting the rate of profits and income distribution to the rate of growth provides us with a bridge to the deep-rooted classical notion of a link between income distribution and capital accumulation. Certainly in our discussion of Ricardo this was a central theme. We see investment as not being determined by savings; savings is not the strategic variable in this sense though it impacts the system via effective demand, indeed investment

304

determines savings via its impact on profits. And as we see in the rate of profit equation, this distributive approach breaks with marginal productivity theory. But let us see how all this turns out when workers save.

The Pasinetti adjustment

The Kaldor savings function involves the distinction between broad categories of income (wages and profits) with aggregate savings divided into categories of savings out of profits and, with $s_w{>}0$, savings out of wages. Thus when the function says that workers as a class of people do save it presumes that they do so out of a single income category called wages, i.e. non-profit income; and while this may appear plausible, it does involve what Pasinetti describes as a "logical slip"[11] in the theory.

If workers save, they do not transfer these savings as a gift to capitalists, nor are these savings confiscated and ownership of them given over to capitalists. However, the assumption that profits accrue totally to capitalists would mean that workers' savings are transferred to capitalists — that workers do not own their savings. But why then would workers save if they are not allowed to own their savings and receive a reward for doing so? If workers as a class of people are not to follow that attribute normally assigned to them, namely, to spend all they receive, then one must see them as being rewarded for their transfers of their savings to capitalists by receiving a part of capitalists' income, i.e. profits. The payment to workers for their accumulation of money capital comes out of profits; the ownership of capital entitles one to a rate of interest and thus a part of the stock of capital (normally indirectly via loans to capitalists) and hence a share of the total profits generated by their share of the capital stock. Let us say again that workers' savings 'purchases' for them and gives them title to a portion of the capital stock and hence a portion of the profits thereby generated.

The necessary adjustment of the Kaldor model via Pasinetti's reformulation involves a restatement of the savings function such to account for the distinction between categories of income (profits and wages) and also for the distribution of this income between categories of people (workers and capitalists). Therefore total profits must be divided between profits which accrue to workers and profits which accrue to capitalists. There are two concepts of the distribution of income; the distribution of income between profits and wages and the distribution of

305

income between workers and capitalists. These two concepts as between categories of income and categories of people, of course, coincide in the particular case where there is no savings out of wages.

So in this adjustment of the Kaldor formulation we let (Wo) stand for workers — as previously the symbol W represented wages — and (C) for 'capitalists'. We maintain the basic divisions:

$$S = S_W + S_P$$

$$Y = W + P \tag{86}$$

and

$$I = S \tag{87}$$

However:

$$P = P_{Wo} + P_C \tag{88}$$

then:

$$S = s_{Wo}(W + P_{Wo}) + s_C P_C \tag{89}$$

or

$$s_{Wo}(Y - P_{Wo} - P_C + P_{Wo}) + s_C P_C$$

$$S = s_{Wo}(Y) + (s_C - s_{Wo}) P_C \tag{90}$$

Equation (90) confronts us with the possibility that the allocation of some part of profits to workers could result in a decline in aggregate savings should workers save a smaller proportion of profits they receive than capitalists would have saved out of these profits had they remained with them. But let us see how it works out.

Regarding the distribution as between categories of people, we can obtain straightaway the profits accruing to capitalists as a proportion of aggregate income. Making use of equations (87) and (90) we have as a proportion of income:

$$\frac{s_{Wo} + (s_C + s_{Wo})P_C}{Y} = \frac{I}{Y} \qquad (91)$$

yielding:

$$\frac{P_C}{Y} = \frac{1}{s_C} - s_{Wo}(\frac{I}{Y}) - \frac{s_{Wo}}{s_C - s_{Wo}} \qquad (92)$$

Interestingly enough, the right side of (92) is the same as that of equation (13) which gave the determinants of profits to income; but it did so under a rather 'unreal' way of considering worker savings. With a realistic consideration of this savings equation (13) gives only a partial distribution of profits; in order to obtain a distribution of income between categories of people we would need to add the share of workers' profits to equation (92). Adding this latter share to both sides of (92) means we obtain an expression for:

$$\frac{P}{Y} = \frac{P_C}{Y} + \frac{P_{Wo}}{Y} \qquad (93)$$

In the same vein we would want a realistic expression for the overall rate of profit in the economy which now must entail a rate of profit on capital paid to workers. We immediately obtain a 'restricted' rate of profit expression — that earned by capitalists — again with the use of equations 87 and 90 with the division by (K). Thus:

$$s_{Wo}(\frac{Y}{K}) + (s_C - s_{Wo})\frac{P_C}{K} = \frac{I}{K} \qquad (94)$$

then:

$$\frac{P_C}{K} \equiv \frac{rK_C}{K} = \frac{1}{s_C - s_{Wo}}(\frac{I}{K}) - \frac{s_{Wo}}{s_C - s_{Wo}}(\frac{Y}{K}) \qquad (95)$$

to which we would need to add the rate of return earned by workers to find the expression for:

$$\frac{rK}{K} \equiv \frac{P}{K} = P_C + P_{Wo} \qquad (96)$$

Let us begin by working out expression (96). As workers' savings are loaned to capitalists and they are rewarded a rate of return (r), their earnings from capital is $\dfrac{rK_{Wo}}{K} \equiv \dfrac{P_{Wo}}{K}$ which we add to both sides of equation (95). Thus:

$$P_C + P_{Wo} = \frac{1}{s_C - s_{Wo}} \left(\frac{I}{K}\right) - \frac{s_{Wo}}{s_C} - s_{Wo}\left(\frac{Y}{K}\right) + \frac{rK_{Wo}}{K} \tag{97}$$

If all workers' savings are invested via loans to capitalists (we assume no 'hoarding'), then $S_{Wo} = K_{Wo}$ which allows us to find an expression for $\dfrac{K_{Wo}}{K}$. With the Pasinetti reformulation we know that:

$$S_{Wo} = s_{Wo}(W + rK_{Wo})$$

$$= s_{Wo}(Y - rK_C) \tag{98}$$

which as a proportion of total savings that is equal to investment in the dynamics of the growth path, means:[12]

$$\frac{K_{Wo}}{K} = \frac{S_{Wo}}{S} = \frac{s_{Wo}(Y - P_C)}{I} = \frac{s_{Wo}s_C}{s_C - s_{Wo}}\left(\frac{Y}{I}\right) - \frac{s_{Wo}}{s_C - s_{Wo}} \tag{99}$$

We need to add expression (99) to (97) to obtain the ruling rate of profit, and we do assume that workers receive the same rate of return on their invested savings, i.e. on their loans to capitalists, as would be rewarded to capitalists. We simply state $r = P/K$ and write equation (97) as:

$$\frac{P}{K} = \frac{1}{S_C - S_{Wo}}\left(\frac{I}{K}\right) - \frac{S_{Wo}}{S_C - S_{Wo}}\left(\frac{Y}{K}\right) + \frac{P}{K}\left[\frac{S_{Wo}S_C}{S_C - S_{Wo}}\left(\frac{Y}{I}\right) - \frac{S_{Wo}}{S_C - S_{Wo}}\right] \tag{100}$$

Equation (100) must now replace the Kaldor formulation of equation (66) or that of another version of (66) which we obtain via equation (6) as:

$$\frac{I}{K} = (S_P - S_W)\frac{P}{K} + S_W\left(\frac{Y}{K}\right)$$

and

$$\frac{P}{K} = \frac{\dfrac{I}{K} - S_W(\dfrac{Y}{K})}{S_P + S_W} \tag{101}$$

or

$$\frac{P}{K} = \frac{1}{S_P + S_W}(\frac{I}{K}) - \frac{S_W}{S_P + S_W}(\frac{Y}{K})$$

And this, of course, is similar to equation (66) as the capital to output ratio is unchanged in the growth equilibrium framework.

Be that as it may, our replacement equation (100) for the rate of profit is somewhat cumbersome; however, with a little manipulation it can be simplified. It resolves itself to:

$$\frac{P}{K} \cdot \frac{S_C}{I} \cdot I - S_{Wo}(Y) = \frac{1}{K} \cdot I - S_{Wo}(Y) \tag{102}$$

Postulating that workers' savings out of their income now consisting of wages and profits do not constitute the whole of savings invested in the economy, i.e. $I - S_{Wo}(Y) \neq 0$, then dividing (102) through by $I - S_{Wo}(Y)$ yields:

$$\frac{P}{K}[S_C(\frac{1}{I})] = \frac{1}{K} \tag{103}$$

and

$$\frac{P}{K} = \frac{1}{S_C} \cdot \frac{I}{K} \tag{104}$$

The reader will notice that the result of equation (104) is formally similar to the Kaldor formulation for the rate of profit but without relating it to that 'uncomfortable' assumption that workers do not save. And if we're to assume that capitalists do not consume, i.e. $S_C = 1$, even though $S_{Wo} > 0$, we have the rate of profit in the growth equilibrium condition determined by the rate of investment. Kaldor's results can be looked upon as a special case of his savings functions, i.e. when $S_W = 0$; well, we now have his case without this assumption.

We do need to adjust the Kaldor distributive equation for profits as a proportion of income in the light of workers receiving profits as equation (93) points out. We need to add the ratio of workers' profits to income to equation (92), so that the equation is now the proportion of aggregate profits to income. This works out as:

$$\frac{P}{Y}=\frac{1}{s_C-s_{Wo}}(\frac{I}{Y})-\frac{s_{Wo}}{s_C-s_{Wo}}+\frac{P}{K}[\frac{s_{Wo}s_C}{s_C-s_{Wo}}(\frac{K}{I})-\frac{s_{Wo}}{s_C-s_{Wo}}(\frac{K}{Y})\ \ \ (105)$$

and with some manipulation can be reduced to:

$$\frac{P}{Y}=\frac{1}{s_C}(\frac{I}{Y}) \qquad (106)$$

which is formally that of the Kaldor equation (67).

But let us arrive at expression (106) in a different way. We have:

$$P=P_C+P_{Wo} \qquad (107)$$

and:

$$\frac{K_{Wo}}{K}=\frac{s_{Wo}}{S} \qquad (108)$$

also:

$$P_{Wo}=\frac{P}{K}(\equiv r)S_{Wo} \qquad (109)$$

then:

$$P=P_C+P(\frac{s_{Wo}}{S})$$

or

$$P_C=P(1-\frac{s_{Wo}}{S_C+s_{Wo}}) \qquad (110)$$

310

Expression (110) can be simplified and stated in terms of aggregate profits. Thus:

$$P = \frac{P_C}{\dfrac{1-S_{W_o}}{S_C-S_{W_o}}} = \frac{P_C}{\dfrac{S_C}{S_C+S_{W_o}}} = \frac{P_C}{\dfrac{S_C}{S}} \qquad (111)$$

then

$$P = P_C \cdot \frac{S}{S_C} \qquad (112)$$

and as

$$S = I, S_C = s_C P_C$$

we have

$$P = \frac{IP_C}{s_C P_C} = \frac{1}{s_C}(I) \qquad (113)$$

and

$$\frac{P}{Y} = \frac{1}{s_C}\left(\frac{I}{Y}\right) \qquad (114)$$

and we are back to Kaldor's distribution equation. With $s_C = 1$, we reiterate the result, that the share of profits is determined by the share of investment in output but we come to this conclusion without the special case assumption that the marginal propensity to save of workers is zero.

The end-all of these manipulations is that in the long run (and we understand this to mean the condition in which the economy has settled into a steady state growth pattern) while the workers propensity to save, though influencing the share of profits accruing to them — equation 92 — and thereby the distribution of income between workers and capitalists, it does not determine the aggregate level of profits, that is, the distribution of income between profits and wages. The act of savings by workers will effect the distribution of income by 'classes of people', but will have no influence on the distribution as between classifications of income. Furthermore, the fact of $s_{W_0} > 0$ is of no influence in the determination of the long-run rate of profit.

These startling results implying the irrelevancy of workers' savings in the formation of the essential propellant of economic growth would compel us to look at the logic behind these equations to get at the economic causes of these results. Pasinetti tells us that his adjustment of Kaldor "has been built on the institutional principle, inherent in any production system, that wages are distributed among the members of society in proportion to the amount of labor they contribute and profits distributed in proportion to the amount of capital they own".[13] Thus when all savings are invested each category of saver will receive profits in proportion to the savings that it provides, thus:

$$\frac{P_C}{S_C} = \frac{P_{W_0}}{S_{W_0}} \qquad (115)$$

Pasinetti's point is that the relation of (115) does not then depend on any behavioral assumption, but follows from the institutional principle that profits be distributed in proportion to ownership of capital. What needs to be determined is the value of the ratio that is to be the same for all savers.

We know that 'capitalists' derive all their income and thereby savings from profits, which means that the ratio of their profits to their savings will set up the overall ratio between profits and savings. If we assume that the workers propensity to save is undifferentiated as between their wages and profit income we have:

$$\frac{P_C}{s_C(P_C)} = \frac{P_{W_0}}{s_{W_0}(W + P_{W_0})} \qquad (116)$$

Thus the source of workers' income has no effect on their total consumption and hence on their total savings. Indeed it can be shown that the act of workers saving will have no effect whatever on the aggregate level of savings in the economy.

Initially when such savings, i.e. $s_{W_0}(W)$, occurs total savings increases; but the income they receive from this savings will itself be saved at the same rate as they save out of wage income which is at a lesser rate than capitalists save out of their profits, that is $s_{W_0}(P_{W_0}) < s_C(P_C)$ and thus the amount saved out of the profit category has diminished as the result of the transfer of saving profits to workers. But the 'excess' consumption out of these workers' profits (in excess of what capitalists would have consumed out of these profits had they not transferred them to workers as payment) as offset by savings out of wages alone in the same proportion. We are saying that:

$$s_{W_0}(P_{W_0}+W)=s_C(P_{W_0}) \qquad (117)$$

the combination of profits and wages received by workers will cause their total savings to be equal to what capitalists would have saved out of these profits had they been retained by capitalists. Thus when we add the total of workers' savings to what the capitalists save out of the profits they retain, we conclude that the sharing of profits does not affect aggregate savings.

This payment of profits to workers can have no effect on the total wage-profit distribution or on the rate of profit as capitalists still determine the rate of investment and the ratio of investment to output. To be sure of our understanding: for capitalists there is a straight relation between profits and investment, there is no other variable involved. So that the proportionality between profits and savings is given by (s_C) which then determines the ratio of profits to savings for workers as well. And as the ratio of profits to income as given by the ratio of investment to income which is the ratio of capitalists' savings to profits, it is then the capitalist that determines the distribution of income between profits and wages. As we said though, workers will as a result of their savings determine the proportion of profits they acquire; what has been referred to as the "social distribution"[14] between workers and capitalists (equation 92 is a social distribution expression). Looking again at (92) it is clear that with $s_{W_0}=0$ we have:

$$\frac{P_C}{Y}=\frac{P}{Y} \qquad (118)$$

and the straight-away relation for a given (s_C). But with $s_{W_0}>0$ the share of profits going to capitalists fall; and this must be coming through the effect on effective demand and possible price changes associated with a given rate of investment. Having mentioned demand we can put forth another way to explain why workers' savings plays no role in determining total profits, though it does affect the profit split. Equation (116) can also be written as:

313

$$s_{W_0}(W) = [(1 - s_{W_0}) - (1 - s_C)]P_{W_0} \qquad (119)$$

The right side of (119) gives the difference in consumption out of profits which is greater for workers, but this difference is offset by savings out of wages so as to leave the workers proportion of total savings no greater than before they received profits. As Pasinetti states it, "Savings out of wages always turn out to be equal to workers' extra consumption (extra consumption meaning consumption in excess of what capitalists would have consumed if these profits remained to them)".[15] Total savings in the system then remains unchanged.

The Kaldor model opened the aggregate nature of the Keynesian approach and thereby focuses our attention on the functional income distribution as to category of income in our understanding the foundations of the long-term growth path. Pasinetti opened matters up even further by going beyond classes of income to look at the classes of people in the ownership of this income; and it is this latter thrust which is of a more important consideration in the modern context. Certainly the activity of workers in the disposition of their income seems in one respect to be irrelevant, for no matter what they do they only share in an amount of profits which for them is predetermined by the activity of the capitalist class. This brings us back to the essence of the Ricardo growth model which linked the savings of capitalists who carry on the production process and that of the process of a capital accumulation via the creation of profits — and without having to assume that workers as a class of people do not engage in the role of ownership of capital.

All this, however, is far from the end of the story regarding the role of class relationships in a growing economy; the Pasinetti paradox has spawned much discussion that has branched out in different directions. It has engendered a neoclassical response questioning the generality of the Pasinetti results; the response demonstrates that while Pasinetti's reformulation of Kaldor is certainly valid, it holds true though for a rather narrow range of values for (s_{W_0}). Outside of this range the savings of workers indeed count for very much; and we may find the economy with only one class of persons who do all the savings (receive all the profits) as well as perform all the labor — the workers. This possibility has led to what is known as the anti-Pasinetti theorem. We also find a neo-Pasinetti theorem which is greatly Kaldor's rebutted to the neoclassical critique whereby he presents a modern version of the Pasinetti conclusion; here we consider the megacorp as the capitalist with its payout of dividends and investment policies. Another development shows the two class savings propensities being positive under the not unreasonable assumption that workers obtain a rate of profit (called interest) on their savings, that is lower than the rate of profit obtained by capitalists on their capital.

While we propose this book to be an 'introduction', we will nevertheless want to consider some of these developments to reinforce a basic post-Keynesian attitude. For notwithstanding that discussions along lines of class differences seems, in our time, to be out of favor, it is still reality that to understand the propagating forces of growth in a free society one has to see the system in terms of class structure.

The anti-Pasinetti theorem

This neoclassical response would seem to have two objectives: one is to reformulate Pasinetti's distributive analysis within a traditional framework, that is, by making use of the usual production function of smooth factors substitutability and that of perfect markets which, as we know, enforces the equality of factor prices to factor marginal productivities; and relatedly to point up the rather limited range over which Pasinetti's long-run results would hold.

Regarding the generality of these results Pasinetti tells us that economists have always thought that the relation between capitalists' savings and capital accumulation depended on "particular simplifying and drastic assumptions about negligible savings by the workers. The novelty of the present analysis has been to show that the relation is valid independently of any of these assumptions. It is valid whatever the savings behavior of workers may be."[16] In other words, that the long-term path of the economy is set out solely in terms of the capitalist class savings behavior; for whatever workers may save, they can only share in an amount of total profits which is predetermined for them; they have no power to influence it all. And, as we pointed out, that whatever amount workers do save, these savings are less than the aggregate level of investment that is generating the long-term growth of the system, that is:

$$s_{W_0}(Y) < I \tag{120}$$

However, the neoclassical reaction was to demonstrate that the word "whatever" by Pasinetti was too general; that there exists a critical value to s_{W_0} at which the rate of growth of capital owned by workers will exceed that of capital owned by capitalists. So that over time workers' savings

315

becomes high enough to overturn equation (120), and it is workers' savings that becomes crucial in generating the capital accumulation and growth of the system. Once past this point, the interesting question is what does determine the equilibrium growth rate of the system? We are now in the 'dual regime' where

$$s_{W_0} = \frac{I}{Y} \tag{121}$$

and if we substitute equation (121) into the basic Kaldor profit ratio of equation (13) we end up with:

$$\frac{P}{Y} = 0, \frac{W}{Y} = 1 \tag{122}$$

And capitalists as a class of people, designated by their income called profits, are out of the picture; profits now become wages (as wages to the state?)

If the two-class structure is to hold in the long term, it is not only that workers' propensity to save meet the conditions of equation (120) but not rise above some particular ratio.

Of course, we immediately see the other extreme of the one-class system by setting $s_p = I/Y$ which by inserting into (13) yields:

$$\frac{P}{Y} = 1, \frac{W}{Y} = 0 \tag{123}$$

Capitalists take it all; all earnings are labeled profits, and what we have is a one-class structure operating a 'slave economy'. If the state (in the guise of being all the people) owns all the capital and receives all the income, it makes no difference whether we call this income 'profits' or 'wages'; what disappears is the different class structure and everyone can be designated as either 'capitalist' or 'worker'.

But let us return to the reality of matters and consider some of the mechanics of this neoclassical response to Pasinetti, that while conceding his results claimed that it was quite limited, and showed the conditions whereby the long-run growth path would be couched in terms of workers' behavior — the workers state? This response was put forth essentially by Meade in 1961[17] along a diagramatic analysis and by Samuelson and Modigliani (S-M) in their quite mathematical paper in 1966.[18] We will attempt to present the crucial features of this counter-analysis and then consider the Pasinetti response.

S-M propose a model in which total output is composed of consumption plus net capital formation; and where production in both sectors is carried on with the same proportion of capital to labor. There is one production technique employing labor and an alike capital in both lines of output. Thus:

$$Y=C+K \tag{124}$$

Putting the factors into the constant returns to scale production function means, as we recall from the discussion of the neoclassical mechanics in Chapter 3:

$$Y=F(K,L)$$

and

$$F(ZK,ZL)=Z^{n}Y \tag{125}$$

$$\text{with } n=1$$

However, in this context capital is disaggregated into:

$$K=K_{Wo}+K_C \tag{126}$$

$$\text{with } K_{Wo}= \text{capital owned by workers}$$

$$K_C= \text{capital owned by capitalists}$$

Then:

$$Y=C+K=F(K_{Wo},K_C,L) \tag{127}$$

Restating in terms of output per unit of 'effective' labor we use the lower case lettering. So $y=Y/L$, and correspondingly with the input variables; then the production function can be written as:

$$y=f(k,1)=f(k), \frac{dF(k,1)}{dk}=f'(k)>0 \tag{128}$$

317

Recall that with our CRS function:

$$ZY = F(ZK, ZL) \tag{129}$$

and letting $Z = 1/L$ yields:

$$\frac{Y}{L} = y = F(\frac{K}{L}, 1) = f(\frac{K}{L}) = f(k)$$

with the marginal product of capital being:

$$MPK = \frac{dY}{dK} = \frac{dF(K, L)}{dK} = f'(k) \tag{130}$$

We have expressions for the rate of profit and the real wage rate resulting from the marginal productivity 'explanations' respectively as:

$$r = f'(k) \tag{131}$$

$$w = f(k) - kf'(k) \tag{132}$$

The increase in capital owned by the capitalist class (their investment) is equal to their propensity to save times their total profits, so:

$$\dot{K}_C = s_C P_C = s_C (r K_C) = s_C K_C (\frac{dY}{dK})$$

$$= s_C K_C [\frac{dF(K_C, K_{W_0}, L)}{dK}] \tag{133}$$

And for workers, the rate of growth of their capital K_{W_0}, is given by:

$$K_{W_0} = s_{W_0}(W + P_{W_0}) = s_{W_0}(W + r K_{W_0}) = s_{W_0}(Y - rK + r K_{W_0}) = s_{W_0}(Y - r K_C)$$

$$= s_{W_0}[F(K_C, K_{W_0}, L) - K_C \frac{dF(K_C, K_{W_0}, L)}{dK}] \tag{134}$$

Thus we have the savings-investment relationship for the two economic classes stated in their neoclassical form; with the understanding that all savings of households are invested in physical capital; and with the given growth rate of the labor force we arrive at a growth rate of the economy under existing technological change. Overall:

$$s_{W_0} + s_C = s(Y) \tag{135}$$

$$\dot{K}_{W_0} + \dot{K}_C = \dot{K} = s(Y) \tag{136}$$

S-M then arrive at the long-term (steady-state) equilibrium values for K, K_{W_0} and K_C. Positing the exponential growth of the labor force (in efficiency units) $L_t = L_0 e^{nt}$, we have:

$$\frac{\dot{k}}{k} = \frac{\dot{K}}{K} - n$$

$$\frac{\dot{k}_C}{k_C} = \frac{\dot{K}_C}{K_C} - n \tag{137}$$

$$\frac{\dot{k}_{W_0}}{k_{W_0}} = \frac{\dot{K}_{W_0}}{K_{W_0}} - n$$

With the use of equations (131) and (133) we solve for the growth rate of capital per unit of labor owned by capitalists substituting for the right side of the second statement in (137):

$$\frac{\dot{k}_C}{k} = \frac{s_C r K_C}{K_C} - n \tag{138}$$

$$= s_C f'(k) - n$$

Similarly for that of capital owned by workers:

$$\frac{\dot{k}_{W_0}}{k_{W_0}} = s_{W_0} [\frac{y - r k_C}{k_{W_0}}] - n$$

$$= s_{W_0} [\frac{f(k) - f'(k) k_C}{k_{W_0}}] - n \tag{139}$$

319

The steady-state solutions of k, k_{W_o}, k_C labelled as $k^*_o, k^*_{W_o}, k^*_C$ are derived by setting $\dot{k}_C$ and $\dot{k}_{W_o}$ in (138) and (139) equal to zero. Thus:

$$\dot{k}_C = s_C f'(k) - n = 0 \tag{140}$$

$$\dot{k}_{W_o} = s_{W_o}[f(k) - rk + rk_{W_o}] - nk_{W_o}$$

or

$$= s_{W_o}[f(k) - rk] + (s_{W_o}r - n)k_{W_o} = 0 \tag{141}$$

with the steady state solution for $k(=k*)$ being solved as:

$$f'(k*) = r* = \frac{1}{s_C}(n) \tag{142}$$

We note that equation (142) is the Pasinetti outcome; the rate of profit is determined by the growth of the effective labor force and (s_C). Of course, along the growth path the growth rate of the capital stock, i.e. rate of investment, is equal to that of the effective labor force. This general result for (k^*) holds for $s_C > s_{W_o} > 0$; should $s_{W_o} = 0$, then $k^* = k^*_C$ and the unreality of workers owning no capital. To this equilibrium value of the rate of profit there corresponds a particular technology, i.e. a particular capital to effective labor ratio and thereby a particular output to capital ratio designated by S-M as $A(k^*) = f(k^*)/k^*$. And in the usual manner, with given savings propensities we can determine aggregate savings and also the distribution of income as the wage rate and the rate of profit will tend to the respective marginal productivities at this capital to output ratio — we read the income distribution from the productivity conditions of the system. Full employment is, of course, assured by the choice of the appropriate capital to labor ratio which absorbs the growth of savings and that of labor.

After these straightaway descriptive equations which set up the equilibrium growth structure, the S-M paper takes on some rather involved mathematical relations; so what we will do (to reiterate) is to present the essential features without an involvement with the underlying mathematical manipulations. Since the result of (142) holds for the condition $s_{W_o} > 0$, $s_C > 0$, S-M proceed to give the steady-state values of $k^*_{W_o}$ and k^*_C respectively as:

$$k_{W_0}^* = s_{W_0} \frac{(\frac{y}{k})^* - \frac{n}{s_C}}{n - s_{W_0}\frac{n}{s_C}}(k^*) = \frac{A(k^*) - f'(k^*)}{\frac{n}{s_{W_0}} - \frac{n}{s_C}}(k^*) \qquad (143a)$$

$$k_C^* = \frac{\frac{n}{s_{W_0}} - A(k^*)}{\frac{n}{s_{W_0}} - \frac{n}{s_C}} k^* \qquad (143b)$$

with the ratio of capital owned by capitalists to that owned by workers given by:

$$\frac{k_C^*}{k_{W_0}^*} = \frac{s_C \alpha(k^*) - s_{W_0}}{s_{W_0}[1 - \alpha(k^*)]} \qquad (144)$$

where

$$\alpha(k^*) = \frac{rk^*}{f(k^*)}$$

Now the equality in (142) is the share of profits in output for a given (k^*); but this given condition of production yields a particular output to capital ratio so that the profit ratio can be seen as:

$$\frac{f'(k^*)}{\frac{Y}{K}} = f'(k^*)[\frac{K}{Y}] = \frac{n}{s_C} \cdot \frac{K}{Y} \qquad (145)$$

We are back to the Pasinetti result whereby the profit ratio is determined by the capitalist class; workers do share in this pool as a reflection of the amount of $k_{W_0}^*$. For this whole analysis to be economically meaningful it must satisfy the non-negativity condition, $k_{W_0} > 0$, $k_C > 0$. The first inequality is directly gathered from (143-a) as the numerator is positive, and for $k_{W_0}^* > 0$, the denominator must be positive which means $s_{W_0} < s_C$ — the reasonable assumption underlying the growth path for a two class of savers economy. The other non-negative condition $k_c>0$ is seen from (144) whereby $s_{W_0}<\alpha(k^*)s_C$ which can be stated as :

$$s_{W_0}\leq[\frac{n}{s_C}\cdot\frac{K}{Y}]s_C \qquad (146)$$

$$\leq n[\frac{k^*}{f(k^*)}]$$

For the growth path to embody the inequality of equation (146), the value of s_{W_0} must not exceed a rather low percentage. Equation (146) is seen to be more stringent than the general assumption of $s_{W_0}<s_C$; for the share of income accruing to capital is less than one, and S-M tell us that it is empirically very much less than one. The "econometrically reasonable" numbers presented are $\alpha(k^*)=.25$ and $s_C=.20$ which means that workers' savings are irrelevant as long as s_{W_0} is equal to or less than .05. More to the point, it is the corporation that essentially constitutes the 'capitalist'; and let us suppose that its dividend pay-out policy is 1/3 of its earnings (in the main the profits of the system) and that individuals save 1/12 of their income composed of dividends and wage earnings. Then:

$$.08\leq\alpha(k^*)\cdot.333 \qquad (147)$$

and we can stay in the Pasinetti regime, if the profit share in income over the long term is about .25.

There are two ways to express the validity of the Pasinetti conclusions in the long term. One is via equation (120) which we restate here as:

$$s_{W_0}<\frac{I}{Y} \qquad (148)$$

and the other is the inequality of equation (146). There is clearly a correspondence here as:

$$s_{W_0}<\frac{I}{Y}=n\frac{k^*}{f(k^*)} \qquad (149)$$

since in the steady-state we have:

322

$$\frac{I}{K} = \frac{\dot{K}}{K} = n \qquad (149a)$$

then:

$$n \cdot \frac{k}{f(k)} = \frac{\dot{K}}{K} \cdot \frac{K}{Y} = \frac{\dot{K}}{Y} = \frac{I}{Y} \qquad (149b)$$

In the long-term the ratio of investment to output takes on a particular value so as to maintain the capital to labor ratio which yields the particular growth rate of the system. And this ratio is one that corresponds to a rate of profit equal to n/s_c. Note that S-M are not necessarily insisting on a marginal productivity explanation of the rate of profit; all they are saying is that the rate of profit be considered an inverse function of the capital to labor ratio. There will be a particular $k=k^*$ that corresponds to the rate of profit determined by the Kaldor-Pasinetti distributive relations for which workers' savings are irrelevant within the two class of savers environment.

Pasinetti in his redesign of the Kaldor results tells us that prior to his correction it appeared that the relation between capitalists' savings and capital accumulation depended on particularly simplifying assumptions about negligible savings by the workers. The novelty of the present analysis has been to show that the relation is valid independently of any of these assumptions. It is valid whatever the savings behavior of the workers may be. S-M would rebut by considering the term "whatever" as too general; they show that the irrelevancy of workers savings is subject to a more stringent condition than that given by equation (146) — stringency that is governed by the nature of the technology that characterizes the equilibrium growth path. This leads to the interesting question as to what happens to the growth path should workers' savings become relevant.

We are now aware that there is a critical value for s_{W_o}, this value dependent upon the rate of growth of the labor supply and the production function, at which the rate of growth of workers' capital will overtake that of capitalists' capital, so that over time the $k^*_{W_o}$ will be the capital to labor ratio reflective of the equilibrium path, i.e. $k^* = k^*_{W_o}$. That is, we are now in the realm of:

$$s_{W_0} > n \cdot \frac{k^*}{f(k^*)} = [\frac{n}{s_c} \cdot \frac{k^*}{y^*}]s_c = \frac{\frac{n}{y}}{k} \qquad (150)$$

The existence of the two class society with their particular raison d'etre eventually comes to an end. The society ends up with a single class of people called 'workers' who do all the accumulation of capital and receive all the profits. Under this condition what determines the growth rate of the economy; and in the transition to the one class system, can the system even maintain the path? Is the structure of equation (149) compatible with long-term equilibrium or does the system break down being plagued by excess savings and chronic unemployment?

To see what happens we begin with the condition of $s_{W_0} = 0$, and then for given values for n and s_c we do consider the implications of increasing values for s_{W_0}. We have the extreme of the Pasinetti regime where, to reiterate:

$$r^* = \frac{n}{s_c}$$

$$\frac{k_c^*}{k^*} = 1 \qquad (151)$$

Now workers begin to save; and as long as their savings propensity remains sufficiently small there is no effect on the equilibrium capital to labor ratio (capital accumulation maintains its proper rate) and the rate of profit is unchanged — the condition of (149) is intact. This is saying that the presence of workers savings does not change the aggregate capital to labor ratio; there is no long-term increase in societies productive capability nor in the level of profits per capita. Yet as workers are accumulating capital and receiving a share of the profits, the level of k_c^* must be receding; capitalists (for the existing s_c) are receiving less of the unchanged per capita wealth. What we have is a transfer of some profits from one class to another. But the interesting question is why no increase in the capital to labor ratio when you are clearly adding the accumulation of one class to that of another? The dynamics underlying this unchanged ratio lies in the response of the capitalists to the increase rate of capital accumulation.

Starting from the state represented by equation (151), the emergence of workers savings drives up the rate of accumulation resulting in $k > k^*$. Now initially output per unit of labor will rise; but concomitantly we will find a decrease in the rate of profit resulting from too great a pace of capital growth (in keeping with the traditional production function) so that the return to capital will decline. Given the savings propensity of capitalists, this will reduce the level of capitalists accumulation. The response to $k_{W_0} > 0$ is $k_r < k^*$; and as s_{W_0} takes on greater values, k_c continues to fall below the state $k_r^* = k^*$. But how far can k_c fall within the framework of the two class of savers?

As long as s_{W_0} does not violate equation (141) which means that as long as it does not exceed .05 the level of k_c will fall to a lower position as determined by equation 143b. We have k_c becoming a smaller and smaller fraction of the unchanging k^* until the state of $k^* = k_{W_n}$. It should be emphasized that in the movement to this point the positive s_{W_0} has no effect on the equilibrium rate of profit, but it does clearly affect the share of the total capital owned by workers. And the ratio of the capital ownership by each class as s_{W_0} takes on different values is given by equation (144).

At this point, Pasinetti's remarkable theorem, as S-M put it (where workers savings have no effect on r^* and k^*) comes to an end. Capitalists are now economically eliminated reducing accumulation, ultimately reducing the system's rate of accumulation to the natural growth rate. Thus the high (s_{W_0}) and the resulting irrelevancy of the capitalists class is not in and of itself inimical to full-employment growth. Workers can provide the proper level of savings required for full-employment growth providing that the economy can adjust the capital to labor ratio (i.e. technique of production) to absorb the initial higher rate of capital growth. Now the profit adjustment mechanism resulting from the behavior of the production function may result in a direct adjustment of the growth of workers capital to that of required capital or it may adjust in oscillatory fashion, but for given growth of the labor force and sufficient flexibility of technique of production the equilibrium growth path is maintainable.

The capital to output ratio is adjusted to where workers savings are now the proper equilibrium savings ratio with the rate of profit declining to its appropriate rate, and the economy carries on with a single classification of people. The determinants of the growth path are:

$$\frac{s_{W_0}}{n} = \frac{k^{\cdot\cdot}}{f(k^{\cdot\cdot})} \tag{152}$$

The double asterisk designating the growth state in the absence of the capitalists class. We point up the essential reasoning here by noting that:

$$\frac{k^{\cdot}}{y^{\cdot}} = \frac{k^{\cdot}}{f(k^{\cdot})} = r(\frac{k^{\cdot}}{y^{\cdot}})\frac{s_c}{n} \tag{153}$$

and then with the use of (151) and (152) it is clear that in the new regime of equilibrium growth:

$$\frac{k^{\cdot\cdot}}{f(k^{\cdot\cdot})} > \frac{k^{\cdot}}{f(k^{\cdot})} \tag{154}$$

$$s_c(r^{\cdot\cdot}) < s_c(r^{\cdot}) \tag{155}$$

adding an additional factor in the adjustment to the equilibrium capital to labor ratio.

What has come to be known as the anti-Pasinetti theorem (or regime) or the dual of the Pasinetti long-term results is represented by equation (152); and certainly the determination of the rate of profit (or whatever it would be called) in the dual regime will be different than in the Pasinetti two-class society — the rate of profit determination in the Pasinetti case is also referred to as the Cambridge (England) equation. Repeating this latter result we have:

$$(\frac{P}{K})^{\cdot} \equiv r^{\cdot} = 1/s_c(\frac{I}{K}) \tag{156}$$

Whereas in the dual regime we find:

$$(\frac{P}{K})^{\cdot\cdot} \equiv r^{\cdot\cdot} = \frac{\frac{P}{Y}}{s_{W_0}}(\frac{I}{K}) \tag{157}$$

326

from the Cambridge equation we can directly find the determinants of the level of profits which is as we would have thought, since profits are a direct result of capitalists behavior. Thus from (156) we see:

$$P = \frac{I}{s_c} \tag{158}$$

But we cannot determine 'profits' from the one class workers society of equation (157). What we see is:

$$s_{Wo}(\frac{P}{K}) = \frac{P}{Y}(\frac{I}{K})$$

$$s_{Wo} = \frac{I}{Y} \tag{159}$$

and the absence of the capitalist class in the steady-state condition. Of course, all income accrues to 'workers'; and we can see this by going through a manipulation that we had done previously, but now in terms of identifying the two ownerships of profits. If we substitute the second equality of (159) in equation (92) we have:

$$\frac{P_c}{Y} = \frac{1}{s_c - \frac{I}{Y}}(\frac{I}{Y}) - \frac{\frac{I}{Y}}{s_c - \frac{I}{Y}} \tag{160}$$

and

$$\frac{P_c}{Y} = 0, \quad \frac{W + P_{Wo}}{Y} = 1$$

In the dual regime it is of little meaning to talk in terms of the share of profits in income, since all income is received by the 'people' as one class of persons so that income is simply called exactly that. However, in the case of the government taking on the role of the capitalist class (and recent history provides much evidence here) we are indeed in some sense back to the Pasinetti regime. Although what is profits would in all likelihood not be labelled as 'profits'. Here the relevant propensity to save, namely that of (s_c), becomes the savings propensity of the state.

We will not venture down this avenue of analysis; instead we return to the dual state as such and again consider the essential characteristics assuming, say, that the economy may be tending towards this state. The growth path of the economy in the dual is determined by the values of (s_{W_O}) and (v) along with the production function; that is, one needs some assumption about technology of production. From (152) we see the growth rate as:

$$G_n = \frac{s_{W_O}}{v^{**}}$$

G_n = natural growth rate   (161)

v = capital to output ratio

And as we pointed out, the system adopts the techniques of production such that the workers accumulation of capital maintains the equilibrium capital to labor ratio (k^{**}) and the capital to output ratio is 'related' to the equilibrium growth path's rate of profit. From the neoclassical view the exuberant savings rate on the part of workers does not destabilize the growth path of the economy.

A look at the Pasinetti regime reveals:

$$G_n = s_c(r)$$ (162)

and the rate of growth is determined irrespective of any assumption on technology.

Should $s_{W_O} < G_n v^*$, the determination of the rate of profit and rate of growth will be given by the non-marginalist condition; i.e., the post-Keynesian (Cambridge) equation holds indeed irrespective of technological considerations. But should $s_{W_O} > G_n v^*$ what happens does depend on technology. And by 'what happens' we mean whether the economy is able to carry on an equilibrium growth path where workers are overwhelmingly providing the required savings. What is the more plausible assumption concerning technology? Is it that the economy in the long term is characterized by a highly flexible capital to output ratio with its inverse relation to the rate of profit, or is it more reasonable to assume a rather constant capital to output ratio?

As a practical matter, we do maintain a two-class economy and the 'capitalist' is far from leaving the stage, though it may be argued that governments in recent times have not been very capitalist (profit) -friendly (this has undergone some change in the decade of the 1990s). If it can be conceptually argued that the capability of maintaining a natural growth rate is seriously impaired when the capitalist class is weakened, then this should raise a cautionary flag in the formation of policies in our mixed economic system. We turn then to consider some of the rebuttle to this marginalist challenge — to this anti-Pasinetti theorem.

The Pasinetti response

As a 'practical' matter, Pasinetti challenged the numbers put up by S-M that seemed to severely restrict the post-Keynesian (Cambridge) outcomes. To recall the point, the S-M numbers of $s_c = .20$ and $P/Y = .25$ imply a ratio of investment to output over the long-term of .05 with the Pasinetti regime failing to hold when:

$$s_{Wo} \geq \frac{I}{Y} \qquad (163)$$

Should we assume a secular growth rate of 3.5% or 4%, we come up with a capital to output ratio of 1.4 or 1.25. Pasinetti's counter-argument is that these magnitudes are clearly less than half of those observed in western capitalist economies and cannot be considered what S-M labelled as "econometrically reasonable". Instead, if we take a capital to output ratio that is closer to reality, say 3.5, and maintain a growth rate of 4%, we arrive at an investment to output ratio of 14%. So that the value of (s_{Wo}) needed to thrust the economy into the anti-Pasinetti regime is in the order of 14%; and this order of the savings propensity to quote Pasinetti, "seems to be far beyond workers' saving propensities either at present or in the foreseeable future".[19] The Pasinetti reaction and the neoclassical replies were carried on mainly in the latter part of the 1960s and into the 1970s when the world appeared hardened in its division between capitalist and socialist economies where in the latter the state assumed the relevant role of the capitalist class.

Yet aside from the issue of the reasonableness of the level of (s_{Wo}), the credibility of the anti-Pasinetti regime was put to doubt on the basis of its theoretical underpinning; that is, on the assumption of the flexibility of the capital to output ratio and on the relationship between this ratio and the rate of profit. First off, we return to a point in our exposition of S-M where we mentioned that the model does not require that the rate of profit be the marginal productivity of capital; that the rate of profit simply be posed as a determinant function of the capital to labor ratio for whatever theory of distribution may be put forth. Now this may seem kind of strange since the savings of workers poses no threat to long-term equilibrium due to the response of $r^{**} < r^*$ as a direct relation to the capital to output ratio in the dual exceeding that of the Pasinetti state. And the rate of profit is 'explained' — supposedly — by the slope of the production function in conjunction with the equilibrium distribution of income as determined by the marginal productivities of factors. Thus the profit earnings of workers adjusts in response to the greater capital intensity of production. All this is what we consider a 'marginal productivity analysis' (the reader may want to review the neoclassical story in Chapter 3). Either the marginal productivity of capital determines what the rate of profit is or it does not; and if it does not, then what S-M are saying is that in the long run, the marginal productivity of capital will be equal to an independently determined rate of profit. Thus the rate of profit determines what the marginal productivity of capital is going to be, which is the opposite of neoclassical reasoning.

Pasinetti's response to the S-M reasoning is "I personally find these arguments unconvincing since marginal productivity is a concept which was invented to explain the rate of profit. Professors Samuelson and Modigliani now seem to turn the problem around and aim at using the rate of profit in order to explain and justify the concept of marginal productivity".[20] What S-M are saying is that the Pasinetti regime is defined as:

$$f'(k^*) = n/s_c = r^* \tag{164}$$

and its dual opposite is:

$$\frac{f(k^{**})}{k^{**}} = \frac{n}{s_{W_0}} = r^{**} \tag{165}$$

when $k_c = 0$. and to reiterate the main relation:

$$r^{**} < r^*$$

in response to

$$\frac{k^{**}}{f(k^{**})} > \frac{k^{*}}{f(k^{*})} \qquad (166)$$

What is basic to the credibility of the anti-Pasinetti outcome is not, it would appear, the issue of what to label that which determines the rate of profit in the long-term condition, as it is the notion of flexibility in technology and the related movement in the rate of profit. And it is here that Pasinetti put forward his counter-thrust.

At this point, it may be advisable for the reader to review the "Some Critical Analysis" portion of Chapter 3 where we discussed the problem involved in the measurement of capital and the concept of reswitching and what all this means for the neoclassical paradigm. What we know now is that the formally established belief that the capital to labor ratio is an inverse function of the rate of profit has been shown to be without foundation; and if there is such a relation, it is not in any event to be drawn as a conventionally smooth function (the ratio should go from near zero to near infinity). Furthermore, the measurement problem makes it clear that we have to rethink what we mean by a production function in the real world of heterogeneity of capital inputs and different ratios of capital to labor in the various output processes. And we certainly have to rethink the idea of reading relative income shares from the productivity of capital curve. The reader is also reminded of the one case where the inverse relationship would hold, which was in the surrogate capital case. But as we pointed out, one cannot generalize from this example to the real world because it is very restricted, holding only when the capital to labor ratios are the same for all output, be it capital or consumption output. Thus the anti-Pasinetti regime becomes credible if we hold to a single valued input ratio, and assume away measurement of capital problems by the presence of homogeneity of capital. We also recall that the lower rate of profit in the anti-Pasinetti case does not have to be associated with a new technique that necessarily requires a higher capital to output ratio; nothing in general can be said on whether a new technique will require a higher or lower capital to output ratio. Thus even if we were to accept the 'workers only' regime as a plausible result (due to the high amount saved from both wages and profits), its relationship to the long-term growth path would need to be based, it would appear, on some rather unreal assumptions.

Let us carry on somewhat further and see how Pasinetti frames his own attack on the S-M outcome. One thing he tells us we can be sure of, and we are aware of this from our introductory discussion of switching of techniques, is that the relation between the capital to output ratio and the rate of profit is nothing like the shape proposed by marginal productivity theorists. This is not to say that there is no relationship here; but that the connection is not clear-cut. A change in the rate of profit will effect the prices of all the physical output of the economy, it will alter relative prices (recall our Sraffian analysis) effecting some prices upward and others downward since the capital to output ratio is a macro magnitude that must be taken in value terms and since we are dealing in vast numbers of commodities (we are not in the 'corn world' where the same output is in part consumed and used as capital), it may be that these changes cancel out so that the capital to output ratio will be no different at higher or lower rates of profit. Pasinetti's overall point is:

> Surely when it is known that a certain magnitude is influenced by hundreds of effects in opposite directions, the most reasonable assumption to make, if an assumption is to be made at all, is that all of these effects will tend to cancel each other out. In other words, when the rate of profit changes, the most reasonable assumption on the capital to output ratio is, after all, Harrod-Domar original assumption that the ratio will remain constant.[21]

Now when the rate of profit changes the technique of production may also change; and one normally thinks of this as bringing into use a different apparatus or type of machine. But does this different piece of capital mean that we are using more capital or less capital? Of course, the matter is in assessing the stock of capital in value terms, and such a calculation requires knowing the rate of return. This rate of return on investment itself enters into the calculation of the cost of any particular array of capital goods. So an essential element in the S-M argument which is to repeat:

$$r = \frac{\text{Total Profit}}{\text{Capital}} = \frac{P}{K} = \frac{P_c + P_{W_0}}{K} \tag{167}$$

$$r = MP_K = f'(k) = \frac{df(K,L)}{dK} \tag{168}$$

is engaging in circularity of reasoning. A quantity from which a marginal product can be derived to determine the rate of profit cannot itself be had without an estimation of what the rate of profit is. Joan Robinson's trenchant comment about this is: "The analysis showed that there is no meaning to be given to the 'quantity of capital' apart from the rate of profit, so that the contribution that the 'marginal product of capital' determines the rate of profit is meaningless".[22] The reader should perhaps review matters along these lines in Chapter 3 and how it has led to the construction of a different kind of production function.

But aside from the capital valuation problem, recent analysis has made us aware that the movement of the capital to output ratio has finite limits. There is a v_{max} and a v_{min} above and below which the ratio will not go. The function relating the ratio to the rate of profit is not smoothly differentiable, is not monotonic. Thus while it moves within a finite range inversely to the change in the rate of profit, the obvious question is how wide is this range likely to be? This brings us into an area of analysis beyond where we want to go with this book; but it is clear that for the Harrod-Domar models this band is taken as exceedingly narrow, so that it is reasonable to picture the *max* and *min* positions as being reduced to a horizontal line. While this approach may be too 'simple', it is one thing to object that (v) may not be entirely constant, and indeed move very limitedly; but it is another thing, as Pasinetti puts it, "to strain exasperatedly such a band (as the marginal productivity theorists have done) and make it cover the whole positive quadrant from zero to infinity".[23]

There are two points here. One is that if the aggregate inverse relationship holds, it would only do so within a finite region, thus the threateningly high workers savings may not be absorbed by the change in technology — as the growth path breaks down. Secondly, there is much question about the negative relationship in the first place. The capital to output ratio may go up or may go down as the rate of profit changes, and since we are dealing with vast numbers of production processes, the overall result may simply be no aggregate change in the ratio.

As part of a symposium on capital theory, Pasinetti published a paper, "Changes in the Rate of Profit and Switches of Techniques", towards the end of which he concludes:

> At any given state of technical knowledge, switches of technique due to changes in the rate of profit do not allow us to make any general statement on changes in the 'quantity of capital' per unit of labor. The new technology may require a lower 'quantity of capital' per unit of labor or it may require a higher 'quantity of capital' per unit

of labor, whether capital is measured in terms of value or in terms of any chosen physical unit, whether we consider any single industry or the economic system as a whole.[24]

The rate of profit does not given an assured signal about the abundance or scarcity of capital with the most profitable technique in use. Hence, why should the capital to output ratio be different at the minimum rate of profit $r=0$ than at the maximum rate of profit $r=Y/K$? So the smooth negative function whereby the capital to output ratio tends to zero as the rate of profit approaches its maximum, and tends to infinity as the rate of profit approaches zero, is, to say the least, misleading marginal productivity analysis. Yet much has been based on such a continuous smooth adoptability.

If we go with the reasonable assumption of long-term constancy of the capital to output ratio then, as Pasinetti puts it, "the answer to our problems becomes very simple".[25] We find the Pasinetti outcome where $v^* = \bar{v}$ with the ratio not exceeding $\bar{v}$. Should $s_{W_0} < G_n \bar{v}$ we have equilibrium growth within the two economic classes of society; with the capitalist class playing the strategic role as the rate of profit is determined via the Cambridge equation — to reiterate $r = 1/s_c(G_n)$. The workers propensity to save does not reach the critical level beyond which they accumulate faster than the capitalists. Should $s_{W_0} > G_n \bar{v}$, equilibrium growth is not possible. There is an in-between case analagous to Harrod's 'knife-edge' growth condition where $s_{W_0} = G_n \bar{v}$. Recall that in the Harrod context the precarious characteristic stems from the instability of the warranted growth rate, while here the matter is the savings propensity of the non-capitalist class.

In the state of $s_{W_0} = G_n \bar{v}$, it is the case of one class replacing another, and in order to carry this out successfully the savings propensity of the wage group becomes crucial, for they are now performing the same functions that capitalists originally undertook. But as we mentioned earlier, the rate of profit is here indeterminate; unless we assume that this knife-edge case is one which is represented by the savings propensity of the state, i.e. a socialist economy (the state in the name of the non-capitalists class takes over the functions of the capitalist group). This brings us back to the Kaldor framework for the two class economy where we have a single source of savings, that being the capitalist class for Kaldor and the state in the knife-edge condition. The state can be represented with a savings propensity equal to unity (the state as such cannot consume) which is equivalent to the condition of $s_c = 1$; the rate of profit being determined by the Cambridge equation, but now $r = G_n$.

But not to stray too far from the central point, the issue is the transition from the Pasinetti to the anti-Pasinetti regime where the savings propensity of workers would have to take on rather high values so that the savings out of profits alone exceeds all capitalists' savings (savings taking on the form of the ownership of physical capital). The question is can the economy change in this way while still maintaining a natural growth rate? Pasinetti's defense of his regime is that the economy cannot do that; thus an understanding of long-term equilibrium growth requires an analysis of economic behavior within the framework of the two economic classes. The anti-Pasinetti state of $s_{W_0} = G_n \bar{v}$ and arrived at via a transition path is of no practical relevance. First equilibrium growth would collapse before the one class society would emerge, and furthermore, we would have a society where capitalists have been eliminated. What should we call such a system if not a socialist system? Certainly not a capitalist system with no capitalists; or do we turn the society upside-down with workers becoming capitalists and capitalists hiring themselves out for a wage and becoming workers rather than, as Kregel puts it, having them "take the honourable way out".[26] So we have a capitalistic system again with different faces occupying the two class position. But this may likely be a too civilized outcome; for even if we could imagine the society in this in-between state, what recent history teaches is that people who recently performed the capitalists' role would indeed take their leave, honourable or otherwise.

Now let us, for the sake of argument, take the approach that there is long-term flexibility in the capital to output ratio. The interesting question then is just how wide (from v_{max} to v_{min}) can we reasonably expect this ban to be; and would it come anywhere near allowing — as a hypothetical considering — the emergence of a workers-only outcome? Marginalists have provided an example of such flexibility hypothesizing a function running from a $v_{max} = 12.5$ to $v_{min} = 3.2$ and portrayed in Fig. (7.4).

We know that the rate of profit cannot exceed that of the Pasinetti regime where workers' savings are relevant to the outcome, so that the line to the right of v^* is of no concern. Seeing this via a more conventional diagram in Fig. (7.5), it is the dashed line below v^* that can be discarded.

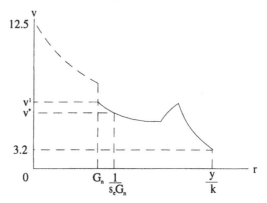

Figure 7.4

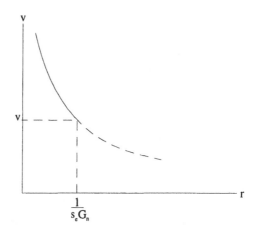

Figure 7.5

While marginalists portray the production function as 'well-behaved' with the capital to output ratio as totally flexibility, in reality it cannot fall below v^*. So it is the area above v^* that interests us.

Now in the in-between state where capitalists have departed we find:

$$\frac{s_{Wo}}{G_n} = v^* \tag{169}$$

then as long as:

$$\frac{s_{Wo}}{G_n} \prec v^* \qquad (170)$$

both classes co-exist and we have the Pasinetti outcome. But the relevant question here is what is the state of affairs when relationship (170) is reversed? Well, we can find:

$$\frac{s_{Wo}}{G_n} > v^* \qquad (171)$$

$$\frac{s_{Wo}}{G_n} > v_{max} \qquad (172)$$

but the latter inequality, as we are aware, results in no equilibrium growth at all. Recalling our growth analysis via the Harrod model where the assumption was that of a fixed v; then the system cannot maintain equilibrium growth when $s/v > G_n$ — which is like the inequality (172). So the range for the capital to output ratio and corresponding rate of profit for which it is possible for the anti-Pasinetti regime to hold is:

$$v^* \preceq \frac{s_{Wo}}{G_n} \preceq v_{max} \qquad (173)$$

But what is the degree of variability in the rate of profit and thereby in the width between v^* and v_{max}. The smaller this band the less possibility of workers being the only category of savers that propels the system along equilibrium growth. We know that the upper bound to the rate of profit reflecting the irrelevancy of workers savings is the $1/s_c(G_n)$ outcome, and the lower limit is that the rate of profit cannot fall below the natural growth of the system (should $s_c = 1$, then $r = G_n$). Thus even if we were to accept a high degree of flexibility in the capital to output ratio in its sensitivity to the rate of profit, what we see is that variability in the rate of profit is itself very limited, which means that the capital output ratio will change within a very narrow range. The variation in the rate of profit is restricted to:

$$G_n \prec r \preceq 1/s_c \cdot G_n \qquad (174)$$

There is not much room for the rate of profit to fall, i.e. for the capital output ratio to rise, so that the economy accommodates the high level of

337

workers savings and maintains the full-employment growth rate. Looking again at Fig. (4), we see that v_{max} is really v'; so that the neoclassical argument for long-term flexibility in the ratio turns out to be an argument for a very limited variability — there is not much support here to justify the anti-Pasinetti theorem.[27] The level of workers savings that will cause them to eventually own all the capital in existence will in all likelihood be incompatible with long-term full-employment growth.

As we previously mentioned, the anti-Pasinetti theorem and the rebuttle to it has spawned much discussion in the literature, but we do not pursue these arguments beyond what we have done. Yet what is it that we want to come away with at this juncture? It is certainly not a matter of avoiding the demise of the 'capitalist'. On the world stage, the battle between capitalism and socialism is over with the latter having been defeated; but it is very much a matter whether capitalism can, so to speak, 'justify' its victory by being able to maintain long-term full-employment growth — and to do so with an overwhelmingly private enterprise framework. And here it is not so much the issue of the distribution of income between categories of income (though this is not unimportant), as it is in the modern context, that of the social distribution of income; what is of primary concern is the distribution of income between categories of people (idealistically within this notion of 'categories' we would include the government). This social distribution will have bearing on the growth and exuberance of that class of people whose role, as it were, is to propel the economy forward.

Now having used the term 'modern context', we want to recast much of this discussion in terms of the behavior of the capitalist as being, to an important degree, that of the 'megacorp', which will have us look again at the categories of savings coefficients.

An updated reformulation

What we will be considering is a further defense of the Pasinetti long-run outcome; one that is based on modern institutional arrangements of finance and will tell us something about the availability of and demand for securities in the context of economic growth.[28] We will more meaningfully come to understand what makes up the level of savings in the economy that is available for investment by the business sector. At the very outset let us engage in a brief recall.

We understand that when workers save and receive thereby a part of the profit income, this will have no effect on the level of savings as a proportion of aggregate income. While it is true that workers' propensity to save out of profits is at a lesser rate than capitalists would have saved out of these profits had they retrained them, so that a sharing of profits means that aggregate savings from profits are lower. It is also true that this excess consumption out of profits (in excess of what capitalists would have consumed out of these profits) is offset by workers savings out of wages alone. The point is that the combination of profits and wages received by workers will cause their total savings to be equal to what capitalists would have saved out of these workers profits. Thus the sharing of profits with workers cannot affect total savings. This is a result of the assumption that workers have a single savings propensity for both wages and profit income. Of course, this means that workers' savings do not impact on the ratio of investment to output (the essential capitalist activity) and will have no effect on the ratio of profits to wage income nor on the rate of profit. The reader can revisit equation (117) in this chapter and the surrounding discussion, which reflect our words here, or we can restate this as:

$$s_{W_0}(W) = (1 - s_{W_0}) P_{W_0} - (1 - s_c) P_{W_0}$$

$$= s_c (P_{W_0}) - s_{W_0}(P_{W_0}) \tag{175}$$

or

$$s_{W_0}(W) + s_{W_0}(P_{W_0}) = s_c(P_{W_0})$$

So workers are spending more out of their profits compared to what capitalists would have spent had they retained these profits.

Now we want to represent the capitalists mainly as the corporation that earns profits, part of which are consumed in the form of the pay-out of dividends and other non-investment spending, and part of which is retained which we consider as corporate savings. We represent the society as consisting of two broad classifications of persons; one is the household classification consisting of workers who receive wages and may also receive property-income, e.g. dividends, and also consisting of rentiers whose income consists solely of property-income. These are lumped together and given a savings propensity (s_H) which was what we previously considered as the savings propensity of workers s_{W_0}. And there is an institutional classification that of the corporation whose savings propensity we designed as (s_I) analogous to (s_c).

339

For the aggregate level of savings to remain unchanged for a given corporate pay-out ratio, households must spend in excess of their profit income; they must, so to speak, overspend their dividend income as long as some of net profits is retained by the corporation. The corporation retention ratio is that of retained earnings to net profits which we define as corporate savings; and it is equal to one minus the pay-out ratio which is the ratio of dividends to net profits. This 'overspending' must hold as long as the households propensity to save is below the retention ratio, and is a direct result of the assumption of a single savings propensity on the part of households.

We set out some relationships. Household income consists of wages plus dividends, thus:

$$Y_H = W + (1 - s_I)P_I \qquad (176)$$

The level of non-wage income is seen here to depend on the institutional (corporate) pay-out ratio of dividends (D) to net profits. So:

$$\delta = \frac{D}{P_I} \qquad (177)$$

and the higher (s_I) the greater retentions and the lower the pay-out ratio. Total net income to the system consists of income to households and retained earnings by corporations; that is:

$$Y = W + \delta P_I + (1 - \delta)P_I \qquad (178)$$

If the savings propensity of households is zero, then the savings of the system is equal to corporate retentions, thus:

$$S = (1 - \delta)P_I \qquad (179)$$

When households save a portion of their income so that their average propensity to consume is less than one $(c_H < 1)$, we have household savings as:

$$S_H = (1 - c_H)Y_H \qquad (180)$$

with aggregate savings being:

$$S=(1-c_H)Y_H+(1-\delta)P_I \qquad (181)$$

Some numbers will be helpful at this point. Suppose we have wage income of 100 and net profits of 70 and a household's savings propensity of .2. Should all profits be paid out we would find:

$$Y_W=100+70$$

$$S_H=s_H(170)=34 \qquad (182)$$

$$C_H=c_H(170)=136$$

Total savings being household savings. Now change the circumstance and suppose that the 'institution' maintains a retention rate of 50%. Then:

$$\delta=.5=\frac{D}{70}$$

$$D=35 \qquad (183)$$

With institutional savings being:

$$S_I=(1-.5)70 \qquad (184)$$

$$=35$$

and household savings are:

$$S_H=s_H(100+35) \qquad (185)$$

$$=27$$

with aggregate savings being 62.

But as we have been saying, when $s_H>0$ and households do share in profit income, this will make no difference with regard to the level of savings. In the Pasinetti regime the rate of profit is independent of the rate of savings of households. The logical consistency of this, when households receive property income, is, to reiterate, for workers to reduce their aggregate savings by spending in excess of (overspending) their profit income; that is, to spend more out of wage income than would be the case if they received no profit income — if the pay-out ratio were zero.

In our little example, household savings will be reduced by 28 for a corporate retention ratio of 50%. This means that households will consume all profit income and increase their spending out of wage income by a fraction required to reduce aggregate savings to 34 — what it was before the change in the retention ratio. Note that 'overspending' will see household consumption increasing by 28 which is equal to $(1-s_H)P_H$. To put the matter another way: this is like saying that households spend additionally out of their non-property income an amount equal to their profit income. Thus where we previously had $c_H=.8(100)$ we now find $c_H=.8(135)=128$ yielding negative savings out of wage income of 28. Thus in the changed circumstance of the 50% pay-out rate we have $s_I=35$ and overspending (negative savings) property income by the amount required to restore aggregate savings to that before the change in the pay-out rate. But it is aggregate income that is really being 'under-saved'; thus where we had $c=.8(135)=108$ we now overspend by 28 so total consumption is 136, which gives us the necessary negative savings to restore the aggregate savings level to 34.

Having entered a world in which the corporate retention effects household savings within the long-term context of the constancy of the savings ratio, we need to see that there is variability regarding the treatment of property income by different types of households within the aggregate.

To say that households overspend their property income is saying that 'workers' — households that also receive wage income — behave this way; and it is also to be presumed that rentiers-shareholder households whose income is derived almost entirely from asset earnings will overspend their gains by selling assets in the face of low earnings. To these 'active' households we add retirees who are overspending their retirement income by dissaving in the form of selling off their past accumulated wealth. And we have active households who are adding to their property income by accumulating assets. So in general we have households that save either directly or through intermediaries and are accumulating assets; and the dissaver households both active and retired.

These activities by different households result in a net savings out of income which provides a demand for securities in the securities market, as well as a net dissaving out of income (reflecting the consumption of capital) which yields a supply of securities. And one must add to this a net supply of new securities issued by the corporate sector. We have a 'market equilibrium' for securities as:

$$s_H(W) = c(g_a) + i(G_K) \qquad (186)$$

It is net savings out of wage income either directly or through intermediaries that sets up a demand for securities, and it is, to repeat, net dissavings out of income (i.e. net consumption out of capital) that gives the supply of securities. And the assumption is that the selling off of assets will be some fraction of capital gains (g_a). As we said one would also have to add the more or less continuous sell-off on the part of retirees. Also we have to reckon with the fact that corporations will finance their current investment expenditures (reflecting a particular growth rate of capital) in part from retentions, and they may decide in addition to finance via the issuance of new securities; so we have a net supply of new issues as $i(G_K)$ — i being the fraction of current investment financed this way.

In this market there is a mechanism that equilibrates the demand for securities essentially attributable to savings out of wages to the consumption of capital minus any new issues by the corporate sector. Such a mechanism is the level of security prices, and the only item in the market equation (186) that is responsive to security price changes is the $c(g_a)$; for (g_a) is nothing else than the change in the market value of securities. But the capital gains element will do more than that; it will be instrumental in relating aggregate savings — now to be considered as the sum of net personal savings plus corporate retentions — with aggregate investment in the economy. Before getting to this, let us set out again just what constitutes net income and savings in this discussion. We restate the savings equation (183) as:

$$S = s_H(W + (1-\delta)P_I) + s_I(P_I) \qquad (187)$$

where

$$s_I(P_I) = \delta P_I$$

telling us that the savings of the household sector available for investment depends not only on that sector's savings propensity, but as well on the retention ratio (the savings propensity) of the institutional-corporate sector. And this latter element depends on the policies of corporations regarding the issuing of new securities. Then if we restate the securities market equation as:

$$c(g_a) = s_H(Y_H) - i(G_K) \tag{188}$$

there will be a level of capital gains that balances the securities market. The corporate issue of new securities plus the spending of capital gains constitutes the supply of securities that adjusts to the demand for securities as governed by savings of households. Thus the purchase of assets by active households will exceed the consumption of capital to the degree necessary to absorb the new issues necessary to finance the growth in the capital stock along the long-term full-employment path. For a given retention policy, and household savings propensity, it is the level of security prices that yields the requisite level of net savings to finance the growth in investment.

As a characteristic of the growth path, within the confines of the Pasinetti regime we find:

$$s_H(W) - c(g_a) + s_I(P_I) = G_K \tag{189}$$

$$s_H(W) - c(g_a) = G_K - s_I(P_I) = i(G_K) \tag{190}$$

[In writing equation (190) we are saying that although active households receive wage income and property income, they accumulate assets out of the former only so that they consume all of their dividend income.]

Thus with given savings propensities it is the level of security prices (the gains) that becomes strategic; and Kaldor, who was instrumental in developing this reformulation of the Pasinetti result, sets up an equation that relates the rise in the market value of securities to the increase in earnings and the pay-out ratio and also to the rise in what he refers to as the 'book value' of assets. This book value which he also labels the valuation ratio (which we designate by (a)) is a particular relation (it is not the financial notion of the book value of common stock); it is the ratio of the market value of securities to the capital employed. We obtain this valuation ratio as:

$$a = \frac{\text{Market Value of Shares}}{\text{Value of Capital}} \tag{191}$$

the capital gains will then be the result of the increase in capital (the growth rate of capital) multiplied by the valuation ratio which gives the increase in the value of existing securities from which one deducts the price of the new securities issued to finance the growth of the capital stock. When some of the investment is financed by retained profits, capital gains accrues to existing shareholders as the capital value per share increases.

We can write:

$$g_a = N\Delta p = a\Delta K - \Delta Np$$

and

$$\Delta K = G_K \tag{192}$$

$$p\Delta N = i(G_K)$$

where iG_K, to reiterate, is that fraction of investment expenditures financed by the issue of new securities; this being inversely related to the retention ratio.

Then:

$$s_H(W) - c(a\Delta K - \Delta Np) = i(G_K) \tag{193}$$

giving us the saving investment equality along the growth path as:

$$s_H(W) - c(a\Delta K - \Delta Np) + s_I(P_I) = G_K \tag{194}$$

It is net savings from the household sector plus retained corporate profits that provide the wherewithal to finance the growth in investment; with that portion financed by retentions being:

$$s_I(P_I) = G_K - i(G_K)$$

$$= G_K(1 - i) \tag{195}$$

There is an interplay among these variables; since the degree of retentions, given the investment demand, will determine the extent of new issue financing which impacts on the change in the market value of securities and influences net savings.

345

With some substitution and rearranging of terms we come to the expression that represents this Pasinetti reformulation which has been termed the neo-Pasinetti theorem. We have $W=Y-P, P=rK, \Delta K=G_K$ and $i(G_K)=p\Delta N$, and by substitution (193) we obtain:

$$s_H(Y-rK)-ca(G_K)+ci(G_K)=i(G_K) \qquad (196)$$

which upon division by G_K yields:

$$\frac{s_H(Y)}{G_K}-\frac{s_H(r)}{G}-ca+ci=i \qquad (197)$$

A similar operation on equation (196) gives:

$$\frac{s_H(Y)}{G_K}+\frac{(s_I-s_H)r}{G}-ca+ci=1 \qquad (198)$$

We can with (197) and (198) solve for the long-term equilibrium rate of profit in this new framework and for the valuation ratio. We need to rearrange terms and subtract (198) from (197); and let us follow through for the determination of the rate of profit. Thus:

$$-\frac{s_H(r)}{G}-ca=i-ci-\frac{s_H(Y)}{G_K} \qquad (199)$$

$$\frac{(s_I-s_H)r}{G}-ca=1-ci-\frac{s_H(Y)}{G_K} \qquad (200)$$

then:

$$\frac{-s_H(r)}{G}-\frac{(s_I-s_H)r}{G}=i-1 \qquad (201)$$

so:

$$-\frac{s_I(r)}{G}=i-1$$

and:

$$r = \frac{G(1-i)}{s_I} \tag{202}$$

By substituting this value for the rate of profit into equation (198) and going through some manipulations we solve for (a) as:

$$a = \frac{1}{c} \left[\frac{s_H(Y)}{G_K} - \frac{s_H}{s_I}(1-i) - i(1-a) \right] \tag{203}$$

How shall we interpret these outcomes? Certainly if there were no new securities issued implying that the retention ratio absorbs all profits, so that the growth in investment is entirely internally financed, then the net savings of the household sector over the long term would be zero. This is akin to the vision of the original Kaldor model where workers played no role in the outcome of the economy because they were assumed to simply not save. Here one sees this net savings of zero as a trading-off of old assets; but having no impact on the financing of future investment to sustain a growth rate from a point in time on.

But realistically the retention ratio is not one so new securities will be issued, and this will have a downside effect on security prices and thereby on capital gains. What this does is to reduce the sale of securities by household dissavers thereby increasing the net savings of the household sector generally to the point of absorbing the new issues by the institutional sector necessary to keep investment expanding at the proper rate. To use Kaldor's own words here, "The issue of new securities by corporations will depress security prices (i.e. the valuation ratio) just enough to reduce the sale of securities by the dissavers' sufficiently to induce the net savings required to take up the new issues".[29] What is happening underneath these movements is that the corporate sector is transferring part of its net profits (and if we had this sector retain all its profits we can then relate net profits to savings so what is being transferred is a portion of corporate savings) to households via a pay-out ratio which then comes back to the corporation in the form of the sale of its securities. Thus while the net savings of the household sector will in part depend on the pay-out ratio, there is no effect on total savings because the retention ratio is less than one, the increase in net savings in the household sector is balanced by the pay-out ratio of the corporate sector. Profits are related to the investment and pricing activity of the corporate sector; it is this activity which determines aggregate savings. The level of savings does not change because households partake in the financing of investment expenditures.

Now the interpretation of equation (203) is clear. In the condition of the long-term full-employment growth path with a given capital to output ratio and particular savings propensities, there exists a particular valuation ratio, that is, a level of security prices, that results in household net savings that when added to corporate retentions results in the aggregate savings-investment equality. The securities market brings into equality net household savings with corporate investment expenditures minus retained profits, i.e. with the level of external finance. We appreciate the behavior of the (a) element as another one of those underpinnings of this steady-state growth path; and its value can be greater or lesser than unity depending on the values of the savings propensities and of the (c) and (i) variables. Relating to the assumption of the Pasinetti regime which, in this framework, we state as $s_H(Y) \prec G_K$, then $a \prec 1$ for a retention ratio of less than unity implying $i \succ 0$ (with (c) being some positive excess consumption over-dividend income, i.e. net consumption out of capital gains).

We see capital gains, i.e. the level of security prices, playing the essential role of maintaining equilibrium in the securities market; that is, in adjusting 'portfolio balances' in the household sector to continuously support the required growth in investment. Yet this terminology of 'security equilibrium' or 'portfolio balance' is a mirror of the existence of a net savings level of the household sector, which is to say that it reveals the level of effective demand that is ensuring full employment on the long-term path.

It is equation (202) that has come to be most representative of this reformulation or neo-Pasinetti theorem; for the determination of the rate of profit is freed from, its dependency on "a class of hereditary capitalists with a special high-savings propensity".[30] The long-term rate of profit depends on the rate of growth, the proportion of external finance and the savings propensity of the institution-corporation and does not involve 'personal' (class of people) savings propensities. The 'capitalists' propensity to save in this reformulation is a measure of corporate investment policy and the availability of finance which itself is a reflection of the corporate pay-out policy. Should all investment be internally financed, then $i=0$ and the rate of profit expression becomes:

$$r = \frac{1}{s_I}(G) \tag{204}$$

348

which is the Pasinetti equation (104) but reached via a different (modern) route. It is instructive here to read Kaldor directly concerning this corporate institution that largely replicates the individual capitalists.

> I have always regarded the high savings propensity as something which attaches to the nature of business income, and not the wealth (or other peculiarities) of the individuals who own property. It is the enterprise, not the particular body of individuals owning it at any one time, which finds it necessary in a dynamic world of increasing returns, to plough back a proportion of profits as a kind of prior charge on earnings. This is because continued expansion cannot be ensured...unless some proportion of the finance required for expansion comes from internal sources. Hence the high savings propensity attaches to profits as such, not to capitalists as such.[31]

Returning to the circumstance of the rate of profit determination of equation (204), we find balance in the securities market as:

$$s_H(W) = c(g_a) \qquad (205)$$

that is, the demand for assets by savers will be equal to the sale of securities by shareholders in order to finance consumption out of capital gains with net personal savings of the household sector equal to zero. In essence, households become irrelevant for the required investment expenditures and determination of the long-term rate of profit. A look behind the scene reveals that the higher level of income generated by corporate investment policy sets up an increased demand for securities resulting in a higher 'offer price'. This means a higher level of capital gains and a greater liquidation of securities by 'inactive' households; and with a net increase in demand, security prices will rise to clear the market. We see a change in the portfolio balance of individual households, but no change in the quantity of securities held by the non-institutional segment of the economy. The required investment to maintain the growth path is equal to corporate savings, i.e. retained profits, for a given distribution of income between profits and wages. Thus while household savings equates with 'household investment', it has no bearing on the determination of the growth condition and on the rate of profit.

However, going to the perhaps more realistic rate of profit determination of equation (204), we find that profit retention falls short of investment expenditures and hence the savings of the household sector becomes instrumental in providing the necessary finances to bring about the corporate spending that generates the level of profits. Thus, in words we have used before, we see again that while households share in the distribution of income between themselves and the corporate sector, they do not determine the level of profits. But we should emphasize an important difference between the original Pasinetti theorem and this reformulation. In the former, the household sector (workers) were 'assigned' a savings propensity through which they participated in profit earnings, but there was no visible connection between the action of the 'capitalist' and the savings of the 'worker'. In the latter, as we have seen, the savings of the household sector is itself influenced by corporate policy. The investment decision by the corporate-institutional sector is crucial not only with regard to the level of investment but with the manner in which it is financed.

Using the relationship concerning corporate savings and pay-out decisions, it will behoove us at this point to take a somewhat different approach to the impact of corporate investment policy. Here we would look at matters more from the income and consumption side; we want to reiterate that we are considering different scenarios for the economy as it is progressing along the full-employment steady-state path.

In a somewhat simpler environment, we now posit a society consisting of a single type of household; one that is 'active' receiving wage income and also receiving profit income in the form of dividends received on securities held. Here all employment is employment by the corporate-institution whose managers are decision makers with regard to the investment decision and the mechanics of finance. Capital gains do not enter into the analysis so that this is not part of income, and these working households will have a single propensity to save applied to their income.[32]

Total net income in the system is equal to household income plus corporate retained earnings (R) which is shown in equation (178) and restated here (omitting the I subscript):

$$Y = Y + R = W + \delta P + (1 - \delta)P \qquad (206)$$

and aggregate savings is that of (181) which we also state here:

$$S = (1 - C_H)Y_H + (1 - \delta)P \qquad (207)$$

Aggregate income can be represented as $Y = C + S$, so that:

$$Y_H + R = Y = c_H(W + \delta P) + (1 - \delta)P + (1 - c_H)(W + \delta P) \tag{208}$$

with household income by itself as:

$$Y_H = c_H(W + \delta P) + (1 - c_H)(W + \delta P) \tag{209}$$

the difference, of course, being that of retained earnings. From equation (210) we see:

$$Y_H + R = Y = W + P \tag{210}$$

and from (209) that:

$$Y_H = W + \delta P \tag{211}$$

with retained earnings as:

$$R = P - \delta P$$

$$= (1 - \delta)P \tag{212}$$

which is corporate savings (as we related previously with equation 179).

What we note straightaway is that a given pay-out ratio (δ) effects both the level of consumption and savings of households and the level of savings for the system as a whole. Should $s_H = 0$, then, to reiterate, all savings is done by the corporation and is equal to retained profits:

$$S = R \tag{213}$$

Looking again at equations (208) and (209) we find the pay-out ratio on the right hand side of both equations, telling us that for a given (c_H) the value of (δ) determines the spending and savings outcome for households and more importantly for the total system. We can then relate the aggregate economy with its propensities as:

$$Y = c(Y) + s(Y) \tag{214}$$

and these propensities will, in the usual run of events, differ from (c_H) and (s_H) depending on the value of (δ).

In the condition of $\delta=1$ there are no retained profits so all savings is household savings as $S=1-c_H(W+P)$. Indeed household consumption propensity is that of the aggregate as a result of the total transfer of profits; as we can say that (s_H) sets the savings propensity as related to aggregate income generated by the economy. In this case aggregate and household propensities converge. At the other extreme where $\delta=0$ there is no household profit income and we find the greatest divergence between the aggregate savings propensity (s) and that of households (s_H) as:

$$S=(1-c_H)W+R=s(Y) \tag{215}$$

Certainly households do not set the aggregate savings ratio. In this case household consumption is at minimum when compared to aggregate consumption when total income is household income. So a state of total retention results in the greatest divergence between (c) and (c_H) and between (S) and $(1-c_H)$. Thus the lower the pay-out ratio the higher the value of (s) which is itself higher than $(1-c_H)$, and the lower the value of (c) which is itself lower than (c_H). The critical point, to repeat, is that the level of the pay-out ratio will determine the savings condition for the aggregate economy which will be quite different from that of the household sector. Of course, the value of (δ) cannot effect the total income in the system to which households have nominal claim; all it does is limit the household's spendable income out of its total income claim.

Some numbers will be helpful in seeing this. Suppose we have an aggregate income of 20 with $W=125$ and $P=75$ and assume $(c_H)=.75$. when $\delta=0, Y_H=125$ with household consumption and savings being 93.75 and 31.25 respectively. But as a proportion of aggregate income we have a consumption propensity $c=.47$ and an aggregate savings ratio of .53. Household savings when added to corporate savings (here equal to P) gives total savings of 106.25 out of the total income of 200. At the other end with $Y_H=200$ ($\delta=1$) household consumption will be maximum and the propensities converge. Household consumption comes to 150 with $(c_H)=(c)$ and aggregate savings equals household savings at a ratio of .25.

Consider the inbetween case of $\delta=.50$. Household income comes to 162.50 with corporate retained profits equal to 37.50. Household consumption is 121.87 which as a proportion of total income gives an aggregate consumption propensity of .60 (thus $c<c_H$). Household savings is 78.12 which out of a total income of 200 yields, a total propensity of .39. Thus the reduction in (δ) increased the value of (s) which is itself higher than (s_H).

352

We can now consider additional characteristics of an economy on the long-term path as a result of differences in the value of (δ). If we presume a policy of $\delta = 1$, then, as we have seen, it is the savings of the household sector that is crucial and sets the savings ratio in the aggregate. Putting this another way, we are saying that given the 'correct' level of investment it is the household sector that accommodates to maintain the economy on the equilibrium path. And this accommodation takes the form of a level of consumption spending such that savings as a proportion of total household income $(W+P)$ is equal to that of the capital sector. But should the level of consumption expenditure be too high for a particular (c_H), then the capital sector as a proportion of total output will be higher than savings as a proportion of household income, aggregate demand rises too rapidly and the economy experiences higher prices and higher profit levels. At a point in time, with the wage rate given, the level of aggregate income will be the same. But its real value declines due to this misalignment of the savings ratio. Yet the result of $\delta = 1$ is simply to recycle this increase in profits back to the household sector in the form of a corresponding increase in dividend income; so that in fact there is no decline in the real value of household income when prices rise, as a result of a zero propensity to save on the part of the corporate section. Interestingly enough, what we are saying is that no matter what the price or the rate of profit is, the savings proportion out of aggregate income will be unaffected. The only question, given this particular pay-out policy, for the nature of the growth path (whether it will be explosive — similar to a Harrod departure — or stable) is whether this constant real savings ratio will be greater or less than investment.

Thus the long-term equilibrium path with constancy in the rate of profit is conditional upon an aggregate savings ratio which, to repeat, is that of the household sector. It is not dependent upon a correct distribution of income between the corporate-institutional sector and the single income class recipients called 'active' households. The idea of altering the real wage to shift resources to accommodate the requisite growth rate (as we analyzed in the Kaldor model) is not workable in this circumstance. The pay-out ratio as it effects or does not effect the real value of income has to be given consideration in our understanding of the steady-state growth picture.

This brings us to the other case where the corporate policy is one of zero dividends, that is, $R=P$. As we have seen, this results in maximum divergence between the aggregate savings propensity and that of households as no part of household income is attributable to profit income.

Should the value of savings now given by $(1-c_H)W+R$ be less than the rate of investment, then consumption will increase along with profit margins, as will the level of savings since retained earnings rise with profits. In this case it is the wage that sets the disposable income while the real value of this income will be affected by the corporate's pricing policy in line with its investment objective. We can presume a scenario in which the household sector via its particular (c_H) triggers the corporate response to increase the mark-up resulting in higher prices and profit levels (given the level of money wages). This reduction in the real value of household income is 'returned' to the system in the form of higher aggregate savings; there is a shift in income via reduced savings on the part of households to higher profits and retentions (savings) to the corporate sector. Should the household sector reduce savings further in an attempt to maintain real consumption levels, then prices, the rate of profit and retentions will increase even further while the real value of income falls all the more. But all this is doing is to accelerate the rate of inflation and the transfer of household savings to the corporate sector in the form of retained profits.

What is happening is that the rate of corporate expenditures plus increased levels of household spending will suffice, for a period of time, to maintain full employment in conjunction with higher rates of inflation. But we would expect that this combination of events cannot continue as the reduction in real income begins to rein-in household expenditures with inflation beginning to weaken. Indeed this process comes to a halt when the income shift is such that the reduced household savings plus corporate retentions cover what was 'excess' investment; and steady growth proceeds with a lower level of household savings but a sufficiently higher level of corporate savings — and this sufficiency is reflected by the fact that profit margins and inflation stop rising. We keep in mind that the increase in profit levels is not 'returned' to the system, it is saved as higher corporate retentions. The question before us was how the economy adjusts when savings is below this rate of investment and changes in spending come out of the household sector.

Of course, the long-term full-employment path relates in one regard to the stability of the rate of profit; so the essential element within the context of this $\delta=0$ policy is that given (s_H), it is a matter of the proper distribution between household income (W) and profits that yields the proper level of savings. Corporate pricing policy, i.e. real wage adjustment, impacts maximally on the household savings ratio and thereby on corporate profits. We reiterate the essential point that along the equilibrium growth path, it is a particular level of household real income that reveals the continued equality of household savings plus retained profits being equal to investment.

Yet the adjustment from an under-savings situation may not occur in a direct manner; so we should consider what happens if there is an excessive transfer of income leading to a decline in effective demand as $R+(1-c_H)W$ exceeds investment. Should the response be predominantly to lower the mark-up while maintaining employment, prices and profits will decline while the real income of households will rise. This fall in the price level is recycled back in the form of lower corporate savings thereby perhaps providing the savings adjustment mechanism to maintain full employment. However, should employment begin to weaken real household income may begin to fall (savings falling all the more) with investment plans now declining as well. One can imagine the system settling into a less than full-employment growth path in the Harrod form of $G=G_W<G_n$. But the point here is that lower profits are simply held as retentions, that when taken with the positive savings, will make the aggregate savings ratio too large to provide the appropriate level of effective demand in relation to the rate of investment. And the issue is whether real income will rise sufficiently or at all to alleviate the problem: The condition of insufficient demand may be tied up with excessive corporate retentions, requiring that the system back away from the policy of $\delta=0$.

An increase in (δ) will, as we showed, decrease the aggregate savings propensity as it increases household income. For a given consumption propensity the economy will manifest higher levels of demand and upward pressure on prices and profits. This effect on real income depending on the rate of inflation relative to the pay-out ratio will adjust consumption levels to the point where aggregate savings balances levels of investment. Thus the question with regard to the full-employment growth path is that given (s_H), what value of (δ) will result in the proper distribution of income between households and businesses so as to generate the necessary level of savings, i.e. to maintain the necessary level of effective demand. On the long-term path the relationship of prices to costs must be such as to yield a level of profits that for the given pay-out ratio results in the continuous equality of savings and investment.

We reiterate that a change in the pay-out ratio does not alter the level of total earnings in the economy. It will, however, change the household's portion of that income and thereby the real value of that income. And it is this change in real value which feeds back to the corporate sector in the form of profits. If the goal is to bring about higher levels of investment and growth, and if firms do link investment decisions to the rate of profit,

355

then this might very well be achieved by raising the pay-out ratio. Yet this leaves the corporation with smaller retentions and a greater dependency on external financing; thus the pay-out decision would also have to reckon with money market conditions as well as the possibility of altering the mark-up policy. Certainly the method of financing investment will have an effect on the savings-consumption decision by households and thereby on the viability of that rate of investment itself.

This neo-Pasinetti formulation presents us with as yet another variable to be brought into play in understanding capitalist-corporate behavior in maintaining a steady-state full-employment path. Certainly the aggregative work of Harrod-Domar (the single propensity to save) in breaking the Keynesian static mold was the essential 'modern' beginning (we say modern to remind us that growth economics was at the core of the 'old' classical analysis to which we are now returning); and our understanding was enhanced as a result of the reality of the distributive (disaggregative) approach of Kaldor and Pasinetti. Our most recent discussion confronted us with an added element that must be thrown up into correct alignment when we replace the corporate-institution for the capitalist-entrepreneurial class (though the latter has by no means disappeared), which is to reckon with the effect of 'shared financing' of investment on the level of savings and thereby on the growth of the economy. This, of course, in relation to decisions concerning pricing and the level of investment itself. Yet the financial decision of the firm is not oblivious to 'money conditions' and the actions of the banking system. We look at this matter in the following chapter.

NOTES

1. M. Kalecki, Theory of Economic Dynamics, Rinehart, New York, 1954, p. 45

2. Ibid., p. 47.

3. Kaldor's writings are many and his influence quite pervasive in the non-neoclassical thinking. Some works pertaining to our discussion in this chapter are: W. Kaldor, "A Model of Economic Growth," *Economic Journal*, 1957. Reprinted in Kaldor, *Essays on Economic Stability and Growth*, Free Press, Glencoe, Illinois, 1960. W. Kaldor, J. A. Meerles, "A New Model of Economic Growth," *Review of Economic Studies*, June 1962. W. Kaldor, "Alternate Theories of Distribution," *Review of Economic Studies*, 1956.

4. Kaldor, "Alternative Theories of Distribution," op. cit. p. 94.

5. Kaldor, *Essays*, op. cit. p. 276.

6. The 3/4 intercept is given by s_w, and with P/Y increasing the slope of the savings function is governed by $s_p - s_w$. The start of the I/Y line is given by the growth rate of output and the last period's rate of profit; now the last term in equation (36) can be written as $\beta'(Y/K - P/Y)$, hence as P/Y takes on positive values, I/Y will increase by $\beta'(Y/K)$.

7. For more detail via a diagrammatic exposition, see G. C. Harcourt, *Some Cambridge Controversies in the Theory of Capital*, Cambridge University Press, Cambridge, England, 1972, pp. 213-214.

8. Kaldor, "Alternative Theories of Distribution", op. cit. p. 94.

9. Kaldor, *Essays*, op. cit. p. 266. The ratio of output to capital will be increasing in the move to print P along the progress function which, in turn, will cause an increase in the ratio of investment to capital. This leads to an increasing rate of growth in output, but diminishingly so. And this movement to full employment is reinforced by increases in the rate of profit which, as well, begins to weaken as the economy loses the impetus towards increasing growth in productivity. At some

357

point then the increase in investment and the rate of capital accumulation will come into line with the growth in the labor force.

10. Kalecki, op. cit, p. 46.

11. Luigi L. Pasinetti, "Rate of Profit and Income Distribution in Relation to the Rate of Economic Growth", *Review of Economic Studies*, 1962, Vol. 29, p. 270.

12. In obtaining the last piece on the right side of (99) we first arrive at:

$$s_{wo}[\frac{Y}{I} - \frac{1}{s_C - s_{wo}} - \frac{s_{wo}}{s_C - s_{wo}}(\frac{Y}{I})]$$

which after some manipulation becomes:

$$\frac{s_{wo}s_c}{s_c - s_{wo}}(\frac{Y}{I}) - \frac{s_{wo}}{s_c - s_{wo}}$$

13. Pasinetti, op. cit., p. 272.

14. See J. A. Kregel, *Rate of Profit Distribution and Growth*, Aldine, New York, 1971, in his analysis of "When Workers Save".

15. Pasinetti, op. cit., p. 273.

16. Ibid., p. 275.

17. J. E. Meade, "The Outcome of the Pasinetti Process", *Economic Journal*, 1966, IXXVI.

18. Paul A. Samuelson, Franco Modigliani, "The Pasinetti Paradox in Neoclassical and More General Models", *Review of Economic Studies*, 1966, XXXIII.

19. Luigi L. Pasinetti, "New Results in an Old Framework", *Review of Economic Studies*, XXIII, 1966.

20. Ibid., p. 303.

21. Luigi L. Pasinetti, *Growth and Income Distribution*, Cambridge University Press, Cambridge, England, 1974, p. 134.

22. Joan Robinson, "Capital Theory Up to Date", *Canadian Journal of Economics*, May 1970.

23. Pasinetti, *Growth and Income Distribution*, op. cit., p. 133.

24. Pasinetti, *Quarterly Journal of Economics*, LXXX, p. 504-517.

25. Ibid.

26. Kregel, op. cit.

27. In the anti-Pasinetti regime we have:

$$v = \frac{s_{wo}}{G_n}$$

and the rate of profit compatible with this condition which is $r < r^*$ and obtained from the inverse of the function relating the capital to output ratio to the rate of profit. We have:

$$r = \frac{1}{f}(\frac{s_{wo}}{G_n})$$

or

$$r = f'(\frac{s_{wo}}{G_n})$$

which yields a solution for the rate of profit representing the workers regime only if the "v" is declining smoothly between $r=0, r=1/s_c \cdot G_n$ is severely restricted to the range of between G_n and $1/s_c \cdot G_n$.

28. Based on the model by Kregel, *op. cit.*, in his appendix D. Also see the analysis by Paul Davidson, "The Demand and Supply of Securities and Economic Growth and Its Implication for the Kaldor-Pasinetti

versus Samuelson-Modigliani Controversy", *American Economic Review*, 1968, LVII.

29. N. Kaldor, *Review of Economic Studies*, October 1966. See Appendix, pp. 316-319.

30. Ibid.

31. Ibid.

32. Based on the model by Kregel, *op. cit.*, in his appendix D. Also see the analysis by Paul Davidson, "The Demand and Supply of Securities and Economic Growth and Its Implication for the Kaldor-Pasinetti versus Samuelson-Modigliani Controversy", *American Economic Review*, 1968, LVII.

8   Money and Keynesian economics

The neoclassical approach and the long term

Throughout our analysis we have not talked explicitly about the role of money; or more to the point how a change in the money stock would affect (if at all) the long-term path of the economy. It is as if we have been considering money as a 'veil' behind which the real activities of the economy regarding investment, employment and growth are taking place. Indeed it appeared as if one need not even consider the existence of money to determine the real outcome of the system; it is simply 'there' as a means to facilitate transactions. We could ask the question, what reason other than to serve as a medium of exchange could possibly motivate people to hold money? A response could be that there is no other explanation; money yields no interest as would a financial asset, and its holding implies the foregoing of tangible physical goods which yields explicit services. Obviously money in and of itself is not a productive asset, financial or otherwise (perhaps it yields some implicit Midas psychic reward), so if people have a demand for money, it must be because it is the means to acquire the assets they really want (purchases and contracts are specified in terms of legal tender). Then the amount of this 'means' that people want to hold would depend on how well it serves this purpose, that is, on its value which is the inverse of the price level. And why not presume that this money-commodity behaves 'normally' in that its value depends on its scarcity which can be enhanced or diminished by the actions of an 'outside' monetary authority with the power to alter the supply of money.

If the only reason for holding some proportion of nominal income in the form of money is that it is a transaction tool, then a change in that proportion will be inverse to the value of money which itself depends on the variation of its supply. The play is to reckon that a change in the money supply solves for the price level which is mirrored in the change in the demand to hold money. Should the money supply be taken as 'fixed', then price changes would emanate from a change in the demand coefficient which we supposed, however, to be motivated by the price change itself. Though one could venture some socio-political reasons that would cause changes in money demand; the center of attention in this context of the singular money demand factor is the supply of money. And coming to the central point of pre-Keynesian classical approach (it seems that Keynes referred to all that came before him as 'classical'): it is that exogenous changes in the money supply will result in an equiproportional change in the price level without changing the level of real output and employment or the rate of interest, i.e. the rate of profit in terms of the long-run vision. So our lack of attention to money in analyzing the steady-state behavior of the real variables would seem to be of no great loss. Quite possibly, the classical model, with some changes in design, would fit well with the post-Keynesian emphasis on the long-term behavior of the economy.

Though before reaching any conclusion let us briefly set out the mechanics of this 'classical-with expectations' model; we append the expectations term because the supply curve of labor within this approach is more realistically designed on an expectations base. At the heart of this analysis is the operation of a labor market which fails to transmit a change in aggregate demand and prices — say due to monetary disturbances — to a change in employment and real output.

The model employs the usual conventional (neoclassical) assumptions: competitive conditions in the buying and selling of labor, profit maximizing firms guided by the usual marginal considerations, and a 'well-behaved' production function in short-run terms describing real output as a function of labor input, with average and marginal derivatives reflecting increasing, and after some level of employment, diminishing marginal returns to labor. While we have argued for an abandonment of this type of construction, we nevertheless use this model to show the role that money and expectations played in 'mainstream' theory; and it will then serve as the base from which we can see what happens when we change some assumptions in line with the post-Keynesian heterodox framework. We are aiming to see what conclusions we can come to about the long period effect of changes in monetary conditions.

In the conventional scheme of things, both the demand and supply of labor are functions of the real wage rate; the implication of this is that workers are presumed to completely adjust the level of expected prices (p_e), to changes in the actual price level (p), and that the nominal wage is flexible in response to labor market conditions.

First we consider the demand for labor.[1] The firm, being a 'bit player' in the marketplace, will take as given data the nominal wage of labor (W) and the selling price of its output (p). With this information the firm will increase its employment guided by the consideration that in doing so it will increase its marginal revenue product (MRP) in excess of its marginal costs (MC). The MRP is the result of multiplying the existing selling price by the increase in output as a result of the higher level of employment; but this increase in output is itself determined by the marginal product per unit of labor multiplied by the additional units of labor hired which yields, in the conventional parlance, the marginal physical product (MPP) as a result of the increase in employment. And, as we pointed out, with the usual configuration of the short-run protection function, we would expect to see a declining MRP as a result of a diminishing MPP as employment increases.

Total costs to the firm will increase linearly with the increase in employment with the rate of increase (i.e. the slope of the cost line) depending on the given money wage (W). Thus we have total cost (C) per level of employment as:

$$C = N \cdot W$$

with marginal cost as:

$$\frac{dC}{dN} = W \tag{1}$$

On the revenue side we have total revenue (R) for a given level of employment as:

$$R = p[\frac{Y}{N} \cdot N] \tag{2}$$

with the change in (R) flowing from the change in (N) being:

$$dR = p[\frac{dY}{dN} \cdot dN] \tag{3}$$

and the increase in revenue per additional unit of employment is:

$$\frac{dR}{dN} = p \cdot \frac{dY}{dN} \tag{4}$$

363

The firm will have an incentive to increase, decrease or bring about no change in employment as:

$$\frac{dR}{dN} \equiv p \cdot \frac{dY}{dN} \begin{matrix} > \\ < \end{matrix} W \equiv \frac{dC}{dN} \tag{5}$$

These decision conditions allow us to represent the demand for labor using either a real wage (w) or money wage (W) relationship. Having both of these demand curves at our disposal will be quite helpful in understanding what happens in this market.

Taking another look at equation (5) the condition of no change in employment is:

$$\frac{W}{p} = \frac{dY}{dN} \quad \text{or} \quad W = p \cdot \frac{dY}{dN} \tag{6a}$$

More employment will be offered under the condition of:

$$\frac{W}{p} < \frac{dY}{dN} \quad \text{or} \quad W < p \cdot \frac{dY}{dN} \tag{6b}$$

and less employment when:

$$\frac{W}{p} > \frac{dY}{dN} \quad \text{or} \quad W > p \cdot \frac{dY}{dN} \tag{6c}$$

We bear in mind that $\frac{dY}{dN}$ is itself a function of the level of employment so:

$$\frac{dY}{dN} = f(N) \tag{7}$$

One demand curve would be drawn with the real wage on the vertical axis as in fig. (8.1).

Every point on this demand curve represents the level of employment that the firm finds most profitable to engage at the existing real wage; the firm carries employment up to its equilibrium hiring condition of the real wage being equal to the marginal productivity of labor (i.e. that $MRP = MC$). A higher level of employment in excess of (N_o) will entail a lower productivity of labor and thereby a lower MRP (the additional employment will add less to the firm's revenue); so that this increase in hiring will have to be, so to speak, paid for either by a higher selling price so as to prevent the MRP from falling below $MC=W$, or the firm would have to see a lower nominal wage to 'compensate' for the declining productivity. Of course, in both scenarios the real wage falls as an inducement to increase employment. Now assuming that the nominal wage is fixed, then changes in the real wage and the corresponding in the demand for labor become functions of the change in the price which, under our competitive conditions, reflect changes in demand for the underlying commodity.

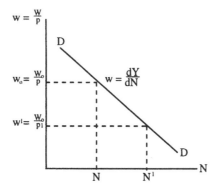

Figure 8.1

We also derive a second demand curve (Fig. 8.2) from the expressions of (6) where the curve is drawn for the money wage on the vertical axis.

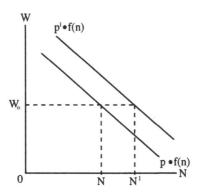

Figure 8.2

365

An increase in the amount demanded as a result in a lower real wage for a given (W_o) in Fig. (8.1) is depicted in Fig. (8.2) by a rightward shift of the demand curve relating a demand curve drawn for a higher price level. So that, the price level enters the money wage version of the demand function multiplicatively.

Our firm can readily identify the real wage confronting it; it knows the selling price which in the reality of the system is controlled by it — though we keep to the competitive story — and is aware of the nominal wage which, again with a bow to reality, is determined via a bargaining or 'conflict' outcome. But for the supplier of labor, i.e. the 'worker', the determination of the real wage is not that simple a matter. The individual worker (again there is no monopoly element in the supply of labor) being a consumer of many products confronts a wide array of prices that change in different degrees from period to period. So our generalist worker faces the question of what price to use to deflate the money wage so as to know what his real income is, but more importantly he has got to make some estimation about price levels in the future so that for the existing money he can make an estimation about the real wage and thereby adjust his offering of labor (in terms of an individual we can think in terms of the work-leisure decision). We could presume that the worker-consumer will be guided in this regard by the consumer price index, but in any event as we turn to the supply curve construction we realize that it has to be based on some formation of expectations.

As an overall configuration we have in Fig. (8.3) a positively sloped supply curve relating the expected real wage (w^e) with the quantity of labor supplied. The g term being the change in the amount of labor forthcoming).

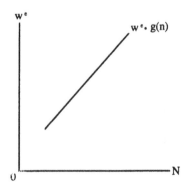

Figure 8.3

But how are expectations formed? In the most straightforward approach we presume that expectations concerning prices in $(t+1)$ are formed at the end of period (t) and are based on the existing price level in that period; and that the expected price is formed 'adoptively'. Adoptive price expectations simply mean that the expected price level in period (t) will be that which is found to exist at the end of $(t-1)$. And should prices at the end of (t) exceed expectations, then expected prices in $(t+1)$ will be equal to that mistaken higher price in (t), and so forth. There is no error correction element in the forecast here, i.e. one does not adjust one's prediction for the error of the previous forecast; the forecast, to reiterate, is based on the actual price level.

One could argue that such a simple adaptive procedure would only make sense in a world of stable prices or one of infrequent changes. But in a world of continuous price increases, this simple approach would perpetuate the same error (if the price increases move up along a trend line) with the underestimation of the true price becoming greater and greater. Some sort of correction procedure is realistically to be assumed in the adaptive procedure, and it could take the form of:

$$p_e t+1 = p_t + \lambda (p_t - p_{t-1}) \tag{8}$$

The expected price in $(t+1)$ is composed of two elements. The first is the actual price at (t) and the second is the corrective factor (λ) times the mistake in forecasting the price level at (t). Should $\lambda = 0$, past errors are not considered in determining forecasts with all weight being placed on past prices, whether that of the immediate post or some combination of past periods.

In the formation of the supply curve we are going to take the approach assuming $\lambda = 1$, so that:

$$p_e = \lambda(p) \tag{9}$$

with

$$\frac{dp_e}{dp} = \lambda' = 1$$

As the actual price level changes, there is a full adjustment of the expected price to the actual higher price. But the adjustment is really to the realized rate of change in prices that results in the actual higher price level.

367

Since the expected real wage will deteriorate (for a given nominal wage) to the degree of the expected price adjustment — here to a degree of 1 — then for the real wage to remain intact, the money wage must rise at the same rate as the expected price increase which is equal to the actual rate of increase. Hence under the full adjustment scenario the real wage will be maintained at the existing level which does bring forth a particular labor supply. We can then redraw the supply curve with the actual real wage level on the vertical axis as a result of flexible money wages to the full adjustment of expected prices. In 'rephrasing' the supply curve we write:

$$w = \frac{W}{P_e} \cdot \frac{P_e}{p} = \frac{W}{p} \tag{10}$$

and from the supply curve of Fig. (8.3)

$$w^e = \frac{W}{P_e} = g(N) \tag{11}$$

then by substitution

$$w = \frac{P_e}{p} \cdot g(N) \tag{12}$$

which gives the supply curve for labor in W,N space in Fig. (8.4).

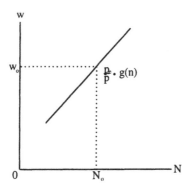

Figure 8.4

368

We can also depict the effect of an expected price change in terms of an existing money wage, which in the space of W,N will show a supply curve shift in response to a change in (p_e). From equation (11) we write:

$$W=p_e \cdot g(N) \tag{13}$$

with the resulting supply curve drawn in Fig. (8.5).

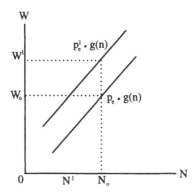

Figure 8.5

A labor supply (N_o) will be forthcoming at (W_o) where this money wage reflects an existing real wage (w_o) as a result of the adjustment to an expected price level. A higher expected price change will, for the adjusted money wage, result in a real wage decline and a reduction in the labor supply to (N') via the inward shift of the supply curve. A fully responsive money wage to the higher (p_e') maintains the existing real wage and labor supply level at (N_o).

In Figs (8.6a) and (8.6b) we see the labor market conditions for an actual change where this change has been fully adjusted to in terms of expectations and money wages. The labor market is in equilibrium as shown in both a real wage and money wage space.

We have a full-employment condition yielding a level of real output that does not result in any unintentional accumulation of inventories. In the simplest accounting statement of the economy we are saying that:

$$Y=C+I=Y=C+S$$

and

$$I=S \tag{14}$$

369

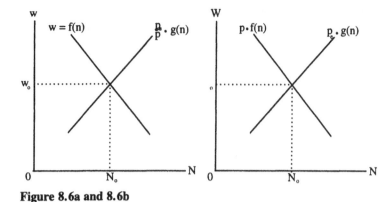

Figure 8.6a and 8.6b

This points up the need to factor in two additional mechanisms to the neo-classical labor market story of Fig. (8.6). One is a means to assure that the part of output not demanded for consumption will be demanded for investment (the savings will be spent to give rise to a level of real investment output), and secondly a means to account for the price level in the reality of a monetary economy. The first is taken care of by the presumption of a loanable-funds (savings) market composed of a demand curve inversely related to the rate of interest implying declining marginal production of capital accompanying greater levels of investment; and a supply curve which treats the rate of interest as a reward for making savings available to finance investment — it is seen as a reward for abstaining for consumption. At the level of income resulting from an employment of (N_o) there will exist a rate of interest that maintains this full-employment level of demand. This interest rate (r) determination is depicted in Fig. (8.7).

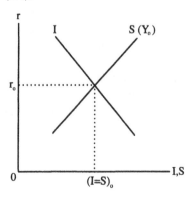

Figure 8.7

And we emphasize that the interest rate — via this very cursory look at the loanable funds approach — is determined by the relation of productivity and thrift in the real sector. This 'reward' explanation for the interest rate suggests that increasing rates would generate more funds to be applied to investment, and thereby reduce to an equivalent extend the amount applied to consumption spending. The interest rate would in this way determine the composition but not the level of aggregate real output which was determined by the real forces of the labor force and the capital stock. The interest simply assured that the proper level of investment demand would be forthcoming to sustain the full-employment state of the system. This was, of course, different from Keynes' argument where in his attack on this approach he insisted that the interest rate be considered a monetary phenomenon which impacts on the real sector through a marginal efficiency of capital explanation for the downward sloping investment schedule.

Turning to an explanation of prices, the classical school relied on the quantity theory of money which considered the use of money as wholly a transaction device. The money supply, i.e. the amount of money held, is in some proportion of nominal income; or can be reckoned as the reciprocal of the income velocity of money (V). Thus in the form of an earlier Cambridge equation (not to be confused with the one used in this book as part of the post-Keynesian discussion), we write:

$$M = k(Y)$$

where

$$k = \frac{1}{V} \tag{15}$$

Thus 'velocity' simply is a measure of the number of times per year a unit of the money supply is spent since an act of spending is an act of income creation, then this velocity is a ratio of the nominal output to the money supply. And this velocity will be greatly influenced by the efficiency of the payment mechanism (how quickly checks clear), the use of credit cards, and the payment practices in the economy. For example, more frequent wage payments means that people can conduct transactions with lower average cash holdings; money circulates faster, i.e. the velocity increases increasing the ratio of nominal income to money.

Putting this into the quantity equation, or more familiarly the equation of exchange, we have:

$$M \cdot V = p \cdot Y \qquad (16)$$

which gives nominal output as the product of the average stock of money times velocity. If we can pretty much take velocity as constant, then we can, so to speak, transform the accounting identify of (16) into a behavioral model as:

$$M = \frac{p \cdot Y}{V} \qquad (17)$$

which gives a direct 'causal arrow' running from a percentage change in the money supply to an equivalent change in nominal G.N.P. But with the classical assumption of the labor market clearing at full-employment, the resulting level of output would be read off the production function for the given size of the labor force and attending level of capital stock. Then with the full-employment output determined by real forces, what the arrow is connecting is a change in the money supply with an equiproportionate change in the price level. It bears emphasizing that with the economy tending to full employment, real output will not rise proportionate with (M); what will rise is the price level as a result of the increase in demand engendered by the money supply change.

To complete the scaffolding of the classical approach we need to account for the transmission from money to prices. In the 'older' pre-Keynesian approach, the increase in (M) means that the economy is holding a supply of funds (savings) in real terms (M/p) that exceeds the demand for these balances as a proportion of nominal income. These excess money balances spill over directly to the goods market resulting in excess demand and higher prices. But the higher price level will serve to reduce the real value of the higher money supply until the amount of real money balances that one holds is equal to what one wants to hold. This signals that the price level has risen to the point of eliminating excess demand and the restoration of equilibrium in the commodities market. We realize that the restoration of market clearing is totally the result of the higher price level squeezing out the excess demand; there is no increase in production due to the behavior of the real wage rate. Thus transactions motive for holding money is stated as:

$$\frac{M}{p} = l(Y) \qquad (18)$$

$$l' > 0$$

Another transmission arrow from money to prices which is Keynesian in design results from the recognition that one also desires to hold real money balances for the purpose of speculation in the securities market; the motive here is that of a 'wealth increasing' mechanism — it is in essence a store of wealth (idle balances). These balances are, of course, not truly idle (they are not hoards); their level will be an inverse function of the investors' expectations regarding the future course of the rate of interest, which is to say that it is positively related to the expected price of securities. The outcome of the securities market reflects the net result of conflicting expectations as individual investors adjust their portfolio balances between speculative balances and securities. A stable rate of interest represents a balanced consensus that it will be no different in the future; and if that is so, it will, as a result of the private market, indeed not change. Should the overriding sentiment be that it is going to fall, then the rate will fall as more investors are adding to their bond holdings than those adding to their liquid balances. And the reverse reasoning holds as well. Thus, to reiterate, the demand for money balances as a store of wealth (not for goods transactions) is dependent on the state of expectations.

Presume that at a given relatively 'high' interest rate (the system is not in the liquidity trap state) the authorities increase the money supply. To the degree that these excess balances are predominantly used to increase security holdings, the interest rate will fall stimulating excess demand (essentially via its impact through the investment function) and higher prices. This condition is as well self-correcting, but here we want to put the emphasis on the impact of the price increase on the interest rate itself. These matters are brought together in Fig. (8.8) where we arrive at the classical model result with the use of our labor market with expectations analysis and the IS-LM demand change mechanism.[2] We will go from a change in demand, to the impact on the labor market and to the input on real output.

We find the economy at a point in time full employment (N_o) resulting in a level of output (Y_o) with a price level (p_o). The interest rate is (r_o) reflecting a simultaneous clearing of both the goods and money markets, that is, where the demand for (C) and (I) goods is equal to production and where, for the resulting level of nominal income, the money stock held by

373

the 'economy' is equal to what it demands to hold. Diagram (8-C) determines the interest rate and corresponding level of demand for a given price level.

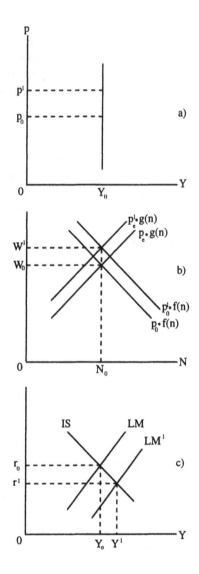

Figure 8.8

Now assume an exogenous increase in the money supply which results in a rightward shift of the LM curve telling us that the interest will fall and demand will increase to Y'. This increase in demand at the existing price level (p_o) is the result of the operation of the multiplier applied to the increase in the money supply where the multiplier expression takes into account the demand response of the goods market to the interest rate change, i.e. the slope of the IS curve. This change will increase prices which in (8-b) shifts the demand curve for labor to the right, reflecting the lower real wage. However, labor's price expectations increase in direct relation to the inverse in actual prices, so that at the existing (W_o) the supply of labor is reduced to the same degree as its demand has increased. The labor market response to the lower real wage which pushes up the money to the point of restoring the real wage to its original level. This will serve to eliminate the excess demand for labor as it eliminates the profitability of increasing employment.

In the commodities arena the higher price level serves to reduce demand both directly, and indirectly, by reducing the real money supply and thereby causing higher interest rates; the system's aggregate demand falls in response to the $(LM)'$ curve. As the demand for increasing employment recedes, so does the demand for aggregate output. The increases in the price level and the interest rate squeeze the monetary determined change in demand out of the system. So the classical approach puts forth a dichotomy or separability in the operation of the economy: employment is determined by the conditions in the labor market with no influence from aggregate demand (assuming the flexibilities that we spoke about); once this is known we find the level of real output from the production function, i.e. the aggregate supply level. What the classical model tells us is that the level of employment and related output is not sensitive to changes in demand conditions.

It is reasonable to suppose that the model would allow for a degree of short-term sensitivity either due to a behavioral assumption that labor does not see the increase in actual prices as a reduction in the real wage, or due to an element of 'stickiness' regarding expectations in that they are not being fully adjusted to the price changes. Thus restating equation (9) we find:

$$p_e = \lambda(p)$$

$$\frac{dp_e}{dp} = \dot\lambda < 1 \tag{19}$$

375

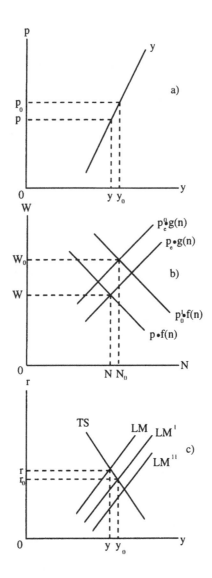

Figure 8.9

In this situation the supply curve shift would be of a lesser magnitude than the demand curve shift, telling us that the money wage increase is not proportionate and the real wage falls. So the monetary induced increase in demand has now spilled over to the real factors of employment and output. Yet for this to have happened implies that there are unused

376

resources to be absorbed by the economy and inability of the labor market to have adjusted to a past decline in demand.

The economy can, in this manner, be moved to higher levels of real activity. Yet the ensuing price increase removes some of the higher demand pressure accruing by shifting the LM curve upward and raising interest rates. But the price increase will itself be limited due to higher levels of supply. The total adjustment reveals more employment, a lower real wage and a higher interest rate (though lower than prior to the increase in the money supply).

We see all this in Fig. (8.9).

This higher level of employment (say the full-employment level) has been 'paid for' by a lower real wage which may not be sustainable should labor decide to restore its relative share of the output. We could then consider monetary disturbances successful in the short-term with labor being 'fooled' and not fully adjusting to prices. Yet over the long-term labor can be expected to act to protect real wages as a priority over any short-term gain in employment. Full-employment at the particular real wage is the result of the assumptions of the model; but if we altered matters and assumed a strongly unionized economy, then the outcome of a constant real wage need not imply full employment. The inflexibility stems from institutional arrangements that do not permit a deterioration of the real wage. Monetary changes (or for that matter fiscal 'IS' shifts) may not work at all even as a Keynesian short-run prescription.

Our main concern though is with the long term, in understanding the influence of various economic elements in sustaining a natural growth path. So we return to the question raised a while back as to what is the role of the money element other than a facilitator of transactions, how is money integrated with the real sides of the economy.

Early efforts to reckon with the monetary influence was via the introduction of money into the neoclassical growth model of the type we discussed in Chapter 5. We want initially to consider the overall effect here.[3] A quick recall of the model's essential characteristics is that markets are always cleared, the production function is standard allowing one to read factor shares from the function, and that the rate of investment (capital formation) equals planned savings — there is no independent investment function. Also there is an exogenous growth of the labor force and a given aggregate savings ratio. For convenience sake, we redraw the diagram depicting the steady-state outcome where we find constant capital to labor and capital to output ratios.

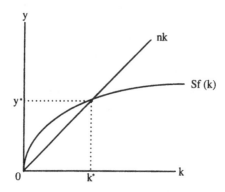

Figure 8.10

The long run path is given for that level of (y) itself a function of (k) for which:

$$sf(k) = nk$$

or

$$f(k) = \frac{n}{s}(k) \tag{20}$$

At $(k*)$ the savings per capita is sufficient to maintain the capital to labor ratio; for a ratio to the left of $(k*)$ savings and hence investment will exceed the growth of the labor force resulting in capital deepening. But this increase in the ratio will diminish due to the declining increase in output per capita, and paradoxically a ratio in excess of $(k*)$ will, due to its effect on output per capita, cause capital to accumulate at a lessor pace than labor force growth. The system will converge at $(k*)$ where the economy is growing at a rate equal to that of the labor force; we have a type of stationary state expanding through time by multiplication.

The correct rate of accumulation in this neoclassical — without money — model results from a particular level of real output which is totally used up between planned consumption and planned savings, i.e. capital formation. In this one sector (no distinction between capital and consumption goods) barter model there is only one asset in the system, that of physical capital. So the notion of wealth per capita designated by (k) has its counterpart in savings per capita. Let us rework this model in terms of output, consumption and investment.

The total level of investment can be composed of two parts, that which maintains the existing capital to labor ratio as the labor force expands, plus an amount which increases the ratio. A point on the (nk) line, as we know, gives us the former, while the total rate of accumulation is read off the savings line. We write investment per worker as:

$$\frac{DK}{N} = nk + Dk$$

$$D = \frac{d}{dt} \tag{21}$$

with output per worker being divided between consumption per worker (c) and investment. So:

$$y = c + nk + Dk$$

$$dk = (y - nk) - c \tag{22}$$

the change in the capital to labor ratio is equal to a surplus in excess of the difference between output and planned consumption. In the steady-state outcome where $dk=0$ we find:

$$y = c + nk$$

and

$$nk = y - c \tag{23}$$

Since (nk) is given as is the production relationship between (y) and (k), then whether a surplus exists to increase the capital to labor ratio depends on the consumption element.

The $y-nk$ curve gives the level of output available for consumption and for having $dk > O$. Thus at a level y_o we find $y-nk > c$ with a positive change in the capital to labor ratio, which in turn results in both a higher level of output and consumption with the former out-pacing the latter, giving a further surplus and still higher (k). However, given the nature of the production function, the surpluses become smaller until point (E) where no surplus is generated and $Dk=0$. For a ratio (k_1) we find $y-nk < c$ with capital accumulating at a lessor rate than the growth of the labor

379

force; the economy will be decumulating capital converging at k^*. Note we have consumption rising linearly with output per capita.

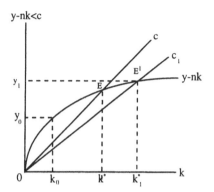

Figure 8.11

Now let us presume that the steady-state solution is at the k_1 position (k_1^*); then at every point the economy would have had to attain a greater surplus which could have resulted from a lower consumption shifting the c curve to c_1, or as a result of an upward shift of the production function. But let us say that neither of these necessary changes will materialize within the context of our barter (real) system; so the question before us is can we bring those changes about with the introduction of money into the system? If the presence of money can somehow change the growth path of the system in real terms when we go from a non-money to a money balance environment, then we may obtain some idea of the role money plays in maintain the long-term path within the reality of a money system generally.

We introduce money into the system as non-interest bearing fiat money that is distributed according to some rule by an outside agency. This money transfer changes our barter system into a monetary one, where prices are established and nominal values are created. Individuals are now in possession of two assets: one is a value of savings originating in the value of output per capita and the other is a level of money stock originating in outside net transfers. The latter being the sum of the money injections minus withdrawals in the form of taxes. We assume that the money stock will grow at some constant rate which has implications for the long-term behavior of prices, with expectations about price changes being equal to the trend of money growth. The actual price change will be equal to the growth of the money stock ($\dot{M}/M$) minus the growth of output ($\dot{y}/y$).

Individuals are seen as managing a portfolio consisting of two assets; that of savings having its counterpart in the 'ownership' of real assets, and the other is the value of cash balances. And this brings us back to the question as to what influences the ratio of real assets to cash balances — what is the desired amount of money balances related to? We can point to two influences: one is the expected rate of return on investment which is itself related to the capital to labor ratio; certainly the greater this rate of interest the greater the desire to hold real assets rather than money balances. But there is also a reckoning concerning the expected cost of holding money balances which reflects expected price changes; when prices are expected to rise the rate of return on holding cash will fall leading to an adjustment in the composition of assets, reducing money holdings in favor or real investment.

Over time real balances will be growing even if the money stock is constant; certainly as output increases (with $\dot{M}/M=0$) the price lever will fall at a rate equal to the growth in real output. This increase in real money balances can be treated as a sort of 'capital gain' since it does increase total wealth, and we would add this increase to the value of current output to obtain total income. The important consideration deals with the ratio of real money balances to real output. The 'pool' of investment funds is composed of savings plus the holdings of money assets, and an increase in the proportion of balances to income implies a corresponding reduction from savings, i.e. from the uses of income to create real capital stock — keeping in mind that real balances are 'held'.

The introduction of money alters the internal mechanics; in the 'real' model the national product is equal to disposable income, in that all of the output is taken up by consumption and investment; but in the money asset model, the disposable income exceeds the national product by the presence of cash balances. It is a feature of the latter approach that not all of that portion of income that is not consumed goes to augment the capital stock. When one makes cash balances a part of assets, one must deduct the full value of these balances from income which, for the given savings propensity, means a lower rate of real capital accumulation. The question is what proportion of income is set aside as an 'inactive' balance? This will greatly be determined by the growth of the money supply itself and the corresponding change in prices.

We see what this means for the long-term equilibrium in Fig. (8.12) where money balances are grafted onto the neoclassical real model result.

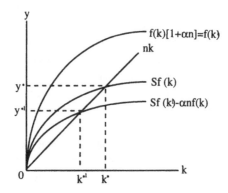

Figure 8.12

The k^* is the without money outcome where savings and accumulation correspond to y^*. However, with money balances income will exceed the output per capita by the increased value (capital gains) of the cash holdings —these gains are factored into the individual's real income. Income is:

$$y' = y + (\alpha n)y \qquad (24)$$

where α is the ratio of real money balances to output.

With a given savings propensity we presumably would see a higher level of savings and capital to labor ratio, but this is not what happens because this increase in the value of the cash component is deducted from savings, and the system ends up with a smaller physical investment and a smaller stock per capita (k^*) and output per capita $(y^{*'})$. Indeed, the increase in the value of cash balances has the same effect as a reduction in the savings propensity in the real model.

To be certain of our understanding let us talk through the move from k^* to a higher level of capital per capita. An increase in the rate of money growth and thereby in the expected rate of price increase will result in a corresponding reduction in the (α) ratio; agents will transfer to real investment (savings) an amount equal to the degree of erosion in the value of cash holdings. We end up with a higher ratio of savings to output available for capital growth.

In a more exact fashion, we have the change in capital intensity and output per head as:

$$\dot{k} = sf(k) + s\alpha nf(k) - \alpha nf(k)$$

382

$$=[s-(1-s)\alpha n]f(k) \tag{25}$$

In long-term equilibrium with $\dot{k}=0$ we have:

$$[s-(1-s)\alpha n]f(k)=nk \tag{26}$$

In a comparison with the outcome of equation (20) we end up with what is depicted in Fig. (8.12), that of a lower output per capita.

There is another way to look at the role of real cash balances by relating to our discussion of Fig. (8.11). Consumption per capita is considered positively related to wealth per capita which we now consider as that of net national output plus real cash balances. In the steady-state condition, real balances per head are not changing, so that, to reiterate, price changes are equal to the rate of money growth. Monetary policy operates to affect the real variables through its ability to influence consumption spending via its impact on wealth. In equilibrium monetary policy will maintain that level of wealth such as to 'release' additions to the capital stock that maintains output per capita at full employment.

Now assume a policy that increases the money supply per capita leading to an even higher expected rate of price increase. Then at the (E) level of the capital to labor ratio in Fig. (8.11) the demand for cash balances as a proportion of wealth will fall with a consequent reduction in consumption. That is, we add the reduction of real balances held to savings to form a larger pool to create real capital stock. The linearly drawn consumption function shifts down to (c_1) with the new long-term outcome at (E'). What is happening is that the increase in the expected rate of inflation causes a re-evaluation of one's portfolio in the direction of a higher proportion of 'holding' real capital (savings) in order to minimize the reduction in one's wealth. Savings becomes, so to speak, a wealth adjustment mechanism brought on by monetary disturbances. Real wealth is built up in the form of material capital goods and reduced in the form of consumption goods. Let us look again to a comparison with the non-money model. An increase in the rate of return on capital at a particular (k) will increase savings and the rate of accumulation via a 'high' rate of growth of output. But in the money model there is the added element of a shift of assets out of money and into real investment.

One can also reckon the impact of money from the production side by considering its presence in the production function as a factor of production complimentary with labor and capital thus:

$$y = f(k, m) \tag{27}$$

In the previous discussion money was treated as a consumer good that generates utility from the interaction between consumers and their real balances. With equation (27) money is treated as a producer good in terms of real balances per capita which is the result of the ratio of real balances to output times output per capita. At this point we want to distinguish between two types of money. We have been referring to outside money in our discussion of the interplay between real money balances and real investment; now we consider as well money of the 'inside' type where economic agents receive money as a result of borrowing from an inside agency as distinct from a costless transfer from the outside. And we make the assumption that a dollar received as a result of borrowing is considered less of an addition to wealth than a dollar received as a transfer (one does not consider any future tax liability in computing wealth).

But what is the rational of (m) as a producer good; how is it in and of itself reckoned to increase production as compared to a non-money system? We have to consider that an explicit medium of exchange results in a more efficient means of distribution. Money replaces the use of real factors as a facilitator to move goods, thus releasing these factors for production purposes, reflecting the idea that more goods will be required in a money system than one under barter (without money firms would have to divert resources to the search for bartering opportunities). This leads us to consider that if real balances were reduced below some level there may be real loss to the economy, in terms of the loss of productive services. So we can consider output as positively related to real balances per worker as they are like the services of capital per worker. A simple approach is to regard money as another input in a linear homogenous production function.

We bring matters together and presume that all money is of the outside type. The change in the capital to labor ratio is now:

$$k = y[k, \Delta m] - nk - c(k, \Delta m) \tag{28}$$

where all of the change in real balances is considered to change one's wealth. What happens when there is an increase in the expected rate of inflation? We have to reckon with two effects, one on consumption and the other on the production side. As we pointed out, the consumption function will shift down thus resulting in more real investment and output per worker; but the other effect is the direct negative impact on output per capita, so that in Fig. (8.11) the $(y\text{-}nk)$ curve shifts down at the existing consumption function resulting in a lower (k).

Which effect will predominate? The magnitude of the consumption shift depends on the degree to which one considers wealth to have been altered by this monetary expansion and expected change in the inflation rate; and we assume that this wealth effect will be greater if money is of the outside type. This effect must be balanced against the degree of sensitivity of real output to the decline of real money balances. The result of a rise in the rate of price change is ambiguous for it can result in a reduction in consumption and output per capita. All we can say is that the net effect here is uncertain; it will depend on the source of funds fueling the higher rate of price changes and how agents view each type of money, and how output responds to a change in real cash balances.

In general we have been looking at a neoclassical category of money growth models that possesses the characteristic of investment equal to planned savings (no independent functions here), and where prices adjust instantaneously to clear all markets. Now the nature of the steady growth path in terms of real outcomes can be altered by a change in the ratio of real cash balances to output, i.e. a change in the composition of one's wealth. This being accomplished by a shift of the consumption function possibly in conjunction with some shift in the production function. Setting the economy on the steady-state path implies the existence of a monetary policy that keeps real money balances in alignment with regard to output growth, and thereby maintains a level of savings that keeps capital growing at the same rate as the labor force. Savings emerge as more than a single dimensional function; real money assets add a realistic ingredient to the neoclassical aggregate output view to account for savings; and it is through this connection that money plays a role.

The introduction of money into the non-money model gave us the paradoxical result of lowering the long-term per capita output; and it bears repeating that this emerges as a result of not treating two obvious major functions of money, that it provides a convenience to consumers so that the national income accounting should include a way to get hold of the service of cash balances held; and that real cash balances may be considered as a productive service in its own right, as we briefly discussed. Once we factor in these functions then a monetary economy would not appear as understated compared to a barter economy.

There is another category of 'conventional' money growth models that we want to consider in reckoning the effect of money and prices referred to as the Keynes-Wicksell (K-W) models.[4] These models postulate independent real savings and investment functions, and that prices rise in response to the excess demand for goods per unit of capital — this excess demand deflated by the stock of capital. This type of model gives us an explicit mechanism to explain the rate of price increases.

Since the excess demand for goods per unit of capital is equal to planned investment minus planned savings, we can write the rate of price change as:

$$\hat{p} \equiv \frac{\dot{p}}{p} = h(\frac{I}{K} - \frac{S}{K}) \tag{29}$$

where

$$\frac{S}{K} = \frac{sy(k)}{K} \tag{30}$$

where (h) is a measure of the speed of market adjustment or that of the rate of price increase.

Fig. (8.13) illustrates the difference between the neoclassical and Keynes-Wicksell models.

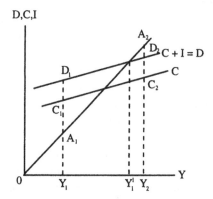

Figure 8.13

In the neoclassical stance, investment demand exists as a mirror image of the level of savings; thus at output level (Y_1) planned consumption exceeds output resulting in negative capital formation equal to C_1A_1. At the level of output (Y_2) investment is equal to positive savings of A_2C_2. The focus of monetary changes is its effect on planned savings and thereby on the level of investment; the investment function is irrelevant in determining capital formation.

But not so in the K-W approach. The state of excess real demand (D_1) will produce a rate of price increase which in turn will impact on aggregate demand including that of investment expenditures. We will need some sort of investment expression that relates the growth of real capital to pricing conditions that reflect the degree to which output is adjusting to the (D_1) demand level. Looking again at Fig. (8.13) we find that at the output level (Y_1) planned consumption is (C_1A_1) with planned investment being (D_1C_1). The excess demand stems from planned investment exceeding planned savings which is seen as negative on the diagram because of the comparison of the two models.

Prices will be bid up in this condition where supply is insufficient and we must then suppose that actual investment spending will turn out to be less than planned (D_1C_1) and as well with planned consumption spending — everyone will be partially frustrated. We can postulate that actual capital accumulation will be less than planned investment, but it will to some degree exceed planned savings (the higher price level plays an inhibiting but not a cancelling-out role in regard to this higher investment demand). The actual level of investment spending will then be some linear combination of planned investment and planned savings; thus:

$$\frac{\dot{K}}{K} = a(\frac{I}{K}) + (1-a)\frac{S}{K} \tag{31}$$

where the (a) term is a measure of the degree to which producer and consumer plans are satisfied when there is excess demand and an increasing proportionate rate of change in the price level with the assumption $1 > a > 0$.

Should $a=0$, then we are back to the neoclassical model approach; the actual rate of capital accumulation is equal to planned savings. Clearly consumer spending plans will be realized, and with the investment-savings mirror there will be no excess demand and no change in the rate of inflation. This would be a position (Y_1') in Fig. (8.13). With $a=1$ producer demands are entirely satisfied; desired capital formation equals actual formation, with the implication that consumer plans are not realized as the fulfillment of planned investment will require a degree of 'consumer sacrifice' to release the necessary real productive factors. Indeed we can picture consumers undergoing 'forced savings' as a mirror of the

387

fulfillment of producer planned investment (of course, here we will see an increase in the inflation rate).

We can see the 'forced element' within the context of the changed rate of price increase by combining equations (29) and (31). Equation (29) can be restated as:

$$\frac{I}{K} = \frac{\hat{p}}{h} + \frac{S}{K} \tag{32}$$

so

$$\frac{\dot{K}}{K} \equiv \frac{I}{K} = a[\frac{\hat{p}}{h} + \frac{S}{K}] + (1-a)\frac{S}{K}$$

$$= \frac{a}{h}(\hat{p}) + \frac{S}{K} \tag{33}$$

where

$$\frac{\dot{p}}{p} \equiv \hat{p}$$

The rate of capital accumulation exceeds that of planned savings by the amount that actual consumers spending falls short of their plans. And we note that when $\hat{p} > 0$ then $a > 0$ with the presence of 'forced savings'. Another way to look at this is simply to say that in this state of excess demand actual capital formation will be less than the planned rate. With some manipulation of (29) and (31) we arrive at:[5]

$$\frac{\dot{K}}{K} = \frac{I}{K} - \frac{(1-a)}{h}(\hat{p}) \tag{34}$$

With all this perhaps the (Y_1) position in Fig. (8.13) becomes even clearer. When the economy is producing at Y_1, the real excess demand is $\hat{p} = h(D_1 A_1)$. Actual capital accumulation will fall short of planned accumulation by $(1-a)\hat{p}$; the closer (a) is to one the greater the fulfillment of producer excess demand and the greater the consumer sacrifice. Thus investment will actually be less than $C_1 D_1$ and actual consumer spending will be less than C_1. The assumption of $a < 1$ tells us that the institutional arrangements are such that consumers will not be 'compelled' to sacrifice whatever real consumption is required to satisfy producer demand.

Now we are ready to examine the impact of a monetary change on the real variables of the system within the above-type model. We place the economy in the steady-state frame: real cash balances per head are constant and the system is expanding with a given capital to labor ratio and output per head. How do we reckon the effect of an increase in the rate of money expansion on the real elements of the economy? We recall that in the neoclassical model the effect of a monetary disturbance is via its impact on planned savings and thus on real investment. However, in the K-W approach, monetary policy can affect the equilibrium capital to labor ratio even if planned savings is considered independent of the rate of money growth. The impact of a money growth change, insofar as it affects the equilibrium capital to labor ratio, will come through its effect on the rate of inflation.

We state the level of capital intensity on a per unit of capital basis, so that it is:

$$1/k = \frac{L}{K} = l \tag{35}$$

then a change in the steady-state labor per unit of capital ratio is:

$$\frac{\dot{l}}{l} = n - \frac{\dot{K}}{K}$$

$$= n - \frac{a}{h}(\hat{p}) - s^* y(l) \tag{36}$$

The third term in (36) is the planned or desired (*) ratio of savings to output, where output per unit of capital (y_1) is a function of labor per unit of capital (l). Thus a change in money growth will impact on capital intensity $(1/l)$ via $(\hat{p})$.

We have the economy in long-term equilibrium with a constant real balance per capita, and now increase the rate of money expansion. The result is a condition of excess aggregate demand and a higher proportional rate of inflation. The analysis of equation (33) suggests that the rate of accumulation of capital will increase though at a rate below that desired by firms $(a < 1)$; and via expression (36) this is seen as an increase in capital intensity. There will exist a degree of 'consumer sacrifice' as household savings are greater than desired or planned savings due to the effect on their demand to hold cash balances. Thus the steady-state capital to labor ratio will change as a result of a change in the rate of inflation; yet from the K-W approach, the result is somewhat less mechanistically (perhaps more realistically) arrived at.

Again, relating to Fig. (8.13), when output is Y_1 there is an inflationary gap D_1A_1. And as we assume full-employment, the reaction of the economy takes the form of price increases and a smaller rate of accumulation than is desired. Prices are increasing as firms seek to accumulate capacity and consumers are absorbing less than C_1 with actual capital formation being less than C_1D_1. This points up, again, the framework that the decision of firms to invest does not presuppose equivalent household decisions to save. It is the function of the market to reconcile the demand for investment with the supply of savings which results in neither investment nor consumption plans being fully realized.

We can relate to the neoclassical real money balance emphasis by reiterating that the higher rate of price increase will reduce real cash balances held and thereby consumption which is presumed a constant fraction of 'wealth' which in part is composed of real balances. So that this decline in balances is added on to savings which gives us what we called 'forced savings'. This all assumes that the ratio of planned savings is indeed influenced by monetary policy and the extent to which prices are adjusting to this aggregate excess demand. For example, if the rate of price change lags that of money growth, then real balances will rise with planned savings falling, with a reduced rate of accumulation. This brings up the asymmetrical result of the K-W model between inflationary and deflationary periods. In Fig. (8.13) the deflationary period is present at Y_2 where planned investment is less than planned savings resulting in the deflationary gap of A_2D_2. Maintain the assumption of long-term full-employment means that the system's response will take the form of price declines as firms seek to reduce their rate of growth of real capital. In other words, firms' planned or desired rate of accumulation will be below the existence rate. Note that consumers absorb a (C_2) level of output, with the actual level of investment being A_2C_2 equal to planned savings — but it is a level of investment that is excess by the difference of the deflationary gap A_2D_2. Thus in equations (33) and (34) $a=0$, and the excess supply will engender price changes that should correct the situation. This comes via the positive impact on the real cash balances that will be reduced from savings; thus rendering actual savings below planned, while firms try to lower the existing capital to labor ratio as the expected rate of return is below the real rate of interest.

Now let us sum up matters regarding these conventional type models. An increase in the rate of monetary expansion should result in the realization of a higher real capital per capita ratio. This is, demand conditions are such that planned investment will exceed planned savings, and we presume that some portion of this higher desired investment will be realized, which implies a degree of 'forced savings' per unit of capital ($a\hat{p}/h$ increases). But this always does depend on the extent to which prices are adjusting to demand conditions and the reaction of consumers and firms.

From the neoclassical more 'mechanistic' perspective, the higher rate of price change can be expected to reduce real cash balances per unit of capital and thereby reduce the ratio of money balances to output. There is a realignment of one's wealth from money balances to capital implying a desired increase in planned savings and an equivalent increase in the actual rate of capital accumulation. Thus, from both viewpoints, the rate of growth of capital will increase relative to the growth rate of the labor force.

It bears reiterating that, in particular for the neoclassical model, the impact of monetary policy comes via the affect on the yield on real money advances relative to the yield in real capital that results in a change in the level of savings. It has been assumed that the return on real money balances will fall relative to the return on money invested in capital. Yet an institutional change concerning how the money supply growth could lead to a different result. What if money is distributed to existing holders of balances as a form of interest payment on these balances; it is as if the 'outside agency' offered compensation for the decline in real balances, i.e. for the rate of inflation. Then the yield on money balances expected, in terms of goods, will be equal to the money supply growth minus the expected rate of price increase. In the steady-state the expected change in the price level is equal to the actual change which is equal to the nominal rate of interest paid. The growth of the money supply per capita is $\hat{M}-n$, with the real return on money balances per head being $\hat{M}-\hat{p}=n$. What this is saying is that a higher nominal rate of interest will be offset by the rate of change in the price level. In other words, the decline in real money balances in terms of goods is balanced by the higher return on investment; there will be no incentive to alter the proportion of real money balances to output and thereby no affect on the steady-state values of the real variables.

So how the money supply grows is important, institutional procedures matter. We can say that the K-W approach is probably a 'richer' way to introduce monetary policy into growth models. It does not rely on the singular neoclassical pathway of a real balance effect in the consumption function; and while it is to be presumed that a rise in the rate of money growth will increase the steady-state capital to labor ratio, it could, depending on institutional arrangements, result in a decline in capital intensity. But the 'normal' outcome tells us that if during the inflationary period we do have $\hat{k} > n$, then in return to the steady-state the rate of capital accumulation must fall, mirroring a decline in planned savings that balances the inflationary induced increase in forced savings $(a/h\hat{p})$ — and again $\hat{K} = n$ but at a higher level of intensity.

Money has come in as an asset that people hold, and thereby influence the portion of one's wealth (income) that remains for savings which, in the neoclassical model, has its equivalence in real investment (there are two stores of value: real balances and real capital). Money plays the role, to reiterate, as a medium for capital gain; the greater the gain in terms of the real value of this asset, the higher the proportion of real balances to output and the lower the proportion of output left over for investment. At the risk of perhaps being somewhat repetitive let us state this again. We have desired consumption per unit of capital as:

$$\frac{C}{K} = (1-s)[\frac{Y}{K} + \frac{\Delta m}{K}] \qquad (37)$$

where Δm is the increase in real balances which we may state as:

$$\Delta m = \hat{M} = \hat{p}(\frac{M}{pK}) \qquad (38)$$

letting the real money balance per unit of capital be designated by (z).

so equation (37) is:

$$\frac{C}{K} = (1-s)[\frac{Y}{K} + (\hat{M} - \hat{p})z] \qquad (39)$$

with desired real savings per unit of capital being:

$$\frac{S}{K} = \frac{Y}{K} - \frac{C}{K}$$

$$= s(\frac{Y}{K}) - (1-s)(\hat{M} - \hat{p})z \qquad (40)$$

and we can see the real balance effect on the rate of capital accumulation via desired real savings. In long-term equilibrium the growth in real cash balances $(\hat{M} - \hat{p})$ will equal that of the labor force (n), with the savings function being:

$$\frac{S}{K} = s(\frac{Y}{K}) - (1-s)nz \qquad (41)$$

This equation being a look-alike to the one in Fig. (8.12), and the discussion around the expressions in (25).

Yet this whole approach concerning the influence of money on the long-term real variables of the economy hinges on the fact that people will indeed hold money as an asset; and a central question for monetary theory is why? Here we have an asset which in and of itself apparently yields no return, but as with any asset, it does have a price relative to other assets which can be calculated by the opportunity cost of holding it, which is the rate of interest foregone as a result of not holding an interest-bearing asset. From this Keynesian point of view the demand for cash balances as a store of wealth is related to expectations concerning the rate of interest (for Keynes the interest rate was a reward for parting with liquidity — cash balances — not for abstaining from consumption). Thus desired savings results from some mix of these stores of value, i.e. dependent upon interest rates which, in conventional reasoning, are equal to the marginal product of capital which is itself a function of capital intensity and real balances that one desires to hold. But the introduction of money this way does not provide a rational reason for its being held. What services-in-kind does it provide? The magnitude of these services is found in the fact that people continue to hold money even under conditions of ultra-high rate of inflation. The attempt to understand this rationale will serve as an introduction to the role of money in the non-conventional post-Keynesian world. Before we move into this area, it may be important to make the point that no matter how technically interesting it is to see the impact of introducing money to conventional models, it does not help us very much to understand the operational reality of the economy in trying to get at the underlying factors that can sustain long-term growth. We have argued throughout that for institutional as well as theoretical reasons the neoclassical structure should be jettisoned; so we need to see how money matters with regard to such elements as pricing, investment and distribution as they have been analyzed within a post-Keynesian framework.

Uncertainty, money and Keynes

There are several interrelated paths through which money has been drawn into the model, one of them is the connection of money to concepts of time and uncertainty. Here it would be worthwhile for the reader to return to Chapter 1 to reacquaint oneself with what was said concerning the use of time in economic modeling. Regarding the neoclassical framework of abstract or logical time as the core of equilibrium analysis we made the point that:

> While this makes for presumably very neat cause and effect relationships which is at the base of equilibrium mechanics, realism does dictate that uncertainty pervades much of decision making, and economic activity stemming from past decisions are to a considerable degree not reversible. Thus time should be treated in terms of historical time where irreversibility and uncertainty provide the framework for decision making. Time flows in one direction — forward; there is no changing of what is, only an awareness of its impact on decisions regarding a future outcome which is uncertain, but is certain not to be a replica of the past. In historical time modeling one goes from an irrevocable past to an uncertain future.

And to draw a sharp distinction between an historical time framework and that of logical time, we reiterate that the latter can move forward or backward (regarding the outcome in equilibrium mechanics); the former can only go forward, i.e. the past is given and cannot be changed and that the future is unknown. But to say that the future is unknown is to say, as Paul Davidson so aptly states, that "human beings have the power to create and control their own economic destiny. They do not have to accept future economic events as the inevitable consequences of some natural law.[6] Professor Davidson sharpens our focus with a further reading of his thoughts:

394

In the post-Keynesian view, economic decisions are made by human beings facing an uncertain and unpredictable economic future, while they are moving away from a fixed and irreversible past. Human beings recognize that they have made errors in the past; and that when one makes errors, one has to live with their consequences.

Post-Keynesians emphasize the fallibility of human nature and the fact that unfettered human economic decisions do not necessarily automatically result in the best of all possible worlds. The developing economic system is an evolutionary process where human expectations regarding an uncertain and unpredictable future will have unavoidable and significant effects on economic outcomes.

In the context of this evolving economy, economic and political institutions play a significant role in shaping expectations about the otherwise and unforeseeable future. Decisions based on these sensible expectations create a path along which the economy travels.[7]

The notion that behavior is based on "reasonable expectations" that creates a path is what we tried to convey by emphasizing the operation of the (v_r) term in the investment equation of the H-D models as a behavior coefficient; that is telling us how entrepreneurs will want to, or let us say can be expected to, react to the experienced change in output. Certainly the reaction is the fundamental propellant to move the system forward at a particular rate, for the induced behavior based on expectations will in a technical sense yield a particular outcome; but it does so because of the accompanying 'supportive' economic and institutional arrangements that are continually correctly aligned along the path. These supports give 'confidence' to the decision maker in dealing with an unknowable result, i.e. the evolving economic structure as history becomes a reasonable basis for shaping investment decisions at every point on the growth path. We have tried to understand these supports such as production arrangements, price determination and the distribution of output. So while an initial reading of simple growth models of the H-D type may give the impression of a mechanistic equilibrium path where outcome is predictable based on the operating the acceleration principle, it is not how we want to see the equilibrium movement nor is it what I would think the original designers had in mind. The accelerator equation, though couched in mathematically predictable terms should be seen as reflecting a response based upon sensible expectations about an uncertain future. Yet saying that investment decisions, for example, are based upon expectations in the face of uncertainty, is not to say that such expectations are drawn from some actuarial predictable knowledge of how things will work out; which brings us to the difference between a world guided by uncertainty and one guided by 'mathematical risk' regarding the real world future events.

By mathematical risk we mean a condition in which the future outcome is simply a statistical reflection of the past. The accumulation of past evidence regarding economic outcomes allows the calculation of statistical averages which can then be used to make statistically reliable statements regarding the mathematical risk or probability of events occurring in the future. Experience or history is regular enough to allow the measurement of the chance or likelihood of the occurrence of any particular form of an event. Of course, this is what we mean by the probability of an event, and probabilities are usually expressed as decimals or fractions and range in value from zero to one. The estimate of probability can be obtained in one of two ways; one of them is to take the 'experiment' though a number of trials and analyze the results to obtain a relative frequency that can be used as an estimate of the probability. Then as the number of trials increases, the relative frequency becomes more and more reliable as an estimate of the probability. Stating this another way, we can say that the probability of an event occurring in a certain way is the relative frequency with which the event occurs in this manner as the number of events is increased indefinitely. Estimation of probability in this manner is referred to as 'experimental probability'. What we have is an event or variable usually called a random or stochastic variable whose different values at different times are determined as if by drawing numbers at random from a container, there being a particular probability attached to each value.

A popular example is the coin-toss experiment. If a coin is tossed into the air, the outcome is that the coin will turn up either heads or tails. The most obvious assumption is that these two events or outcomes are equally likely, which means that we may state the probability (β) of a tail outcome as:

$$\beta = 1/2 \tag{42}$$

and the possibility of a head as:

$$1 - \beta = 1/2 \tag{43}$$

This statement of probability tells us that if the experiment (the coin toss) were undertaken, many many times the fraction of the tosses that resulted in a head would approach one half. Thus if the coin is perfectly balanced there is equal probability of either event turning up with any single toss; however, based on the data of relative frequency as a result of a number of trials, one approaches this chance-determined outcome with some degree of confidence-based on empirical knowledge used to form the probability. In our coin toss example, it is the relative frequency of a particular outcome which is the basis for the empirical knowledge. If an event occurs (b) times out of (n) the relative frequency of its occurrence is (b/n). If the event fails to occur (c) times out of (n) — thereby giving us the other outcome — the relative frequency of the other outcome is (c/n). Since the sum of these two events equals the total number of trials we have:

$$c + b = n \tag{44}$$

$$\frac{c}{n} + \frac{b}{n} = 1 \tag{45}$$

so:

$$\frac{c}{n} = \beta, \frac{b}{n} = 1 - \beta \tag{46}$$

We can imagine a point in time when the experiment is done, when the probabilities have been formed; and so for all times forward this particular kind of activity carries with it the same probability of outcome, it becomes a part of 'natural law of behavior'. One does not, so to speak, 'check in with history', i.e. one does not redo the experiment to reaffirm the probabilities before engaging this activity. These probabilities are simply determined or assumed from a consideration of the factors involved, which in this case is that the coin is perfectly balanced and that the die is of uniform density. Such probabilities which are based on historical empirical information (or historical law) can be called 'a priori probabilities'; and their presence imparts a sense of certainty about the future. To repeat: "knowledge about the future involves the relating of statistical averages based on past and/or current realizations to forthcoming events".[8]

The conventional (neoclassical) understanding of economic relationships is that the basis for decision making (more broadly the basis of economics as a science) is the existence of these a priori probabilities (or simply probabilities), i.e. a world of predictable uncertainty. Entering into economic decisions involves probabilities or calculable risks, so that the future becomes, to a degree, knowable or ergodic. In his paper on a 'Technical Definition of Uncertainty", Davidson makes the point, "In an economic world governed entirely by ergodic processes, therefore, economic relationships are timeless or ahistoric in the sense that the future is merely a statistical reflection of the past".[9] He relates Samuelson's argument that "the basis for economics as a science is the ergodic hypothesis".[10] And this approach is the basis for much of the analyses in economics revolving around immutable economic laws that will, over the long term, yield predictable outcomes so that we can confidently predict future consequences for behavior in the aggregate economy or for particular economic agents, e.g. consumers. Thus we have much economic reasoning built up around such 'unalterable' economic laws as the law of diminishing returns, or that of Say's law, or that relating to utility marginization which underlies consumer behavior, and that of the quantity theory of money which purports to establish the long-term neutrality of money (money does not matter) with regard to real income. While there may be some deviation from the predictable outcome in the short-term period, the ergodic characteristic will hold true in the long run. Over any given number of coin tosses, over half the outcomes may be of a particular type, but over a greater and greater number of tosses, the predictable probability will hold.

We turn once more to Professor Davidson's words for a most enlightened description of what is at the heart of this neoclassical structure of economic reasoning based on 'natural law' and the existence of an ergodic world. He writes:

> All neoclassical theories presume that the economic system resembles the mechanical systems analyzed by nineteenth century physical scientists. The movement over time of such systems is determined by events and laws existing at the initial instant in time. A presumption of neoclassical theories is that the future path of the economy is already predetermined by the conditions exhibited at the initial instant.
>
> This neoclassical initial instant concept is equivalent to the 'Big Bang' view of the creation. In this 'Big Bang' conceptualization, the future path of all heavenly bodies is determined in this initial and unique heavenly explosion and, consequently, the future position of any star or planet is predictable. By analogy, therefore, the future position of the economy is, in principle, already known or knowable by individuals analyzing market signals. Thus when neoclassical

theorists describe people as having 'rational expectations' or 'being able fully to anticipate' the future, they are reasoning via this astronomical analogy. [11]

Thus the universe is analogous to a mechanical system obeying immutable laws so that the existence of a calculable future can be shown. And the 'hard' sciences such as astronomy and physics study and understand the operation of these laws. Well, if economics is to be similarly a hard science, it too must be governed by fixed laws of behavior so that one can comfortably calculate future outcomes. Neoclassical theory claims to have discovered and developed such laws and consequently believe that the only remaining purpose of economic research is to analyze existing data to estimate the quantitative parameters necessary to predict.

By contrast, let us briefly consider an understanding of the post-Keynesian economic world which is one guided by uncertainty (that is, unpredictable uncertainty) and where decisions are made within the context of historical time. For post-Keynesians decisions are made, in general, in a nonergodic environment; it is not that the future is uncertain (it always is), it is that history and/or current events do not provide a sufficient guide to the future so that one cannot venture probabilities about outcomes — one cannot project statistical averages to forthcoming events. As Davidson puts it:

> Our knowledge about economic events occurring through time is, however, asymmetrical: although we know the past, we cannot be sure that we have any reliable knowledge about the economic future. The future remains to be created by human actions and is not merely determined by some immutable economic laws. [12]

Economic decisions are taken with the understanding that sufficient information about future outcomes does not currently exist; indeed, decision makers act with the belief that unforeseen events will intrude during the lapse of time between decision and outcome.

We put up two quotes, one by Hicks and one by Keynes to embellish the post-Keynesian approach that economic processes take place in a nonorgodic world. First Hicks:

> "....people do not know what is going to happen and know that they do not know what is going to happen". [13]

And from Keynes in the General Theory before the existence of post-Keynesian school:

> It would be foolish, in forming our expectations to attach great weight to matters which are very uncertain....By 'very uncertain' I do not mean the same thing as 'very improbable'. It is reasonable, therefore, to be guided to a considerable degree by the facts about which we feel somewhat confident, even though they may be less decisively relevant to the issue than other facts about which our knowledge is vague and scanty. For this reason the facts of the existing situation enter disproportionately into the formation of our long-term expectations....The state of long-term expectations, upon which our decisions are based, does not solely depend, therefore, on the most probable forecast we can make. It also depends on *confidence* with which we make this forecast....The state of confidence, as they term it, is a matter to which practical men always pay the closest and most anxious attention....There is not much to be said about the state of confidence a priori. Our conclusion must mainly depend upon the actual observation of markets and business psychology....The outstanding fact is the extreme precariousness of the basis of knowledge on which our estimates of prospective yield have to be made. Our knowledge of the factors which will govern the yield of an investment some years hence is usually very slight and often negligible. [14]

So Keynes is describing a world in which macrodecisions are made and where the laws of probability do not generally apply. In this nonergodic situation decisions are guided by what we mentioned as a state of reasonable expectations which for Keynes is that state of confidence. And this confidence, or lack of it, is greatly the result of current behavior reactions of economic agents and existing institutions. At a point in time the system may be going to work itself so as to fulfill or so as to disappoint those reasonable expectations. The longer the period of time between decision and outcome, the more likely the presumption of a nonergodic environment and the possibility of those reasonable expectations being dashed. Keynes was then very clear about rejecting the assumption that expectations can be given a definite and calculable form and thereby reducing uncertainty to the same calculable status as that of certainty itself. He tells us:

By 'uncertain' knowledge, let me explain, I do not mean merely to distinguish what is known for certain from what is only probable. The game of roulette is not subject to uncertainty, in this sense....The sense in which I am using the term is that in which the prospect of a European war is uncertain, or the price of copper and the rate of interest twenty years hence, or the obsolescence of a new invention....About these matters there is no scientific basis on which to form any calculable probability whatever. We simply do not know.[15]

Well, we are now prepared to relate this world of decision making under uncertainty to the existence of money balances and the long-term non-neutrality of money. We have demonstrated that change in money balances will have a long-run effect on the real variables of the system; but this was done within a conventional framework which in and of itself should make us somewhat uncomfortable, and there was also no rationale for the existence of these balances — why do people hold money as a vehicle for storing wealth even under the most adverse conditions? In answering this question we will come to appreciate the possession of money and/or liquid assets and the existence of explicit money contacts as means to allow agents to cope with the unknowable, i.e. to function in a nonergodic world.

We begin to understand this via Keynes' liquidity preference explanation for the rate of interest. What is by now accepted doctrine is the approach that the rate of interest is not to be thought of as a price which equates the demand for resources to invest with the propensity to abstain from consumption; it is to be understood as a price which equates the demand to wealth in the form of cash balances with the available quantity of these balances being held — it is to be seen as a reward for parting with liquidity. The implication of this being that should the rate of interest be higher, i.e. if the reward for parting with liquidity were higher, the amount of cash balances which agents desire to hold would be less than what they do hold, so that there is a surplus of cash that nobody is willing to hold. In Keynes' words, "Thus the rate of interest at any time, being the reward for parting with liquidity, is a measure of the unwillingness of those who possess money to part with their liquid control over it".[16] So that liquidity preference taken with the quantity of money determines the actual rate of interest.

The question now is why should such a thing as liquidity preference exist? In the usual explication, one falls back to the distinction between the uses of money for the transaction of current business and its use as a store of wealth. The former reflects the need for money balances to be used as a means of payment for personal and business exchanges (designated L_1) and is seen to depend essentially on the level of economic activity. Keynes also put into this active balance 'account' a demand for money as a result of a precautionary motive, which he puts as "the desire for security as to the future cash equivalent of a certain proportion of total resources". But the demand for money as a store of wealth (idle balances designated by L_2) had the objective of using money as a means of securing profit via the investment in an interest-bearing asset. This speculative motive for holding money was dependent on the state of expectations concerning the future course of the rate of interest which in a nonergodic world cannot be known beforehand. And we reiterate that uncertainty for Keynes implies ignorance about forthcoming events, not probabilities about future outcomes which involves knowledge, that is, calculable risks.

Certainly up to some point it is worthwhile to sacrifice investment for liquidity (or highly 'near' liquidity assets) because of the convenience of it. After all, advanced societies have created money and money contracts as instruments to facilitate distribution and production. But, as Keynes poses the question, "given that the rate of interest is never negative, why should anyone prefer to hold his wealth in a form which yields little or no interest to holding it in a form which yields interest (assuming that the risk of default is the same in respect of a bank balance as of a bond)?".[17] His answer is that the necessary condition without which the presence of a liquidity preference for money is a store of wealth could not exist is the existence of uncertainty as to the future rate of interest, i.e. the inability to infer the future rate from the present rate.

Individuals may have expectations about the future rate of interest that differs from the one determined by mass psychology (not knowledge) as reflected in the bond market. People who believe that the interest rate will be below that assumed by the market will have a reason to purchase bonds, while those with an opposite opinion will have a reason for holding their liquid cash if not enhancing their liquidity position. Thus, as Keynes puts it, "the market price will be fixed at the point at which the sales of the 'bears' and the purchases of the 'bulls' are balanced".[18] Of course, this is what makes the market; bond prices and interest rates will be what the consensus of speculators expect them to be. Another way to put this is to say that the market will set the price of bonds and the rate of interest at the level at which the demand to hold liquid balances (due to the 'bearish' outlook of the future of bonds) is equal to the amount of cash held for the speculative purpose. From this expectational point of view the inverse liquidity preference schedule may be explained by the condition that every increase in the interest rate will persuade a growing number to reduce their cash position as the mind-set for future higher bond prices begins to take hold.

Thus an inherent 'utility' of cash balances is that it permits the individual to reap profits by taking advantage of opportunities in the future. Of course, it also provides a sense of security against uninsurable unseemly events. Should an individual not maintain cash balances and be invested in non-marketable assets, then the person has locked himself into a non-flexible position limiting both opportunities and self-insurance against misfortune. "Accordingly, when economic decisions makers think that future events can be generated in nonergodic circumstances, then anyone with sensible expectations will have a positive demand for liquidity (including money as idle balances) to maintain freedom and flexibility of response".[19]

Certainly the existence of uncertainty will play an influential role in how the household agent will store its wealth as between money and/or financial assets (near money) and a physical asset. If it is stored in the form of a physical capital good then the agent would presume the existence of a dependable well organized 'spot' or cash market (at the instantaneous time of the transaction) for that good; one must have confidence of being able to convert the good to (i.e. the store of wealth) money. But as a rule the agent will have to pay transaction costs in the conversion to and back from that physical store of wealth; in addition at a future conversion date the selling price could very well differ from the current purchase price (there is no probability assignment to the future price). All this is reducing the effective yield of storing wealth in physical assets. Thus, as long as agents are free to store wealth in the form of money or securities (where well-ordered markets exist), it is more likely that they will do just that rather than turn to physical goods. The institutions of money and dependable cash security markets, in an uncertain world, permits agents to store part of their income without the simultaneous commitments to purchase produced goods. "The human propensity to use some portion of current wealth to purchase (and maintain) liquidity (idle balances for precautionary and speculative purposes) instead of committing income completely to the purchase of currently producible goods and services, reflects a sensible behavior by decision makers (in a nonergodic world); a behavior which negates Say's Law".[20] We reiterate the salient point that the utility value of money stems from its ability to provide flexibility for further action and protection in the event matters turn out badly — there is clearly a place for this 'special' type of asset.

One can apply the term 'special' because of the essential properties of money. First money has a zero elasticity of output and employment. There can be an increase in the demand for liquidity (or near money financial assets) without necessarily implying an increase in the 'production' of money; or if there is to be an increase in supply, it can be brought about without causing more employment. Secondly, it is reasonable to assume zero (or close to zero) substitutability with other assets when the price of money increases; and this is the result of the unique characteristic of money (or similar financial assets) in the face of uncertainty. Thus a change in the demand for this particular asset has no real impact in and of itself; but certainly money is not neutral as an increase in the demand for liquidity will have negative direct and indirect (via interest rate movements) effects on real production and employment. And the released resources of the real sector cannot be deflected into the production of money. So we have this 'instrument' of money assets interdicting itself between income and spending on goods and services, i.e. people are purchasing something with their income that provides them with 'utility' but which does not generate employment. Thus in an aggregate sense money would seem to be necessary for the difference between full employment income and spending resulting in unemployment (as we said, a negation of Say's Law). Ironically, this man-made instrument, so necessary for the operation and evolvement of modern society, may itself be a cause for the recurrent difficulty of the system's inability to provide full employment of its resources.

In terms of long-term considerations structured via the steady-state growth path, we did see that money is not neutral; that the ratio of real balances to output will determine the net amount of liquidity that remains for real investment along the path. But the proportion of output that serves as a store of value in the form of liquidity (as opposed to that of real capital) is best understood in terms of behavior towards uncertainty. And the uncertainty in this context is in terms of the expected rate of inflation and thereby the expected rate of money growth. Along the long-term path the ratio of real money balances to output is constant, thereby releasing the appropriate growth rate of capital to maintain full employment; but this implies a working out of the rate of money growth equal to overall expectations. Thus an additional ingredient in the steady growth context is an ongoing 'level of uncertainty' which itself implies an overall fulfillment of expectations or, perhaps better put, of 'guestimates' about the future. The importance of uncertainty and its relation to money has bearing both in the short and long term.

Let us go a bit further in our thinking about the effects of money by considering the existence of explicit money contracts in the organization of production and exchange. In this regard, we will see money as a tool with which to reduce the amount of uncertainty in carrying on business activities. Entering into a production process normally involves a reasonably long time between the organization of input to begin and maintain the process and the product outcome and sale, that is, production involves a long gestation or carrying-out period of time. Whether we think in terms of single unit of output (e.g. the construction of a building) that will be completed and sold at an estimated future time period, or in terms of a flow of output per unit of time over a future span of time, what is required to fulfill these production plans is some assurance of a continuous flow of material and labor inputs into the future, thereby setting up an associated stream of cost-expenditures.

We can think of our megacorp organization with a given production capacity and being able to form some estimation as to cost of output as a result of a particular level of production (i.e. utilizing the plant at some degree of capacity) based on estimation of future demand. The organization undertakes this production with some target rate of profit in mind so that it has some expectation of sales proceeds in relation to costs and hence an understanding of the price at which it will sell its output. Aside from the possibility of disappointment on the sales revenue side, there are immediate uncertainties (in this real nonorgodic world) on the cost side that the organization would like to reduce if not totally eliminate.

The organization would like to be able to count upon the required physical flow of labor and material inputs and to be able to have some money cost control over the entire process. Certainly expectations regarding unit costs could be based on existing price arrangements; but it is far from certain whether actual costs would work out this way due to the unknown future regarding the availability and pricing of labor and materials. Thus at the outset the organization can reduce the uncertainty by entering into 'forward contracts' with input suppliers. This contract in the case of materials, for example, will then stipulate the quantity and sequence of delivery dates as well as the dates of payment. In the case of labor the money wage forward contracts can be one where the wage is based on a per unit production or 'piece rate' approach where the nature of the output lends itself to this arrangement, thereby removing the uncertainty about labor costs per unit of output. Or the contract could be based on a wage per unit of time which only partially reduces the labor cost per unit unknown; for at some point in the future labor productivity could change unexpectedly.

What we have in the notion of a forward money contract is a legal obligation between contracting parties that specifies the future dates for both delivery and payment. As Davidson puts it:

> Since production takes time, the hiring of labor and the purchase of materials to be used in any productive activity must precede the date when the finished product will be available to the entrepreneur for delivery to buyers. For any lengthy production process, hiring and raw material purchase transactions will require forward contracting to permit entrepreneurial control of the production operation and the efficient sequencing of labour, capital and raw material inputs in producing the final product for sale.[21]

In the absence of forward contracts, the organization would be quite hesitatant to begin a long duration production process without knowledge of future costs. Such contracts are modern institutional arrangements which permit agents to reduce uncertainty in their operations and to deal with and limit liabilities in the event of a negative outcome in an uncertain (unpredictable) future.

Certainly the parties entering into a production relationship are presumed to be willing to abide by the provisions of the covering money contractual arrangements. But should one party be unable or unwilling to fulfill his obligation, then it is legal enforceability of the agreement under civil law which gives the 'aggrieved' party the assurance of a just monetary compensation. Thus a seller of material inputs, for example, is given the confidence to enter into a long-term relationship with the producing unit, being assured of a future cash flow even if unforeseen events causes the organization to be unable to meet its obligation say with regard to payment and/or the acceptance of a particular quantity of delivered goods. And from the viewpoint of the buyer (the organization), forward money contracts generally will determine and limit its cost liability (though there may be surprises on the productivity front). If we think back to the conventional analysis of the profit maximizing firm with its marginal revenue-marginal cost relationship (accepting all the make-believe assumptions here), one could ask the question how is the firm able to calculate its marginal costs if it were not able to read these costs off of price and nominal wage contracts for material and labor inputs? Are we to presume that all payments for inputs are made before each production step, so that we have a world in which there are no contractual obligations due at any future date? And if all contracts are settled at the beginning of each production undertaking at every point in time, there is no uncertainty about future income and no need for liquidity balances as a store of value to safeguard against the unknown. But money does matter because 'inactive' liquid balances do exist and effect production and employment levels. Economic activity proceeds within an environment of uncertainty which is a reflection of the condition that not all contracts are settled at the same time they are entered into; and furthermore, from the payee's side, it is not presumed that, in the event of unforeseen happenings, the contract will be 'automatically' renegotiated if at all.

It would seem that the producing unit through these contractual agreements can greatly assure its costs of production; however, it is on the sales revenue side that most of the uncertainty prevails. The basic concern is whether it will be able to sell its production at the end of the process so as to cover its costs and yield an expected level of profits. Here it can greatly assure its future cash income by forward contracting to sell its output at a stipulated cost-markup price; but it still faces the inherent uncertainty about levels of demand which are subject (from its perspective) to uninsurable exogenous disturbances.

However the future may turn out, the beginning of a production cycle supposes that the organization has the finance (the liquidity) to meet its contractually controlled cost flow. This may be the case due to previous expectations being realized and, with a given pay-out policy, the organization will have generated sufficient internal funds to finance its operations. But failing this (perhaps due to heightened expectations) it must be able to borrow the necessary credit money from banks to carry out its production operations. The availability of this money is then an essential ingredient in furthering real production and employment, while its 'shortage' will retard real growth as firms may be unwilling to undertake long-term contractual commitments in the absence of long-term financial backing even if they expected their production plans to be warranted by a future increase in demand. So this 'debt money' is certainly not neutral as its increase is essentially related to production contracts for both working and fixed capital. We relate the rise and fall in the money supply to increases and decreases in economic activity which differs from the conventional line of reasoning which runs from money (determined from 'outside' the production system) to economic activity either directly or indirectly through interest rate changes. The money

407

supply should be considered as endogenous to levels of activity as this is mirrored in the myriad of forward financial contracts that serve to intertwine economic agents in society.

In the next section of this chapter we take a close look at this post-Keynesian approach to handling money, but now let us consider our discussion of a contractual money economy in terms of some macro-relationship that we touched upon earlier. Recall our earlier analysis of the 'neoclassical synthesis' where we related the conventional labor market apparatus (which, for a given price level, will have the money wage and hence the real wage determined by market forces of supply and demand) with the IS-LM portrayal of Keynesian economics. We concluded that the real elements of output and employment are, in the long term, to be considered as insensitive to demand variations, where these variations relate to changes in the money supply which comes through to the model in the form of LM shifts. What is behind the resulting totally inelastic aggregate supply curve via the LM movement is that 'inactive' money balances are not a means to hold wealth, they are a means to acquire wealth in the form of bonds guided by expectations regarding future prices of bonds. Changes in the money supply alter the demand for financial asset wealth which then impacts upon aggregate demand and prices. We pause to reiterate this relationship, to recall the difference with the approach of handling money in the neoclassical growth model where wealth is stored in a combination of money balances and real investment.

In a condition of unemployment, the real wage is too high to clear the labor market; this is simply saying that production costs (of which labor costs plays the dominant role) are too high relative to expected sales proceeds, thereby inhibiting the undertaking of production processes and employment. The conventional response would be for wage rates to fall in the face of this excess supply, thereby increasing the profitability of production which can then be expected to lead to an increase in employment. It behooves us to revisit Keynes' argument that counters this market-wage adjustment solution to the unemployment problem. For an understanding of the role of money and forward money contracts in the operations of a modern economy gives added support to Keynes' approach that flexible money and real wages are not, and indeed cannot be, the solution; as it underpins his view that the solution to the unemployment difficulty lies with effective demand. We conclude that money matters both in the short and long-term, so that a construction of a natural growth path must explicitly deal with how money 'supports' the path.

The straightaway neoclassical approach is that a reduction in money wages reduces the overall costs of production which, in the competitive framework, will mean lower prices which results in increased sales. More sales will lead to more production and more hiring. Employment will be increased up to the level where the lower wage is just offset by diminishing marginal productivity of labor as output increases. And this increase in production will be worthwhile because lower money wages are presumed to result in lower real wages which increases profits; for certainly prices do not change in exact proportion to wages. So through a process of falling money wages accompanied by rising profit and output levels, the economy restores itself to full employment.

This neoclassical sequence of events can take on what we may think of as a crude and less crude form. In the former, the increase in employment and profits comes through a reduction in costs as the firm adjusts its input choice decision in seeking the least cost production technology. From this view the reduction in money wages is assumed to leave demand unaffected. And 'monetarists' would maintain that there is no reason why demand should be affected, since there is no obvious reason why a wage rate reduction should reduce the money supply and/or income velocity of money which themselves determine aggregate demand.

But it is not very useful to consider matters this way, since increases in employment are normally associated with increases in production and sales; thus in the less crude form we would presume that money wage reductions will have a positive effect on aggregate demand. There is no sense in describing the neoclassical affect in terms of increased output and employment unless there is some increase in aggregate effective demand. The rationale here is that while the general reduction in wages reduces the purchasing power of 'workers', there are other agents whose money income will not have fallen and will in fact find their real income rising and positively affecting their demand. Yet even with regard to the grouping of people affected by wage rate changes, there is the assumption that the volume of employment will increase to an extent that will more than offset the reduction in the wage rate. Thus total demand will be greater at the lower wage rate thereby sustaining the greater level of employment. There is the assumption of an elasticity of demand for labor greater than unity with an increase in aggregate workers' income. And this higher income, i.e. this higher buying power, will bring higher equivalent levels of demand for both consumption and investment output. The accompanying higher level of savings will 'buy' an equivalent amount of investment goods via the lower interest rate in the loanable funds market (the implicit assumption is that investment expenditures would take the values required for full employment). Thus with a combination of an elastic demand for labor and the operation of Say's law, a reduction in money wages (and the real wage) can be expected to increase aggregate effective demand and employment.

One facet of the Keynesian revolution was a rejection of the assertion that overall wage reductions (even if they could be brought about) can be a significant factor in restoring full employment. And his reasoning was that the neoclassical presumed too much, and indeed did not have a realistic supportive theory, concerning the response of aggregate effective demand. Keynes points out that while he could accept the wage reduction argument in a single industry, the logic of this may very well fall apart when applied to the economy as a whole. He tells us:

> For, whilst no one would wish to deny the proposition that a reduction in money wages accompanied by the same aggregate effective demand as before will be associated with an increase in employment, the precise question at issue is whether the reduction in money will or will not be accompanied by the same aggregate effective demand as before measured in money. Or, at any rate, by an aggregate effective demand which is not reduced in full proportion to the reduction in money wages...But if the classical theory is not allowed to extend by analogy its conclusions in respect of a particular industry to industry as a whole, it is wholly unable to answer the question what effect on employment a reduction on money-wages will have.[22]

Keynes felt that 'orthodox' theory had no method of analysis to tackle the problem of unemployment on an aggregative basis.

So let us step back and see in a bit more detail why Keynes asserted that the cost reduction rationale (via money-wage declines) to increase employment was basically flawed. A particular industry (say industry A) estimated its demand schedule as well as its supply schedule relating the prices which will be asked for the sale of different quantities of goods, on the basis of given costs of production which we take to be essentially labor costs. The particular market outcome reflects the position of the supply curve implying a particular profit per unit of output on the basis of a particular wage structure. A fall in the wage rate in (A) increases profits per unit and will lead to more employment in (A); but output will also increase in response to reduced cost and higher profits (Keynes used the neoclassical competitive framework). Bear in mind that we have reduced the wage costs in (A) but not generally, so the real income of consumers overall in terms of A's output has gone up stimulating more demand and production in industry A. In this way, one can construct a demand schedule for (A) and reason a change in the amount demanded as a function of a change in its costs of production. But we can do this only on some fixed assumption of the nature of market schedules in all other lines of activity.

Yet this is exactly where the problem lies, for we do not reduce wage rates in any one sector; what is proposed is an overall wage decline affecting all workers. This means that there will be a fall in income and demand generally with the possible consequence of decline in demand for the output of (A) in the face of its lower selling price. Indeed any benefits to employment that result from lower costs may be overwhelmed by a reduction in demand for its output. And there is every likelihood to see a fall in A's prices being more severe and equaling that of wages so that the real wage remains unchanged thereby taking with it the incentive to increase output and employment.

Again, matters regarding employment may work out well in any one sector assuming aggregate demand does not fall, or increases for its product due to its price falling relative to other prices. But as Keynes argued, you cannot transfer the possible positive result in a single sector to the economy as a whole. The demand curve for any one sector cannot be constructed on the assumption of all other things being the same. So the entire approach must clearly be on a macro level, with the onus on orthodox theory to show that aggregate effective demand will remain buoyant or increase in the face of a general wage reduction so as to justify higher levels of employment.

Keynes' point was that orthodox theory could not make a case as to the practical significance of wage reductions in restoring full employment. He poses a condition that would seem most favorable to the orthodox outcome, and then asks whether, even under these most favorable terms, the policy would work out. And for the policy to succeed it would have to increase effective demand by virtue of the repercussions of wage-rate reductions or the aggregate propensity to consume or on the schedule of the marginal efficiency of capital or on the rate of interest — effective demand being the sum of expected consumption and expected investment.

The favorable condition is the supposition that firms believe that they can attain higher profits via wage reduction; and acting on this belief they cut their wage rates and increase employment and expand output. The individual entrepreneur will certainly see that a wage reduction will lower his costs, but he is not likely to reckon the effect of an economy-wide wage decline on the demand of his particular product. He may very well expect to sell a larger volume at a greater net profit. As Keynes puts it, "It is indeed not unlikely that an individual entrepreneur, seeing his own costs reduced, will overlook at the outset the repercussions on the demand for his product and will act on the assumption that he will be able to sell at a profit larger output than before".[23] Assuming then, that all entrepreneurs act this way, the economy will see a greater level of employment — at least initially.

The question is, will firms obtain the higher profits they expect so as to justify and maintain their higher levels of employment? Keynes was quite explicit in his analysis of the circumstances determining the answer to this question. The expectations of profits that give rise to a particular level of employment are realized under one supposition that the marginal propensity to consume is equal to unity so that there is no gap between the higher level of income due to the higher level of employment and the increase in demand to absorb the higher level of output (the crude version of Say's law assuming no investment output is required; we will shortly relate our discussion of money and uncertainty to this 'law'). But more meaningfully, under a second supposition that there is an increase in investment expenditures corresponding to the gap between the increase in income and that of consumption, so that the economy will be able to sell all of the addition to output that was expected to be sold with the realization of expected proceeds (the less crude version of Say's law). But for investment expenditures to take on the value required for full employment there would have to be an increase in the marginal efficiency of capital relative to the rate of interest that is traceable to the reduction in the wage rate. In the absence of this latter circumstance (in reality the increment of savings is not zero) firms will find that their proceeds are less than expected, inventories will unintentionally increase that cannot be sold except at losses and output will be reduced with an associated decline in employment. As one expositor of Keynes states it:

> The practical refutation of the classical logic reveals itself in the form of business losses. The proceeds from the added output have fallen short of the cost of producing the added output. There is no sustaining basis for the employment of a greater number of workers as a consequence of the economy-wide cut in money wages.[24]

Any conclusion concerning the effect of wage reductions would have to be reckoned through its impact on those determinants of effective demand; and assuming the analysis is restricted to a closed system, then, as Keynes notes, the most favorable results from a decline in money wages would have to be based mainly on an increase in investment expenditures due to either an increase in the marginal efficiency of capital or a decline in the rate of interest.

With regard to the former the best outcome would be if the cut in money wages was seen as a one-time move. Wage rates are judged to have hit bottom with future changes expected to be in an upward direction. In this circumstance firms would take advantage of lower costs to bring into being investment projects whose 'internal' rate of return (that Keynesian marginal efficiency of capital rate) now exceeds the rate of interest. This higher MEC rate on capital stems in part from low costs, but more importantly from the higher expected earnings due largely to higher future demand. For the firm to postpone capacity adjustment in the light of such wages expectations could very well subject it to a loss of market share as it may not be able to meet higher demand and, of course, it will be subject to higher costs as a result of having waited. The point is to stimulate higher investment expenditures in an environment of wage reductions, that is itself a signal of weakening effective demand. The motivation to look to the longer term and act on investment expenditures in the present, is the anticipation of higher production costs and levels of demand in the future.

Certainly if wage reductions were expected to be followed by further reductions, the MEC rate would deteriorate powered by reduced expected earnings, and investment spending would fail to accommodate whatever level of employment emerges. Aggregate demand would be insufficient, firms would again reduce employment triggering further wage reductions, and the economy slips further into the cyclical downturn. Keynes' statement is that "The most unfavourable contingency is that in which money-wage rates are slowly sagging downward and each reduction in wages serves to diminish confidence in the prospective maintenance of wages".[25]

Keynes appreciated that as a practical matter we are not going to get a one-time large reduction in money wages in a system of free labor-management bargaining; wages are not set by administrative decree, nor are worker organizations handmaidens of the state. This leads him to remark that:

On the other hand, it would be much better that wages should be rigidly fixed and deemed incapable of material changes, than that depressions should be accompanied by a gradual downward tendency of money wages...It follows that with the actual practices and institutions of the contemporary world it is more expedient to aim at a rigid money wage policy than at a flexible policy responding by easy stages to changes in the amount of unemployment — so far, that is to say, as the marginal efficiency of capital is concerned.[26]

The wage rigidity, rather than emerging as a negative characteristic impeding the adjustment to full employment, is in reality a necessary trait to impede the increase in unemployment by maintaining relatively buoyant effective demand, which then provides a greater possibility for the success of other measures to increase demand and reverse the decline. But Keynes did not follow through his thinking about wage inflexibility in the operation of a modern monetary economy; he relates to this in terms of a 'money illusion' or simply acknowledging downside rigidities. We will therefore want to link his discussion of the efficacy of a flexible wage policy to our understanding of the role of money and money contracts.

Before considering this it is interesting to recall that the effect of wage flexibility on employment via its impact on interest rates was also considered by Keynes to be not very promising. The uncertainties here are the extent to which rates would fall as a reflection of the fall in money wages, and the elasticity of the investment demand schedule which relates to considerations about confidence and expected yield. The necessary reduction in wages required reduces interest sufficiently to stimulate the required level of investment could itself shatter confidence and result in a highly inelastic investment response. Overall, flexible wages offered no grounds for the belief of being capable of sustaining full employment. One can, theoretically, produce the same effect on the rate of interest by increasing the quantity of money while leaving the level of wages unchanged; but monetary policy action would be prone to the same uncertainties and limitations as that of flexible wages.

Getting back to the central point about the role of money, we understand that it does matter with regard to the real outcomes of the economy. And its importance stems greatly from the realization that money (and the banking system) is a society-produced institution put in place to make possible the flow of production and employment through time. Money is the basis upon which those forward contracts are negotiated for the purchase of material inputs and hiring of labor on a time-use arrangement;

and as a result of our previous discussion, we now appreciate the necessity of such contracts in a realistic world of uncertainty. So the availability of 'money' or lack thereof in response to organizations' demand for liquidity as they contemplate production increases and thereby enter into cash commitments through time, will certainly be an important inhibiting or encouraging element regarding the growth of real output and employment.

But the very presence of liquidity and the contractual basis for employment help to explain why the economy may from time to time evidence less than full-employment and can become mired in under-employment equilibrium. The presence of these human institutions can be seen as providing support to Keynes' objection to the two main orthodox propositions concerning the labor market and unemployment; to reiterate: that real wages depend on the money wage negotiation in the labor market, and that labor can increase its employment by reducing its real wage as a result of accepting a lower money wage.

We will look somewhat closer at these institutions as they relate to wages and employment so that we obtain a realistic notion of what is meant by the term 'labor market', indeed whether such a market exists as the term is normally understood; to also connect 'sticky' or the rigidity of wages to liquidity, and to obtain a true vision of the connection between the price level and the money wage. Of course, in contemplating these discussions we are setting ourselves in the short-term cyclical frame and not in our steady-state balanced growth path. But it is proper to take this approach in refuting the neoclassical constructions, and thereafter to see how a realistic appraisal can be supportive of long-term equilibrium — as we have tried to do throughout this book.

Let us again revisit our earlier IS-LM-labor market model. The examination of the labor segment of the economy using the standard market demand and supply curves with the real wage on the vertical axis is, to say the least, misleading in the light of the way things really work. The demand for labor is related to the level of output that the organization plans to produce within the framework of a pervading technology that is characterized by a high capital to labor ratio and level of capitality that results in rather constant labor costs per unit of output (and hence constant marginal costs) up to the level of full-capacity production. The reader may want to revisit the "setting of prices" section of Chapter 6 for a reminder look at the cost curves of these oligopolistic market structure 'megacorp' organizations (as footnoted in Chapter 6), a detailed analysis is provided by Eichner and the exposition by Bober). For a broad range of output levels prime costs per unit of output are constant; thus one can meet an increase in demand for one's product by increasing output at the prevailing cost level. However prices are determined in this framework — and we are now aware that they are set via a mark-up pricing arrangement — we want to stress that they are not, within the operational range of the existing capacity, cost-driven as in the usual neoclassical manner. We do not in general have rising marginal costs which both limits the expansion of output and requires that prices rise as production increases.

The real linkage is that once the organization determines the price, the level of production (and amount of employment) is determined by the amount of output that the market is expected to take. The demand for labor is determined by the production plans of the organization without reference to any marginal productivity of labor notion; indeed, with the nature of the cost structure as it is, this conventional basis underlying labor demand completely misses the mark.

At times we have referred to the firm as the 'megacorp' or the organization to distinguish this enterprise from the neoclassical 'atomistic' family-owned firm. The megacorp's objectives are of a wider scope than the usual assumptions of profit maximization or loss minimization. An essential aim is a rate of return, and very likely to increase market share in the various lines of its operations; and it will look to withdraw from those lines whose growth rate of sales are deemed to be insufficient given the projected growth of the aggregate economy. Yet this aim of maintaining market share and branching out into more rapidly expanding areas serves a more fundamental aim which is the growth of the organization itself and measured by growth of sales and market share and/or that of cash flow.

Thus given the share of market which it plans to command and estimating the growth of the total market on the basis of a projection about the growth of the aggregate economy, the firm then estimates its output over a future period of time and puts its production plans into motion; and we now appreciate that it is in a state of uncertainty that these plans are set, as the organization attempts to reckon with occurrences in the economy at large that may cause its sales and profit levels expectations to be unfulfilled. Yet with this uncertainty it will set prices in its various lines of operations by means of a mark-up over average variable costs that covers fixed costs and will yield a profit target for that level of output (again it might be worthwhile to review the mechanics of this procedure and related discussion in Chapter 6).

As we talked about previously , the organization will try to lock-in, in so far as possible, its costs of production over the planning period; and

416

with regard to labor costs this takes the form of those explicit forward financial wage contracts between the organization and 'labor'. Thus for a true understanding of matters we need to abandon, as a primary tool of analysis, the view that money wages are determined by market forces; wages are the result of an administered price process between the organization and 'labor' with the resulting contractual outcome prevailing over some period of time. There is an implicit understanding that goes along with this wage contract to the effect that if the organization's expectations are not being met it will not look to abrogate the agreement. Of course, contracts are entered into with a clear understanding of their legal enforcement; but in the operations of one's business it is always best to avoid this state. Attempts at reducing the money wage may very well impart a bad reputation to the firm and would probably be harmful to worker productivity.

If sales are disappointing the firm may simply decide to reduce production and employment with no effect on unit variable costs. The excess labor supply does not translate into a lower money wages and there is no affect on the real wage as the firm may opt to minimize the reduction in net profits by maintaining the existing mark-up at the expense of sales. Given the nature of the cost curves, unit total costs will increase as a result of an increase in unit fixed costs when the plant is being operated at less than expected intensity. The essential point is that changes in output and employment over some moderate range can leave prices and wages unchanged, though it will affect net profits. There is no 'market clearing' operation due to a fall in the price of labor — the price does not fall in the face of excess supply.

But suppose [and this is more of a reflection of Fig. (8.8) in this chapter] that output exceeds anticipated sales with the plant operating at greater than expected capacity with the associated increase in employment; and the organization sees conditions as ripe for it to increase its price and enjoy a higher average cash flow (say in anticipation of the need for additional investment funds). Overall, prices will rise and the real wage will fall. Clearly we cannot look to the middle frame of Fig. 8.8 to explain what will happen both to the money wage and to the real wage. Labor does not, in light of this lower real wage, so to speak, withdraw its labor, thus shifting the labor supply curve to the left thereby creating conditions to increase the money wage so as to leave real wages unchanged. Even in terms of the traditional competitive labor market, it is a "somewhat distorted perspective which views the individual or household as weighing the disutility from additional work against the utility

417

obtained from additional income thus earned and offering fewer hours of labor or dropping out of the labor force entirely if real wages fall".[27] The conventional analysis ignores other essential kinds of satisfaction that work provides; and very few households can afford to supply less labor as real wages decline — this is not the means to eliminate an excess supply of labor.

But even if we think in terms of a 'union-model' there is no way to ameliorate the decline in the real wage accept by striking to re-open the contract to change its terms. And the unpopularity of abrogating a contract will in all likelihood hold for unions as it does for the megacorp. Indeed the choice is stopping work entirely or for the union to accommodate the increase in the demand for its 'product' at the existing wage.

Thus the vertical aggregate supply curve in Fig. (8.8) is an inaccurate result based on the faulty assumption that the real wage remains unchanged in the face of a higher level of demand and prices brought on, as we might recall, by an increase in the money supply. With the profitability of higher employment levels evaporated there would be no increase in real output; hence the vertical curve and the conclusion that money does not matter. But we now understand the framework that would cause us to abandon this neoclassical synthesis and its implication concerning the real economy. At the risk of being somewhat repetitive, what we come away with at this point is that the demand for labor depends on the level of aggregate economic activity having essentially nothing to do with a marginal productivity of labor notion; and that labor supply as well must be understood in a framework divorced from marginal utility or disutility concepts.

This is very much a Keynesian result reached via a different line of reasoning. As Keynes noted in his rebuttal to the argument that the demand for labor can only increase via a reduction in the money and real wage rates, overall the amount of employment at any money wage depends on the availability of jobs which translates to the organization's assumptions about the future course of sales. One can observe changes in employment in the real world without any obvious changes in the productivity of labor or the real wage. And we can see that money has a direct relation to employment and output via the ability of the banking system to create the finance required by the megacorp if it is to undertake those forward money contracts and begin production.

Now this brings us to reckon the outcome of Fig. (8.9) in a somewhat different way. When the money wage contract is again negotiated say at the beginning of a new production period, labor will have presumably formed some outlook about expected price changes in the light of actual price changes. As we pointed out, if it is blessed with perfect foresight, it will negotiate a money wage such as to leave real wages unchanged and thereby yield the vertical aggregate supply curve [though in the story of Fig. (8.9) demand and prices go up first and then with labor immediately recognizing the fall off in the real wage it adjusts its supply to increase the money wage to completely compensate — a story that we want to put aside]. This supposes that labor bargainers somehow anticipate, say, an average of the price mark-up policies. But this is a very unlikely explanation as the administered price is subject to quick adjustment in the event of demand changes that were very difficult to anticipate in an uncertain world, plus the organization may decide to alter the projection concerning market share. Unions cannot be assumed to correctly anticipate prices so as to strive to maintain the real wage. It would seem that organizations determine a price based on some net profit goal (given costs) and anticipated sales, generally looking ahead under conditions of uncertainty; while labor in all likelihood forms a price projected change based on some form of realized price behavior. How can these different perspectives result in a constant real wage; and all the more, when we realize that the mark-up is based on variable costs so that prices adjust to money wages rather than the converse which is the basis of Fig. (8.9).

The long-run outcome of Fig. (8.9) is based on the conventional approach that an exogenous change in the money supply triggers endogenously determined equations that simultaneously solve for relative prices, with money wages being one such price. In such a model, monetary change (acting upon demand) in the long run (when agents have had time to adjust) can only affect the absolute price level. But in the reality of matters prices are administered to the economy based on real considerations. To reiterate: the organization sets the price to yield a certain net profit in conjunction with an understanding concerning market share and sales. Money wages are a negotiated result which, from the organization's point of view, will evidence a demand for labor based upon the existing technology, and the megacorp's projection concerning demand and expected profits. The supply of labor — generally through some sort of 'worker organization' — depends on demographic and cultural factors dealing with specific skill attainment. There is no uniform type of labor responding along a neoclassical labor supply curve. An additional point that we want to keep in mind is that the organization (as we previously pointed out) does not have as its primary goal the maximization of short-term profits; it is as likely if not more so to be pursuing to maintain or increase its market share, hence an increase in demand larger than anticipated is likely to be met with an increase in production rather than price. But this would depend on whether additional capacity is to be constructed and whether the organization wants to generate more internal funds for this purpose via higher mark-up. In any event, prices will not change in any straightforward fashion with demand (which is presumably altered via monetary policy) over the business cycle. Thus the role of money will have to be understood primarily in terms of its impact on real demand and support of real production whether over the long or short-term time frames.

In Fig. (8.9) we presented what was referred to as the Keynesian (or short-term) case where employment and production can be positively affected by monetary actions via the reduction in the real wage as a result of increased and prices. The assumption of that analysis is that labor is under a money illusion or is not fully adjusting to realize price increases. But the reasoning for this possible sequence of events is that in the event firms take advantage of the increased demand to put through a higher mark-up, money wages will simply not be able to adjust because of the existence of fixed wage contracts without which production would not be undertaken in the first place. This decline in the real wage has little if anything to do with an 'illusion' or with 'imperfect foresight' where labor does not process fully the higher price increase, so that even if we assume a reopening of the wage contract 'immediately' upon the realization of higher prices, labor does not in its bargain expect prices to rise in the future to the same degree. Thus the labor supply curve shifts to the left by a lessor increment than the rightward shift of the demand curve resulting in the real wage decline. Here, as with Fig. (8.8), the results are based on flawed theoretical reasoning.

At this juncture we want to relate the inflexibility of money wage rates and the store of value explanation for liquidity demand as it all reflects on the negation of Say's law. It is, as we know, sensible behavior in an uncertain world for organizations to lock-in their costs of production in the form of forward financial contracts in money terms, which to some degree (depending on internal finance conditions and the mark-up policy) requires the assurance of the banking system's ability to 'create' the supportive financial means. But this very way of carrying on production results in the expectation of stable or 'sticky' wage rates in the presence of uncertainty about future prices. For if money wages were to be presumed to be totally flexible in response to prices, then people would be unwilling to hold a portion of their wealth in the form of a depreciation money asset (or in the

420

form of very liquid-close substitutes for non-interest bearing money). It is this institutional way of carrying on economic activity which itself can be cause for insufficient aggregate demand and involuntary overall unemployment. Money functioning in this store of value way yields a 'return' in and of itself; and as such we have to reckon that the act of maintaining liquidity today is not a decision to postpone spending today in order to spend tomorrow. There will be a gap between the increment in income and the increment in consumption which, though explainable via Keynes' fundamental principle about the marginal propensity to consume, is now given more credibility in terms of the role of liquidity in an uncertain world. The question is whether sufficient investment expenditures will be forthcoming to keep production levels from falling (or, in terms of the long view path, to maintain the proper growth in real output). Post-Keynesians eschew any mechanism that automatically brings into play the compensating level of investment expenditure. In fact, increased liquidity demand by consumers (i.e. the reallocation of income from purchases of goods to liquid assets) and its affect on sales will signal organizations to postpone investment and cut current production and employment — and this is not likely to be alleviated by any reduction in the rate of interest.

In modern capitalist economies investment is essentially influenced by business confidence regarding the growth of market demand and not by the level of savings. Indeed, as we have pointed out in our discussions of distribution and savings, post-Keynesians argue that it is investment which limits or determines savings rather than the reverse. So what we come away with is that the negation of Say's law is a natural outcome of the operations of the economy, and not particularly the fault of any 'rigidities'.

As an overall approach, post-Keynesians view money as an essential non-neutral feature of an advanced market economy. It is not to be treated as a 'veil' behind which real economic activity is occurring; instead it must be understood to have a direct affect on the economy's real output and employment both in the short and long time frames of analysis (from the latter perspective, of course, one can ignore the cyclical movements in the economy). One therefore has to track both the real and monetary flows as they relate to each other; and through this interplay we can put another gloss on the Keynesian relation between savings and investment.

The basic Keynesian vision is one of equilibrium mechanics wherein one would understand the forces that would maintain the economy in a particular condition in a given historical setting, and then observe the mechanism of moving the system to a different equilibrium outcome. Now one can alter this basic design to one of 'dynamics' in two ways. One is to maintain the equilibrium mode, but, so to speak, 'get into the transition period'; that is, to see the process of disequilibrium or transition rather than focusing on and comparing static positions. So that the elements of savings and investments while not in equality at any point in time can be depicted as moving in the direction of balance. Here we are talking about a process of temporal equilibrium adjustment where the variables are lagged in an economically meaningful way. More realistically would be the construction of a dynamic system with induced investment and consumption lags, with a range of values assigned to the investment coefficient that can produce conditions of perpetual cyclical movements (or the possibility of expansion at some proportional rate). In these macro-models either the balance of savings and investment is never achieved, which is in keeping with actual historical experience, or it is always achieved on the long-term path of continuous forward motion. The latter (steady-state) being a quite useful theoretical construction for interpreting the trend movement of the economy.

But keeping to the actual events, this constant imbalance between savings and investment can be looked at via the Federal Reserve Board's flow of funds accounts which can serve as the means to highlight the interconnections between the final and real sectors of the economy, and the lead-in to post-Keynesian monetary analysis.

The Board constructs balance sheets for twelve major sectors of the economy (financial and non-financial) in which, for each sector, there are estimate of total assets, liabilities and net worth held at a point in time. Assets are divided into financial and real (non-financial) assets. The next step in the preparation of the flow of Funds Accounts is to put together a sources and uses of funds statement for each sector. The uses of funds is equal to the net change in total assets, consisting of the net change in real assets (or net real investment) plus that of financial assets (or net financial investment). The sources of funds consists of the change in outstanding liabilities, i.e. net borrowing (plus sign telling us that total borrowing is larger than debt repayment) and net current savings (or the change in current surplus cost). So for each sector we have a change in total assets equal to total uses of funds; and a change in liabilities and net current savings equal to the total sources of funds. In the balance of the Flow of Funds account we have (in more recognizable terms):

$$Net\ real\ investment\ +\ Net\ financial\ investment$$
$$=\ Net\ borrowing\ -\ Net\ current\ Saving \qquad (47)$$

422

or

Total use of funds = Total source of funds

In terms of a non-financial sector (with no financial investment), the net cash inflow is the change in the current surplus account which reflects current savings, while net real investment is net purchases of plant and equipment; so we have a comparison of the change over time between net cash inflow and its expenditures on durable goods, i.e. tangible investment. Then:

$$\textit{Net real investment} - \textit{Net current saving} \qquad (48)$$
$$= \textit{Net borrowing.}$$

This relation between the use of funds in terms of a sector's outlay on durable goods (discretionary spending) and its source of funds as reflective of current saving is akin to the relation between investment and savings in the simple Keynesian model. When any one sector's outlay exceeds its cash inflow, the sector is contributing positively to the spending stream; and this addition to spending will in the Keynesian manner increase the level of economic activity. But if this "cash-flow feedback effect" is negative, then expenditures on durable goods falls short of the sector's cash inflow, which is similar to when investment is less than savings and the level of economic activity is dampened.

Yet a sector's negative balance between durable goods outlay and cash inflow will not only be expected to have a real impact, but it will also have a corresponding financial impact. If we imagine a flow of funds accounting for an economy of non-financial sectors, then in the aggregate their uses of funds would have to equal their total sources. Thus if one sector had a cash deficit this would necessarily have to be offset by another sector's cash surplus. But in the reality of an economy with a developed banking sector, there need not be offsetting transfers of cash (if one can imagine this) between sectors. With outlays exceeding cash inflows (current savings), the resulting deficit can then be financed by loans from the banking sector, with the result that sources of funds (i.e. money) is now greater by the amount of positive borrowing. This increased 'money' then goes into circulation as a result of its expenditure on tangible assets. "Thus one finds a strong correlation between the size of the deficit in the various sectors of the economy — in the business and household sectors as well as in the government — and the money supply."[28] If we look at the balance of (48), then the cash deficit could be made up by selling off financial assets (having a negative change in financial investment); but this would simply be a transfer of cash between agents and not a change in the money supply. One can combine borrowing plus net current savings into a total called 'gross savings', with the difference between this total savings and outlays on investment being equal to net financial investment.

Thus the increase in the source of funds via borrowing is seen to be in response to the cash deficit which itself reflects an increase in 'asset' purchases (through those forward money contracts), and when this deficit is accommodated, the money supply increases. This sequence does not place the money supply change in its accustomed causal role with regard to real output and employment in the short-term, nor with regard to the level of nominal income in the long-run (assuming that the income flow corresponds to capacity use at full employment) — as in the conventional monetarist approach. What we see is the change in the money supply in a respondent position to the change in the demand for 'credit money' which itself is greatly related to the level of economic activity as a result of production plans made by firms in accordance with their expectations. This brings us to the post-Keynesian way of handling money and the rate of interest.

Post-Keynesian monetary theory and Re-thinking Keynes

It will behoove us to first briefly overview the standard approach to monetary matters employed in economic texts which contains, as we will see, a basic misunderstanding regarding the causal changes in the money supply. The usual exposition is that the Federal Reserve System (the 'Fed') has at its disposal monetary tools which it can employ to determine the size of the money base which itself is equal to reserves of commercial banks plus currency in circulation. The currency directly contributes to the money supply while the reserves are controlled by the Fed essentially via its open-market tool; and it is the bank reserve ingredient that forms the basis for demand (checking) and other deposits. In 1993, the size of the money supply (at times spoken of as the money stock) was $1,128 (in billions) with the combined demand (checkable) and other deposits being 70% of the total money supply with the remaining 30% being composed of currency and traveler's checks — we are considering the money supply in its most common (though narrowist) M1 definition. And all this gets wrapped up with a money expansion multiplier formula which relates in a rather automatic way the relation between a change in the money stock to a change in the money base as a result of a change in bank reserves through the Fed's open market operations, given the banking system's reserve requirements against their demand deposits. Between the years 1985 and 1993, this multiplier ranged from a low of 2.74 to a high of 3.24. There is the usual partial disclaimer that some leakage can be expected as some banks may build up excess reserves, so that the actual money supply may be somewhat less than potential; but the clear impression is that an increase in the money base will eventually increase the money stock by approximately the size of the deposit multiplier. This multiplier can be worked out in the following way: We have the M1 stock consisting of currency (cu) + deposits (d), and we presume a reasonably stable ratio of currency to deposits (ψ) so the money supply is:

$$M = \psi d + d$$

$$= d(1 + \psi) \tag{49}$$

The money base consists of currency plus bank reserves which is in some fixed ratio (i) to deposits, giving a money base (MB) as:

$$MB = \psi d + id$$

$$= d(\psi + i) \tag{50}$$

If we divide (M) by (MB) we obtain the multiplier:

$$\frac{M}{MB} = \frac{1 + \psi}{\psi + i} \tag{51}$$

Supposing the reserve ratio (i) is .2 and the currency ratio (ψ) is .3, then the multiplier is:

$$\frac{1 + .3}{.3 + .2} = 2.6 \tag{52}$$

An increase in the base of $100 million would increase the money supply by $260 million. And as we pointed out a change in the base is normally linked to the Fed's open market action, so the multiplier provides that link between action on the monetary base and the money supply in the

425

economy. As one text puts it, "As long as the currency to deposit ratio and the reserve ratio do not change, the Fed can control the money supply by adjusting the monetary base...the whole money supply is built on the monetary base".[29] Of course, the multiplier would also be increased as a result of reducing the reserve to deposit ratio. Whatever the mechanics, it is on this reasoning that monetarists hold the money supply to be properly viewed as an exogenous variable.

Although post-Keynesians acknowledge the generally stable relationship between the money base and the money supply, and between the money supply and nominal income, the causal relationship implied is the reverse of the conventional view. Both the money stock and the money base are to be considered endogenous; that is, determined by conditions 'inside' the system. Seeing this from the bank's balance sheet, the post-Keynesian approach would have the causation run from the liability side to the asset side; banks first extend credit thereby creating demand deposits and increasing the money supply and look to obtain reserves later. Or, to put the matter somewhat differently, banks first make loans (appearing on the asset side) and then search for the required reserves to cover the increase in their assets. Banks provide the necessary credit demanded at a given price (i.e. at a given rate of interest), while the Fed supplies the amount of base money induced by this very creation of additional money. As Lavoie summarizes this approach: "In a nutshell, the main post-Keynesian view of endogenous money can be presented as follows. Money is credit-driven; loans make deposits; deposits make reserves. The supply of and the demand for credit money are interdependent. This control instrument of the central bank is not a quantity but a price, the price of interest".[30] As Keynes pointed out in the *Treatise on Money*, "money comes into existence along with debts".[31] The supply of money is essentially related to those forward money contracts and any debts which they necessitate. Returning to our flow of funds view, it is the presence of deficits that determines the demand for credit, i.e. money, and thereby the endogenous response of the banking system in its creation. Thus the demand for 'money' creates its own supply, at least up to the limit set by the reserve ratio. Again, in contrast to orthodox theory, the supply of new loans and thus the increase in the money supply is not seen to be dependent on the availability of free reserves. Reserves, in reality, pose little if any constraint; the central bank as a lender of last resort is presumed to provide the reserves required to accommodate the money supply which is dependent on demand as governed by the level of economic activity and the rate of interest.

426

We briefly want to look at evidence in support of this reverse causality emphasis. In a paper entitled "Unpacking the post-Keynesian Black Box: bank lending and the money supply",[32] Moore cites several pieces of evidence in support of this reverse approach. There is the operational understanding of the Fed's open market committee itself. Managers of this operation "insist that in the short run, money stock creation is a joint result of a complex interaction among households, business corporations, financial institutions, the Treasury and the Federal Reserve. They emphasize that most of the reported short-run movements in monetary aggregates are primarily the result of statistical 'noise' and estimating errors in the data, and argue that the view that the central bank determines changes in the money stock in the short run is simply inaccurate".[33] Then what is also 'wrong' is the assumption that the banking system expands the money supply (i.e. loans) only after the Fed has increased the money base (has put reserves into the system).

In fact, in the workings of the banking system, the amount of reserves required to be maintained at the end of a given statement week are predetermined by the level of deposits activity several weeks earlier. Since banks have to meet their reserve requirements at the end of each week, and since they cannot alter their requirements being based on earlier deposit levels, the total amount of required reserves simply has to be available. Certainly, the central bank will have the freedom as to how these reserves are to be acquired. These reserves can be supplied through a combination of ways, but to suggest that open market operations would be used as a means to prevent a rise in reserves is illogical in the face of this predetermined requirement that must be accommodated. In reality, the change in the money base is not to be viewed as a tool to directly affect a future change in the money supply, but essentially as a required response in support of an already existing change in some money aggregate.

Moore also brings to bear evidence concerning various formal causality tests between bank reserves and bank deposits with the finds that the money supply is exogenous with respect to reserves. There is much evidence in support of the one direction causality from each of four definitions of the money supply to the money base, and from bank lending to the monetary aggregates. This underscores the primary supportive and stabilizing role of the central bank. Attempts to determine the money supply via vigorous control of reserves would subject the economy to wide fluctuations in the rate of interest which would enhance rather than limit the uncertainty about future costs. And a determining factor in setting up the Fed system was to enable firms to count on a sufficient supply of funds in line with their borrowing requirements. The fact that the central bank determines the reserve base and also what proportion of reserves can be used as earning assets (as means to create money) conveys the wrong impression that the central authorities somehow exercise direct control over the money supply by injecting or withdrawing reserves. Of course, they do alter reserves but not with monetary aggregates as the basic target; the essential reason is that of a supportive role. "Once deposits have been created by an act of lending, the central bank must somehow ensure that the required reserves are available at the settlement date. Otherwise the banks, no matter how hard they scramble for funds, could not in the aggregate meet their reserve requirements".[34]

What the central bank does target and control is the rate of interest; its controlling instrument is not a quantity of money but its price. Given the price of its choice, it stands prepared to supply the reserves necessary to support whatever the amount of bank loans demanded at that price. Thus the ability of the Fed to control the rate of growth of monetary aggregates depends on its ability to control the rate of bank lending via the rate of interest; and not through the monetary base. The supply of money should then be depicted as a horizontal line being infinitely elastic at every existing (exogenous) rate of interest; it cannot in fact be distinguished from deposit creation which reflects the demand for bank credit. It bears repeating that the central bank can determine the short-term interest rate at which it will stand ready to supply liquidity; but the money supply itself is not the controlling device. What is lost sight of is when reserve requirements come into effect, the loans inducing such requirements have already been made.

We illustrate this post-Keynesian view of endogenous money and exogenous interest rates in Fig. (8.14).

On the vertical axis in (8.14) we have a set rate of interest $(\bar{r})$ by the central bank, with the level of 'credit money' on the horizontal axis translated to a level of money stock in panel (ii). The demand curve for bank loans is related to a given level of nominal income and drawn negatively related to the rate of interest; in that the higher this administratively determined price the greater the retarding effect on bank lending. At the given interest rate the banking system will supply the amount of deposits or bank credit demanded (again we note the interdependence of the supply and the demand for money) while the central bank provides the money base induced by this increase in money. Thus in panel (iii) we find the reverse causality with the money base (M_b) being endogenous to the money aggregate, with the base money being equal to the reciprocal of the money multiplier (M_m) times the money stock. So that at every set rate of interest there exists a supply curve of money parallel to horizontal money axis; and this stemming from the primary role of the central bank which is to provide the money base sufficient to protect the liquidity of commercial banks. The term 'horizontalists' has been put forward to designate this post-Keynesian endogenous view of money, in

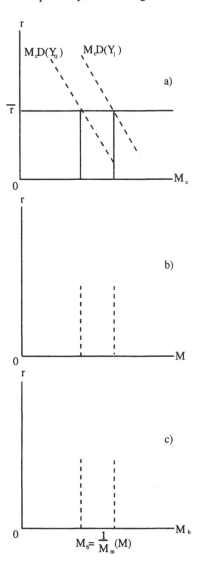

Figure 8.14

contradiction to the traditional 'verticalist' approach that views changes in some money aggregate as attributable to a specific action by the central bank. Let us reiterate the characteristics of this endogenous money approach: "Loans make deposits; money makes money base; the money supply curve is horizontal; the rate of interest is exogenous".[35]

In the light of this endogenous approach we will need to rethink those standard explanations as to how money matters. The quantity theory, as we are aware, sets up a link running from the money supply to nominal income. As we showed earlier, with real output taken at its full-employment rate, the general price level is found to be dependent on the supply of money. Money does matter but, in the long-term, not with regard to the level of real output. And, in any event, this link to prices assumes a rather stable velocity of circulation determined by 'institutional factors'.

But we now understand that this is not totally accurate even if we confine ourselves to the long term consideration and making use of the neoclassical production function and the savings-investment relationship. What we learned from those neoclassical long-run models is that money matters with regard to real output per capita where the system is on its long-run growth path, via the result of a change in the money supply on the rate of inflation. The rate of general price changes affects the demand to hold cash balances as an asset with its impact on planned savings (i.e. investment) and on the capital to labor ratio. On the steady-state path, full employment output is prescribed for a particular rate of technical progress and a rate of capital accumulation.

If we look again at Fig. (8.8) we realize that there were some matters not explicitly considered with regard to that vertical real output result in panel (a). We can see that as a point-in-time on the steady growth path yielding a particular real output per capita. And this is reflective of a ratio of real money balances to output such as to yield the level of investment that maintains full employment. Thus maintaining a movement along the path, from this neoclassical angle, means that the economy maintains the 'correct' inactive money balance ratio which itself is determined by the growth of the money supply and the corresponding rate of change in prices. We reiterate a point, made earlier in this context, that in the long term we have a particular rate of inflation to which wages are fully adjusted, with the money supply expanding at the same rate as the labor forces. But money growth models with their causality from money to prices and the savings-investment identify should not be the means to enhance our understanding of the role that money plays on the secular growth path; certainly in the light of the criticism levied on neoclassical mechanics. Of course, the growth of money in an accommodating or supportive role to counteract the always present sense of uncertainty is one of many essential ingredients in maintain steady growth balance; but this is far removed from neoclassical models.

Let us, however, back away from the secular balanced growth vision, and look at the short-term (cyclical) transmission mechanism from money to real output. There is the basic monetarist relation of a direct transmission; one version being that central bank policies increase the money supply resulting in the economy finding itself with 'too much money' in real terms relative to the demand for real money balances. This excess money supply spills over directly to the goods market at the existing rate of interest and prices raising demand and real output. The movement being from a change in the money base to a change in the money supply to that of real Gross Domestic Product. Of course, a reduction in general prices has the same impact on the supply of real money balances held, causing economic agents to alter their portfolio of assets in the direction of goods.

We confront some difficulties with this transmission mechanism via the real balances effect resulting from post-Keynesian thinking. Since the supply and demand for money are co-determined at any exogenous short-term interest ratio, i.e. the quantity of money is demand determined, there cannot be an excess supply of nominal cash balances that in a sequential sense translates into a demand increase. The unfortunate image one has, I believe, with this excess money supply approach, is that nominal money is 'dropped' from a helicopter and then exercises its influence on demand and prices. What is dropped, if you will, is base money in response to a prior increase in bank financing (money) traceable to cost and demand changes within the economy.

Another problem arises with the real balance effect as a result of price changes which underpins that standard teaching device of the aggregate demand and supply curves; which is presented as an apparatus analogous to that of the micro-market model, and as such suffers from the same theoretical defects. Once the aggregate model determines a general price level and gross domestic product (GDP) — which need not be one of full employment — then an increase in demand will send the economy to higher levels of prices and real output. The new equilibrium position emerges as a result of the real balance effect acting on the higher demand curve, and the increase in the aggregate production and employment in

431

response to higher prices (falling real wages) stemming from the demand change.

Now given our post-Keynesian understanding of the cost curves for those megacorp entities and the nature of administered mark-up pricing one can, to say the least, call into question the accepted outcome of such a demand shift. As a general rule, higher levels of demand will be met with higher utilization rates as a result of bringing existing excess capacity 'on line' with no change in selling prices. We recall our discussion of the production arrangements normally characteristic of the megacorp organization; it is that total costs per unit fall as output increases with prime costs per unit remaining unchanged as employment increases. Thus profits per unit of output increase as a function of employment and output. The essential point resulting from the fixed technical coefficient function is that the demand for production workers is proportional to the level of output that firms plan to produce, while overhead costs (managerial and highly skilled technical personnel) do not vary directly with planned production. Increased utilization will not alter direct production costs per unit; thus there is no underlying cost rationale for any increase in prices. And we might add that policies leading to a reduction in aggregate demand, while reducing output and increasing unemployment, will also generally be ineffective in reducing prices and wages.

Re-thinking some Keynesian relationships

Let us work up a production function reflective of those non-neoclassical cost curves that will give us a means to clearly see the relation between prices, employment and demand. We differentiate between the permanent overhead employment that is related mainly to the technological nature of the operating plant and can be reckoned as a function of full capacity operations, designating this employment as (N_o); and production employment representing the variable factors of production that is directly linked to the utilization rate of capacity — designating this as (N_v). Writing (l_o) and (l_v) as the respective labor coefficients which are indexes of productivity, and Y, Y^* as the level of output and full-capacity output level respectively, we have the following equations:

$$N = N_o + N_u \tag{53}$$

$$N_u = \frac{Y}{l_v} \qquad (54)$$

$$N_o = \frac{Y^*}{l_o} \qquad (55)$$

The numbers of overhead or permanent employment are unaffected by changes in production levels; indeed, as we depict our production function we would show no possible positive output for a level of such employment below (N_o). Then the relation between total employment and production would come through the degree of capacity utilization given the existing capacity of the system, which is a characteristic putting us into the short-term. Note that the ratio of actual output to full capacity (or potential) output is the rate of capacity utilization (u); so:

$$u = \frac{Y}{Y^*} \qquad (56)$$

We extract a utilization function which mirrors the level of production employment as:

$$Y = [N - N_o]l_v \qquad (57)$$

or

$$Y = [N - \frac{Y^*}{l_o}]l_v \qquad (58)$$

and as the second term within the bracket is constant, the change in output with respect to total employment is:

$$\frac{dY}{dN} = l_v \qquad (59)$$

The variable labor coefficient (l_v) is a constant, thus total employment will increase in proportion to output for a given (N_o) up to the maximum level of output. As output levels increase, the number of (N_o) remains unchanged, so output will increase at a faster rate than total employment and average productivity (the overall productivity per worker) will increase. It will do so even if we took $l_v = 1$. Hence, output per unit of total employment is an increasing function of the utilization rate. We show this result with some manipulation of equations (53) to (59). Thus:

$$\frac{Y}{N_o + N_v} = \frac{l_v \cdot N_u}{N_o + N_u} \qquad (60)$$

from (55) and (56) we can write:

$$N_o = \frac{Y}{u l_o} \qquad (61)$$

and by substitution we have:

$$\frac{Y}{N} = \frac{l_v \cdot N_v}{N_v + \dfrac{l_v N_v}{u l_o}} \qquad (62)$$

which upon division by N_u gives:

$$\frac{Y}{N} = \frac{l_v}{1 + \dfrac{\dfrac{l_v}{l_o}}{u}} \qquad (63)$$

Another way to arrive at this conclusion is by dividing (60) directly by N_v showing:

$$\frac{Y}{N} = \frac{l_v}{1 + \dfrac{N_o}{N_v}} \qquad (64)$$

Now the 'productive operatives' at a point in time will be some proportion of their numbers under conditions of full-capacity operation, so we write:

$$N_v = u N_v^* \qquad (65)$$

434

and by substitution into (64):

$$\frac{Y}{N} = \frac{l_v}{1 + \dfrac{N_o}{uN_v^*}}$$ (66)

Since the permanent staff (N_o) is exactly that, its ratio to production workers at full operations is a fixed ratio which is designated by (f); then overall productivity per worker is:

$$\frac{Y}{N} = \frac{l_v}{1 + f/u}$$ (67)

with this expression being an increasing function of the utilization rate (u).[36]

In Fig. (8.15) we depict the relation between production and employment through the utilization function.

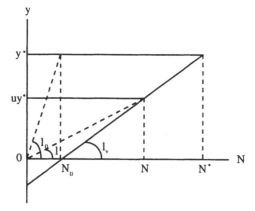

Figure 8.15

We have that required level of permanent staff (N_o) with no positive output for a level of employment below this number. The angle (l_o) represents the productivity of this staff reflecting the number of this labor required for a level of full capacity operations. A smaller angle implies the requirement of a larger number of this overhead labor, reflecting a decline in its productivity (the $N_o Y^*$ vertical line moves to the right). For a utilization rate (uY^*) we have production worker employment as $(N-N_o)$

435

with the angle (l_v) giving the constant marginal product of such labor. The overall rate of labor productivity for that level of utilization, reflective of total employment ON is given by the angle (l). And as we see the smaller the utilization rate and total employment level the smaller the total labor productivity (l) angle.

The output per unit of labor is then given by the angle from a point on the utilization function to the origin. Interestingly enough, an increase in the amount of overhead labor shifts the entire utilization function to the right, with no change in the relation between overall productivity and utilization; however, when it is the productivity of production workers that is declining (the l_v falls), then the slope of the function is flatter, indicating the need for more such labor for the same utilization rate, or the same employment level mirroring a smaller utilization rate. From either view this reduces output per worker.

Fig. (8.16) shows us the resulting production function relating output per unit of labor to the utilization rate, which is to the increasing use of labor for a given 'structure of operations'. And what we find is increasing returns to labor up to 'full-operations'.

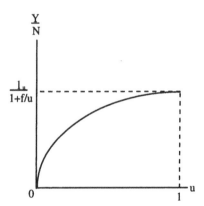

Figure 8.16

Taking the first and second derivatives of either (63) or (67) reveals that output per worker is increasing at a decreasing rate up to the $u=1$ level. While this function looks like the conventional neoclassical production curve, it is not that at all. It is not based on decreasing returns to labor derived from the 'fantasy' of flexible technical coefficients of production in a modern economy. What we have is a framework of increasing returns to the use of labor until all 'machines' are being utilized.

With this realistic micro-analysis in hand, we return to our discussion of the macroeconomic transmission effects. First of all we re-emphasize that in view of mark-up pricing and forward money contractual arrangements, it is quite realistic to presume that real wages are independent of the level of demand and output when the economy is adjusting to higher levels of demand by activating existing excess capacity. In general, changes in demand will affect the level of output and employment but will not alter the relation between prices and wages.

Here the reader may want to re-visit the pricing discussion in Chapter 6; but simply put, with the marginal cost in money terms given and with megacorp's target rate of return, the mark-up and selling price are determined. The given marginal cost (and thereby AVC) resulting from the money wage contract and our modern production function. But it would be helpful to restate some relationships here. As we said, prior to full capacity operations we take the marginal costs (MC) as constant; then the selling price is:

$$p = (1 + \Theta)MC \qquad (68)$$

where (Θ) is the profit margin. And this margin of profit can be considered as a proxy for the percentage mark-up (m). The mark-up is:

$$m = \frac{p - MC}{p} \qquad (69)$$

The price being the result of considering the mark-up as a percentage on AVC or MC, with the equation normally written as:

$$p = (1 + m)MC \qquad (70)$$

The proxy relation between (m) and (Θ) is simply that:

$$\Theta = \frac{m}{1 + m} \qquad (71)$$

which can be stated as a function of (m) as:

$$m = \frac{\Theta}{1 - \Theta} \qquad (72)$$

437

Now the important connection for us at this point is between the real wage, the mark-up and the constant marginal product. These appear straightaway by considering the real cost of labor to employers as the money wage divided by the marginal product (MP). Thus:

$$MC = \frac{W}{MP} \tag{73}$$

And by substitution into equation (69) we have:

$$m = \frac{p - \dfrac{W}{MP}}{p} \tag{74}$$

leading to:

$$w = MP(1 - m) \tag{75}$$

$$(w = \text{real wage})$$

As long as increases in demand can be met with increased utilization rates, the (MP) and (m) can be taken as constant; it is then evident that real wages are independent of demand changes. We see this pricing behavior in Fig. (8.17).

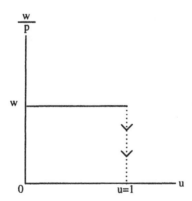

Figure 8.17

Next we need to set out the determinants of demand, and the relationship of demand changes to capacity utilization and profits. This will allow a

438

realistic understanding of the 'Keynesian' *IS* -curve shifts, as we set this type of analysis within a post-Keynesian framework. In our particular approach we first construct the 'potential' profit equation and related profit curve.[37]

We state gross profits (P) as the nominal value of output (Y) minus nominal wages in real terms $(wN=W)$; with this value of output at a particular level of utilization and employment, given by equation (58) and a particular set price. For simplicity of the equation we omit taxes and depreciation, so that gross profits are equal to net profits which are available for capital accumulation, i.e. for increasing capacity. We keep in mind that this level of output in anticipation of expected sales has been 'supported' by the required liquidity made available by the banking system. Profits are:

$$P = Y - W \tag{76}$$

with the rate of profit (π)

$$\pi = \frac{Y - W}{K} \tag{77}$$

the (K) being the given capital stock (i.e. fixed number of machines) representing the existing capacity.

The total employment at a given utilization rate is $(N_v + N_o)$ which we substitute into (77):

$$\pi = \frac{Y - w(N_v + N_o)}{K} \tag{78}$$

We know that the real cost of labor is given by equation (75) — for $u < 1$; which by substitution in (78) gives:

$$\pi = \frac{Y - MP(1 - m)(N)}{K} \tag{79}$$

With some manipulation of (79) we obtain an expression for the rate of profit as:

$$\pi = \frac{m}{\iota}(u) - \frac{(1 - m)f}{\iota} \tag{80}$$

439

where (f) and (ι) are defined parameters with (ι) being the capital coefficient that tells us the amount of capital required per unit of output at full capacity. That is:

$$K = \iota(Y^*) \qquad (81)$$

The amount of production has got to be defined both in terms of (l_v) as well as (ι) as increasing employment brings into use an increasing number of machines. And it is, so to speak, inside our labor productivity function. Indeed, the amount of overall employment needed per utilization rate or needed at the full-capacity rate can be considered as greatly determined by technology inherent in the capital stock. We can imagine a situation where a technological change brings into being radically different capital requiring less labor (both overhead and operational); then output per worker would increase at some rate. But let us not stray from the primary discussion about the impact of demand changes (though certainly one would need to reckon these within the even more realistic context of ongoing technological progress).

The profit curve reflective of equation (80) is shown in Fig. (8.18).

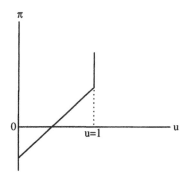

Figure 8.18

There is a linear relation of profits and capacity utilization, with the intercept of the curve in the negative zone and the positive slope of the curve given by the ratio (m/ι). Points on this curve are realizable or potential on the assumption that demand is adequate; i.e. that the organization will sell all of its output at current prices so that it can realize the profits or loss reduction that it has 'created' as a result of production at a certain rate of capacity utilization.

440

Increases in demand will propel the economy up along the curve realizing higher rates of profit; but the way in which these higher rates come about depends on the state of capacity. Assuming that megacorp organizations normally carry a built-in degree of excess capacity, then higher levels of demand will result in higher output levels via the production equation (58) with increased levels of overall labor productivity and an existing price markup arrangement. Money wages are given to the system via explicit wage contracts, so that real wages can be taken as constant as production and employment increases. So that utilization rates, employment and profits are all increasing as a result of higher levels of average labor productivity. This is the point we made with regard to Fig. (8.18) and equation (75), with the increasing rate of profit read off equation (80). Thus higher levels of economic activity are not predicated on a reduction of the real wage, as in the conventional neoclassical synthesis, but upon a more extensive and efficient use of labor, i.e. upon the technical relationships governing production. However, should nominal wages begin to increase as employment expands, then prices can be expected to increase proportionately on the assumption of a constant mark-up, thus leaving the real wage unchanged and maintaining the firms gross profit margin. We recall that given the nature of the production function higher money wage would necessarily make for higher prime costs per unit requiring higher prices to maintain profit levels. Once wage contracts have been negotiated the rate of inflation is predetermined.

Certainly the exogenously determined rate of interest will influence money demand and thereby the money aggregate, but higher levels of money demand need not necessarily lead to higher rates of interest. There is an analogy that can be drawn between the interest rate set by banks which can be viewed as a price mark-up over the cost of funds determined by the central bank (this 'spread' reflecting the commercial bank's profit target and degree of its market power) and the price setting operation of our megacorp organization. In both cases the mark-up is not explained by short-term demand conditions. And we now understand that we can no longer count on a line of reasoning that runs from an exogenous change in the money supply to an impact on national income through changes in the interest rate. Yet there is the further issue as to whether the interest rate is at all a significant variable in determining investment spending and aggregate demand. This brings us back to our profit-utilization curve and demand changes.

Whether the 'created' profits along the curve will materialize depends upon conditions of demand, and here we assume the simplifying (but not damaging) basic Kaldor approach that there is no saving out of wages, so that all savings are out of profits and that it is the change in the level of investment demand that drives the change in output and capacity utilization. We have an aggregative one sector model which accounts for all of the investment and employment and where a constant fraction (s_p) is saved out of profits (P) by firms. The level of savings is determined by the level of profits which is related to output and capacity use given the appropriate level of demand. And in equilibrium the amount of savings generated for a particular level of profits is equal to the amount of spending undertaken by firms for investment purposes. Thus:

$$s_p(P) = I \qquad (82)$$

leading to our familiar 'Cambridge Equation':

$$\pi = \frac{G}{s_p P} \qquad (83)$$

This brings up the need to specify an investment function to capture the incentive to invest which is clearly shaped by a multiplicity of considerations. We did specify such a function in our analysis of the Kaldor model which seemed to capture the essential ingredients. The approach was to formulate investment decisions as being related to the rate of profit and the need to adjust the capital stock between what is on hand and what is desired given the growth of demand. Now in terms of our overt discussion of capacity these influences show up as investment becoming a function of the rate of profit and the current level of capacity use.

Current profits give rise to the savings to finance capital expenditures; in other words, internally generated funds, as they flow from demand and the organizations pricing and pay-out policy, form the essential finance for capital accumulation. Furthermore, current profit levels may influence the expectation of the profitability of future investment and thereby influence future investment. Higher expected profits based on current performance may make it easier for the organization to obtain bank credit to increase capacity. Yet while the profit and investment elements are intertwined, the capacity factor in itself may play the crucial role in investment decisions. There is the point of view stemming from the Kalecki influence that advanced capitalist economics are by and large demand constrained. The degree of realized rates of utilization certainly in the short term (except for

442

the peaks of very strong expansions) will not equal full or come close to full utilization; in fact even on the long-term path the system can maintain full employment with a degree of residual capacity. In economies of imperfect competition, it is assumed that producers tend at all times to hold a planned and deliberate reserve of excess capacity. Thus the current level of capacity use may very well tell the organization whether it does or does not have sufficient excess capacity in terms of its overall strategy and the possibility of new competitors. The capacity influence on investment is two-fold: one is through its effect on profits and the ability to finance additional investment; and secondly in a direct way in that the greater the current utilization rate the greater the demand to put additional capacity in place in order to maintain the longer term extra margin of capability (a temporary inability to satisfy demand could result in a permanent loss of market share).

An investment function encompassing these influences can be set out as:

$$\frac{I}{K} = G = I(u, \pi) \tag{84}$$

$$I = I_o + I_u(u) + I_\pi(\pi) \tag{85}$$

Then:

$$s_\pi(\pi) = I_o + I_u(u) + I_\pi(\pi)$$

$$\pi = \frac{I_o + I_u(u)}{s\pi - I_\pi} \tag{86}$$

(stating the relationship in terms of a rate of profit π)

Returning to our profit curve as it is reflected in equation (80) we can determine, to reiterate, what the rate of profit will be for a given level of capacity use providing a sufficient level of demand at current prices; and with equation (86) we see the rate of profit that will actually be realized as a result of demand being sufficient. The equality of savings out of profits with investment levels is a mirror of aggregate demand equalling aggregate supply yielding an equilibrium (Keynesian type) outcome for a given rate of capacity use. We see this utilization rate equilibrium (u^*) in Fig. (8.19), where we re-label out potential 'created' profits curve as the

443

aggregate supply (AS) line, and the realized profits curve the aggregate demand (AD) line.

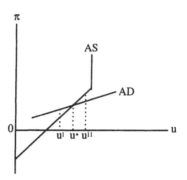

Figure 8.19

Note that at (u') profits realized exceeds attainable profits reflecting a condition of excess demand for goods; this prompts an increase in capacity use and employment leading to the realization of higher rates of profit with no change in the real wage rate. At capacity use rate (u') and for all points below the AD curve investment exceeds savings leading to higher levels of profit and correspondingly higher levels of saving. For an output level to the right of (u^*) realized profits are below potential profits as all the goods that have been produced cannot be sold at current prices. This insufficiency of demand means that the firm is losing some of its created profits and will respond by reducing capacity utilization and employment with corresponding reduction in the rate of profit. For all points above the (AD) savings exceed investment, reducing profits and savings.

Looking again at our profits curve, we see that it indicates the amount of profit which can be realized at a given level of capacity utilization with existing technology and the real wage rate. But whether a particular level of potential profits will be realized depends upon the level of demand; and for an output level at a utilization rate of (u'') the organization will be left with unsold goods that represent unrealized profits. Now given this state of technology and costs, the AS or profits curve is positioned, and the system will be at some point on it. There is then a particular utilization rate that simultaneously puts the economy on its AD or 'realization curve' so that it is in equilibrium in the sense that profits realized is equal to potential profits for that level of output — the u^* point. And this level of utilization rate and employment relates to a particular real wages rate and income distribution. This is similar to our analysis of the Kaldor model where savings and investment are brought into line via changes in the distribution of income.

We picture the economy evidencing stability of equilibrium; that is, displacements along the profits curve will pull the system towards its equilibrium position. Starting from a point (u') the economy will move up on the profit curve as a result of realized profits leading to higher utilization rates and employment. And these factors will have a positive effect on investment; however the increase of savings as a result of the higher profit level will be more sensitive. Though savings will be less than investment, i.e. excess demand will be present for higher capacity use rates, the degree of this excess demand will diminish reducing the difference between realized and created profits. One can speak in terms of the acceleration effect on investment stemming from higher rates of profit increasing at a lessor rate than savings. Conversely, if the economy is displaced from (u^*) to (u'') it will generate more additional savings than additional investment with insufficiency of demand and lower realized profits. This will lead to lower levels of output and profits with the reduction in savings being at a greater rate than the reduction in spending out of the lower level of profits; this reduces the excess production at lower utilization rates reducing the system to the equilibrium (u^*) position. So that if the economy is realizing an incentive to invest, thus giving rise to a higher rate of capital accumulation, the distribution of income has to change in favor of profits thereby adjusting the savings of the society to investment. Thus, as we have mentioned in other contexts, the equilibrium point (u^*) is reflective of a particular distribution of income and accompanying real wage rate. Of course, at the (u'') position the incentive to invest decreases, necessitating a change in distribution in favor of wages in order to bring about the required reduction in the insufficiency of demand (savings rates out of profits can be safely taken to be greater than out of wages, or we may assume zero savings out of wages).

Figure (8.19) reveals the relationship between effective demand and employment differently from the conventional Keynesian approach as it stresses the impact of income distribution and profits on employment. The real wage consideration is not at the core of the analysis in effecting employment which reflects the reality of the megacorp-oligopolistic structure of the economy rather than the neoclassical micro-foundations of Keynes. Money is in the picture by virtue of the amount of credit money that agents want to acquire at the given rate of interest in support of a level of demand. But let us replay this relation between demand and

445

employment along more familiar lines where we explicitly bring in the production function of Fig. (8.15). We will in a more direct way see that unemployment is related to conditions of demand and the structure of production rather than to an excessive real wage rate.

We have a system where demand is equal to the spending of wages (we assume zero savings out of wages) plus investment expenditures. Then aggregate demand in nominal terms is:

$$D = wN + pI \qquad (87)$$

The level of output in real terms for a given utilization rate is determined via equation (58) with the nominal value of output (Q) being:

$$Q = pY \qquad (88)$$

And the condition of an equilibrium utilization rate tells us that:

$$wN + pI = pY \qquad (89)$$

which is that (u^{*}) position in Fig. (8.19) where the level of output is equal to expected sales. The level of effective demand will, for a given production technology, effect employment via the relation of levels of employment to higher rates of capacity utilization. Fig. (8.20) shows the connection between demand and employment reflecting the production mechanism of equation (58).

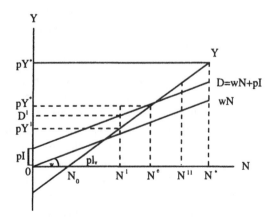

Figure 8.20

446

The (Y) line shows the increase in real output (given the constant labor coefficients) as capacity utilization and employment increase, resulting in an overall increase in output per worker. The wage bill (wN) rises linearly with higher levels of employment of production workers given the wage rate. Aggregate demand increases with employment being equal to the wage bill plus higher levels of investment spending as profits rise reflecting the investment function of equation (85). The level of what we referred to as potential or created profits is read as the vertical distance between the (Y) or (AS) line (the nominal value of aggregate supply) and the cost curve here designated by the wage bill line. However, realized profits will be read off the realization curve or the aggregate demand line as in Fig. (8.19). So for a level of employment (N') realized profits exceed created profits as related to the current level of output, as demand is more than sufficient to absorb all production; that is, the reduction in inventory levels represents additional realized profits. The equilibrium level is represented by employment level (N^e).

For levels of production beyond (Y^e) realized profits deteriorate as demand is insufficient to absorb all production with the corresponding build-up of inventories representing unrealized profits similar to position (u'') in Fig. (8.19). So if the economy is displaced to an employment level (N'') it will find savings to have increased too rapidly leading to insufficient demand and reducing the incentive to invest and giving way to a lower rate of accumulation. This will, in and of itself, alter the distribution in favor of wages, thereby working to reduce the insufficiency of demand as production and employment decline. Fig. (8.20) does present us with a more detailed picture of the analysis.

Should the nominal wage rate increase, it causes the wage bill curve to become steeper and correspondingly increases the slope of the aggregate demand curve. This clearly increases the amount of realized profit and prompts an increase in utilization rates and employment. The system will produce a higher level of equilibrium employment which, we now see as corresponding to a level of output which results in maximum realized profits. And should the economy realize an increase in investment spending, say autonomous expenditures (I_o) as in our investment function, then the entire AD curve shifts up again producing higher levels of employment. But what we want to stress is the positive relationship between the demand for labor and the real wage rate, in contrast with the conventional formulation. For example, in Fig. (8.9) the analysis shows an increase in demand via a monetary change resulting in higher levels of output and employment, but only in conjunction with a lower real wage

447

rate. But the driving force behind employment, as we now reckon, is the principal of effective demand. While a higher real wage reduces potential profits for a given level of production, there is the offsetting factor of the increase in aggregate demand which reduces inventory levels and increases realized profits. This stimulates greater levels of output and employment, leading to increasing potential profits (via increasing productivity) with the re-establishment of the realization of these potential profits at higher levels of employment. This result is shown in Fig. (8.21) with the economy moving from point (A) to (B).

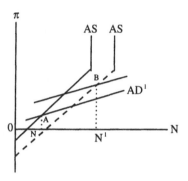

Figure 8.21

So to reiterate: if the economy is presumed to be operating with excess capacity as a general characteristic increasing employment and profits are positively related to aggregate demand without 'requiring' any reduction in the real wage. However, should real wages increase, this will not (as is normally presumed) have a negative input; indeed there is a positive relationship between economic activity and the real wage rate. To put this in sharper focus: a policy to reduce the real wage in order to alleviate a condition of excess supply of labor and restore the 'labor market' to full-employment is a wrong policy, as it will lead to lower levels of demand and realized profits that will drive employment to even lower levels. The point is not that a lack of 'flexibilities' in the economy prevents the restoration of full employment; on the contrary, it is a realistic approach to argue that it is just such flexibilities that prevent the realization of full employment.

Additional restructuring

Clearly we need a new design to replace the neoclassical synthesis which, to reiterate, links changes in demand via *IS-LM* (integrating monetary and commodities markets) to the labor market and to production. Our restructuring of this Keynesian economics is drawn from the discussion around Figures (8.20) and (8.21) requiring a different way to link up real wages and capacity utilization (and employment) from demand considerations (based on different savings propensies out of wages and profits), and an investment function which is itself based on utilization rates and profitability.

However, before any further construction we might want to take as yet another look at some aspects of the conventional approach. The *IS* curve shows a negative relationship between changes in aggregate real output and the rate of interest; thus all points on the curve represent a working-out of the investment spending multiplier yielding combinations of interest rates and real national product (i.e. national income) that keep the commodities market in equilibrium. By equilibrium we mean in the sense that planned investment plus government spending equals planned savings plus tax revenue at that level of income (the micro-orthodoxy of market equilibrium carried to the aggregate). And what is perhaps standard procedure, one then goes on to demonstrate that the slope of the *IS* curve is subject to change based on a change in the size of the multiplier itself (perhaps due to tax rate changes) and changes in the investment coefficient link to the interest rate. The latter demonstration pointing out that even if the interest rate could be lowered it may not have much of an affect on the level of investment demand, and thus for a given size of the multiplier there would be a small impact on the level of income.

But in support of the negative slope of *IS* is the Keynesian investment demand function; and it is not sometimes fully appreciated that Keynes' investment schedule is an intension or ex-ante schedule at different rates of interest, so when the rate of interest is specified, the amount of investment that firms will want to undertake is also specified. Yet we need to understand that the basis for the schedule in an aggregative sense stems from its rationale with regard to a single firm (similar to the neoclassical aggregate demand curve resulting from an adding-up process of individual demand curves). We can then pose the following question in line with Keynes' reasoning: how can the system bring about an increase in planned investment? Well, one approach would be to reduce the interest rate with the result of improving the stream of future discounted net returns and hence (given costs) the present discounted values. Another way would be to increase the expected future net yield which increases that marginal efficiency of capital rate (*mec*) so that at the existing interest rate (*r*) investment projects which may not have been profitable before become so now. But given expected yield and costs, it is the fall in the rate of interest that is strategic; it is the lower rate of interest that calls forth the increasing positive investment intentions as it is presumed to 'compensate' for the expected lower *mec* rate resulting from the additional investment. This allowed interpreters of Keynes to draw a downward sloping investment demand curve akin to a commodity demand curve with points on this schedule reflecting the equality of *mec=r*.

Now why should the anticipated marginal efficiency of capital rate fall as the firm anticipates increasing investment? Keynes offered some answers along two lines. One in terms of a fall in the expected yield as the supply of investment increases, and the other is that the cost of capital can be expected to increase because as he put it, "pressure on the facilities for producing capital will cause its supply price to increase".[38] He considered the second point to be more influential in the short-term, reflecting the assumption that capital goods are produced under increasing marginal cost assumptions. Thus, as Keynes tells us, "one can construct for each type of capital a schedule showing the increase in investment and the related decline in the marginal efficiency of capital; we can then aggregate all the different types of capital so as to provide a schedule relating the type of marginal efficiency of capital in general which that rate of investment will establish".[39] This standard approach places the rate of interest in the central role in determining aggregate demand through its influence on investment decisions.

A question that one must ask is whether the Keynesian analysis really does explain investment decisions in the individual firm, keeping uppermost in mind the pure competitive framework within which the firm operates and the 'decision' ex-ante nature of the investment schedule. Certainly for the individual firm a calculation of expected future returns must presume the existence of a level of capital stock; in the competitive framework the firm sees itself as too small a player in that whatever amount of investment it intends to undertake is not conceived to significantly alter the aggregate level of that particular type of capital. At a future point in time the firm will find the larger capital stock resulting from the investments undertaken by all firms which is an ex post reality. At the time the individual firm is considering the profitability of an investment, its expected return is not seen to be affected by the size of its own investment; its anticipated decline in the (*mec*) rate stems from elsewhere. Keynes made the point that a drop in the present discounted values should not be considered as the result of a fall-off in prospective yields, which he assumed to be independent of the level of capital stock, certainly not in the short term.

Then the support for the firm's investment demand schedule must rest with the anticipated rising supply price which erodes the prospective rate of return as more investment is contemplated. One reads the investment schedule as telling us how much additional investment the firm can be expected to undertake at different rates of interest; but what this is saying is how much of an increase in the cost of capital is anticipated by the firm and thereby requiring a particular rate of interest to motivate the undertaking.

But this raises a rather serious point regarding Keynes' investment schedule. Why should an individual firm, which does not contemplate a meaningful change in the aggregate stock of capital as a result of its own investment, be assumed to anticipate an increase in the supply price of capital when formulating investment decisions? If the firm is too small a player from one point of view then it is certainly that from the other. To assume that the firm is able to foresee the increase in the price of capital goods, which reduces the profitability of investment, would have us suppose that the firm is aware that other firms in its industry and in other industries as well are making similar investment decisions; and certainly that the particular firm can accurately anticipate the impact on prices of these decisions taken over the whole economy. I would think these to be unrealistic and offer unconvincing support for the investment demand curve.

The firm experiences rising supply prices only as a result of other firms having acted upon similar investment intentions, i.e. the rise in costs comes about as a result of investment ex post while the expected future returns which form the basis of the lower (*mec*) rate are clearly ex ante. So what we have with the Keynesian function is a confused construction; being a mixed bag of ex ante and ex post considerations that is not very likely to explain investment decisions in the individual firm. And if it cannot do that then there is no way we can go from the behavior of the individual firm (supposedly interest rate driven) to an aggregate investment curve. The individual firm curve is more the result of investment intentions on the part of all other firms, the realization of which is ex post. One cannot add up because of this very lack of independence. It is misleading to see a similarity between a market demand curve for a commodity derived from putitive independent individual curves (though in Chapter 2 we have put even this conventional approach to some critical inquiry) and that of an aggregate investment demand schedule, the subdivision's behavior of which are dependent on the actions of others, that is, on the aggregate itself.

It is perhaps reasonable to downgrade, if not abandon, the interest element in the formation of an investment function, and to propose an explication of investment based primarily on the shift variables of the function. The investment function that we encountered in studying the Kaldor model, and the one represented by equation (85) are indeed structured around these other variables.

A further point needs to be emphasized in this re-design of our thinking about a basic macro model. The marginal efficiency of capital rate rests on expectations about the future, as we have been saying it is an ex ante consideration. These expectations in an uncertain (nonergodic) world are very insecurely based; thus the conventional notion of adjusting the capital stock up to the point where the (*mec*) is equal to the rate of interest implies a thought 'process' which is mainly unreal, for it assumes confidence about the knowledge of the factors governing the yield of investment years hence, thereby leading to a 'calculated' response to the change in the rate of interest. But in the real world our knowledge about long-term expectations is more often than not very negligible and, in any event, should long-term expectations fail they are not likely to be offset by changes in the rate of interest. Aggregate investment levels are best thought of as a result of investment on the individual firm level being governed by the 'animal spirits' of the organization as it seeks to penetrate new markets and gain a competitive advantage and/or not lose existing market share, rather by a calculated decision or yield. We can say that current economic conditions affect the 'buoyancy' of these spirits and related investment decisions, with the preferred financing being via internal funds which is largely determined by profits. Thus profits are an essential determinant of investment (via financial considerations) which has impact on future profits. "Firms increase their capital stock as finance becomes available which arises as profits are made and savings undertaken. Thus some potential investment delayed in the past because of a lack of finance can now proceed as finance becomes available."[40]

A recent study concerning the investment-finance link as it relates to fiscal policy is supportive of our position about interest rates and the investment function.[41] One finding is that the evidence shows that interest rates and the cost of capital play a small and uncertain role in the determination of investment compared with the influence of the firm's financial condition and the growth of their sales, which we can relate to in terms of capacity utilization rates. And the problem of aggregation that we spoke of is further highlighted by the fact that the strategic variables affecting investment will differ across firms. The study points out that for the fastest growing firms capital spending does not appear to be negatively impacted by higher interest rates or capital costs; however, these firms are most sensitive to sales and financial determinants of investment. Regarding fiscal policy, it appears that the organization with the most exuberant of spirits may be most negatively affected by deficit reduction policies that retard the growth or demand, while they may benefit little from the supposed reduced interest rate effect of such policies. Overall the study offers three major points:

1. The most important determinant of investment is the strength of the economy. The indirect impact of taxation and spending initiatives on overall economic activity is likely to have a greater effect on investment than the influence of taxes or interest rates on the cost of capital.

2. For similar reasons, the negative (crowding out) effect of government deficits on investment is likely to be small . . . the drag on the economy from tax increased and government spending cuts will probably overshadow any stimulus to investment that occurs from falling interest rates. Therefore, in today's economy, deficit cutting is more likely to reduce investment than to increase it.

3. Policy to stimulate investment directly should focus on robust policies designed to get cash into the hands of investing firms. Accelerated depreciation allowances and the investment tax credit are examples of this kind of policy since they not only reduce the cost of capital, but also increase firms' cash flow.

The study concludes that:

> The view that interest rates and cost of capital constitute the most important policy lever for the determination of private investment is, unfortunately, an example of a dominant hypothesis that underlies current policy positions even though it lacks strong empirical support in the research presented here. I have argued that in the light of new

evidence about the determinants of investment, the policy discussion should place greater weight on cyclical movements of the macroeconomy and the financial conditions of the corporate sector, and less emphasis on the cost-of-capital channel.[42]

This conclusion is in line with post-Keynesian analysis regarding the investment function and modeling of the economy generally.

We should also point out that the price level as well does not appear in the investment function nor in our aggregate demand equation as an initiating force for changes in demand. In conventional analysis the level of aggregate demand is determined via the interplay of two equations; one expressing equilibrium in the commodities market (*IS*) and the other showing equilibrium in the money market (*LM*). Thus we have two equations in three variables: that of the rate of interest, the level of income and the price level. The price level usually enters the picture via the construction of the (*LM*) curve which depicts the liquidity demand and money supply equality for different levels of income and interest rates, where this money supply is taken in real terms. Thus an increase in the price level for example has the same effect as a nominal reduction in money at given prices; it reduces the real money supply which then increases the interest rate via upward shift of the *LM* curve with resulting negative effects on investment demand and aggregate output. Thus the approach to construction of a negatively sloped aggregate demand curve plotting the change in the price level and the change in aggregate income resulting from the assumed positive relationship between changes in the price level and interest rates.

Of course, post-Keynesians eschew this entire apparatus; and we have in our discussion in this chapter shown why this conventional approach does not fit in well with reality. But let us again run through some points. There is no predictable 'automatic' relationship between price levels and demand changes. The markup which explains the actual level of prices is itself not explained by short-term demand conditions. Then aside from any direct impact, the price will not influence demand in an indirect way via interest rate changes. We should not think along a line of reasoning which runs from a change in prices due to an increase in demand, to a change in the real value of the money supply to a higher rate of interest which then feeds back to influence demand and real output, thereby serving as an equilibrating mechanism for the aggregate economy. The (*LM*) curve is 'suspect' because it pictures the interest rate changing (in a competitive-market fashion) as a result of a change in liquidity demand in response to changes in the level of income in relation to an exogenously determined money supply. The money supply though is itself not independent of the level of economic activity — it is endogenous to the system and not a factor that influences the economy from the 'outside'. It is the interest rate that is the exogenous factor and should be taken as the independent variable in any causation scheme, which means that the liquidity preference notion loses importance in the monetary analysis of the economy. Post-Keynesians see the interest rate as politically determined distribution variable and not as a market determined price.

We now understand why the price level and interest rate do not appear in our investment demand analysis, which leads to a design for the aggregate demand or (IS) curve that differs from that of the neoclassical synthesis. So let us consider the alternative post-Keynesian construction.

Looking again at Fig. (8.19), we have a state of equilibrium at (u^e) defined as a condition where realized profits are equal to potential profits that level of capacity utilization rate and corresponding level of employment; but more importantly for a given level of variable labor employed. This reflects a condition of $AD=AS$ regaining the equality of savings equaling investment which is, of course, associated with a particular distribution of income, i.e. a particular rate of profit and real wage rate. With Fig. (8.21) we see that a higher level of demand results in higher levels of employment and utilization rate that is associated with a higher rate of profit that is itself a function of the higher level of output. And at point (B) in Fig. (8.21) we find the correct distribution of income such that equilibrium is maintained at this higher output level, i.e. demand is sufficient to cause realized profits to be equal to potential profits.

If we then take prices as given, then an increase in aggregate demand, say due to an increase in the wage rate, would lead to higher levels of utilization rates (real output), employment and profits. Certainly a higher wage rate increases wage costs, but it also increases aggregate demand which leads to higher levels of employment and an overall increase in output per worker sufficient to yield a higher rate of profit, and thereby that necessary distribution of income which maximizes realized profits for the existing demand condition. The higher level of profits while resulting from the higher level of employment and output will itself give rise to higher levels of investment demand.

We should be able to construct a curve representing a positive relationship between real wage rates and levels of employment with the resulting levels of output at each point on the curve representing the equilibrium condition which, to reiterate, is the equality of realized and

455

potential profits that has its equivalence in investment equals savings. So we have an upward sloping (*IS*) curve positively relating levels of employment and output to the real wage rate. Using equations 53, 54 and 87-89, we construct the (*IS*) equation as:[43]

$$\frac{w}{p} = \frac{(N-N_o)l_v}{N} - \frac{I}{N} \tag{90}$$

Real output increases as the ratio of (N_v) to total employment (*N*) increases, i.e. as given by the first term on the right side of (90). And the higher levels of output are correspondingly associated with 'correct' distribution of income, and in particular the real wage rate so as to result in the sufficient level of aggregate demand. It is not a matter, to reiterate, of demand being automatically adjusted via 'flexibilities' in the system; it is a matter of the distribution of income bearing the brunt of adjusting the savings of society to investment and thereby the level of demand. We see this post-Keynesian (*IS*) curve in Fig. (8.22):

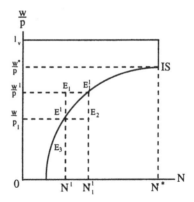

Figure 8.22

At all points on the curve such as a point E' the economy is in equilibrium (*S=I*) corresponding to a real wage rate $(w/p)'$. For a point off the curve such as (E_1) the economy finds itself with a too high real wage rate implying an excess demand for goods over the production levels associated with (*N*) employment. This will induce higher capacity utilization rates and employment levels moving the economy to E_1' where aggregate supply has increased to accommodate the higher aggregate demand with a higher level of employment. And we immediately see how different this is from the neoclassical scenario where the excess demand for goods would trigger higher prices which reduces the real wage and excess demand for the given level of employment — thus sending the system from (E_1) to (E'). It behooves us to jettison the conventional price adjustment approach as being out of line with the institutional arrangements of a modern economy, and to rely on the output adjustment explanation to eliminate excess demand at the existing real wage rate.

On the other hand, if the economy is at point (E_2) we find too low a level of aggregate demand due to an insufficiently high real wage rate $(AS \! > \! AD)$. The economy will be induced to reduce utilization rates which reduces the overall output per worker and the rate of profit. The level of output and employment falls, thereby eliminating the excess supply at the existing low real wage rate. The movement is from (E_2) to (E') rather than the orthodox price response by increasing the real wage rate and increasing demand to absorb the available output — moving from (E_2) to (E_1').

In Fig. (8.22) a comparison of points (E') and (E_1') mirrors points (A) and (B) in Fig. (8.21). Structural changes which cause an upward displacement of the realization (AD) curve (and this may be the result of factors other than a higher wage rate) will, in the usual circumstance of excess capacity, be met with increasing levels of output and profits. This improved profits condition stems from the nature of the production function of the modern organization and not, in the main, from higher prices. At (E_1') there is again the proper combination of the real wage rate and rate of profit that clears the commodities market. Thus along the curve there is a positive association between the real wage rate and the rate of profit, such that for different levels of employment and output aggregate demand is equal to aggregate supply; with the levels of employment being Keynesian demand determined rather than real wage determined.

Money is ever present in the move along the (IS) curve in line with our understanding of the horizontal nature of the money supply curve, in its supporting role of those forward contracts entered into by firms as they respond to increasing demand conditions. As we pointed out, in the operations of a modern economy one cannot look to price level changes to adjust markets, whether for goods or labor. In terms of goods, selling prices are in general not altered in response to demand changes in the face of excess capacity (a degree of which is built in to the operations of the organization); and post-Keynesian monetary theory realistically rules out demand adjustment via change in the real value of the money supply and respondent interest rate changes. The money aggregate changes in response to the shift of the *AD* curve, it is not a causal factor either directly or via price changes.

In terms of labor, Fig. (8.22) presents us with some non-conventional observations. Let us consider that full employment is at N^* commensurate with the full-capacity operations of the economy, and that the real wage rate is $(w/p)_1$. The economy is in a state of less than full employment by the difference between N^* and N_1'. Now according to conventional market theory, this excess supply of labor should reduce the real wage rate (by reducing the nominal wage) until the real wage rate is again equal to the marginal productivity of labor, thus restoring full employment. This, supposedly, reflecting an employment level by each firm that maximizes its profits. Putting aside, for the moment, whether this kind of real wage adjustment has any validity in the real world, what would be the impact of such a move in terms of the analysis in Fig. (8.22)? The effect would be a decline in effective demand shifting the realization curve downward, resulting in a lower rate of profit and level of employment. The unemployment picture worsens as the economy finds itself at a lower point on the (*IS*) curve such as (E_3). To use Lavoie's words here, "There is unemployment because of a deficiency of effective demand, not because real wages are too high, as in the neoclassical story".[44] And with this kind of unemployment, the usual market response is helpless to correct matters, since the cure is higher wages, not lower ones.

Our discussion has been about an economy with margins of spare capacity where higher levels of demand (say investment demand) can be accommodated by changes in output. And this adjustment of aggregate supply is characterized by higher employment levels and higher profits which are obtained through greater production. So in this framework we can say that, given the savings propensities, the required savings will be generated via changes in the level of output as the latter affects profit levels.

Suppose, though, we face an economy with no spare capacity so that we are on the vertical section of the profits curve in Fig. (8.18) with a level of (N^*) in Fig. (8.22). In this circumstance an increase in demand cannot be adjusted to (at least within a reasonable period of time) by increasing output. Firms will either stand for the presence of unsatisfied customers or they will raise prices. What may be the rationale for the price change? As we pointed out in our analysis of the megacorp pricing policy, it is at this output level that firms will opt to increase the mark-up in order to generate more internal funds with which to finance additional capacity. Mark-up policy can be expected to change based on long-term projections of growth in demand. As well, it is with this full capacity utilization rate that increased demand spills over into higher unit prime costs which threaten existing profit margins necessitating a price response. But what this price increase will accomplish is to reduce the excess demand as the additional capacity is being put into place. What this policy does is to leave the organization with that built-in spare capability to meet future increases in demand and not have unsatisfied customers with the possibility of losing market share.

What we want to understand in this framework is that it is aggregate demand that is being adjusted to aggregate supply, with profit levels increasing as a result of higher prices and, at what might be supposed, a lower real wage rate. So that it is via a change in the distribution of income (in a negative relationship) for a given level of aggregate supply that savings is made equal to investment.

In terms of conditions for labor, we now have to presume a real wage in excess of $(w/p)^*$ in Fig. (8.22) which indicates excess demand for goods relative to output at (N^*). The level of supply cannot adjust being limited by the shortage of labor which is simply a mirror of the excess demand for goods. Now what happens if, as convention dictates, prices in both markets change by the same amount (since the excess demand for labor results from the excess demand for goods)? There will be no change in the real wage rate — rate of profit relationship and neither the goods or the labor market can be returned to 'normal' clearing conditions, that is, the excess demand remains what it is. Thus, even if we did have price flexibility, the real wage rate would not be restored to full employment-clearing state. This highlights what we have said in a different context, that the solution is not in terms of internal market mechanics; here the system requires a downward displacement of the realization (AD) curve. This could be engineered via an increase in the exogenously determined rate of interest which increases the cost of external funds financing and could act to reduce investment demand, although other actions of a fiscal nature would most likely be more effective in reducing the demand for goods and hence the demand for labor. Since the firm does not realize a higher rate of profit (assuming no change in methods of production), its incentive to increase its capital stock may decline when faced with a higher cost of borrowing.

This lack of market clearing regarding employment is evident in Fig. (8.23).[45]

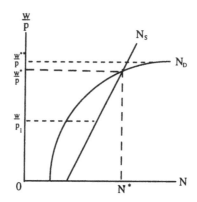

Figure 8.23

The labor demand curve is in line with our analysis in Fig. (8.19) and (8.22) and the supply curve is the normally postulated one. At the real wage rate $(w/p)_1$ there is excess supply of labor; and as we can observe, allowing the real wage rate to fall will only worsen matters. And in the condition of excess demand for labor at $(w/p)^{**}$ the normal response of an increasing real wage rate cannot correct the matter, as the excess demand increases. The labor market is clearly unstable, and the fault is not that of 'imperfections'; indeed, 'perfections' will serve to aggravate exogenous shocks that throw the system off full-employment.

We want to call attention to another aspect of conventional analysis that falls away in the face of post-Keynesian reality. And here we look at the notion that firms increase hiring to the point where the real wage rate is equal to the marginal product of labor which results in optimization of profits. Of course, this 'law of employment' is conventionally associated with the pure competitive industrial set-up where firms are price 'takers', and the notion of a uniform labor input. We are appreciative that this approach is unreal on all accounts; but what is perhaps not fully held up to scrutiny is the singleness of labor. Our utilization-employment function in Fig. (8.20) makes us aware of the difference between the productivity of overall labor and the productivity of the 'productive' variable labor. In the orthodox approach all labor is the variable labor, and the change in profits (P) to that of employment is:

$$\frac{dP}{dN} = pl_o - w \tag{91}$$

with profits being maximized by setting (91) equal to zero so:

$$w = pl_o \qquad (92)$$

While the overall productivity of labor increases the greater level of employment and utilization rate, this overall productivity is less than the marginal product of the variable labor itself. Thus if the firm pays a wage equal to the value of the marginal product of labor which, in the usual sense means variable labor, its costs would be greater than the value of output. The firm is not maximizing profits, it is making losses. This is another means to point out that the neoclassical labor market apparatus is totally mis-structured; and its inclusion in the neoclassical-Keynesian synthesis causes one to miss much of the 'true Keynes'.

There is another issue that we briefly want to look at in its impact on employment and the rate of profit; and that is the result of a displacement of the (AS), or what we referred to as the profits curve. Factors that shift this curve upwards increase the level of created profits at any given level of utilization rate. Such factors may be a decline in the amount of fixed labor required to produce a given output, lower taxes on a higher established mark-up indicating a heightened degree of monopoly. In Fig. (8.24) we note two possible effects of such a shift within the condition of excess capacity.

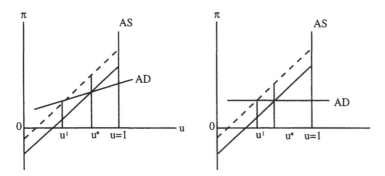

Figure 8.24

We find an increase in realized profits at utilization rate (u^*); and this change in distribution will necessarily alter the savings and investment balance which will then affect the sufficiency of demand for the prevailing level of output. As we pointed out earlier in connection with Fig. (8.19),

461

the stability of the system requires that savings out of profits exceed the investment propensity out of profits; but this means that the increase in profits will cause savings to increase by more than investment with the result of an insufficiency of demand.

We know that in general organizations will respond to this lower demand by reducing output and employment which, via a reduction in the efficiency of labor, will cause profits to fall and eventually return to their original level. This result is evident in Fig. (8.24) where the level of output falls to compensate for the higher profits (lower costs) — certainly a nonconventional scenario. Yet it is quite possible that the reduction in utilization rates will trigger a reverse 'accelerator effect'; that is, the lower level of demand will negatively impact investment plans in a manner as to overcome whatever positive effect from the initial higher rate of profit. When the economy does stabilize, it will be with a lower rate of profit and lower level of investment than originally, as in Fig. (8.23). The increase in the rate of profit will not be sufficient to increase investment levels if it becomes associated with insufficient levels of aggregate demand. Looking back to our investment equation (85), we are talking about the term $I_u(u) \succ 0$.

Rowthorn refers to this as the "paradox of costs".[46] Matters that lower the cost of production will be followed by a reduction in output and a lowering of the utilization rate which reduces the overall productivity per worker that more than offsets the lower costs. As a result the rate of profit will decrease, thus lower costs will lead to lower profits. In a more direct way, if we are achieving these lower costs through lower wages, then the detrimental effect of reduced demand is more telling than any positive impact of immediate higher profits. Cost reduction will increase the rate of profit which can be achieved at any given level of output; but they will also decrease the level of output itself, and because of this (in the light by what we know about production arrangement in the modern firm) the actual rate of profit will fall. Of course, this entire reasoning works in reverse, in which higher wages emerge as benefits to capital in that they lead to higher profits.

There is another paradox in this story stemming from the savings side, considered the "paradox of thrift". Starting from the equilibrium (86), suppose capitalists save a larger share out of profits (s_π increases). This reduces demand which in turn will reduce profits and thereby the level of investment. A higher savings propensity (more thrift) leads to less savings because it leads to lower profits. We see this demand parameter change in Fig. (8.25).

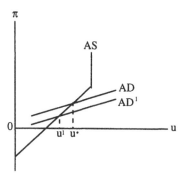

Figure 8.25

Let us follow through again on this distinction between a shift in profits and investment due to variations in the potential profits curve and that caused by a change in the realization (*AD*) curve. With regard to the former, we simply reverse our previous analysis. An increase in overhead costs shifts the profit curve downward which, if the utilization rate were to remain the same would lead to a lower rate of profit. But what has to be considered, and is at times lost sight of, is that these higher costs correspond to increased revenues distributed to households. These additional revenues result in additional demand which induces a higher rate of capacity utilization and corresponding higher rate of profit. "Additional costs cannot reduce overall profits if we take effective demand into account".[47] And we are reinforcing this increase in demand by our assumption that investment responds to changes in the utilization rate.

Now let us alter the framework to one where the normal condition is one of full-capacity operations, so that our concern is with the vertical section of the profits curve, and run through these structural shifts. First we reiterate some thoughts on how we might expect prices to behave. While real wages may be considered independent of demand when there is excess capacity, this is not the case at full capacity. In the latter condition, increased demand will be met with higher prices via an increase in the mark-up with the intention of curtailing the excess demand and simultaneously providing greater internal finance to increase capacity, so the mark-up then is geared to long-run considerations and directly affected by demand conditions; and as Rowthorn points out, it cannot be directly influenced by such influences as union pressure on workers. Indeed, if money wage rates begin to rise, prices will go up in the same proportion and real wages remain unchanged. But in the absence of this, higher

463

demand levels at around the full-capacity operating rate will cause real wages to fall. In Fig. (8.17) we have the real wage falling at the $u=1$ operations level.

In this situation there is no spare capacity to accommodate higher levels of demand, so that at a point in time it is demand that is adjusting to aggregate supply via changes in the distribution of income. Higher profits now become the essential force behind investment demand (the capacity utilization factor drops out of the investment function) which increases capacity. If we put the economy on the steady-state path, than at all points in time it is in the condition of full-capacity operations; the economy is thereby maintaining a particular distribution of income so as to result in the necessary growth of aggregate demand to absorb the growth in capacity. Yet we do note that there is room for 'conflict' over the distribution element; a lower rate of profit may be extracted, but at the penalty of reducing the rate of investment and economic growth — Fig. (8.24) tells this story.

In contrast, when the economy is operating below full capacity, there need not be any direct conflict over the distribution of income. The rate of profit can be increased with higher rates of capital accumulation without reducing the real wage rate. Indeed, as we have analyzed, it is an advantage to increase real wages as a means to increase demand which results in greater levels of output, and this will lead to greater profits that result in more investment — with the positive impact of higher utilization rates also taken into account.

What we are dealing with is two different views of what is the 'normal' circumstances of the economy. If it is supply constrained, then the distribution of income becomes the central element, with labor perhaps having to accept a lower proportion of a growing output in order to keep investment growing at, say, the Harrodian natural rate.

If it is demand constrained, then higher real wage rates can invigorate the economy resulting in higher levels of output as well as higher rates of profit and investment. The issue here is to prevent the growth in demand from overwhelming the growth of productive capacity so as to revert the economy to the supply constrained circumstances. But it is certainly plausible to argue that the economy is rarely on that vertical section of the profits curve, what Rowthorn refers to as the inflationary growth condition. We can presume that higher levels of demand-driven investment always carry with it planned spare capacity which, though in and of itself increases demand, does not do so to the point of absorbing all of the higher level of capability. The steady-state path can be set out in terms of full-employment with a constant presence of spare capacity.

We can work up an equation that relates the rate of profit and the real wage. Using equation (89) which we restate here:

$$pY = wN + p\pi K \tag{93}$$

we divide through by pK to obtain:

$$\Pi = \frac{Y}{K} - \frac{wN}{pK} \tag{94}$$

Equation (94) can be restated as:[48]

$$\Pi = \frac{Y}{K}[1 - \frac{w}{p} \cdot \frac{N}{Y}] \tag{95}$$

with the bracketed term giving the share of profits in output. From our production relationships we formed equation (67) that related the overall productivity per worker as a function of the utilization rate. Then inverting (67) and inserting into (95) gives:

$$\Pi = \frac{Y}{K}[1 - \frac{w}{p}(\frac{1 + f/u}{l_v})] \tag{96}$$

Recalling the (f) term as the ratio of overhead labor to variable labor at full capacity operations, means that in (95) we need to relate the level of output and that of the capital stock to the full capacity level of output. In the formation of our profits equation (80) we noted:

$$Y = u(Y^*)$$

$$K = \iota(Y^*) \tag{97}$$

So equation (96) reads:

$$\Pi = \frac{u}{\iota}[1 - \frac{w}{p}(\frac{1 + f/u}{l_v})] \tag{98}$$

which, after manipulation, becomes:

$$\Pi = \frac{u}{\iota}[1 - \frac{\frac{w}{p}}{l_v} - \frac{\frac{w}{p}(f)}{ul_v}] \qquad (99)$$

Equation (99) is a variation of our profits equation (80); it is as Lavoie relates "a three dimensional equation which links the rate of profit to the real wage rate and the utilization of capacity".[49] The technologically determined parameters indicating the importance of fixed capital and the ratio of overhead to variable labor are given by (ι) and (f).

It is clear that given (u), the negative relation between changes in the real wage rate and the rate of profit and thereby the rate of investment, holds. But the matter to bear in mind is that the utilization rate is not a given, but is endogenous to the system being influenced by the change in the real wage itself. And as we pointed out, profits are positively related to the utilization rate; thus the rate of growth of the economy must now be seen as positively related to real wage changes. But it need not only be a change in the real wage rate (given prices); any positive changes in the components of aggregate demand (for a given real wage) will impact positively on utilization rates and hence on the rate of profit and investment. The usual approach of requiring a reduction of the real wage rate to increase the actual rate of profit and economic growth is, in general, a mis-reading of the operation of the economy.

To appreciate the influences on the utilization rate through the effect on aggregate demand, we make use of our rate of profit Cambridge equation (83) which we repeat:

$$\Pi = \frac{G}{s_P} \qquad (100)$$

and substitute into (99) to solve for the utilization of capacity. So:

$$\frac{G}{s_P} = \frac{u}{\iota}(\frac{1 - \frac{w}{p}}{l_v}) - \frac{\frac{u}{\iota}\cdot\frac{w}{p}(f)}{ul_v} \qquad (101)$$

than

$$\frac{u}{\iota}\left(\frac{1-\dfrac{w}{p}}{l_v}\right) = \frac{G}{s_P} + \frac{\dfrac{w}{p}(f)}{\iota l_v} \tag{102}$$

and

$$u = \frac{G\left(\dfrac{\iota}{s_P}\right) + \dfrac{\dfrac{w}{p}(f)}{l_v}}{\dfrac{1-w/p}{l_v}} \tag{103}$$

Given the parameters that define the level of employment to production, what we termed the utilization function; the rate of utilization is then seen to depend upon the propensity to save out of profits, the wage rate and the rate of growth.

Our investment equation (85) points out the essential determining influences on the investment decisions as the rate of profit and the rate of utilization. Certainly these are interdependent influences as they affect the rate of growth of the system and are, as well, influenced by the growth rate itself. With equations (95) and (103) we can see these linkages in more detail. From (95) to (96) we observe that the share of profits changes positively with the rate of capacity utilization, with the latter depending on a given rate of growth via equation (103). Then the profit share becomes a function of the growth rate of the economy; we note the positive relation between the rate of profit and utilization rate in equation (99).

Interestingly enough, we also see that the economy can maintain a higher rate of investment and growth for a given real wage rate. As we made mention, the real wage need not go down to bring into being the higher rate of profit associated with the higher rate of growth, due to the endogenous behavior of the utilization rate (via equation 98 where we take the real wage as given).

If we place the economy on that long-term steady-state path then the rate of profit and the rate of capital accumulation are given which, as we can now appreciate, also involves a constant rate of capacity utilization. Additionally, the money supply would be expanding at a rate commensurate with the growth in external financing which means that the monetary authorities have pegged the rate of interest to accommodate the particular demand for debt to expand capacity. Yet the degree of debt financing is itself in part tied to the organization's pay-out policy, as this policy, in one regard, impacts on consumption demand. Certainly there are numerous variables that can go awry and throw the economy off the steady-growth track, so that, hopefully, we are able to appreciate that long-ago Harrod-Domar growth model in a deeper way.

It is with this thought that we bring our discussion of the 'alternative way' to a close; mindful that this work is intended to be introductory that began with the question "What is Economics About?" Hopefully, the reader at this point will feel somewhat secure about putting into question, if not discarding, the usual conceptual apparatus to understanding the workings of the economic system. We fully close with some end-thoughts in the following chapter.

NOTES

1. We retell some of the conventional story concerning income distribution as set out in Chapter 3. This enables us to have the tools at hand for our immediate analysis.

2. This particular presentation of the labor market and its relation to the aggregate system is modeled after that of William H. Branson, *Macroeconomics*, Harper and Row, 1989. We repeat some of the material of Chapter 3.

3. Basic references are J. Tobin, "Money and Economic Growth," *Econometrics*, October 1965; H. G. Johnson, "The Neoclassical One-Sector Growth Model: A Geometrical Exposition and Extension to a Monetary Economy", August 1966, *Economics*. Also, Johnson, *Essays in Monetary Economics*, Cambridge University Press, 1967; David Leuhari and Don Patinkin, "The Role of Money in a Simple Growth Model", *American Economic Review*, September 1968.

4. See Jerome L. Stein, "Monetary Growth in Perspective", *American Economic Review*, March 1970. Also, Stein, "Money and Capacity Growth", *Journal of Political Economy*, October 1966. As well, the *Journal of Money, Credit and Banking*, May 1969, which is devoted to a discussion of monetary growth economics.

5. As:

$$\frac{\dot{K}}{K} = a\frac{I}{K} + \frac{I}{K} - \frac{\hat{p}}{h} - a\frac{I}{K} + \frac{a\hat{p}}{h}$$

$$= \frac{I}{K} - \frac{(1-a)\hat{p}}{h}$$

6. Paul Davidson, *Controversies in Post Keynesian Economics*, Edward Elgar, 1991, p. 32.

7. Ibid.

8. Davidson, "Sensible Expectations and the Long-Run Non-Neutrality of Money", *Journal of Post-Keynesian Economics*, Fall 1987.

9. Davidson, "A Technical Definition of Uncertainty and the Long-Run Non-Neutrality of Money", *Cambridge Journal of Economics*, 1988, p. 331.

10. Ibid., p. 332.

11. Davidson, *Controversies* . . . op. cit., p. 33.

12. Ibid., p. 35.

13. J. R. Hicks, *Economic Perspectives*, Oxford University Press, 1977, p. viii.

14. John M. Keynes, *The General Theory of Employment*, Interest and Money, Harcourt Brace, New York, 1936, particularly the chapter on long-term expectations.

15. Ibid.

16. Ibid., p. 167.

17. Ibid., p. 168.

18. Ibid., p. 170.

19. Davidson, "Sensible Expectations . . ." op. cit., p. 152.

20. Davidson, "A Technical Definition . . ." op. cit., p. 333.

21. Davidson, *Controversies* op. cit., p. 58.

22. Keynes, op. cit., p. 259.

23. Ibid., p. 261.

24. Dudley Dillard, *The Economics of John Maynard Keynes*, Crosby Lockwood, London, 1950, p. 212.

25. Keynes, op. cit., p. 265.

26. Ibid.

27. Eileen Appelbaum, "The Labor Market", in *A Guide to Post-Keynesian Economics*. Edited by Alfred S. Eichner, M. E. Sharpe, Armonk, New York, 1979, p. 111.

28. Alfred S. Eichner, *Towards a New Economics*, M. E. Sharpe, New York, p. 121.

29. John B. Taylor, *Economics*, Houghton Mifflin, Boston, 1995, p. 833.

30. Marc Lavoie, *Foundations of Post-Keynesian Economic Analysis*, Edward Elgar, Aldershot, England, 1992, p. 170.

31. John M. Keynes, *A Treatise on Money*, Macmillan, 1930 (Vols. 1 and 2). Also the discussion in the *General Theory*, Chapter 13.

32. Basil Moore, "Unpacking the Post-Keynesian Black Box: Bank Lending and the Money Supply" in *Post-Keynesian Economics*, Edited by Malcolm C. Sawyer, Edward Elgar, Aldershot, England, 1988.

33. Ibid., p. 127.

34. Ibid.

35. Lavoie, op. cit., p. 174.

36. This analysis follows that found in Lavoie, op. cit., Chapter 5, dealing with effective demand and employment.

37. We follow the basic design put forward by R. Rowthorn, "Demand, Real Wages and Economic Growth", *Thames Papers in Political Economy*, 1987. Reprinted in *Post-Keynesian Economics*, edited by Malcolm C. Sawyer, Edward Elgar, Aldershot, England, 1988.

38. Keynes, *The General Theory*, op. cit., p. 136.

39. Ibid.

40. Malcolm C. Sawyer, *Unemployment, Imperfect Compensation and Macroeconomics*, Edward Elgar, Aldershot, England, 1995, p. 45.

41. Steven Fazzari, *The Investment-Finance Link*, Public Policy Brief, The Jerome Levy Institute of Bard College, No. 9, 1993.

42. Ibid., p. 35.

43. In equilibrium:

$$D = wN + pI$$

where

$$wN = pY - pI$$

then

$$w = \frac{pY - pI}{N}$$

as

$$Y = (N - N_o)l_v$$

so

$$w = \frac{p(N - N_o)l_v}{N} - \frac{pI}{N}$$

with

$$\frac{w}{p} = \frac{(N - N_o)l_v}{N} - \frac{I}{N}$$

44. Lavoie, op. cit., p. 238.

45. Based on Lavoie's discussion, op. cit., Chapter 5.

46. Rowthorn, op. cit., p. 180.

47. Lavoie, op. cit., p. 315.

48. Since equation 95 is seen as:

$$\pi = \frac{Y}{K} - \frac{Y}{K} \cdot \frac{wN}{pY}$$

$$= \frac{Y}{K}(1 - \frac{w}{p} \cdot \frac{N}{Y})$$

49. Lavoie, op. cit., p. 299.

9 End thoughts

The conventional thought process whether regarding price determination, the distribution of output, or, in a broader scope, that of the neoclassical Keynesian synthesis, is to account for economic outcomes in terms of market models based on predictable behavioral assumptions on the part of agents specified by independently positioned supply and demand curves. The overall activity of the system is seen as the result of 'harmonizing' these models. And this approach is clearly evident in the Keynesian synthesis which regulates the real and money flows of the economy through the markets for goods, labor and finance. Yet we come away from our deliberations quite suspect of, and in all likelihood we would entirely eschew, this market hypothesis upon which to base our understanding.

We are aware that in the predominant operation of the economy, i.e. where goods are industrial products, there are no independently placed demand and supply functions that jointly determine price and output levels. Indeed, that it is the level of demand that determines supply, and it does so independently of the prevailing price. And this prevailing price is the result of a mark-up price arrangement given the organization's target profit rate and finance needs. In the credit market, as well, this basic hypothesis must be jettisoned; as it is the demand for new loans that determine the increase of demand deposits and thereby the growth of the money supply and, again, at an institutionally determined price. In the labor 'market' it is the level of demand for each organization's output that determines employment, again, independently of the prevailing real wage. The supply curve for labor as a separate behavioral function cannot, in reality, be structured in the neoclassical fashion of an upward sloping backward bending curve. It is best to treat the labor supply curve as vertical in the short term, and concentrate on the demand aspects (as we have done) of the labor market. Despite the human characterization of this arena, neoclassicists insist on treating this analysis in the same manner as they treat a market for goods such that a change in the actual real wage relative to its equilibrium condition would result in market forces that would restore the equilibrium real wage. But this requires the existence of the accustomed separate supply curve which, as we said, cannot be structured. To support the contention that such a supply curve represents a realistic analytical tool, whether in the market for goods or labor, "economists are forced to invent stories that are caricatures of reality — such as the story that industrial firms are subject to decreasing returns when they expand output or the story that workers who cannot obtain jobs are merely exercising their preference for leisure".[1] In fact, the exchange of labor services and the determination of wages do not take place in the context of a market as this term is normally understood; post-Keynesians then prefer the term 'labor sector' rather than 'labor market'. While in an earlier chapter there was some discussion of the Keynesian approach to the labor sector, we did not get into a detailed analysis of the realistic way to model a labor supply curve.

We would conclude that the standard market model with its independent supply and demand functions must be jettisoned as the basic construction of analysis. Eichner comes straight to the point here when he tells us:

> It is often useful to separate the factors influencing the quantity supplied from the factors operating on the demand side — as long as one does not assume that the two will be brought into balance with one another through a change in the market price. It is the latter error that permeates the entire body of orthodox theory that has led to the present intellectual bankruptcy of economics.[2]

In almost all situations, the idea of specifying a supply curve which is independent and separate from the demand curve, is a wrong construction.

We can perhaps relate our sentiments to some history of economic thought. In *Capital* Volume I, Marx in writing about the determination of prices contrasted the reality of the classical political economy represented best by Ricardo, with that of the "vulgar economy". He considered the latter to represent a construction that dealt in appearances which, willfully or otherwise, prevented its practitioners — those bourgeois economists — from penetrating into the internal essence of what constitutes prices. Marx did show that although prices of production normally deviated from the value of labor inherent in the production of the good, so as to equalize the rate of profit, this mechanism does not remove (though it might obscure) the essential fact that prices are ultimately derived from or determined by these labor values.

Marx believed that the competitive pricing overhang hides the reality of this "prior concrete magnitude" that determines and limits the aggregate level of those profit and rent revenues; this magnitude coming out of the values of the commodities. After the payment of wages there remains the surplus value which constitutes the source of profits which is redistributed to equalize the rate of profit, via the transformation of these values into prices and surplus value into profits; and this is accomplished via the competitive process. Thus in Marx's thinking, some capitalists would end up with more surplus value than their workers had produced and others with less. But this surplus value is the result of the amount of extra work which the work force is forced to do. Marx wanted to reveal and stress the exploitive nature between profits and labor; and hence one must begin by abstracting from those aspects of the competitive process which disguise the exploitive origin of profit.

Now why was it so difficult for all to see what for Marx was at the heart of the capitalistic system? Here Marx speaks about economists being "blinded by competition" which results in their unrealistic theories of price. At best these theories would say that prices have their basis in supply and demand; and at worst that they have their origin in, and are the result of, an adding-up of wages, profits and rent, as if each of these components were produced by their respective inputs. Of course, for Marx this trinity approach was an apologetic approach; he considered it a total distortion that something called capital produces its own profit. In Marx's thinking, once wages have been paid, there remains a surplus value which constitutes the ultimate source of profits; he argued against considering the level of wages and profits as independent entities and thereby being capable of being added up.

It is not at all our desire to get involved in an analysis of Marxian economics, except to relate to his belief that economists could not see the 'truth' about the political economy of his time because they were taken up with illusionary models upon which they built their understanding. His complaint resonates with post-Keynesians of our day as the world enters a new millennium. In general, economists remain blinded by the glare of neoclassical market models and a pervasive sense of 'rationality' in behavior. This prevents a realistic understanding of how the system works for it does not account for the behavior of 'institutions' (and interest groups) in the formation of economic results. Whether in consideration of the labor sector, or in understanding mark-up procedures, or in analyzing

477

the distribution of income, or in comprehending the cost curves of the producing unit, or regarding monetary theory, or in reckoning the commercial relations between states, and so on; one cannot base an understanding of these matters on the neoclassical approach. The realistic players on the economic stage are in the form of quasi-monopolistic organizations of production and finance, and governmental and quasi-governmental, agencies with direct links to, and substantial influence on the economic decisions of 'private' units in the economy.

Post-Keynesians value explanations of the economic system as it exists, rather than predicating behavior on normative assumptions that may be regarded as 'natural'. Indeed, post-Keynesians consider the anomic as normal. We are facing a different world than that which formed the core of orthodox economic analysis. In the light of constant changing technology, it is rather meaningless to look at the world through the scarcity lens with the allocative mechanics at the center of analysis. The human specie is ever less dependent on nature, and more and more on himself, with the development of new knowledge and the learning process as the essential forces of economic change. This translates into models of production and distribution in an environment of almost unlimited capability; we are in need of realistic hypothesis to model the institutions of this different world. If we are to talk about 'limitations' then it is a limit that stems from the political and social framework dealing with the production and distributive mechanics in society. Post-Keynesians do not separate what one may think of as pure economic science from the political-institutional arrangements of the economy; the formal modeling of the former must reflect the reality of the latter.

NOTES

1. Eichner, *Towards a New Economics*, op. cit., p. 7.

2. Ibid.

For Product Safety Concerns and Information please contact our EU representative GPSR@taylorandfrancis.com Taylor & Francis Verlag GmbH, Kaufingerstraße 24, 80331 München, Germany

Printed and bound by CPI Group (UK) Ltd, Croydon, CR0 4YY

08/05/2025

01864382-0002